BRITISH PRIVATEERING ENTERPRISE
in the
EIGHTEENTH CENTURY

EXETER MARITIME STUDIES

General Editor: Stephen Fisher

EXETER MARITIME STUDIES No. 4

BRITISH PRIVATEERING ENTERPRISE
in the
EIGHTEENTH CENTURY

David J. Starkey

UEP

First published 1990 by the
University of Exeter Press

© David J. Starkey, 1990
University of Exeter

British Library Cataloguing in Publication Data
Starkey, David J.
British privateering enterprise in the eighteenth century
– (Exeter maritime studies; no. 4)
1. Privateering, history
I. Title   II. Series
910.45
ISBN 978 0 85989 312 1

University of Exeter Press
Reed Hall
Streatham Drive
Exeter, Devon EX4 4QR
UK
www.exeterpress.co.uk

Printed digitally since 2010

Typeset by Kestrel Data, Exeter

Printed and bound by CPI Group (UK) Ltd, Croydon, CR0 4YY

For Jill

CONTENTS

Appendices

Maps

Figure

Plates

Tables

Abbreviations and Dates

ACL   Avon County Library, Bristol
BL   British Library, London
DRO   Devon Record Office, Exeter
LRO   Liverpool Record Office
LSF   Library of the Society of Friends, London
PRO   Public Record Office, London
SMV   Society of Merchant Venturers, Bristol

The Gregorian, or New Style, system of dating has been adopted in this study in preference to the Julian, or Old Style, method utilised by contemporaries prior to 1752. Thus, 1 January, rather than 25 March, is taken as New Year's Day in years up to and including 1751.

The dates cited for war years refer to the periods during which letters of marque, or privateer commissions, were issued rather than the years in which conflicts formally commenced and terminated. For instance, '1756–1762' is used to denote the Seven Years' War in this study and not the more conventional '1756–1763'.

Preface

In many ways, this study is the culmination of a research programme established in the Department of Economic History at the University of Exeter during the mid-1970s. Initiated by Walter E. Minchinton, the aim of this project was to investigate a well documented, though largely neglected aspect of economic and military history—British privateering activity in the eighteenth century. Various people laid the foundations for this enquiry; in particular, Professor Minchinton and Celia King transcribed and codified the letter of marque declarations made in the wars of the mid-eighteenth century, while Ray Burnley designed the computer database in which this information was stored and thereafter offered indispensable guidance in the utilisation of the file. On the basis of these efforts, a number of research students completed graduate dissertations on various facets of the privateering phenomenon; as one of the chief beneficiaries, I would like to express my gratitude to those who established the sturdy framework around which my post-graduate work was constructed. Furthermore, and in an intellectual sense, my special thanks are due to Professor Minchinton who not only introduced me to the subject of privateering, but also supervised the master's and doctoral dissertations on which the present book is founded; and to Dr Stephen Fisher for the critical assistance he provided during the preparation of these theses.

A further research initiative has been instrumental in bringing this book to fruition. In 1985, the Departments of History and Archaeology, and of Economic History, at the University of Exeter, generously funded by the Leverhulme Trust, commenced a reassessment of the maritime history of the county of Devon. As Research Fellow in this Project, I have been able—amidst other duties—to pursue my interest in privateering history, expanding the scope of my PhD thesis to consider more and broader issues with the incorporation of additional material. In this, I have received the unstinting help and encouragement of the Project's Directors, Dr Basil Greenhill, Professor Joyce Youings and Dr Stephen Fisher. Under their influence, moreover, Exeter University's interest in maritime historical studies has flourished as witnessed by the establishment of the *Exeter Maritime Studies* series in which this monograph appears. Here, I am indebted to the Publications Committee of Exeter University for accepting my volume for inclusion in the series; to Barbara Mennell, Publications Officer, for her patience and guidance during this work's long gestation period; to Dr Michael Duffy for reading various drafts of the study and offering sound, objective appraisals which have undoubtedly enhanced the final product; and to Dr Stephen Fisher, general editor of the series, who has stimulated and enriched my work over many years.

That assistance has been forthcoming from beyond the confines of Exeter University is suggested by numerous other debts which I have incurred. I am grateful to the British Academy for providing a generous subvention towards the publication costs of the volume. The personnel of the Public Record Office, the British Library, the India Office Library, Devon Record Office, Liverpool Record Office, the West Country Studies Library, and the Society of Merchant Venturers of Bristol, have been unfailingly helpful in locating and retrieving bundles, parcels and volumes of documentary evidence for my perusal. The cartographic and photographic services of Rodney Fry and John Saunders were at once accurate and efficient, and are much appreciated. Warm thanks are due to John Appleby, Tony Barrow, James Derriman, Ray Freeman, Eric Graham, William Meyer, Tony Pawlyn, Peter Raban and Maurice Schofield—fellow researchers whose kindness in forwarding information and exchanging ideas has been both remarkable and heartening. Finally, I would like to acknowledge the contribution of my wife, Jill Howitt; as well as assisting in the collection and interpretation of data, she has cheerfully provided the less tangible factors—time, space and support—essential for the completion of this study.

David J. Starkey
Exeter, September 1989

Introduction

Maritime warfare has assumed many guises over the centuries. One of its manifestations, and one which was commonly practised from medieval times until the nineteenth century, was privateering. The base of this generic term, coined by the English in the mid-seventeenth century and used anachronistically and somewhat indiscriminately ever since, identifies the chief characteristic of this activity. It was essentially private, a form of enterprise in which individuals might deploy their own resources to attack and seize the vessels and goods of foreign subjects, acquiring for themselves the rights to any property thereby appropriated. Such hostile acts were not random, however, for this predatory business was conducted within the international law of the sea, its practitioners authorised and regulated by the legal and administrative institutions of their respective states. If this official sanction distinguished privateering from piracy, it also implied that government perceived some utility in the activity beyond the personal enrichment of its citizens. In accord with the mercantilist sentiments prevalent in the seventeenth and eighteenth centuries, this utility was deemed to accrue from the destruction wrought upon rival shipping and commerce—injury which was inflicted, moreover, at no expense to the state. Privateering, therefore, might serve public as well as private interests; at once a business opportunity, a tool of war and a factor in the diplomacy between nations, the place of this activity in the maritime experience of the British Isles—principally during the 1702–1783 period—is the subject of the study which follows.

Historians have been tardy in their treatment of this aspect of the economic and military past. In the 1920s, George N. Clark complained that 'no satisfactory information is available on the numbers and strength of British privateers',[1] a call to arms echoed by John S. Bromley some twenty years later.[2] Yet, despite the valuable work of Bromley and others on the privateering endeavours of the Channel Islanders, John Brewer's recent comment that 'more work needs to be done on English privateering'[3] points to the large gap in our knowledge which still remains. This disregard stems chiefly from the factionalism which tends to afflict maritime historical studies; as a multi-faceted activity, privateering fits uneasily into a fragmented discipline, straddling the artificial fences which divide students of the maritime dimension of economic, military and political history.

A transient business, confined almost entirely to wartime, commerce-raiding enterprise features only fleetingly in considerations of the more permanent aspects of the maritime economy—trade, ports and the shipping industry. Naval historians, similarly, have all too readily turned a blind eye towards the private vessels-of-war encouraged by the state to augment the Royal Navy, while analysts of eighteenth-century international relations have rarely appreciated the role of private commerce-raiding on the diplomatic stage. Consequently, assumptions and generalisations have taken the place of facts. For instance, to some, privateering was 'eliminated' in the eighteenth century,[4] though, to others, the scale of the activity was 'probably extended',[5] with privateers not only more numerous by the 1770s but also 'larger and infinitely better armed than they had been 20 years before';[6] in most eyes, moreover, particularly those of the Navy and its historians, this legitimate activity was merely the province of the 'reckless gambler', a 'well known . . . haven for all sorts of criminals'.[7]

An abundance of evidence exists to clarify these vague and misleading assertions. The archives of the High Court of Admiralty contain hundreds of thousands of documents pertaining to the privateering phenomenon, for it was in this idiosynchratic bastion of the civil law—Dickens's 'cosey, dosey, old-fashioned, time-forgotten, sleepy-headed little family party'[8]— that privateering was administered. Here, shipowners obtained letters of marque, or privateer commissions, the licences which authorised them to send forth private vessels-of-war; here, also, the ships and goods taken in pursuance of these licences were adjudicated along with the properties seized by the Navy and by non-commissioned captors. The survival of the records generated at each stage of the legal process facilitates a comprehensive assessment of the extent and effectiveness of British privateering activity in the eighteenth century. Supportive and additional evidence is widely available; contemporary newspapers offer a wealth of information, with items of news, the views of correspondents and advertisements affording valuable insights into the conduct and fortunes of privateersmen; articles of agreement, muster rolls and mercantile correspondence provide a clear impression of the internal workings of privateering ventures; while business accounts—though relatively few have survived—indicate the range of costs and profits associated with this speculative form of enterprise.

Utilising such a rich array of source material, this study addresses three central issues. The character of eighteenth-century British privateering is the concern of Part 1 of the work. Here, the origins and evolution of the activity are traced to place its eighteenth-century form in a long-term context, to establish its legal and theoretical basis, and to explain the measures adopted to regulate its practise. Attention is focused on the composition of the privateering fleet; a vital distinction is drawn between the private man-of-war set forth specifically to prey on the enemy's sea-borne property, and the commercially-oriented 'letter of marque', the merchant ship commissioned to stimulate the defensive or opportunist energies of her crew; further classification is attempted, with typologies established to denote the aims and means of the various kinds of vessel afforded the status of 'privateer' by the commission they carried. Whatever her function, each licensed craft possessed a prize-taking potential, a dimension imbued with extraordinary risks and rewards which gave rise to a particular and unusual organisational form. Concluding this discussion of the character of the privateering business, therefore, is a consideration of the structure of the commerce-raiding venture and the implications this held for the shipowners and seafarers—or, more properly, the venturers—concerned.

The scale of British privateering enterprise is the second broad area of scrutiny. In Part 2, the 'input' and 'output' of the commerce-raiding business in the five wars of the period 1702–1783 is assessed.[9] Based on legal records—those of the High Court of Admiralty archive—the measures presented are necessarily crude, with 'inputs' expressed in terms of the number, tonnage and manning requirements of commissioned vessels, and 'output' determined by the number of enemy properties subject to common condemnation in the London Prize Court. By refining this data, however, such matters as the regional distribution of privateering investment, the complexion of the commissioned fleet, the fluctuating rate of predatory activity and the contribution of commerce-raiding venturers to the prize war are illuminated. A comparative perspective, moroever, is adopted to identify the long-run trends apparent in the business during the eighteenth century, and to place it in the wider context of the commercial and military developments of the era.

Such assessments provide a platform for a broad analysis of the significance of British privateering enterprise in the eighteenth century, the third element of the book. Consideration is given to the many and varied factors which served to condition the scale and form of the activity. The military efficacy of privateering is discussed, with particular attention paid to the differing, often conflicting, attitudes of the state, the Navy and the merchant shipowner to the operations of private men-of-war, and the far from cordial relations which generally prevailed between the private and public arms of the naval service. Finally, commerce-raiding is placed in its most important context, as a branch of the shipping industry in which shipowners and seafarers risked their capital and their labour in the quest for speculative profits. A consumer of shipping, manpower and other resources, a source of profit and loss, privateering enterprise assumed a significant place in the wartime economies of many British ports during the eighteenth century.

Notes

1. G. N. Clark, 'War Trade and Trade War' *Economic History Review*, first series, I (1927-1928), 264.
2. J. S. Bromley, 'The Channel Island Privateers in the War of the Spanish Succession' *Société Guernesiaise Report and Transactions*, XIV (1947), 444.
3. J. Brewer, *The Sinews of Power. War, Money and the English State, 1688-1783* (Unwin, 1989) 272n.
4. J. F. Shepherd and G. M. Walton, *Shipping, Maritime Trade, and the Economic Development of Colonial North America* (Cambridge UP, 1972) 74.
5. R. Davis, *The Rise of the English Shipping Industry in the Seventeenth and Eighteenth Centuries* (Macmillan, 1962) 333.
6. A. C. Carter, *Neutrality or Commitment. The Evolution of Dutch Foreign Policy, 1667-1795* (Edward Arnold, 1975) 99.
7. N. A. M. Rodger, *The Wooden World. An Anatomy of the Georgian Navy* (Collins, 1986) 185.
8. C. Dickens, *David Copperfield* (Chapman and Hall, 1850) 249.
9. 'Inputs', in terms of the number of vessels commissioned, into the privateering business in the 1793–1801 and 1803–1815 conflicts are presented in Appendices 7 and 8.

Part One
CHARACTER

One

Origins and Regulation

A privateer is a kind of private man-of-war, though the commission be not reckoned very honourable . . . and some persons account those but one remove from pirates.

Malachy Postlethwayt, *The Universal Dictionary of Trade and Commerce* (1774), II, 'privateer'.

That privateering was, and still is, confused with piracy is hardly surprising given the similarities in the aims and methods of the two activities. Both privateersman and pirate were intent on enriching themselves at the expense of other maritime travellers, an end which was often achieved by violent means, the forced appropriation of ships and merchandise. However, there had always been a theoretical distinction between the two forms of predation and during the seventeenth century this demarcation became more apparent in practice. While the privateersman assumed a place within the developing code of international maritime law, his legitimate prey being restricted largely to enemy property in wartime, the pirate's indiscriminate and unauthorised business was increasingly outlawed. Such developments occurred as the maritime powers sought to protect their growing interest in overseas trade from the stateless sea-robber and to expand it at the expense of their commercial and colonial rivals. The growth of state navies, and the concomitant advance in the administrative efficiency of marine departments facilitated these advances; thus, the laws against piracy were more rigorously enforced, while privateering enterprise was better regulated.

By the 1730s, therefore, piracy had been largely eradicated from the North Atlantic and privateering had been incorporated into the framework of international relations, a recognition of its potential utility as a tool of war. This integration, however, was not achieved by the imposition of a new system of regulation; rather, the measures traditionally employed to restrict private maritime warfare were increasingly formalised and a code of conduct more clearly defined. The basic tenets of control, and much of the terminology which applied to eighteenth-century privateering, were deeply rooted in the various forms of private conflict at sea that had been apparent since medieval times.

The ancient right of reprisal clearly underlay the eighteenth-century form of privateering enterprise. This was a means by which an individual could redress, by force if necessary, a proven grievance against a foreign subject. It was a measure of last resort, for the wronged party could only petition his sovereign for 'letters of marque,[1] and reprisal' once all efforts to obtain satisfaction using the legal processes of the foreign state had failed. Once granted, this authorisation empowered the petitioner to recover the amount of his loss from any of his transgressor's compatriots, with any surplus accountable to his own sovereign. In 1295, for instance, Bernard D'Ongressil of Bayonne was despoiled to the extent of £700 by some Portuguese sailors, proved his loss to the satisfaction of his lord, Sir John of Brittany, and was granted 'letters of marque, and reprisal' permitting him to make good his injury at the expense of the subjects of the King of Portugal.[2] Such rights were regularly granted to individuals during the Middle Ages and the practice survived until the late sixteenth century at least when Elizabeth I thought fit to authorise numerous private reprisals against the Spaniards.[3]

The device of reprisal made possible minor acts of war without breaking the general peace existing between nations.[4] Thus, it was distinct in theory from privateering, an activity limited to periods of declared war. Yet the rationale of private reprisals was clearly apparent in eighteenth-century commerce-raiding. From the concept of the redress of individual loss by reprisal in time of peace, there had evolved the notion of 'general' reprisals against an enemy in wartime. Nations justified acts of war as retaliatory measures against alleged aggressors, and therefore unlimited reprisals against the subjects of the offending state were permissible. In July 1739, for example, general reprisals were granted against Spanish commerce in retaliation for the depredations purportedly committed by the Spanish *guarda-costas* in the West Indies, while in December 1780 the failure of the United Provinces to respond to a series of published British grievances provoked the authorisation of general reprisals against Dutch trade and shipping. The language of private reprisals,[5] moreover, survived and continued to be applied to the 'general' reprisals of the later era. Thus, the terms 'letter of marque', 'letters of marque, and reprisal' and, occasionally, 'letters of reprisal' were used to describe the licences issued in wartime to seventeenth- and eighteenth-century privateersmen, though this usage was inappropriate in the strictest sense, as the rights originally implied by such titles were only applicable in time of peace.

While the right of reprisal was an important antecedent of eighteenth-century privateering, a further origin of the activity is to be found in the utilisation of private ships by the state for purposes of war in the days when royal navies were non-existent or inadequate. In England, the Norman kings depended upon the coast towns, particularly the Cinque Ports, to mobilise a set number of ships during an emergency, at times, as in 1242, ordering all the vessels of the Channel ports to commit every possible injury upon the enemy at sea.[6] In the fourteenth and fifteenth centuries, there were several instances of 'putting out to contract the keeping of the seas',[7] while Henry VIII made use of a large number of hired merchant ships to augment his fledgling Navy in the French wars of the 1540s. It was customary for the state to hire or impress private vessels, therefore, authorising them, by virtue of 'commissions', to act as ships of war. With the growth of navies in the seventeenth century, the state became less reliant on the merchant service and by the 1660s only purpose-built warships were powerful or adept enough to serve in line-of-battle. However, the facility to commission merchant vessels was retained and occasionally it was invoked to justify acts of private maritime warfare. Thus, in the American Revolutionary War, when it was theoretically impossible to grant reprisals against the inhabitants of the rebellious North American colonies, who were still considered to be subjects of His Britannic Majesty, the Admiralty Court issued 'commissions' to authorise the seizure of goods carried in contravention of the 1775 Prohibition of Trade Act.[8]

If the letter of marque and the privateer commission derived from separate origins, the difference in the application of their respective powers was purely technical by the eighteenth century. Indeed, it was the Admiralty's practice to address the 'commanders of such merchant ships and vessels as may have letters of marque, or commissions, for private men-of-war.'[9] This elasticity in nomenclature was stretched further by the adoption of the term 'letter of marque' to describe a particular form of eighteenth-century privateering vessel—the armed merchantman—as well as the document she carried. Again, the origins of this strain of the activity can be traced back over the centuries. Commercial vessels had long since carried arms to resist pirates or enemy craft, particularly in the long-distance trades in which cargoes were generally more valuable, and predators consequently more numerous. When called upon to use their weapons, merchantmen occasionally mounted successful defensive actions resulting in the capture of their assailants. However, it became a principle of maritime law that a captor without a commission had no legal title to his prize, which was usually condemned as a 'droit and perquisite' of the state. Therefore, to reap the rewards of such an encounter, or to profit from a meeting with a weak or incapacitated hostile vessel, it was commonplace from the 1620s onwards for owners of these armed traders to take out 'letters of marque, or commissions' in time of war. Though the conveyance of cargoes remained the priority of these vessels, the right of reprisal embodied in their privateering licences added a prize-taking potential to their voyages which might benefit owners and crew alike.

Privateering, in its eighteenth-century guise, was thus descended from a variety of distinct, though closely-related, origins. In the process of this evolution, a system of regulation developed by which states sought to restrict the attentions of their private forces to legitimate targets, thereby maximising their utility as a tool of maritime war. In eighteenth-century Britain, general reprisals were variously granted by a Royal Proclamation (1702), a Royal Declaration (1744), a Royal Proclamation and Declaration (1756), or by His Majesty's Order-in-Council (1778, 1779, 1780) issued at the commencement of hostilities and subsequently enacted by Parliament.[10] Though differing in detail, these Prize Acts incorporated the general principles which had long since governed privateering activity; thus, a privateersman required a letter of marque, or commission, to legitimise and benefit from his predatory activities;[11] this authorisation applied only to the vessels and goods of a specified adversary; arrested properties were to be adjudicated by the due process of law as laid down in the legislation; and prizes, from 1708 onwards, were to be the 'sole interest and property' of captors.[12]

The Lord High Admiral, or the Commissioners who executed the office for much of the century, was responsible for the administration of these Acts, a power exercised through the High Court of Admiralty and its colonial subsidiaries, the Vice-Admiralty Courts.[13] This institution dated back to the mid-fourteenth century, though its jurisdiction was limited until the 1520s. Thereafter, the Court gained cognizance over a wide range of cases arising from maritime activity, and prize adjudication became one of its principal functions. It developed an expertise in handling such business, which was often complex and politically delicate, requiring flexible procedures, quick results and a specialised knowledge of the sea and seafarers. In the seventeenth century, this expertise was recognised in the creation of a distinct 'Prize' division within the Court, the remainder of its civil and criminal work being conducted in the 'Instance' division. Prize sessions, from the 1670s, were held at Doctors' Commons, the residence of the doctors in civil law, situated to the south of St Paul's Cathedral, London.[14]

It was in these sessions that the business of privateering was administered throughout the eighteenth century. By this juncture, the Court's procedures had been formalised and the means by which it controlled privateering activity well established. To obtain his licence, the intending privateer commander—or someone acting on his behalf—was required to attend the Admiralty Court in Doctors' Commons, London,[15] and produce a 'warrant from the Lord High Admiral . . . for the granting of a commission or letter of marque'. Then he was obliged to make a declaration before the Admiralty judge consisting of a 'particular true and exact account of the ship or vessel'[16] to be commissioned. The information contained in these sworn statements varied from war to war, though they retained a basic form throughout the period 1689–1815. Declarants were required to state the name of the vessel concerned, the date the application was made, the tonnage of the vessel, its crew size, its armaments (including small arms and cutlasses), the period for which it was victualled, the type and quantity of ammunition and tackle carried, and the names of the commander, officers and principal owners. Such detail facilitated the regulation of privateers by providing the Admiralty Court with an accurate register of vessels licensed to attack enemy property on the high seas, and nominating the persons responsible for the promotion and conduct of such ventures. Thus, if complaints were made about the activities of a commissioned vessel, the authorities possessed the means to identify the vessel concerned and, more importantly, the individuals accountable for its operations.

The declaration also permitted the Court to restrict the issue of letters of marque to vessels of a particular quality or size if the need arose. In the latter stages of the Nine Years' War, for instance, the Admiralty attempted to divert seamen from the mercantile sector into naval service; accordingly, declarants were required to specify whether their venture was commercial or predatory in design, as commissions were valid for one voyage only in the case of 'letters of marque', while private men-of-war were allowed to cruise 'until further orders'.[17] Similarly, the declaration identified the vessels of under 100 tons burthen, 12 guns and 40 men which might only be commissioned at the discretion of the Lords of the Admiralty as a consequence of the Privateers' Act of 1759. This legislation, intended to curb the activities of small commerce-raiders, further added to the regulatory significance of the declaration, by making an inspection of the vessel and its documentation compulsory before embarkation. If everything was in order, a clearance pass was issued, though if vessels were found to be of an inferior strength to that stated in the declaration, the letter of marque was to be deemed null and void, while commanders sailing without a clearance pass were liable to a year's imprisonment.[18]

As well as making his declaration, the privateering commander was required to provide a bail to guarantee the good conduct of himself and his crew. This surety had been a customary feature of privateering regulation since the fifteenth century, but it was not until 1674 that the Anglo-Dutch Marine Treaty fixed its amount at £3,000 for a vessel with 150 men or more, or £1,500 if a lesser complement was carried. Its significance as a controlling device was clear; thus,

> without any security whatever having been given for their conduct, which is uniformly required and taken in the most solemn manner from every Privateer . . . non-commissioned vessels would be roving about, committing Acts of Violence and depredation on such ships as they might fall in with . . .[19]

Two reputable guarantors, whose circumstances and worth were to be investigated by the Marshal of the Admiralty Court, were to offer this bail which was liable to execution should it be proven that the privateersmen concerned had exceeded their authority.

The limits to this authority were expressed in the 'instructions to privateers' compiled by the Lords of the Admiralty and issued to each recipient of a letter of marque. Though the instructions were modified over time, and additional orders were issued to meet the particular circumstances of a war, they incorporated a consistent core of regulatory provision in force throughout the eighteenth century.[20] They constituted a code of practice intended to guide the behaviour of the privateersman at sea and to ensure the proper adjudication of prizes. Within this code, the Admiralty's concern to maximise the military utility of commissioned vessels is evident. Thus, commanders were instructed to give 'aid and succour' to any British vessel 'found in distress by being in fight, set upon, or taken by the enemy or by reason of any accident'. Commanders were further ordered to maintain 'a correspondence by all conveniences and upon all occasions' with the Admiralty, tendering accounts of their proceedings, particularly any information they might glean 'of the designs of the enemy, of any of their fleets, ships, vessels, or parties'. Moreover, prisoners taken from enemy private ships-of-war were to be identified and conveyed to a British port where they were to be delivered into the 'care and custody' of a civil magistrate or military commander.

Most of the instructions, however, related to the arrest and adjudication of vessels and goods suspected of belonging to enemy subjects. In particular, a sufficient body of evidence was required for the Judge of the Admiralty Court to decide whether the seized property should be condemned. To this end, the instructions laid down that three or four of the prize vessel's crew, including the master and mate if possible, were to be brought or sent to a home port 'to be sworn and examined upon such interrogations as shall lead to the discovery of the truth concerning the interest or property' of the seized ship or goods. These witnesses were obliged to respond to a set of 'standing interrogatories', up to 34 questions administered in the port of landing by local officials authorised by an Admiralty Court warrant, or by the British Consul in overseas bases. This standard examination, to be undertaken within five days of the warrant's issue, was designed to establish the nationality, destination and ownership of the arrested vessel and its cargo, together with the location and circumstances of the capture. In this way, the liability of seized vessels and goods to condemnation might be proved 'out of the prize's own mouth', by the direct admission of witnesses that the property in question was owned by an enemy subject; alternatively, liability might be determined by presumption,[21] if resistance to arrest had been offered, if papers had been concealed or if contradictory testimonies had been given by detainees. To support this information, the Court required documentary evidence, and captors were instructed to submit for examination 'all such papers, passes, sea briefs, charters, bills of lading, letters and other such writings' found on board the arrested vessel, making oath that the documents were 'brought in as they were received and taken without any fraud, addition, subduction, or embezzlement'.

In general, greater emphasis was placed on the submission of evidence as the century proceeded. Accordingly, the option of ransoming vessels and goods was gradually restricted. Common in the early years of the century, and legitimate provided a hostage was taken and a properly accredited ransom bill was presented to the Admiralty Court, ransoming was 'found, by experience, to be liable to great abuses' for the property at issue was released without examination by impartial authorities. Moreover, there was 'reason to apprehend that, upon the whole, it operates more to the Disadvantage than to the benefit of His Majesty's subjects.'[22] Greater control was thus inevitable and the ransoming of neutral vessels was forbidden by the 1759 Privateers' Act, while the practice in general was prohibited during the American Revolutionary War.[23] Increasingly, therefore, captors were required to deliver all the ships and goods they had seized 'into such port of this realm of England or some other port of our dominions . . . as shall be most convenient'. Captured property was to be 'kept and preserved and no part . . . sold, spoiled, wasted or diminished and the bulk thereof shall not be broken before judgement be given in the High Court of Admiralty'.

In following the 'instructions to privateers', the captor was able to supply the Admiralty Court with documentary evidence and the depositions of witnesses—the 'preparatory examinations' upon which a judgement could be made. The matter was then out of the privateersman's hands and subject to the process of adjudication laid down by the 1708 Prize Act and re-enacted at the outset of each subsequent conflict. In uncontested cases, a definitive sentence of 'common condemnation' might be passed within two or three weeks of the prize's landing. Otherwise, if claims upon the seized property were lodged by neutral subjects or rival captors, or if irregularities were alleged to have taken place in the conduct of the arrest, long and complex proceedings might ensue, particularly if the evidence of witnesses from overseas was required. In such cases, the disputed property was released to the claimants by interlocutory decree, on the provision of security, while the Judge reserved his final decision until all the evidence was available. Even then, the case could continue, for aggrieved parties might exercise their right of appeal to the Lords Commissioners of Prize Appeals.[24]

Thus, from the issue of his letter of marque to the final condemnation of his prize, the privateersman's business was sanctioned and controlled by the High Court of Admiralty. This ancient and somewhat quixotic bastion of the civil law appears to have discharged its duties with some efficiency in the eighteenth century. Certainly the marked internal consistency of the archive it generated suggests the orderliness of its proceedings; here, each declaration is supported by a bail, while the adjudication process can usually be traced from libel to appeal in the Court's minute books with the documents themselves, and the evidence presented, preserved separately in a systematic fashion.[25] However, contemporaries found occasion to complain about the idiosyncratic ways of this tribunal. Apart from an appearance to make his declaration and offer bail, the privateersman did not attend the Court. Rather, his interests, and those of claimants, were represented by one of the doctors of civil law who were afforded the monopoly right to undertake the business of the Court. Charges, quite naturally, were levied for the services of these proctors whose privileged position was often resented by their clients. In the 1702–1712 conflict, for instance, there were bitter complaints that the privateering business was impeded by a cumbersome legal process which served 'the private interests of a few useless persons',[26] while in 1745 the death of Everard Sayers moved one newspaper to remark that his office of proctor was a 'place of considerable profit.'[27] Administrative problems also arose from time to time; thus, in 1778, a dispute among the Admiralty clerks 'about the division of the fees of the said commissions'[28] slowed down the procedure, and applicants were further frustrated when

> the warrants granted to letters of marque, privateers, etc, for making reprisals on the French were, either through negligence, inattention or design, sealed with a wrong seal; the consequence thereof is that they must be re-sealed, which will protract their sailing for seven or eight days at least.[29]

The volume of business in the Admiralty Court might also hinder the smooth operation of the system. In one instance, Peter Tessier, commander of the *Spitfire* of Dartmouth, acted on the assumption that his agent had appeared at Doctors' Commons and obtained a commission; alas, he was denied his share in *De Twee Gesusters*, which

> he would have been entitled to if the multiplicity of business in the Admiralty Office had not prevented his letters of marque against the Dutch being sealed until the day next after the capture.[30]

In spite of such bureaucratic lapses, the Court was reasonably effective as an administrative unit, particularly after the reforms of 1708 had expedited its process. However, its ability to enforce the 'instructions to privateers', to control the behaviour of privateersmen, was inevitably limited by the problems of detecting offences committed at sea. Such policing as occurred was undertaken by naval officers who might receive specific orders to apprehend known offenders such as John Patrick, commander of the *Fame*.[31] Alternatively, they might visit a private man-of-war to search for deserters or stragglers, to press men or to check for procedural irregularities. In the course of these encounters misdemeanours might come to light leading to the detention of miscreants like James Verco, commander of the *Fox* privateer, who was arrested by Lord Hervey of the *Daphne* man-of-war on suspicion of illegally removing goods from a neutral vessel.[32] Similarly, customs officials helped to restrain the activities of private commissioned vessels, checking their documentation on clearing and entering port, and occasionally assisting at sea; the *Dreadnought*, for instance, was escorted back to Leith by the *Princess Royal* revenue cutter charged with the unlawful possession of two bags of dollars worth £400.[33] Informants were also encouraged to disclose the transgressions of privateering crews by the prospect of a share in the proceeds of an illegal action; if collusion, for example, between prize and captor was revealed, the source of such information stood to gain half of the value of the property at stake, the remainder being condemned as a droit of the Admiralty.[34] Though the evidence supplied by these policing agencies might be devalued by their own interest in the property at stake, it was often the only 'third-party' information upon which the Court could act.

Penalties were laid down to punish the errant privateersman and to deter would-be transgressors. In cases of serious misconduct, offenders were prosecuted according to the criminal law, with death or imprisonment awaiting those found guilty of murder, mutiny, rape or other crimes of violence. Robbery was sometimes deemed an act of piracy warranting the death sentence as William Lawrence, commander of the *Pluto* privateer, discovered at Execution Dock after he was convicted of stealing goods worth £700 from a Dutch merchantman in 1759.[35] If these sanctions applied to all seafarers, there were specific measures designed to keep the privateersman within the prescribed code of conduct. The privilege and potential advantage afforded to him by the grant of a letter of marque might be withdrawn if the Admiralty Court decided his behaviour warranted the revocation of his commission. In the Seven Years' War, for instance, the letters of marque issued to the *Fame* and the *Sampson* were declared null and void as a consequence of improper conduct,[36] while in 1780 the Lords of the Admiralty ordered the Court to cancel the licences issued to Thomas Short for 'boarding and plundering neutral ships', to Richard Kendall for forcing the Impress Officer at Lancaster to seek refuge in the County Prison, and to William Reynolds for threatening to fire upon a press gang at Faversham.[37]

Such a penalty effectively negated the primary or supplementary aim of these ventures by extinguishing the right of reprisal, a serious proposition for investors and seafarers intent on securing profits from their investments in commerce-raiding. The Court had other means of impairing the financial viability of these enterprises. It could proceed against the bail provided to guarantee the privateersman's good conduct, thereby adding significantly to the costs of promoting the unsuccessful venture. Moreover, the Court ultimately had control over the earnings of privateering venturers, for it was in its power to condemn property to captors or to restore it to claimants should no justification for the seizure be established or a transgression of the 'instructions to privateers' be proven. Compounding this threat to the privateersman's rewards was the possibility that costs and damages might be awarded against him, a substantial deterrent given the heavy legal expenses, and the loss of income, accruing to a claimant from a protracted case.

If such prospects curbed the privateersman's wilder excesses, a further measure of self-regulation was instilled into the privateering business by the owners and setters-out of commerce-raiding ventures. Indiscretions committed aboard their vessels clearly threatened the profits of these privateering entrepreneurs. Accordingly, the articles of agreement[38] drawn up by promoters, and signed by seafarers, generally sought to prohibit the distortion of evidence, plunder, mistreatment of prisoners and other improprieties which might precipitate costly actions in the Admiralty Court. Fear of financial penalty also pervaded the orders given by privateer owners to their commanders, the rights of neutral traders being a particular concern. Thus, in 1703, Patrick Galloway was warned not to 'bring in any free ships', for

> it will never answer our ends, & on the contrary would make us odious to all traders heere [London], & at the Court of Admiralty, & putt us to great charges & damages.[39]

Richard Fitzherbert, on taking command of the *Dreadnought* of Bristol in 1758, received orders to search for contraband goods, and to

> endeavour to get out of the Ship's Company what Secrets you can but we desire you will act very cautiously that we may not be brought into trouble and expense.[40]

In 1780, James Haslam, commander of the *Enterprize* of Liverpool, was

> strictly order'd not to meddle with any neutral vessel whatever unless you are certain by her papers or other indisputable information (freely given without bribery, promised gratuities, or Force) that she has taken in her loading in North America.[41]

To supplement the Admiralty's 'instructions to privateers', managers sometimes provided further information to guide the behaviour of their captains, particularly with regard to contraband goods. John du Grave was consulted by the owners of the *Sarah Gally* regarding neutral trade; subsequently, he advised Patrick Galloway that Sweedes or Danes if you find going to France with Tarr pitch hemp Oake plant and long spruce planks or masts you may bring them in. And if coming from France and have any red wine brandy molasses ginger or Indico or Walnutt tree planks these you must bring in.[42]

Richard Fitzherbert was given more formal advice in the form of a copy of *Naval Trade and Commerce*, a publication containing the 1674 Anglo-Dutch Marine Treaty; he was ordered to refer to this agreement, noting that the Dutch

> have power to carry all sorts of goods to and from our Enemys except Ammunition, but it is different with the Danes, Swedes, Dantzichers, Bremenors, Hamburghers or Italians, any of these carrying to our Enemys any Masts, Sails, Rigging, Cables, Anchors, Cordage, Lead, Pitch, Tarr, Hemp, Guns, Powder, Ball, or any other Ammunition are Contraband Goods and lawful prizes.[43]

Irregularities occurred, however, and numerous cautionary tales emerged from Doctors' Commons. Patrick Galloway was warned not to arrest any more

> troublesome ships & pray for the future be cautious to bring none but such as you have reason to suspect for we finds the Court resents it.

Accordingly, the '*Morning Starr* was released and discharged with her Cargoe . . . & will cost us money', while the master of a detained 'linseed ship speaks bigg & says to make you pay Deare if his ship has been riffled of the least thing.'[44] Later in the century, William Catell, commander of the *Terrible* of Yarmouth, was accused in the Appeal Court of acting 'expressly contrary' to the general 'instructions to privateers', and contravening the additional order of 20 November 1780, in arresting the *Iwan Dawicks*, a neutral Russian vessel.[45] Costs and damages were awarded against Benjamin Buttell, commander of the *King George* of Exeter, for failing to submit Peter Vanden Bussche's property for examination, and attempting to conceal this transgression by placing the penniless, and neutral, Ostender on a Dutch merchantman bound for Norway.[46] A similar inconvenience almost befell Thomas Goldsmith, commander of the *Snap Dragon* of Dartmouth, who neglected to place a signed and dated copy of his letter of marque, let alone a prize crew, aboard *Die Lieffde* as an unidentified sail approached, precipitating a lengthy, expensive, but ultimately successful, suit with the owners of the *Bird*, the unknown ship and alleged joint-captor.[47]

In such cases, the adjudication process served to punish privateersmen for their excessive or careless behaviour. Whether the sanctions built in to the system—substantially supported by the complex legal and bureaucratic provisions which increasingly bounded the shipping industry as a whole—were fully effective in restricting the depredations of privateers is uncertain, for those who were successful in bending or breaking the rules left little trace of their extra-legal activity. Nevertheless, it is clear that a well-developed body of law underlay and circumscribed the privateering business in the eighteenth century; moreover, there were considerable economic incentives to encourage privateering venturers to operate within the regulatory framework.

Notes

1. This was sometimes 'mark', 'mart' or 'march'. The etymological source of the term is unclear, though various explanations have been put forward. The most convincing are Stark's contention that it derived from 'marchare', to mark or set apart certain goods as compensation, or, alternatively, that the term originated from the German 'mark', a boundary or frontier which the petitioner might cross to redress his grievance. F.R. Stark, *The Abolition of Privateering and the Declaration of Paris* (New York: Columbia UP, 1897) 52-3. Partridge suggests that the term is closely akin to the Old French 'merc', or Old Provencal 'marcha', meaning 'seizing, reprisal'. E. Partridge, *Origins, a Short Etymological Dictionary of Modern English* (Routledge & Kegan Paul, 1958) 381.

2. Stark, *Abolition of Privateering*, 52.

3. The 'letters of reprisal' granted to Robert Kitchin of Bristol permitting him to recover £6,500 from the Spaniards in 1585 are reprinted in J.W. Damer Powell, *Bristol Privateers and Ships of War* (Bristol: Arrowsmith, 1930) 345-6. For a detailed discussion of Elizabethan privateering see K.R. Andrews, *English Privateering Voyages to the West Indies, 1588–1595* (Cambridge UP, 1959), and *Elizabethan Privateering during the Spanish War, 1585–1603* (Cambridge UP, 1964).

4. For a detailed analysis of the theory and practice of reprisal in medieval Europe, see M.H. Keen, *The Laws of War in the Late Middle Ages* (Routledge & Kegan Paul, 1965) 218-38.

5. The term 'particular' reprisals is used by Damer Powell, *Bristol Privateers*, xvi.

6. Stark, *Abolition of Privateering*, 50-1.

7. R.G. Marsden, *Law and Custom of the Sea* (Navy Records Society, 1915), I, 115-18.

8. 16 George III, c.5. 'An Act to Prohibit all Trade and Intercourse with the Colonies . . . now in Rebellion'. Privateering commissions against the rebel colonists were authorised by 17 George III, c.7. 'An Act for Enabling the Commissioners for Executing the Office of Lord High Admiral of Great Britain to Grant Commissions to the Commanders of Private Ships and Vessels . . .' No mention is made of 'letters of marque' or 'general reprisals' in this legislation, in contrast to the Prize Acts passed against the sovereign states.

9. For instance, see the 'Instructions to privateers', 29 March 1744. PRO, HCA 26/4; 'Instructions to privateers', 27 March 1777. PRO, HCA 26/60.

10. These Acts are collected in a bound volume of 'Acts Relating to Prizes, 1707-1832'. PRO, HCA 30/524.

11. Enemy ships and goods taken by uncommissioned vessels were normally condemned as 'droits et perquisites' of the Admiralty, the captor having no entitlement to the proceeds of his prize. However, he might petition the state, praying for some reward for the service rendered by his action. Thus, in attacking the islands of Demerara and Essequibo in 1781, four Bristol privateers acted without Dutch letters of marque, trusting 'to the honour of the Government, that no advantage would be taken of that defect, while they only did what appeared to them, to be good service to their country as well as to themselves'. Damer Powell, *Bristol Privateers*, 252-3.

12. British vessels re-captured from the enemy reverted to the original owners provided salvage was paid to the captors. The amount payable varied according to the length of time the vessel had been held by the enemy. Thus, one-eighth of the value was to be paid to the captors if the vessel had been detained for less than 24 hours; one-fifth was payable if 24 to 48 hours had elapsed since the capture; one-third was payable if she had been held for 48 to 96 hours; and one-half was payable if the period of capture had exceeded 96 hours. See 13 George II, c.4. 'An Act for the Encouragement of Seamen and the Speedy and more Effectual Manning of His Majesty's Navy'.

13. The Vice-Admiralty Courts are discussed by C.M. Andrews, *The Colonial Period of American History* (Yale UP, 1938), IV, 222-71.

14. For the early history of the Court, see R.G. Marsden, *Select Pleas in the Court of Admiralty* (Selden Society, 1894 and 1897), I, xi-lxxxviii, and II, xi-lxxxviii; the rise and fall of Doctors' Commons is discussed by F. Wiswall, jr, *The Development of Admiralty Jurisdiction and Practice since 1800* (Cambridge UP, 1970) 75-95; the High Court of Admiralty archive is discussed by J.C. Appleby and D.J. Starkey 'The Records of the High Court of Admiralty as a Source for Maritime Historians' in D.J. Starkey, ed., *Sources for*

a New Maritime History of Devon (Exeter: Devon County Council, 1986) 70-85.

15. To expedite the authorisation process in the outports, declarations could be made before local officials, usually the mayor or customs collector, specifically warranted by the Admiralty Court to undertake this duty. This was a common practice in the later wars of the century, with some 60 per cent of Bristol declarations made in the city in the Seven Years' War, and about 25 per cent of Liverpool declarants appearing before local officials in the 1777–1783 conflict. In these cases, the declaration, and details of the sureties, were posted to Doctors' Commons, and verified by the Court before the formal issue of the letter of marque. Declarations made in the outports are packed with their respective bail documents in PRO, HCA 25. Colonial privateers were authorised by letters of marque, or commissions, issued by the Vice-Admiralty Courts. See Appendix 1.

16. 'Instructions to Privateers', 27 March 1777. PRO, HCA 26/60.

17. PRO, HCA 26/3.

18. 32 George II, c.25. 'An Act for the Encouragement of Seamen and the Prevention of Piracies by Private Ships-of-War'. A handwritten clearance pass issued at Gravesend is preserved with the papers of the *Trimmer* in PRO, C 108/60. Thus,

'Port of London

These are to certify that I have been on board the Schooner *Trimmer* of London whereof Francis Clarke goes Commander bound on a cruize for three months and found her built man'd and arm'd as set forth in a letter of marque dated the Fourteenth day of June in the year one thousand eight hundred & three.

June 19 1803   Thos Porter'

19. PRO, HCA 45/12.

20. Quotations in this section are taken from 'Instructions to Privateers', 27 March 1777. PRO, HCA 26/60.

21. See R. Pares, *Colonial Blockade and Neutral Rights, 1739-1763* (Philadelphia: Porcupine Press, 1975) 115-21.

22. Preamble to 22 George III, c.25. 'An Act to Prohibit the ransoming of Ships and Vessels captured from HM's Subjects'.

23. Ransoms were deemed to be acts of piracy in each of the Prize Acts of the 1777-1783 war. 17 George III, c.7. 'An Act for Enabling the Commissioners . . .'; 19 George III, c.23, 20 George III, c.23, and 21 George III, c.15. Acts 'for the Encouragement of Seamen and the more Speedy and Effectual Manning of His Majesty's Navy'. However, the practice was permissible in exceptional circumstances; thus, if the captor's crew was depleted and a prize crew could not be spared, the prize might be ransomed. An additional question was added to the standing interrogatories to cover this eventuality. See 'Instructions to Privateers', 27 March 1777. PRO, HCA 26/60.

24. The system of adjudication was clarified, with time limits set for the various

stages of the process, in 1708. 6 Anne, c.37. 'An Act for the Encouragement of Trade to America ...'

25. See Appleby and Starkey, 'Records of the High Court of Admiralty'.

26. *Observator*, 6 May 1702.

27. *Penny London Post, or Morning Advertiser*, 11 February 1745.

28. *Morning Chronicle and London Advertiser*, 14 August 1778.

29. *Morning Chronicle and London Advertiser*, 19 August 1778.

30. PRO, HCA 45/12.

31. Damer Powell, *Bristol Privateers*, 210-11.

32. PRO, HCA 45/12.

33. *Newcastle Chronicle*, 9 June 1781.

34. 13 George II, c.4. 'An Act for the Encouragement of Seamen'.

35. *Gentleman's Magazine*, 29 (1759), 496, 604.

36. The crew of the *Sampson* killed four members of a press gang in New York. See J. Press, *The Merchant Seamen of Bristol, 1747–1789* (Bristol UP, 1976) 17. John Patrick, commander of the *Fame*, was guilty of various depredations in the Mediterranean. See Damer Powell, *Bristol Privateers*, 207-13.

37. In the American Revolutionary War, the Lords of the Admiralty instructed Sir James Marriott, Judge of the High Court of Admiralty, to revoke a number of letters of marque and privateer commissions. Some of these instructions are preserved in PRO, HCA 25/210(2).

38. 'Owners and captors' were obliged by the Prize Acts to divide prizes according to 'private contracts'.

39. PRO, C 108/318. Creagh & Fallet to Patrick Galloway, 2-3 March 1703.

40. ACL, Papers of the *Southwell* Privateer, 24651. These documents are printed in Damer Powell, *Bristol Privateers*, 355-67, 370-3.

41. LRO, Account Books of the *Enterprize*, 387 MD 45. Extracts from these documents are printed in G. Williams, *History of the Liverpool Privateers and Letters of Marque with an account of the Liverpool Slave Trade* (Heinemann, 1897) 18-31, 661-4.

42. PRO, C 108/318. John du Grave to Patrick Galloway, 3 January 1703.

43. ACL, Papers of the *Southwell* Privateer, 24651.

44. PRO, C 108/318. Creagh & Fallet to Patrick Galloway, 4 March 1703.

45. PRO, HCA 45/9.

46. PRO, HCA 42/147; HCA 45/9. See D. J. Starkey, 'A Note on the Privateering Career of the *King George*, 1779' *Devon and Cornwall Notes and Queries*, 35 (1986), 10.

47. PRO, HCA 42/135; HCA 45/9.

Two

Private Men-of-War and 'Letters of Marque'

The provisions which regulated British privateering enterprise in the eighteenth century applied to all commissioned vessels, irrespective of the scale and ambition of individual ventures. Thus, the commission, instructions and process of prize adjudication circumscribing the activities of the four-ton *Jolly Sloop* of Jersey in 1704, were similar to those governing the cruise of the *Fame*, of 1,000 tons burthen, in 1744, and the voyage of the 723-ton *Ceres* to Madras and China on account of the East India Company in 1781.[1] Given that such diverse undertakings, by virtue of their letters of marque, formed part of the same privateering business, a broad consideration of the composition of the commissioned force is clearly pertinent. Though the classification and quantification of the licensed fleet by its constituent elements is rendered difficult by the nature of the available sources, and by the ambivalent character of some ventures, distinctive branches of the business can be identified and their significance assessed. In the first instance, it is useful to separate 'private men-of-war' from 'letters of marque'; further division is then appropriate, for these broad categories comprised various discrete, if closely-related, subsidiary elements.

Private Men-of-War

The principal concern of the private man-of-war was to make prize of enemy ships and goods encountered on the high seas. To this end, the commissioned predator embarked on a cruise rather than a voyage, with no set destination and no cargo. To fight the ship, and to navigate prizes to a home port, substantial crews were invariably carried—much larger than the complement of a merchantman of an equivalent tonnage. Generally, though not always, the private man-of-war's company received no wages for its commerce-raiding endeavours; instead, the net receipts of the cruise were divided between the owners of the vessel and the ship's company, with each crew member owning a pre-determined share in the proceeds of the venture. As this was his principal reward, the privateersman was more interested in taking his prize intact than in sinking or destroying enemy craft; thus, surprise and subterfuge were often as vital to his purpose as the carriage and swivel guns, cutlasses and small arms, with which his vessel was normally equipped.

The vessels employed as private men-of-war came from various sources. Some were built to serve as commerce-raiders; the *Caesar* of Bristol, for instance, was described as a private ship-of-war and 'built for that purpose',[2] while the *Swallow* of Exeter 'was a known prime sailer, being built purposely for a privateer'[3] and the *Dragon* was equipped for a six months' cruise, being 'just built for that purpose, and now ready to be launched in the Harbour of Teingmouth.'[4] Naval vessels were sometimes bought and fitted out as private men-of-war; in 1779, for example, a former Russian man-of-war, 'built at Revel by English shipwrights', was purchased by private owners and adapted for privateering,[5] while the *Enterprize* of London was originally the *Aquilon* frigate, and 'when in the King's service mounted 28 guns with 200 men, but has now 32 guns and 220 men.'[6] Prize ships were often fitted out as commerce-raiders, with some, such as the *Dover's Prize* of London, and the *Fly's Prize* of Dover,[7] having their names altered to reflect their origin. The majority of private ships-of-war, however, were merchantmen built primarily for other trades, and modified for cruising against the enemy. This involved little effort in the case of the diminutive cutters, luggers and sloops set forth on short cruises in home waters. In larger craft, it usually entailed the provision of additional armaments, with ports cut for carriage guns or carronades, swivels installed on the quarter deck, or even in the topsails,[8] and cohorns fitted on the main deck. Defensive measures were also taken, with vessels' sides strengthened by extra planking, and reinforced fences erected on the rails to offer protection to the deck crews from enemy musket fire at close quarters.[9]

Whether newly-built, of foreign extraction or re-deployed from other service, private men-of-war embodied a distinct form of enterprise which had no peacetime equivalent. Three strains of this predatory business can be detected in the eighteenth century, with the 'Channel' privateer, the 'deep-water' private ship-of-war and the 'expeditionary force'

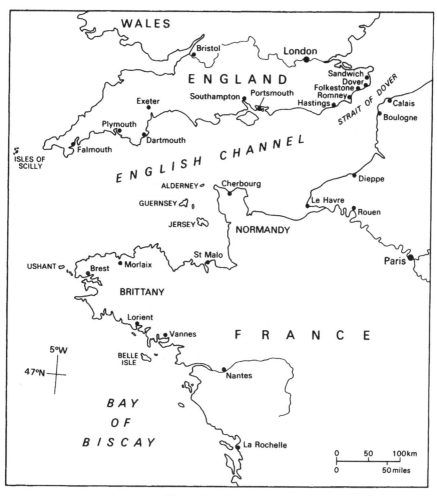

Map 1 – The English Channel
Locational advantages stimulated 'Channel' privateering enterprise in Guernsey, Jersey and the
ports of southern England during Anglo-French wars.

distinguished by their targets, their range and the scale of their operations. It must not be presumed, however, that every private man-of-war fitted precisely into one or other of the sub-groups, or that each venture conformed rigidly to type; indeed, substantial 'grey' areas are apparent at the margins of these categories, as numerous ventures crossed the loosely-drawn boundaries between the various branches of the activity.

1. 'Channel' Privateers

'Channel' privateering was an important and persistent feature of British commerce-raiding enterprise in the eighteenth century. It was largely a function of Anglo-French conflict, for the small craft which participated in this activity preyed on France's coastal and fishing vessels, and on larger neutral merchantmen carrying contraband goods between north-west Europe and the Bourbon ports to the south. Locational advantages dictated that these predatory operations should be undertaken from two principal centres; thus, the ports of Kent and Sussex were ideally placed to mount short forays into the Narrows and across to the French coast, while the Channel Islanders enthusiastically sought to exploit their knowledge of the shores of nearby Brittany and Normandy, and their relative proximity to the ports of the Bay of Biscay. Such enterprise was not exclusive to these bases, however, for the ports of south-west England sometimes engaged in the activity; indeed, during the Anglo-Dutch War of 1780–1783, the West Country emerged as the leading centre of 'Channel' commerce-raiding, while the nature of the prey in this particular conflict also moved entrepreneurs in North Sea ports to invest in small-scale ventures. Moreover, vessels from other bases participated in this business, with diminutive London predators regularly operating from Kentish ports, and similar craft from further afield frequenting the Channel when predatory prospects were bright, commonly using southern havens as their operational bases.

The vessels employed in this branch of the privateering business ranged from the 'cockleshells' and 'row-boats' of less than 10 tons burthen to more substantial craft of up to 130 or 140 tons burthen which possessed an ocean-going capability and might easily function as 'deep-water' private ships-of-war.[10] Most 'Channel' vessels, however, were in the region of 20 to 70 tons burthen, victualled to sustain short cruises of two weeks to three months in duration. Generally, they were equipped with a small number of armaments—perhaps four to eight small carriage guns, and a similar number of swivels—though they normally relied upon their superiority in manpower to subdue small, poorly-defended enemy or neutral vessels. To this end, 'Channel' privateersmen were provided with anti-personnel weapons such as cutlasses, 'musquets' or other small arms to suppress any resistance encountered on boarding a detained vessel. Crew size might vary from a dozen to 80 or so seafarers though, invariably, the ship's company was large relative to the tonnage of the craft and often it included specialists such as a gunner or a surgeon whose duties were associated with fighting rather than handling the ship. In this study, a 'rule of thumb' derived from the 1759 Privateers' Act has been applied to the letter of marque declarations to identify vessels engaged in this form of predatory enterprise; accordingly, licensed craft of the burthen of 99 tons or less, carrying at least one man per 2.5 tons, have been deemed 'Channel' privateers.

While such characteristics were evident in most of the ventures mounted from the South East and the Channel Islands, the impact of the privateering forces set forth from the two regions was somewhat different. In the eastern reaches of the Channel, predators based in ports like Dover, Folkestone, Hastings and Rye took a heavy toll on neutral trade as it passed through the Strait of Dover. Neutral vessels were stopped in these waters and searched for evidence of enemy property concealed on board, or for any contraband goods carried.[11] Though these actions were legitimate in time of war, the excessive zeal with which many privateersmen conducted their examinations, the pillage of innocent vessels and the inconsistencies displayed by the Prize Court in the adjudication of seized property increasingly served to jeopardise Britain's relations with the neutral states. Even if many of these depredations were committed by non-commissioned craft acting illegally, the finger of blame was generally pointed at the small-scale privateering ventures launched from Channel ports. In the Seven Years' War, the situation reached crisis point and to appease the outraged neutral powers Pitt's administration was obliged to pass the Privateers' Act,[12] thereby curbing the activities of private men-of-war of less than 100 tons burthen and 40 men. This measure failed to settle matters, and when the issue revived in the American Revolutionary War, Dutch adherence to the Armed Neutrality of 1780 led to the outbreak of the Fourth Anglo-Dutch conflict and a new phase of the privateering war.

Though not averse to arresting and searching passing neutral vessels, the Channel Islanders directed much of their privateering energy against French coastal traffic. The diminutive predators fitted out in Guernsey and Jersey—and in Alderney from the 1740s—were ideally suited to navigating the shallows of the Breton or Biscay shore, while the Island seafarers were adept at negotiating the rocks and shoals of these treacherous waters. Here, off the headlands and islets of a much indented coastline, the Island privateersmen might dream of capturing the valuable West Indiaman heading fully laden with coffee, cotton or sugar for a French Atlantic port. Occasionally, such fanciful thoughts were realised, particularly from the 1740s onwards as Channel Island venturers grew in ambition and set forth larger craft to cruise further south. More normally, however, it was the humble coasting vessel or fishing shallop which succumbed to Island predators. Though such captures were relatively insignificant in themselves, the cumulative effect of these continual attacks on coastwise traffic was considerable, as supplies of coal, grain, salt and other necessaries were regularly interrupted. At times, indeed, this disruption had a demoralising effect upon the maritime communities of Brittany, Normandy and as far west as the Gironde, as 'some thousands of Frenchmen suffered in their persons or in their purses'.[13] Conversely, the commerce-raiding business was an important feature of the Channel Islands' wartime economy throughout the eighteenth century. A dearth of alternative investment opportunities, together with their advantageous strategic location, meant that the Islanders engaged in the 'new vocation' of privateering with increasing enthusiasm and success from the 1690s.[14] In the face of such an irritant the French seriously considered invading the Islands in 1759 and again in 1778.

2. 'Deep-water' Private Ships-of-War

The 'deep-water' arm of the privateering business comprised relatively large-scale ventures set forth to seek the valuable cargoes of colonial produce returning to Europe from the Caribbean, South America or the East Indies. Though these opportunist craft might prey on the small fry which sustained the 'Channel' privateers, it was the prospect of capturing the consignments of bullion, cotton, spices and sugar carried on the trans-oceanic routes that principally motivated their activities. Such 'capital' prizes[15] were generally conveyed in large, well-defended vessels, often sailing for France or Spain in convoys with further protection afforded by naval escorts in home waters. Assailants required some considerable force to apprehend these rich cargoes; accordingly, 'stout' vessels with heavy armaments and substantial crews were fitted out to cruise the shipping lanes of the north-eastern Atlantic in search of homeward-bound 'Martinicomen', East Indiamen or register-ships.

Such predators varied in size, with 100- or 120-ton craft cruising in the same stations—with similar, if lesser, goals—as the more typical

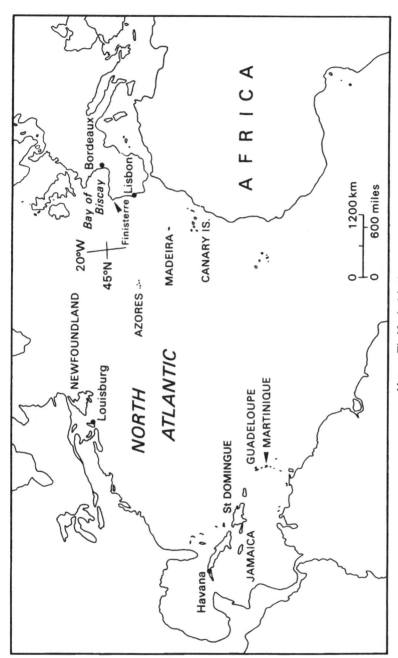

Map 2 – The North Atlantic

Cargoes bound from the West India islands of Guadeloupe, Martinique and St Domingue for France's Atlantic ports were the principal target of British 'deep-water' private ships-of-war cruising in the Western Approaches and the Bay of Biscay.

'deep-water' vessels of 200 to 450 tons burthen and the mammoth private ships-of-war burthen in excess of 500 tons. Manning was the principal signal of 'deep-water' intent, however, as large numbers of seafarers were invariably recruited to work the guns and man prizes as well as handle the ship. In the present work, the 1759 Privateers' Act again provides the guidelines by which this commerce-raiding genre has been determined; thus, vessels exceeding 100 tons burthen, exhibiting tons-per-man ratios of 2.5 or less in the letter of marque declarations, are deemed to have operated as 'deep-water' private men-of-war. Furthermore, to take account of the scale economies apparent in the larger vessels, a benchmark of 100 seafarers has been applied to the declarations; unless there is conclusive evidence to the contrary, complements of this or a greater magnitude—larger, that is, than the 99-strong crew of the era's largest merchant vessel, the East Indiaman—are assumed to have served aboard 'deep-water' predators.

As relatively substantial quantities of capital and labour were required to promote the large-scale enterprise, London and Bristol, where such resources were available in some abundance, tended to dominate the 'deep-water' form of predation. In particular, it was from the Thames and Bristol's chief roadstead, Kingroad, that the most powerful units of the commissioned fleet—the 'privateers of force'—set forth, with complements of at least 150 men eager to profit at the expense of the more valuable elements of the enemy's trade. Armed with at least 24 carriage guns of 9-, 12- or even 18-pounds weight of shot, these powerful vessels—many of which were former men-of-war purchased from the Navy or captured from the enemy—were particularly prominent in the propitious conditions of the 1740s and 1750s.

'Deep-water' companies were consciously organised along naval lines to maximise the prize-taking capacity of the venture; thus, a hierarchical command structure, specialisation of task and co-ordination of effort were held to be vital to the ship's operations. This is clear in the advice offered by William Hutchinson to the intending privateer commander. In the view of this experienced mariner and sometime privateersman, an optimum complement of 160 men was required to fight and handle a private ship-of-war of 24 carriage guns; during action, he opined, 33 seafarers should be deployed on the quarter deck under the commander's direction, with 80 on the main deck in the charge of the first and second lieutenants, and a further 43 stationed on the forecastle under the boatswain's command. An important feature of Hutchinson's ideal quarter bill was the role of the specialist crew members and their mates; thus, the master was to 'assist and work the ship according to orders', the carpenter and his crew were 'to attend the pumps and the wings about the water's edge, fore and aft, with shot plugs', while 'in the powder room' the gunner's mate and an assistant were 'to fill and hand powder to the boys, carriers'.[16]

Though it is unlikely that any private ship-of-war was manned or handled precisely in the fashion of Hutchinson's model predator, his basic premise of the efficacy of the measured recruitment and orderly deployment of labour is apparent in the surviving muster rolls and articles of agreement appertaining to such ventures. The articles of the *Tygress* of Dartmouth, for instance, specifically stipulated that 200 men were needed to work and fight the 28-gun commerce-raider,[17] while in the contracts relating to ventures such as the *York* of Dover, and the *Tyger* and *Tygress* of Bristol, the quality and intended share allocation of officers and specialist crew members was determined before enlistment took place.[18] These 'deep-water' crews were hierarchical in character, with the structure of the larger complements—of over 200 men—similar to that evident in the typical naval fifth- or sixth-rate of the mid-eighteenth century.[19] Thus, the commander was aided by up to four lieutenants, with the further support of trainee officers—dubbed midshipmen or servants—normally available. In common with all substantial sailing craft of the time, both naval and mercantile, the master, boatswain and carpenter, with their respective mates, crews and yeomen, were responsible for the handling, rigging and maintenance of the vessel.[20] Craftsmen were also recruited to co-ordinate the belligerent facets of the private ship-of-war's business: as in naval vessels, the carriage guns were in the charge of the gunner, his mates and the quarter gunners; the master-at-arms, or 'captain of maraines', assisted by a sergeant and corporals, drilled the seamen and landmen in the use of small arms, cutlasses and other anti-personnel devices; such weapons were maintained by the armourer and his crew; while the surgeon and his mates dealt with the sick and wounded. Lesser rates such as quarter master, linguist, steward, clerk and cook were generally recruited,[21] and most 'deep-water' private men-of-war had some provision for music, with a 'French Horn', drummers and trumpeters shipped aboard to sustain morale.

Subservient to the officers and craftsmen were the 'ship's people' who constituted the bulk of the complement. Able seamen were the most skilled and valued element of this group of privateersmen; fully-trained men with at least two or three years experience at sea, their services were generally much in demand during wartime and in privateers they normally commanded a full share in the prize fund. The less experienced mariners were rated variously as 'ordinary', 'three-quarter', 'two-thirds' or even 'one-quarter' seamen—ranks which equated their share entitlement with their expertise. Inferior still were the landmen and boys who were fresh to the sea; unskilled in the arts of seamanship, these ratings normally warranted a half-share, or less, in the net proceeds of a venture. The balance between the skilled and the inexperienced elements of the 'ship's people' varied widely, though it was unusual for landmen and boys to outnumber 'able saylers' and 'ordinary' ratings. In the *Alexander*, for instance, 55 able seamen served alongside 26 'part seamen', 10 landmen and 13 boys, while another Bristol ship, the *Sheerness*, was manned by 106 able and ordinary seamen, 44 landmen, and some 33 'sea lads' and 'land boys', and the London vessel *Hardwicke* mustered 60 full, and 23 ordinary, seamen, as well as 47 landmen.[22]

If the crews of these substantial predators were similar in structure to the companies of the lesser rated naval vessels—the principal difference being that landmen were carried instead of marines—the transient, speculative nature of privateering enterprise made it unlikely that they ever approached the fighting efficiency of the King's ships. However, attempts were made to enhance the effectiveness of 'deep-water' private ships-of-war. Drill was recommended by William Hutchinson; commanders should therefore

> take the first opportunity to have all hands called to quarters; the officers in their stations to have everything made properly ready and fit for action; to have a general exercise, not only of the great guns and small arms, but the methods of working and managing the ship.[23]

Captain Finmore of the *Lord Nelson* was instructed to 'practice the men with guns at all times',[24] while the commander of the *Southwell*, John Engledue, was ordered to organise the crew 'as soon as you get under sail', appointing 'every man his station in time of Action or Engagement'. Engledue was further advised

> that all opportunities may be embraced for Instructing your Men in the use of the small arms, and that others be exercised with the great Guns that they not be at a loss when they come to engage with an Enemy.[25]

Clearly, such preparations might be a vital factor during battle when life, limb and profit could depend upon the smooth integration of the various navigational, handling and fighting skills of the crew. A further means of enhancing the potency of 'deep-water' predators was effected by cruising in company with a vessel of similar intent. Some commerce-raiding projects comprised two or more ships fitted out specifically to operate in consort; if the *Royal Family* squadron—five vessels mustering 112 guns and 853 men[26]—was the most notable example, lesser combinations, such as the *Warren Gally* and *Saltash*, the *Brutus* and *Little Brutus*, both of London, and the *Ellis* and *Gregson* of Liverpool, were common. Other liaisons were arranged on meeting at sea, the *Southwell's* owners being

> of the opinion 'twill be for the benefit of the Cruize if you could be in conjunction with another good privateer, therefore if you meet one at sea of equal or superior (not less) force than ours that will join, you have our consent so to do and enter into a written agreement with the Commander and Officers of such, that what you take in conjunction be equally divided.[27]

The cruising stations in which the *Southwell* might meet her fellow 'deep-water' private men-of-war were a further distinctive feature of this form of privateering enterprise. In general, these large-scale ventures operated beyond the confines of the English Channel, seeking to intercept their homeward-bound prey in the north-eastern Atlantic. Occasionally, this entailed cruising to the west of the Azores where the French West Indiamen and Spanish register-ships might be encountered before they could meet up with naval escorts. The more powerful concerns tended to adopt this tactic, with the *Duke* and the *Prince Frederick*—of 48 guns and 399 men in total—striking such a target to the west of the Azorean island of St Mary's in 1745 as they cruised between the Western Islands and Newfoundland.[28] Commonly, however, the Azores marked the western boundary of the 'deep-water' vessel's operations; thus, the *Enterprize* was to depart Liverpool by the North Channel, gain the longitude of 20°W and cross the latitudes 'under an easy sail' to the Azores. As her owners considered that 'the odds is considerably against rambling in the wide ocean', the *Enterprize* was to proceed to the latitude of Ushant, at longitude 16°W, and cruise between that station and the Western Island of Corvo.[29] Further to the east, the Bay of Biscay was much frequented by private men-of-war; some, like the *Dreadnought,* sailed across the Bay between latitudes 48°N and 46°N, within longitude 10°W 'unless you see cause or give chase',[30] while others hovered close inshore, the *Enterprize* heading for Belle Isle in her second cruise 'as it is the place where all vessels bound for Nantz and Bordeaux take in their pilots',[31] and the *Southwell* despatched to steer as near the French coast as wind, weather and the safety of our ship will admit, more especially when you are to the Southward of Ushent.[32]

'Deep-water' predators also operated south of Finisterre, particularly during Anglo-Spanish hostilities, with predators cruising between Cape St Vincent and the Azores to ensnare vessels approaching enemy bases from a southerly direction;[33] indeed, at times when the prospects of taking prizes in the Atlantic diminished—in 1758–1759, for instance—some private ships-of-war were despatched to cruise in the Mediterranean.

Thus, it was largely off the Atlantic seaboard of western Europe, in a variety of locations, that the 'deep-water' private ships-of-war were to be found. Here, they cruised for anything between three and nine months in search of the valuable prizes which alone could cover the substantial costs incurred in mounting such enterprises and provide a return for the owners and seafarers who invested their capital and labour in the venture. Limited trading options faced these craft, for the only available cargoes were the wines and fruit of the Azores, Canaries or Madeira—of insufficient value to offset seriously the losses of a barren cruise. Their prospective prizes, moreover, were often reluctant to yield without a fight; thus, high financial and physical risks were intrinsic to this element of the commerce-raiding business.

3. 'Expeditionary' Forces

A relatively small portion of British privateering enterprise in the eighteenth century manifested itself in the mounting of 'expeditions'. These highly ambitious attempts to plunder Spanish America and the East Indies were rarely undertaken, for capital requirements were high, the logistical problems associated with despatching two or more vessels to distant and largely unknown waters were immense, and the returns to be earned were uncertain and inevitably deferred. Accordingly, only a handful of 'expeditionary' ventures were assembled in the eighteenth century, with Bristol and London again the principal sources of capital and other outfitting resources. Yet this branch of the business has left an indelible mark on privateering history, for the expeditions of Dampier, Rogers, Shelvocke and Comyn were very much in the heroic tradition of Drake, Hawkins and the other celebrated sea-dogs of the Elizabethan era. Moreover, in these voyages some of the most enduring legends of British privateering were born: thus, it was during William Dampier's ill-fated cruise of 1703–1706 that Alexander Selkirk was marooned on Juan

Fernandez, to be rescued after four years and four months of solitude by Woodes Rogers and subsequently immortalised in Defoe's *Robinson Crusoe*; similarly, the morbid black albatross shot by Simon Hatley as it stalked the *Speedwell* in 1719 lives on in Coleridge's *Ancient Mariner*.

As business concerns, these ventures were characterised by their scale and their ambition. The vessels employed in this long-distance enterprise were not necessarily large, ranging from the *Cinque Ports Gally*—bearing the hallmarks, at 130 tons burthen, 20 guns and 90 men,[34] of a modest 'deep-water' predator—to Phillips Comyn's flagship, the 1,000-ton *Fame*, carrying 56 guns and 400 men. They all operated with consorts, however: the *Cinque Ports Gally* accompanied Dampier's command, the *St George*; the *Duke* and the *Dutchess,* mustering 600 tons, 54 guns and 270 men, departed Bristol in 1708 with instructions 'in everything to behave yourselves one toward another as a kind Duke regarding his beloved Dutchess';[35] George Shelvocke's *Speedwell*, of 200 tons burthen and 100 men, embarked for the South Seas in the company of the slightly more powerful *Success*;[36] while the mammoth *Fame*'s principal consort was the *Winchelsea*, a substantial vessel of 550 tons burthen, 32 guns and 200 men.[37] To sustain their sizeable complements each vessel was laden with considerable quantities of provisions and stores, sufficient to last, in theory, for a cruise in the Pacific of up to 18 months' duration. In practice, supplies were often inadequate and replenishment was accomplished by plunder or purchase *en route*, a frequent bone of contention between owners and men when the fruits of the venture were finally assessed.

In this quest to secure the riches of the Indies, the venturers who instigated these 'expeditions' invariably devised a plan of campaign. Dampier's two small craft sailed round the Horn in a vain attempt to seize the Acapulco-Manila register-ship in 1704;[38] despite this failure, a similar scheme was taken up by the Bristol fitters-out of the *Duke* and the *Dutchess* who informed their captain, Woodes Rogers, of 'our grand design being to seek out one or bothe the ships belonging to Acapulco in South America'.[39] A decade later, the *Speedwell* and the *Success* set out to reach the Peruvian base of Payta by March 1720 and there to intercept the

> King of Spain's ships [which] sail from Lima for Panama with the Kings treasure, which ships carry the revenues of Peru.[40]

If these treasure ships escaped, the private men-of-war were to emulate Woodes Rogers' success in plundering the garrison of Guayaquil.

In 1744, the '*Fame* and her consorts' embarked with an even more ambitious plan; thus, 'in the best concerted scheme that was ever undertaken by a body of merchants', a syndicate of wealthy London shipowners intended that the 'expedition' should initially cruise in the Western Approaches,

> from thence to look at Madeira or St Jago for water ... if time was to permit to cruise for a season at or near Buenos Aires, but to be sure to get time enough to the Straits of Sunda or Banda to meet the French homeward bound ships from East India.[41]

When these plans came to nothing, Commodore Comyn, in desperation, revived the 'grand design' of 40 years earlier and tried to rally his beleaguered forces to cruise in the *Winchelsea* 'among the Phillipine Islands to intercept the Acapulco ship bound to Manilla'. Further failure 'broke the heart' of the Commodore, 'dampened his spirits and carried him off in a fit of fever' on 28 May 1746.[42] Subsequently, the 186 survivors of his expedition struggled back to London in the damaged and leaky *Winchelsea* to demand retribution from the ship's owners in a bitter and violent meeting at the King's Arms Tavern in London.[43]

While the demise of Comyn and his venture was the most abject, it was not the only expedition to fail amidst acrimony and litigation. Indeed, conflict and tension plagued relations between the various parties to these long-distance ventures, with Shelvocke accused of piracy by his owners,[44] Dampier marooning his sailing master Selkirk, and the owners and the men of the *Duke* and the *Dutchess* vigorously contesting the division of their spoils. That Rogers' expedition was the only one to achieve its objectives indicates the high-risk character of this form of commerce-raiding. Essentially, it was an anachronistic activity, an attempt to seek the treasures which had drawn the Elizabethan adventurers to the New World. It was a form of enterprise confined to the Anglo-Spanish wars of the first half of the eighteenth century[45] when incursions into the Pacific to pillage Spanish trade and settlements might realistically be expected to produce rewards. Increasingly, as the century wore on, it was in home waters and in the Atlantic that British privateering venturers focused their attentions, with France's trans-oceanic and coastal trades their principal targets.

'Letters of Marque'

By the 1770s the term 'letter of marque' was commonly applied to a commercial vessel issued with a privateer commission, or letter of marque. The *Tartar*, for instance, was a 'letter of marque warranted to sail with the first convoy for Smyrna and Constantinople';[46] the crew of the 'letter of marque' *Emperor* paid sixpence each to the Bristol Hospital Fund on their return from Jamaica;[47] while a bounty of £185 rewarded the owners and men of the *Marianne* and *Achilles* 'letters of marque of London' for their capture of an enemy *corsaire*.[48] Such a designation referred to a particular form of enterprise in which an overseas trading vessel was imbued with a prize-taking facility by the privateering licence held by her captain. Widely practised throughout the eighteenth century, this activity combined the conveyance of goods with predation upon the enemy's seaborne property. Typically, therefore, foreign-going craft embarked upon voyages to specified destinations, though time might be set aside for cruising in search of prize; cargoes were generally loaded, yet hold space might be restricted by the carriage of additional men for defensive or offensive purposes; and crews invariably served for a regular monthly wage, with the prospect of a share in the net proceeds of a prize to encourage their valour or opportunism.

The balance between the trading and commerce-raiding components of such ventures varied considerably, however. Whereas the predatory function was largely incidental to the predominantly commercial purpose of some enterprises, in others the reverse was true as vessels set forth to seek prizes, with the secondary intention of picking up a cargo should their principal quest prove fruitless. Though delineation by motive is somewhat difficult using the letter of marque declarations, a range of other sources makes it possible to distinguish the more predatory 'cruising voyage' form of 'letter of marque' from the essentially commercial 'armed trading vessel'; in addition, the numerous commissioned vessels engaged in restricted trades or in non-commercial occupations—the 'specialist vessels'—can be identified and considered as a separate strain of 'letter of marque' enterprise.

1. 'Cruising Voyages'
The vessels engaged in 'cruising voyages' had close affinities with 'deep-water' private ships-of-war. Heavily-manned and armed, they were substantial craft of some 300 to 500 tons burthen, set out with the principal aim of apprehending the enemy's sea-borne commerce. In contrast to the 'deep-water' predator, this was not the sole purpose of the exercise, for the 'cruising voyage' was undertaken to the Caribbean, the Mediterranean or even to the waters off Newfoundland—stations where there existed

prospects of securing a cargo of sufficient value to offset the losses which might accrue from a barren cruise. This trading option, and the distance of their chosen stations, held ramifications for the organisation of the 'cruising voyage'. Thus, regular wages were paid to seafarers—'which is an advantage privateers have not', as one recruiting notice pointed out[49]—who also owned a stake in the net prize fund. As in other 'letters of marque', however, the crew's portion of the spoils was normally limited to a fifth or a quarter of the net produce, compared to the half-share generally owned by 'deep-water' privateersmen. Consequently, to restrict the wages bill, and to improve the value of shares for those enlisting, crews were relatively limited in size, with 70 to 120 men recruited where a 'deep-water' private ship-of-war of an equivalent size might be served by 150 to 250 seafarers.

This distinctive form of commerce-raiding venture was largely deployed in the Mediterranean in the early part of the eighteenth century, with a number of substantial craft also operating off the Newfoundland Banks. As European trade with the Caribbean and North America increased during the course of the century, and the focus of the Anglo-French struggle shifted from Europe to the colonial theatre, so 'cruising voyages' to the West Indies were increasingly undertaken. Whereas the 1702-1712 war had seen vessels such as the *Diligence*, of 330 tons burthen and 140 men, heading for the Straits,[50] and the 400-ton *Camberwell Gally*, with 85 men, carrying prizes into St John's, Newfoundland,[51] the Seven Years' War witnessed a growing number of ventures like the 400-ton *Britannia*, engaged on her 'present cruising voyage to Nevis and St Christopher',[52] with 88 seafarers signing her articles. In the 1777–1783 war, the vacuum left by the defection of American colonial privateers to the ranks of the enemy stimulated Caribbean 'cruising voyages' as never before;[53] thus, the *Hercules* required men 'for a cruize and a voyage to Jamaica', the *Renown* cleared 'for the island of St Vincent and a Cruize', while in Jamaica there 'arrived the letter of marque sloop *Gayton* from a cruize, with three valuable prizes'.[54]

Such ventures were mounted from the major overseas trading ports where merchants and shipowners with considerable experience in long-distance commercial enterprise, as well as access to the necessary capital and manpower resources, ran their operations. Accordingly, London entrepreneurs were heavily involved in this dual-purpose element of the privateering business, particularly in the vessels despatched to cruise and trade in the Mediterranean. Bristol's extensive interests in the trans-Atlantic trades were reflected in the outset of a growing number of

'cruising voyages' to the Caribbean from the 1750s onwards, while
Liverpool's commissioned fleet, especially in the 1777–1783 war,
contained a high proportion of vessels fitted out to cruise in the West
Indies or to take in a cargo if, like Richard Woods of the *Hector,* through
'misfortune . . . I can't meet up with the Enemy'.[55] In adopting such a
flexible approach, venturers were responding to the high risks involved
in long-distance commerce-raiding projects by seeking to ensure that their
vessels generated an income, be it prize or freight.

2. 'Armed Trading Vessels'
'Armed trading vessels' formed a considerable part of the commissioned
fleets set forth from the British Isles in the eighteenth century. These
ships were principally concerned with overseas trade, and the conveyance
of goods to a specified destination remained their master's priority
notwithstanding the right of reprisal afforded him by the grant of a letter
of marque. As in peacetime, therefore, the chief remuneration for owners
of these vessels was the profit earned from the freights charged to
consignees, while the crew's labour was rewarded by the payment of
monthly wages. Privateer commissions were taken out in an attempt to
supplement these earnings by adding a prize-taking facility to such
commercial ventures; accordingly, to enhance the predatory potential of
the operation, armed merchantmen generally forsook the restrictive
company of a naval convoy.[56]

In some cases, trading vessels might engage in commerce-raiding
activity for set periods of their voyages. William Hutchinson, for instance,
wrote of the experience he gained in an East Indiaman 'fitted out first to
cruise three months off the Western Islands',[57] while in March 1781 it
was reported that Thomas Frocks, captain of the *Marlborough* of Whitby,
had sailed 'about three weeks since in order to cruize against the Dutch
before he went to the whale fishery'.[58] Other vessels might seek prizes
at the captain's discretion; thus, the articles of the *Sarah* of Liverpool,
commanded by John Taylor in her passage to Barbados, had it that

> whereas the said John Taylor has obtained a letter of marque and hath
> armed ye said ship, it is agreed that he shall if he thinks proper, cruize
> on his voyage.[59]

A defensive motive also underlay the issue of letters of marque for
trading ventures. Enemy naval and privateering activity persistently
threatened commercial operations in wartime, and shipowners were often
obliged to take precautionary steps, fitting additional armaments in their

vessels and recruiting extra hands to man the guns and otherwise ward off assailants. To encourage crews 'to behave gallant and brave in defending the ship . . . in case she shall be attacked', shipowners took out commissions, thereby obtaining for themselves and their employees the sole right to the net proceeds of enemy ships and goods taken in the course of a successful defensive action. In providing financial incentives, therefore, it was intended that seafarers should 'defend and fight the ship as though she was actually one of His Majesty's Ships of War'.[60]

Ships engaged in all branches of overseas commerce were commissioned in wartime. Though imbued with a secondary commerce-raiding purpose and primed for defence—functions which implied the enlistment of extra hands—these 'armed trading vessels' were similar in character and mode of operation to the ships normally employed in their respective trades. Thus, slavers of 80 to 250 tons burthen and 30 or 40 men embarked from Chester, Jersey and Lancaster as well as from Bristol, Liverpool and London on their 'triangular' voyages to the coast of Africa and the West Indies; Newfoundlandmen of 50 to 100 tons burthen, with crews 15 to 25 strong, left West Country ports with salt, fishing equipment and 'bye-boatmen' for the fishery, some returning via Southern Europe where their cargoes of dried cod were exchanged for wine, fruit and specie; capacious ships of up to 500 tons burthen—with companies as small as 20 men—left east coast ports to convey coal to London or to cross the North Sea to pick up timber and naval stores from Scandinavia; whalers, with harpooners, spectioneers and boatsteerers in their complements, were fitted out in the Tyne to ply the waters of the Davis Straits; and a variety of craft departed Kingroad, the Mersey or the Thames for the West Indies and the Mediterranean with cargoes of British manufactures to exchange for the exotic produce of those regions. Diverse, dispersed and preoccupied with trade, these armed merchantmen nevertheless constituted an important—at times, preponderant—element of British privateering enterprise in the eighteenth century, for vested in each was the right to make prize of the enemy's sea-borne commerce.

3. 'Specialist Vessels'

Vessels in government employment, and the ships owned or operated by the chartered trading companies, were a prominent aspect of 'letter of marque' enterprise. Engaged in specialist occupations, these craft possessed a prize-taking capability in the manner of the 'armed trading vessel'. Thus, the privateer commission they carried added a predatory dimension to their prescribed duties, a means by which both owners and seafarers might augment their income. Many privately-owned ships leased to the government to convey troops, ordnance stores and provisions to foreign and colonial theatres of war enjoyed this privilege. Such vessels were particularly evident in the American Revolutionary War when the state, faced with immense logistical difficulties, hired an unprecedented number of merchant vessels, many of which were provided with commissions to stimulate the opportunistic or defensive qualities of the crew as occasion might demand. Similar reasoning explained the issue of letters of marque for the *Owner's Adventure*, a craft 'constantly employed between Harwich and London as Surveyor of Her Majesty's anchors',[61] while it also underlay the licensing of the *Falmouth*, a government advice boat charged to sail from 'Plymouth with the trade to Portsmouth',[62] and the grant of a commission for the *Rose* and other vessels in the service of the Customs Commissioners. However, commerce-raiding was not to impede the regular duty of these vessels; thus, in allowing Richard Wallis, commander of the cruizer *Rose*, to take out letters of marque, the Customs Board warned their employee

> in the strictest manner not to quit his station and Duty as a Revenue Officer under pretence of looking for captures, it being our Resolution to recall the Permission hereby granted as soon as it shall be discovered in any Instance to be prejudicial to our service.[63]

Whether such permission was required by commanders of chartered trading company vessels is unclear; if so, it was rarely refused, for the majority of ships operated by the Hudson's Bay Company and the East India Company sailed from London with privateer commissions. These distinctive 'letters of marque' were engaged in highly regularised trades, a factor reflected in the declarations made by their commanders in the Admiralty Court. Thus, the Hudson's Bay vessels were normally commissioned in the late spring as they prepared to leave the Thames in May, intent on reaching Albany, Fort York or Churchill by August. There, the lading of trade goods and supplies for the Canadian settlements was exchanged for the return cargo of furs, the vessels departing for London as soon as possible to avoid the ice which blocked the northern seas in the winter months.[64] The ships engaged by the Company were relatively small, ranging from the *Mary Frigat*, of 130 tons burthen, to the 290-ton *Sea Horse*,[65] though they were generally worked by 40 to 60 men, comparatively large crews suggesting that the Company, in common with other employers, recruited extra men in wartime.

East Indiamen normally left the Downs during the winter, the ships bound for China sailing in November or December, with a second division of vessels leaving for India in February. In wartime, these outward-bound detachments might amalgamate to suit the Admiralty's convoy schedule. Typically, the cargoes carried to the Company's eastern settlements were provisions or ordnance stores, though, on occasion, Indiamen carried troops and stores to the East Indies for the government.[66] After unloading at Madras, Bombay, Calcutta or Canton, the Indiaman's hold was filled up with 'fine' wares, such as silks, piece goods and spices, or the 'gruff' goods—saltpetre, sugar and rice in India, or tea in China—leaving for London early in the New Year to arrive home in the summer after a round trip of some eighteen months. The vessels undertaking these arduous voyages were built specifically for the East Indies trade, and were owned by an elite group of City merchants, the 'shipping interest', which had the monopoly right to supply the Company's shipping requirement. In general, Indiamen were the largest, most costly and heavily-armed British merchant ship of the day, their tonnage increasing from some 300 to 500 tons burthen in the 1702–1712 conflict, to over 700 tons burthen, on average, in the American Revolutionary War.

In the middle decades of the century, the tonnages declared by captains of Indiamen applying for letters of marque exhibited a remarkable degree of uniformity, the vast majority falling between 490 and 499 tons burthen. In fact, the tonnage declared in these cases was not the true burthen of the vessel, but the basic tonnage chartered by the Company. The standard charter party of the mid-eighteenth century provided that only 404 tons was paid for at the going rate, with a further 80 tons of iron kintledge or ballast carried out and home at a very low rate, and an allowance of 15 tons made for the private trade of the ship's officers. Beyond this guaranteed freight, the Company 'had the right but not the obligation to fill the ship up, paying for most of the cargo over 499 tons at half the charter party rate.'[67] It was therefore in its interest to hire larger ships, as a higher proportion of the total was paid for at half price; thus, the majority of Indiamen were probably from 600 to 800 tons builders' measurement,[68] though the figure of 499 tons, or thereabouts, was generally declared. Uniformity is also apparent in the manning and armament details given by the Company's captains; however, these figures were more accurate, reflecting the strength of the Indiaman, which was normally armed with 26 to 30 carriage guns, often 12- or 18-pounders, and worked by 99 men.

Indiamen were equipped with such powerful weapons and large crews primarily to defend the valuable cargoes of the Orient. However, like other 'letters of marque', the privateer commission they normally carried gave them the right to attack enemy shipping. It also vested in the owners and men of these vessels the sole right to the proceeds of prizes taken as a result of such opportunistic actions as well as those seized in essentially defensive engagements. Thus, an element of these commissioned trading or specialist voyages was concerned with the apprehension of prize. However marginal it might be to the vessel's main purpose, this element constituted a privateering venture in which investors risked their capital, and seafarers their labour, in a quest for profit. Clearly, therefore, the commerce-raiding dimension of the 'letter of marque' was based on the same principle as that which underlay the operation of the overtly predatory private man-of-war. In practice, the peculiar character of the risks and rewards inherent in prize-taking endeavour was common to all branches of the privateering business; moreover, it governed the organisation of individual enterprises as venturers attempted to curtail the hazards and realise the profitable potential of their speculations.

Notes

1. Declarations 6 July 1704, 2 April 1744, 3 October 1781. PRO, HCA 26/19, 4, 69.
2. *Felix Farley's Bristol Journal*, 18 September 1756.
3. *Exeter Flying Post*, 19 February 1779.
4. *Exeter Flying Post*, 5 March 1779.
5. *Exeter Flying Post*, 25 June 1779.
6. *Morning Chronicle and London Advertiser*, 2 September 1778.
7. Declarations 20 September 1744, 19 October 1757. PRO, HCA 26/22, 8.
8. The *Mars Privateer* of Guernsey was fitted with 'two brass 3-pounders in each top'. *Exeter Flying Post*, 18 February 1780. However, William Hutchinson warned that swivels located in the topsails were potentially dangerous, a source of fire and self-destruction. *A Treatise on Naval Architecture* (Liverpool, 4th edn, 1794) 218.
9. See Hutchinson, *Naval Architecture*, 217-18.
10. In the 1740s, for instance, Dover venturers fitted out five vessels of over 120 tons burthen, all of which operated in the fashion of the 'Channel' predator.
11. See W.R. Meyer, 'Mascall's Privateers' *Archaeologia Cantiana*, XCV (1979), 214-5.
12. 32 George II, c.25. 'An Act for the Encouragement of Seamen and the Prevention of Piracies by Private Ships-of-War'.

13. Bromley, 'Channel Island Privateers', 447.
14. See J. S. Bromley, 'A New Vocation: Privateering in the Wars of 1689–97 and 1702–13', and A. G. Jamieson, 'The Return to Privateering: Channel Island Privateers, 1739-83' in A. G. Jamieson, ed., *A People of the Sea. The Maritime History of the Channel Islands* (Methuen, 1986) 109-72.
15. A 'capital' prize was worth £10,000 or more according to Francis Ingram, managing owner of the *Enterprize* of Liverpool. LRO, Account Books of the *Enterprize*, 387 MD 45.
16. Hutchinson, *Naval Architecture*, 224-7.
17. PRO, ADM 43/5(1).
18. PRO, ADM 43/5(1), 6(1).
19. For instance, compare the muster roll of the *Royal Family* squadron in Appendix 6 to the naval complements presented in Rodger, *Wooden World*, 348-51.
20. See Davis, *Shipping Industry*, 111-32, for a discussion of the manning of merchantmen; and Rodger, *Wooden World*, 15-29, 348-51, for the composition of crews aboard men-of-war.
21. The muster roll of the *King George*, 'flagship' of the *Royal Family* squadron, included the 'Commodore's Barber' and the 'Commodore's Taylor'. PRO, ADM 43/13(2). See Appendix 6.
22. PRO, ADM 43/5(2).
23. Hutchinson, *Naval Architecture*, 225.
24. PRO, C 108/104. Isaac Blackburn to Captain Finmore, 9 January 1804.
25. ACL, Papers of the *Southwell* Privateer, 24651.
26. These figures refer to the second cruise of the squadron. PRO, HCA 26/24, 25; PRO, ADM 43/13(2). During the first cruise, 102 guns and 970 men were mustered. H. S. Vaughan, ed., *The Voyages and Cruises of Commodore Walker* (Cassel, 1928) 95. See Appendix 6.
27. ACL, Papers of the *Southwell* Privateer, 24651.
28. *Gentleman's Magazine*, 15 (1745), 418-19, 428-9.
29. LRO, Account Books of the *Enterprize*, 387 MD 45.
30. ACL, Papers of the *Southwell* Privateer, 24651.
31. LRO, Account Books of the *Enterprize*, 387 MD 45.
32. ACL, Papers of the *Southwell* Privateer, 24651.
33. The *Royal Family* squadron cruised in these waters during both of its sorties. In particular, it was to operate between 'Cape St Vincent in Portugal and Cape Cantin, on the coast of Barbary' during the first cruise. Vaughan, *Voyages and Cruises*, 96.
34. Declaration 11 January 1703. PRO, HCA 26/18. Originally, it was intended that the *Fame* should accompany the *St George*. However, after quarrelling with Dampier, Captain Pullein withdrew the *Fame* from the expedition and sailed independently; the *Cinque Ports Gally* joined the expedition on meeting the *Fame* at Kinsale. See B. M. H. Rogers, 'Dampier's Voyage of 1703' *Mariner's Mirror*, X (1924), 366-81; and C. D. Lee, 'Alexander Selkirk and

the Last Voyage of the *Cinque Ports Gally*' *Mariner's Mirror*, 73 (1987), 385-99.

35. Declaration 28 April 1708. PRO, HCA 25/20. Rogers' sailing instructions are to be found in PRO, C 104/36(2).

36. Both vessels were commissioned on 1 January 1719. PRO, HCA 26/29.

37. Declaration 2 April 1744. PRO, HCA 26/4.

38. Rogers, 'Dampier's Voyage', 369.

39. PRO, C 104/36(2).

40. W. G. Perrin, ed., *A Voyage Round the World by way of the Great South Seas performed in the Years 1719–1722* (Cassel, 1928) xii.

41. PRO, C 103/130. Richard Taunton to Thomas Hall, 27 October 1746. See also C. Gill, *Merchants and Mariners of the Eighteenth Century* (Edward Arnold, 1961) 146-9.

42. PRO, C 103/130. John Brohier to his brother, 4 January 1747.

43. PRO, C 103/130. Richard Taunton to Thomas Hall, 26 August 1747.

44. See Perrin, *Voyage Round the World*, xviii-xix.

45. The promoters of the *Tartar* apparently had plans to send their vessel to the East Indies in 1780. However, these came to nothing as 'gaol fever' decimated the 230-strong crew in Lisbon. See Jamieson, 'Return to Privateering', 159-60.

46. *Morning Chronicle and London Advertiser*, 14 August 1778.

47. SMV, Muster Rolls, 1777–1783.

48. PRO, ADM 43/29.

49. Advertisement for the *Hercules*. *Felix Farley's Bristol Journal*, 26 September 1778.

50. J. S. Bromley, 'Prize Office and Prize Agency at Portsmouth, 1689–1748' in J. Webb, N. Yates and S. Peacock, eds, *Hampshire Studies* (Portsmouth Record Office, 1981) 177.

51. PRO, HCA 34/27-29.

52. PRO, ADM 43/18.

53. Colonial privateers operated to great effect in the Caribbean and North American waters during the 1739-1748 war, thereby reducing the scope for predators based in the British Isles. See C. E. Swanson, 'The Profitability of Privateering: Reflections on British Colonial Privateers during the War of 1739–1748' *American Neptune*, 42 (1982), 36-56; and C. E. Swanson, 'American Privateering and Imperial Warfare, 1739-1748' *William and Mary Quarterly* third series, XLII (1985), 357-82.

54. *Felix Farley's Bristol Journal*, 8 August, 26 September, 3 October 1778.

55. LRO, Tuohy Papers, 380 TUO 1/17. Richard Woods to David Tuohy, 1781.

56. Legislation passed in 1798 and 1803 made it obligatory for foreign-going vessels to sail in convoy unless a letter of marque was carried. Those traders intending to 'run', therefore, required a privateer commission. 38 George III, c.76 and 43 George III, c.57.

57. Hutchinson, *Naval Architecture*, 211.

58. *Newcastle Chronicle*, 3 March 1781.

59. PRO, ADM 43/21.
60. PRO, HCA 30/663. Articles of Agreement, *Royal George*, 19 November 1747.
61. Declaration 23 February 1710. PRO, HCA 26/14.
62. PRO, ADM 43/11(2).
63. PRO, ADM 43/25(2).
64. See K. G. Davies, ed., *Letters from Hudson's Bay* (Hudson's Bay Record Society, 1965); and B. Wilson, *The Great Company, 1667–1871* (Smith, Elder, & Co., 1900).
65. Declarations 27 April 1744, 15 May 1782. PRO, HCA 26/32, 70.
66. D. Syrett, *Shipping and the American War, 1775–1783. A Study of British Transport Organisation* (Athlone Press, 1970) 71-6.
67. Davis, *Shipping Industry*, 264. Vessels of 500 tons burthen or more were obliged to carry a clergyman; by citing the figure of 499 tons, the Company avoided this requirement, much to the disgust of William Hutchinson. See Williams, *Liverpool Privateers*, 147.
68. In 1751, there was an unsuccessful attempt to check the building of ships of over 600 tons burthen. L. S. Sutherland, *A London Merchant, 1695–1774* (Oxford UP, 1962).

Three

Risks and Rewards

The onset of war in the eighteenth century generally disrupted the British shipping industry. Operating costs normally rose as enemy commerce-raiding activity led to increased insurance rates, and the need to employ larger crews and more armaments to defend both vessel and cargo. Other precautionary measures, such as sailing in convoy, could lead to delays and unseasonal voyages, while the fluctuating military situation might result in the loss of established markets and trading partners, depressing commercial confidence and activity. To the maritime labour force, war often entailed high employment levels and rising incomes, but these short-term gains were offset by the fact that the increased demand for seamen came principally from the Royal Navy. Thus, relatively few mariners enjoyed the high wages of wartime as many enlisted for—or were pressed into—potentially dangerous and comparatively low paid naval service.

War did present opportunities to the shipping industry, however. Shipowners could seek profits in trades peculiar to periods of hostilities; for instance, they might lease their vessels to the government to serve as transports, or they might despatch them as 'runners', sailing without escort in a highly risky, though potentially lucrative, attempt to reach market before the convoy, and the glut, arrived. A further option for entrepreneurs was the procurement of letters of marque for their ships, thereby acquiring for themselves, together with the vessel's crew, the sole interest in any enemy property that might be seized on the high seas. Many invested in this right of reprisal, setting forth private men-of-war specifically to seek prizes, and adding a prize-taking potential to the voyages of their commercial vessels, or 'letters of marque', many of which operated as 'runners'.

An element of each of these commissioned ventures was concerned with commerce-raiding, whether it constituted the *raison d'être* or just an incidental facet of the enterprise. The unusual nature of this predatory element conditioned the structure and administration of privateering ventures, setting them apart from other maritime endeavours. Whereas shipowners' earnings normally accrued from charges levied for the carriage of cargo, and seafarers' labour was procured for a wage paid by the shipowner regardless of the profit generated, privateer owners and privateersmen were rewarded from the same source, the prize fund generated by their commerce-raiding activities. Technically, therefore, activity authorised by virtue of letters of marque was undertaken not by employers and employees, but by venturers who invested their capital or their labour (and sometimes both) in privateering enterprises, and thereby owned an agreed portion of any profit earned. Such an arrangement was by no means unique—it was practised in the fishing industry, for example; nor did it seriously alter the supply of the factors of production, for capital was invested largely, though not entirely, by merchants and shipowners, and labour was provided chiefly by men accustomed to work at sea; however, it imposed a distinctive stamp on the privateering business as those who invested their capital or their labour in this enterprise sought to limit the extraordinary risks inherent in the activity, and to maximise the rewards it promised.

Risks

The risks facing privateering venturers were of two main kinds—physical and financial. In this, the commerce-raiding business was not unusual, for the the natural hazards of the sea and the prospect of trading losses threatened all forms of maritime enterprise. Yet the very nature of the privateering business accentuated these dangers to a marked degree. It was a violent occupation; even seafarers serving in the most benign of 'letters of marque' might be called upon to defend their ship, while men entered into private men-of-war in the expectation that they would have to fight for their prize. Thus, privateersmen faced the very real prospect of death, maiming or capture at the hands of the enemy, as well as the normal perils of injury and disease which beset the working lives of all mariners.

On occasion, these hazards confronted shipowners in the prize-taking business, for it was quite common for a captain to hold shares in his own vessel. In general, however, it was not the physical but the financial risks which concerned venturers of privateering capital. Principal among these was the fear that their commerce-raiding enterprise might well yield little or no income as prizes were not always forthcoming; if this did not unduly worry investors in 'armed trading vessels', whose stake in prize-taking was very much secondary to their interest in the carriage of goods, it was a prime consideration for speculators in private men-of-war whose return depended almost entirely upon the condemnation of enemy property. On the other hand, costs were inevitably incurred in the promotion and duration of these ventures and had to be met whether or not prizes were returned. Given this potential for financial loss, capital investors sought to limit their liabilities by spreading the burden of a variety of costs as far as possible; it was this quest which largely determined the organisational structure of privateering ventures.

Three forms of expense were generally evident in the privateering business, though the scale and precise character of each varied according to the extent of the commerce-raiding dimension of the individual enterprise. In the first instance, there were the initial costs of the venture. A suitable vessel was obviously required, together with a letter of marque, or commission, to authorise her commerce-raiding activities, the requisite number of men to navigate and fight her, and a sufficient quantity of victuals and provisions to supply the crew for the duration of the voyage or cruise. The costs of this initial outfit naturally varied with the scale of the project and such exogenous factors as the state of the shipping market and the availability of labour. Relatively little expenditure was generally involved in purchasing the extra guns and enlisting the additional hands necessary to enhance the prize-taking capability of the merchantmen employed as 'armed traders' or 'specialist vessels'. Similarly, 'Channel' privateers might be purchased cheaply, fitted with swivels or small carriage guns, and expeditiously sent out on short-range sorties. Messrs Seale and Ougier, for example, laid out a mere £157 10s on the outfit of the 40-ton *Snap Dragon* of Dartmouth in 1781,[1] while the cutter and lugger privateers of the Channel Islands were usually 'small and inexpensive.'[2] Inevitably, the initial costs rose with the ambitions of the promoters. Thus, the *Enterprize*, a 215-ton 'deep-water' commerce-raider of Liverpool, was fitted out for £4,083 13s 8d,[3] while the promoters of Woodes Rogers' 'expedition' expended £13,188 12s on the outset of their vessels,[4] and an estimated £40,000 was invested in the initial outfit of the *Royal Family* squadron.[5] (see Appendix 3).

Labour costs were another significant factor in the initial outfit of privateering vessels. Seafarers were often relatively scarce in time of war as the demands of the Navy, the merchant service and the privateering business generally exceeded the supply of trained mariners. In such a market situation, financial inducements were often necessary to entice seamen to ship aboard 'letters of marque' and private men-of-war. Bounties were occasionally offered, the owners of the *Dreadnought* of Newcastle, for instance, promising six guineas to every able seaman entering her service, with four guineas available for ordinary seamen, and three guineas for landmen.[6] The sum of five guineas was paid to each seaman joining the *Lark* of Falmouth, with half forwarded on enlistment and the other half payable on the completion of the three months' cruise.[7] Money was also advanced to privateersmen; thus, each 'good able seaman' entering the *Bellona* of Teignmouth received seven guineas,[8] and five guineas were advanced to all officers and able seamen joining the *Dursley Gally* of Bristol.[9] In 'letters of marque', wages were advanced to the crew, the men of the *Sarah* of Liverpool receiving a total of £65 0s 6d before embarkation,[10] while the officers and men engaged in the 'cruising voyage' of the *Brittania* of Bristol were paid an advance of two months' wages, ranging from the £12 received by Captain William Olive to the sum of £1 10s paid to William Wade, rated as 'boy'.[11] The costs of recruiting labour were further enhanced on occasions when owners were obliged to engage the services of crimps, and when they were forced to search beyond their own localities for seafarers. Francis Ingram, agent for the *Enterprize* of Liverpool, used both of these devices, spending £16 16s 6d on crimpage, and a further £160 18s 11d on the enlistment and transport of men from Chester and Whitehaven.[12]

Such expenses formed part of the initial outfit, the costs met by promoters before the vessel put to sea. The second set of costs were incurred in the course of the voyage or cruise. These 'running' costs might accrue from the calamities of war, the hazards of the sea, or the mismanagement, ill-conduct or bad fortune of the crew. Repairs were often necessary as a result of engagement with the enemy, navigational error or simple wear and tear. Contemporary newspapers abound with accounts of damaging encounters with hostile craft rendering vessels holed between wind and water, shattered in their rigging and steerage, or dismasted. In other instances, vessels were immobilised by poor seamanship, the *Prince Frederick*, for example, a member of the *Royal Family* squadron, foundering on the 'Welch Hook' in the Severn estuary due to the incompetence of her pilot.[13] In addition to the expense of the necessary repairs, costs accrued from the detention of vessels in port, their crews idle but not discharged—'eating up our provisions in a harbour', as one agent put it[14]—wasting crucial time while rivals were at sea seeking prizes.

Further charges might result from the profligacy of the commander and his crew in the consumption of stores and provisions, such excesses leading to the disruption of cruises for re-victualling and the purchase of additional supplies. Thus, commanders were instructed to use the ship's provisions

in such a manner that nothing may be squandered or given in profusion, to that end keep a watchful eye over the steward.[15]

The third element of cost in privateering ventures emanated from the very success of the enterprise, for the apprehension, detention and condemnation of prizes invariably entailed expenses. 'As an encourage-ment for the valour of the seamen, or mariners, and landmen',[16] and 'to excite a laudable emulation among the ship's company',[17] rewards were offered to those sighting, and to the first men aboard, a vessel which was subsequently condemned. Such additional payments varied in amount, though a guinea was the normal rate for vigilance, and anything up to 15 guineas might be paid to courageous hands. To further stimulate the efforts of the crew, benefits were offered to men seriously injured in fighting the ship, and to the widows or executors of those killed in action. Permanent disability—the loss of an eye or limb was usually cited—was the minimum qualification for these payments which varied according to the rank and, in some cases, to the marital status of the individual concerned. In the *Blandford*, for instance, 'to excite the whole Company to courage and bravery' an award of £50 was payable in the event of the disablement or demise of the captain or lieutenants, with £30 granted in the case of other officers, and £20 offered to compensate the losses suffered by other ranks;[18] meanwhile, the married seamen aboard the *Britannia* were entitled to twice as much benefit as their bachelor shipmates if injured or killed in action.[19]

Once secured, the prize, particularly if it appeared to be a 'capital' prize worth £10,000 or more, was sometimes escorted by the captor to a home or neutral port, the disruption of the cruise being of less import than the safe return of the spoils. On other occasions, a prize crew was placed on board and charged with the responsibility of navigating the captured ship to a port of landing. This could impair the fighting efficiency of the captor, for the despatch of a number of prize crews might seriously diminish the complement of a privateer, leaving it vulnerable to enemy attack and less able to apprehend further prizes. In one instance, the depletion of the *Enterprize*'s crew not only led to the escape of the *Juffrow Martinico*, but also obliged Captain Thomas Eden to order the removal of the crew from the *Vrow Barbara and Hendrina*, an irregular action which he was required to explain to the Admiralty Court.[20] In another case, the loss of 17 of the 42 strong crew of the *Fox* induced her commander, James Verco, to lift the cargo out of a detained vessel resulting in his arrest by Lord Hervey, in the *Daphne* man-of-war, and three months' imprisonment. Though he was acquitted on 28 March 1781, this confinement proved costly, for Verco effectively missed the most active period of the privateering war.[21]

As soon as the arrested property was landed, a series of charges was laid at the captor's account. Handling a detained vessel incurred costs; thus, £488 11s 8d was paid by the captors for 'Pilotage & Men to bring *Carnatic* from Downs to Longreach', while a 'Boatage' fee of £1 17s 6d was charged to the captors of the *Prudent*. Valuable prizes like the *Carnatic* were insured, the premiums on two policies taken out to provide cover of £57,000, amounting to £1,194 13s 3d. 'Wharfage, landing, housing and weighing' the prize cargo were further items of cost, while sundry expenses such as 'coach hire for prisoners', 'ale for landwaiters', 'carriage of trunks' and 'soldiers keeping guard' also had to be met.

The process of adjudicating detained property incurred further costs for captors, with proctors' bills, witnesses' expenses and sundry court fees adding to the debit account. Even in cases of common condemnation where there could be no doubt as to the validity of a prize, these expenses were relatively high; thus, proctors' bills were amongst the largest charges laid against the four French prizes condemned to the *Ellis* and the *Gregson* of Liverpool in 1778, ranging from £71 10s 9d for the *Prudent* to £96 3s 3d in the case of the *Ville du Cap*.[22] In more complex actions, the legal expenses rose accordingly. The owners of the *Snap Dragon* of Dartmouth, in responding to the *Bird's* claim and appeal as joint-captor of *Die Lieffde*, had spent £750 on proctors' bills by August 1781, and were charged at least another £200 before the case was determined in 1782, while Peter Ougier's journeys to Shrewsbury to collect witnesses, and to London to brief his proctor, further added to the costs of the case.[23] An adverse verdict, moreover, might involve the payment of compensation to the wronged party. Thus, Benjamin Buttell was condemned in costs and damages for sending Peter Vanden Bussche to Trontheim in Norway, rather than to Falmouth with the *El Alesandro* prize, an indiscretion which left the Exeter privateersman some £1,042 8s 8d poorer.[24] In another case, the demurrage, freight and sundry disbursments arising from the detention of *De Eendraght* amounted to £1,638 4s, almost a third of the total value of the prize.[25]

The condemnation of property meant that duties had to be paid on
prize cargoes, warehousing facilities arranged and the sale of vessel and
goods organised. This necessary process often proved expensive; duties
on the *Carnatic's* cargo, for instance, amounted to over £22,000,[26] while
the prize goods brought home by the *Duke* and the *Dutchess* produced
nearly £27,000 for Her Majesty's Collector of Customs.[27] Moreover, the
administration of these matters invoked a further expense in that an agent
was appointed to co-ordinate the condemnation and disposal of prizes,
and a commission was normally paid to recompense this individual for
his 'care, pains and trouble'.[28] The amount of this agency fee varied
between 2.5 and 5 per cent of the net prize fund, though in some cases
the agent was also responsible for supervising the initial outfit, and
commission was accordingly charged against the gross costs of the
venture. Hence, Peter Ougier agreed to a fee of 5 per cent of the whole
cost of the *Snap Dragon* and her outfit, as well as 2.5 per cent of the
owners' part of any prizes condemned.[29]

At least as agent, Ougier was assured of some form of income even if
the *Snap Dragon* failed to take a prize; as part-owner, however, he was
guaranteed only a share of the various charges incurred in the outset and
life of the venture, while a return on his investment was highly uncertain.
In this latter respect, of course, Ougier, like other speculators in
commerce-raiding activity, was in a similar position to those who invested
in more regular sea-borne trades. Yet while the fixed costs involved
in the general avenues of trade might be passed on in the form of a
freight rate, and the unforeseen costs of wreck or damage might be
underwritten by insurers, such options were not readily available to
venturers of commerce-raiding capital. Their enterprise served no
consumer upon whom a surcharge could be levied. Moreover, the absence
of a cargo and the sheer physical risk involved in the activity meant that
many predatory vessels sailed uninsured. Thus, in the financial accounts
relating to a variety of such craft—from the 'expedition' of Woodes
Rogers, to the 'deep-water' enterprise of the *Southwell,* to the 'cruising
voyage' of the *Mentor,* to the 'Channel' sorties of Zephaniah Job's Cornish
privateers—no reference is made to insurance, while the disastrous
outcome of the *Fame's* 'expedition' left Richard Taunton reflecting
that 'my loss will be £2,000, though I did not insure a penny.'[30] Even
when private ships-of war were underwritten, the cover provided was
sometimes inadequate and the premium invariably high; in 1756,
for instance, the case of the *Mercury* privateer prompted one observer
to assert that 'our present method of insurance upon privateers is

greatly defective',[31] while in August 1780 Richard Newman was informed that

> the many privateers that have been lately captured have determined the underwriters not to touch them but at advanced premiums.[32]

Nevertheless, financial risks could be restricted in other ways. The very structure of commerce-raiding ventures effected a reduction in costs and a dilution of risk, for part of the financial gamble—as well as much of the physical hazard—was borne by the labour force. Seafarers received no wages for their work in private men-of-war, while in 'letters of marque' any work in the prize-taking component of the enterprise was also unpaid as no increase in wages was made in respect of the extra duties this element might entail; instead, their labour, or additional labour, was rewarded with a share in any prize taken. Thus, privateersmen, like shipowners and merchants, invested their productive resources—their labour—in these ventures knowing that failure to take a prize meant that no income would be earned, the only recompense being the victuals and accommodation provided for the duration of the cruise or voyage. Moreover, they engaged in this 'no purchase, no pay' contract at a time when demand for their services from the other maritime sectors, notably from the Navy, was high. By selling their labour for a share in the net product of a commerce-raiding enterprise, therefore, seafarers were gambling the wages they might have earned elsewhere against the chance that they might locate and seize enemy goods of sufficient worth to render their shares more valuable than the amount of wages forsaken. An opportunity cost of at least 22s 6d per month, the net rate earned by an able seaman in the Navy,[33] would thus accrue to each privateersman from a barren cruise; essentially, this represented his minimum financial stake in the project, an investment which significantly reduced the initial and operating costs of the enterprise, costs borne by promoters in more conventional trades.

Entrepreneurial risks were also spread by the division of privateering ventures into shares, with each subscriber responsible for a part of the expenses involved and a proportionate part of the rewards generated. This practice was to be found in all branches of overseas trade, but it was employed to a much greater degree than normal in the privateering business, particularly in the promotion of relatively high-risk private men-of-war. While 'letters of marque' were generally instigated and organised on similar lines to peace-time trading operations, the more overtly predatory elements of the business were characterised by a broader diversification of ownership. Thus, Channel Island privateers were divided into as many as 64 shares;[34] capital for the *Royal Family* squadron was raised in 120 lots, though 30 shares were apparently unsubscribed;[35] the 'expedition' of the *Duke* and the *Dutchess* comprised 256 shares, divided among 17 investors;[36] and in 1778 Messrs Worrell & Co of London advertised for sale 400 shares in an unnamed private ship-of-war at £50 each.[37]

The majority of shareholders, quite naturally, came from the maritime community, as shipowners and merchants simply shifted their resources from other trades into privateering ventures. Consequently, bulwarks of the shipping industry such as Thomas Hall, Aaron Franks and Sherman Godfrey of London, John Bachelor, William Freake, and Abraham and Isaac Elton of Bristol, Thomas Ridge of Portsmouth, the Newmans and Holdsworths of Dartmouth, and the Gregsons, Tarletons and Backhouses of Liverpool, were frequently nominated as owners of commissioned vessels in the letter of marque declarations.[38] Alongside such characters, however, there stood a large number of investors from widely differing backgrounds. Members of the nobility and gentry held shares in private ships-of-war; thus, the Dukes of Bedford, Chandos, and Northumberland were cited in the declarations, together with baronets like Sir Lawrence Dundas of London and Sir John Rogers of Plymouth, and a host of 'gentlemen' and 'esquires'. 'Several ladies of the first rank', moreover, were reported to be

> opening subscriptions for fitting out privateers; and it is expected in
> a very little time several will be manned and sent to sea against our
> perfidious enemies, meerly by British *pin-money*.[39]

Officials such as Sir John Birtles, His Majesty's Consul at Genoa, and Sir Owen Buckingham, Lord Mayor of London, speculated in the activity, while Sir Cloudesly Shovell and Lord Anson were among the naval officers designated as 'owners and setters out' of privateers. Capital was also forthcoming from other social ranks as bakers, bankers, butchers, cheesemongers, coal merchants, dyers, grocers and haberdashers invested in commerce-raiding activity, and in Guernsey

> the shares of privateers are divided like lottery tickets in London, and
> a number of servants club together to buy one.[40]

Shareholders, great and small, formed partnerships or, more commonly, 'companies', with one of their number delegated to act as 'managing owner', *armateur* or director of the project. In the American Revolutionary

War, a further form of shareholding became apparent. Designed to limit the individual's risk and to mobilise the funds of the small investor, privateering 'associations' were established in various localities. Thus, in 1779, 'the city of Edinburgh, by a private subscription, are raising a sum to enable them to purchase four stout privateers', while the 'gentlemen and ladies' of Poole and 'the merchants of Dublin' devised similar schemes.[41] Proposals were put forward for the establishment of the 'Exeter and Devonshire Naval Association' to equip a number of privateers by general subscription, each share in the enterprise to be worth £25. To attract funds, and 'to render this plan as broad bottom'd, and universal as possible', it was envisaged that

> those whose circumstances will not admit of their subscribing a whole
> share, may join with their Friends and Acquaintences, and raise a share
> between themselves . . . Thus too those who have never been in sight
> of Salt Water, nor had the least Hand in Commercial or Naval
> Transactions, nay even the LADIES, and Female delicacy itself, may
> lend effectual Assistance to drub the French.[42]

In London, there were numerous meetings of 'respectable maritime traders . . . to consider about fitting out some stout privateers'[43] by popular subscription, and it is clear that at least one society, the 'Reprisal Association', was 'regularly formed by the members having executed a deed of settlement enrolled in HM's Court of King's Bench'. Potential subscribers were informed that members of the Association's governing committee—who were required to be merchants of the City of London and owners of five shares in the society—with Mr Wells, Secretary to the Association, would

> attend every day from 12 to 2 o'clock to receive subscriptions and
> transact business at the Reprisal Association Offices, late the African
> Company's, opposite to the London Tavern, where printed abstracts
> of the deed of settlement, the names of the Committee, etc, are ready
> to be delivered, and all other necessary information given.

'Upwards of £10,000' in subscriptions had been lodged with the London Exchange Banking Company by 1 September 1778 and two 'deep-water' private ships-of-war—the *King George*, of 24 guns and 150 men, and the *Queen Charlotte*, of 32 guns and 200 men—were subsequently purchased for the Association by 'gentlemen who are entrusted with this part of the business of the society', and despatched on cruises.[44]

Having formed their society to spread the risks inherent in commerce raiding activity, and to raise capital expeditiously, the committee and members of the Reprisal Association were soon confronted by another hazard which from time to time threatened the investments of privateering entrepreneurs—the conduct of their fellow venturers, the ship's company. Though co-operation apparently marked the relationship of owners and men as they strove towards a common goal, conflict occasionally arose, especially if cruises were proving unproductive. Thus, on 20 March 1779, 'an Act of Mutiny and Piracy' was committed by members of the *King George*'s crew who confined the captain and officers in irons, steered the vessel to north-west Ireland, and made their escape in the ship's cutter armed with pistols, musquets and cutlasses.[45] Clearly, the actions of these 'atrocious offenders' impaired the efficient operation of the venture, raising costs and reducing the chances of prize apprehension. The episode also exposed the relatively vulnerable position of privateer owners, in that their financial investment depended largely upon the physical effort of their co-venturers, the crew, whose labour was expended at sea beyond the direct supervision of investors. Promoters therefore sought to extend their control over ventures by exerting the right to manage the operation, and by imposing a degree of discipline upon the crews of their vessels. To a certain extent, the structure of the privateering business facilitated these aims, for it was the *armateurs* who instigated proceedings and dictated the terms on which seamen might venture their labour, as stipulated in the articles of agreement drawn up on behalf of the promoters and signed by recruits as they joined the vessel. Moreover, privateersmen were afforded a prime productivity incentive in that they owned part of the profits of their commerce-raiding efforts, and this was their only recompense. As many were experienced mariners, they must have been aware that disorganisation and ill-conduct not only diminished the prize-taking capability of the venture, but also jeopardised the safety of the vessel and ultimately their own lives.

On the other hand, the inherently speculative and violent character of the activity, together with the short, 'free-ranging' nature of cruises, and the very size and variable quality of crews, might serve to undermine shipboard discipline. Men's expectations were often high as they sought to grasp a rare opportunity for instant wealth, intoxicated by the 'spirit of privateering' into believing that pickings were easy and plentiful. When such hopes were not realised euphoria and diligence might turn to disillusionment, insubordination and mutiny. In seeking to avoid such costly diversions, privateer owners relied heavily on the commanders and senior officers of their vessels to manage and motivate the crew at sea, the promoters of Woodes Rogers' 'expedition' going so far as to send their agent, Carlton Vanbrugh, on the cruise with a specific brief to prevent embezzlement and to keep regular accounts.[46]

Furthermore, owners used the articles of agreement to assert their right to manage the venture, and invariably prescribed a series of penalties for misdemeanours committed at sea. Accordingly, a destination was normally specified in 'letter of marque' agreements, and sometimes the aim of the voyage; thus, the *King William* was bound from 'the port of Bristol to Newfoundland and to any other port or ports in the Mediterranean', though the crew also agreed to work in 'any Cruize or cruizes Captain Thomas Cornish shall think proper and advisable to make'.[47] On occasion, commanders of private men-of-war were given similar authority, George Hudson, for instance, having it 'entirely in his power to cruize wherever he thinks most beneficial for the interest of the Owners and ship's company'. This was rare, however, and probably due to the fact that Hudson was a part-owner himself,[48] for owners normally retained for themselves the

> sole direction in what manner and latitudes or Parts of the World the said ship shall cruize in and give the necessary instructions relating thereto to the Captain.[49]

These written orders were often very precise, detailing the targets which the 'expeditionary forces' were to try and secure, and the latitudes and longitudes of stations in which 'deep-water' private ships-of-war were to cruise. They also carried weight, in that a captain ignoring his orders was accountable for his actions; thus, the owners of the *Lord Cardiff* successfully sued the vessel's commander to recover £623 in costs and damages incurred on the restitution of a neutral ship taken against their orders.[50]

In their instructions to commanders, owners also stressed the importance of the establishment and maintenance of good order aboard ship. This was crucial to the operational efficiency of commerce-raiding vessels, for much of the work, particularly during engagements, depended upon the co-ordination of the crew's effort. Commanders were charged, therefore, with the management of their people, to instil into them a measure of common purpose, which might enhance their performance at critical junctures. Woodes Rogers, for instance, was to ensure that 'concord and good harmony' prevailed on board the *Duke* and the *Dutchess*,[51] while Patrick Galloway was advised not to 'insult' his men, but to 'caress them & give them good words & Civill usage' to win their loyalty,[52] and John Engledue was encouraged to cultivate 'a good understanding and harmony' with his officers, though he was to be wary of any 'familiarity between them and the seamen, as it may be of very dangerous consequence'.[53]

Naturally, the smooth operation of the cruise required that

> the Captain, Officers, seamen and Adventurers shall and will honestly and diligently do and perform their work and business and Faithfully and Courageously do their respective dutys on board the said ship according to their respective stations.[54]

To ensure that such obligations were observed, privateer owners incorporated a series of disciplinary provisions, detailing misdemeanours and punishments, into the articles of agreement governing the cruise. Desertion, absence without leave for as little as eight hours, and cowardice in the face of the enemy, were normally cited as offences, while 'those who shall get Drunk or so affected with liquor that they shall not do their duty in driving away or attacking the enemy' were deemed to have transgressed their contract.[55] Insubordinate behaviour likely to 'disturb and divide the harmony and mutual agreement that ought to be amongst the Company'[56] contravened all agreements, though such ill-conduct might range from disrespect shown to the commander or senior officers, to a refusal to obey the commands of a superior, to outright mutiny. Control was also exercised over the crew's rights to plunder captured property, and in the treatment meted out to prisoners. The embezzlement of prize goods was invariably outlawed, though in some ventures petty or private plunder was allowed, with each crew member given the right to relieve an opponent 'of the same degree or station' of his wearing apparel, buttons, buckles, watches, bedding and plate.[57] Captains, moreover, were entitled to plunder their opposite number's cabin, with a limit, usually £50, placed on the value of their private adventure. This practice, however, was not universal, and in some agreements it was expressly forbidden, for

> allowing small plunder on board hath produced very ill consequences amongst the ship's company, and stripping the enemy and taking their cloaths and bedding is inhuman.[58]

The behaviour of privateersmen towards prisoners was further proscribed by clauses which suggested that 'courage and bravery shows itself in nothing more than in treating the Vanquished with tenderness and Humanity'.[59] Captives were 'not to be treated with severity' therefore, and more particularly there was to be 'no violence to male prisoners, or indecency to female prisoners.'[60]

Procedures were laid down for determining cases of alleged misbehaviour. Privateersmen accused of serious misconduct, such as mutiny, murder or assault, were normally proceeded against according to the criminal law, though in the *Boscawen*'s articles it was agreed that all offenders should be tried by the entire ship's company and 'that no action at law . . . shall ever after commence'.[61] Breaches of shipboard discipline were normally decided in this fashion, with the precise mechanism of arbitration stipulated in the agreement. In some instances, cases were judged by the democratic will of the entire complement, while in others a committee comprising a specified number of officers and men was instituted to consider the alleged misdemeanours of crew members.

Offenders were punished according to the penalties specified in the agreement. For most transgressions, the miscreant was discharged his service, and forfeited his shares in the venture, and his wages if he served in a 'letter of marque'. In the *Surprize* of London it was lawful for the captain and officers to inflict corporal punishment 'or pecuniary mulct at their discretion' upon cowards and mutineers.[62] Fines were imposed in other ventures; thus, men who signed the articles, but failed to ship aboard the *Success* of Jersey were to suffer a fine of 30 livres,[63] while those absenting themselves from the *Two Henrys* of Hastings were liable to a £5 fine.[64] In another example, the crew of the *Assistance*, if found guilty of embezzling goods, were to submit three times the value of the stolen property to the prize fund,[65] though in the *Brutus* and *Little Brutus* such an offence was deemed a felony to be proceeded against at law, with half of the criminal's shares going to the informant as a reward, and the other half adding to the 'dead shares' set aside for injury benefits and encouragements.[66] This was unusual, for in most ventures forfeit shares were either submitted to the prize fund or, on occasion, to the account of the owners. To underline the financial basis of these punishments, and to provide a deterrent should shares prove worthless, privateersmen were usually bound to the agreement in a penal sum; the amount of this bond varied from £50 per venturer in small-scale enterprises to the £2,000 in which the men of the *Tygress* of Dartmouth agreed to bind themselves to the owners of the vessel.[67]

Such a security might persuade the most reckless of seafarers to abide by the rules governing the enterprise. If so, it would not only dispel one of the principal risks associated with the privateering business, but also improve the prospects of fulfilling the main or supplementary aim of the venture, the seizure and condemnation of a prize. Once this goal was realised, the administration and distribution of the rewards could commence.

Rewards

If the physical and financial risks associated with privateering ventures were unusually high, the rewards to be earned were potentially very great. A strong correlation existed between these two critical aspects of the business, as great expense and immense physical effort was generally required to capture the treasure ships of the South Seas or the valuable cargoes returning from the East and West Indies, while more modest exertions might only yield the lesser prizes of home waters. There was invariably a margin, however, between the value of the intended target and the costs the predator expected to incur; moreover, there was always the possibility that the odds might be upset, and through fortunate circumstance the glittering prize might fall to the commercially-oriented 'letter of marque' or the private man-of-war of moderate force and limited intent. Thus, it was the prospect of profits, and the dream of windfall profits, that encouraged investors and seafarers to chance their capital and their labour in commerce-raiding activity. To some degree, of course, such incentives induced capitalists to engage in all overseas trading ventures, but it was only on rare occasions that seafarers were offered the opportunity to make large, speculative gains. Privateering, though it afforded no guarantee of income, held the potential to raise the ceiling which the payment of wages normally imposed on the seafarer's earnings.

The extent of the seaman's share in the profits of a commerce-raiding enterprise was laid down in the articles of agreement which determined, among other matters, the distribution of rewards between the various parties to the venture. Initially, this entailed the creation of a prize fund. The principal constituent of this general account was the gross proceeds of prize goods seized and condemned, supplemented in some cases by sundry items such as fines or shares forfeited by miscreants. In certain ventures, a fund might be created even if the cruise proved barren; thus, 'by the articles of agreement the *Fame* and *Winchelsea* was to be sold to pay sailor's wages in case no prizes were taken',[68] while the *Tartar*

> on completion of her cruize & returning to London shall be valued & appraised & the amount shall be part of jt. stock.[69]

Charges were then deducted from this fund, and the residue, the net proceeds, divided between the venturers according to the shares each held in the enterprise. In effect, the deduction of charges from the common stock meant that all parties to the venture were sustaining a proportion of its costs. Thus, the privateersman, having staked his forsaken wage in the undertaking, bore a further part of the financial risk in that each expense met out of the general account reduced the net returns of the venture, and therefore his, as well as the promoters', income.

The range of costs shared in this fashion varied widely. In all cases, the charges associated with the detention and condemnation of prizes, and the sale of condemned property, were paid out of the common stock. This provision was extended, in certain instances, to the costs resulting from the prosecution and restitution of goods deemed free by the Admiralty Court.[70] The prize fund generally covered the encouragement offered to stimulate the vigilance and valour of the ship's company; thus, a guinea 'for sighting' was debited from the proceeds of each of the *Ellis* and *Gregson*'s four prizes,[71] while 'smart money' was to be taken out of the gross account resulting from the *Tygress*'s captures 'if the majority of the Ship's Company shall think such encouragement ought to be paid, but not otherwise.'[72] Benefits paid to dependents of men killed in action, or to those injured in fighting the vessel, were generally drawn out of the common stock, which also bore the cost of provisions taken in during the course of some cruises.[73] However, supplies obtained from a prize vessel were to be appraised as prize goods, and the appropriate portion paid to the crew on the completion of the cruise.[74]

While such arrangements covered many of the costs incurred in the course of a cruise and in the processing of prizes, the general account was often used to re-imburse promoters in their initial costs. Thus, on the creation of a prize fund, owners were able to reclaim a portion of the expenditures made in the outfit of the venture. This re-imbursement varied in degree, and in form. The *Hardwicke*'s articles had it that the product of the first four months of the cruise was to cover the owners' fitting-out costs, any further or subsequent proceeds to be divided in the proportions agreed.[75] In two other London 'deep-water' private ships-of-war, it was agreed that the first prize taken should defray the initial costs of the enterprise. The extent of the recompense varied, however; thus, the owners of the *Swift*, 'having victualled the ship' were to 'be re-imbursed that charge out of the first prize taken',[76] while the *Lowestoff*'s promoters could also draw 'out of the first prize that shall be taken ... the whole charge of warlike stores (great guns and small arms excepted) victualling

and advance money.'[77] In the case of the *Surprize*, also of London, the
bulk of the outfitting costs of the owners were to be paid; thus,

> out of the neat produce (of prizes) there shall in the first place be
> deducted and reimbursed all every and whatsoever sums as shall have
> been laid out and expended in victualling the said privateer and in
> furnishing her with powder, shott and medicines.[78]

The prize fund was thus utilised to share many of the operating costs
incurred in privateering ventures, and, in some cases, to re-imburse
owners for part of their initial expenditures. The net proceeds were then
distributed according to the articles of agreement, which specified the
proportion of the spoils belonging to the two sets of venturers, owners
and ship's company. This varied widely, the extent of each party's share
being determined by the nature of the venture, the payment of other
rewards and local practice. In general, the crews of 'letters of marque'
were entitled to a smaller portion of the prize fund than their counterparts
in private men-of-war, reflecting the supplementary nature of prize-taking
activity in many of these ventures; naturally, they received wages for their
sailing and cargo-handling duties, while the relatively small complements
carried meant that each share in the prize fund was that much more
valuable. Thus, the men of the *Sea Nimph* and the *Dutchess*, two London
'letters of marque' bound for the Mediterranean in 1711, and the
Ambuscade of Portsmouth, bound on a 'cruising voyage' to Lisbon, were
to share in one-sixth of the prize fund on top of their normal wages.[79]
In other examples, a larger fraction was allocated to 'letter of marque'
crews, the men of the *George Dogger* sharing in one-fifth of the net value
of prizes taken,[80] while able seamen joining the *Royal George* of London
in 1747 agreed to a monthly wage of 55 shillings, and a single share in
the quarter portion of prize money payable to the ship's company.[81]
During the Seven Years' War, a similar division applied in the 'cruising
voyages' of the *Brittania* of Bristol, and the *Deal Castle* of London, and
also in the *Sarah*, an 'armed trading vessel' of Liverpool, though wages
were higher in all three cases, able seamen earning some 60 to 65 shillings
per month.[82]

Crews serving in private men-of-war normally received a larger share
of the spoils, though wages were rarely paid. Local variations were
apparent, however; while in most Bristol and London commerce-raiders
the two groups of venturers received 50 per cent of the net prize fund
each, in Dartmouth the net proceeds were divided into eight equal parts,
with the promoters owning five, and the crew sharing in the remaining

three-eighths. The 'Channel' privateers of Dover generally operated with a 50:50 division, though the crew of the *Dover* were entitled to five- eighths of the net prize fund.[83] An even larger proportion, 75 per cent, was owned by the men of the *Eagle* and *Two Henrys* of Hastings, presumably as compensation for their agreement to provide their own musquets and to find their own victuals after the first fortnight of the six months' cruise.[84] In Liverpool, on the other hand, the 'cruising voyage' mode of operation appears to have been adopted in the port's 'deep-water' private ships-of-war; thus, the crews of the *Ellis* and the *Gregson* received just 25 per cent of the net proceeds of prizes taken,[85] though it seems probable, as in the contemporary case of the *Enterprize*,[86] that wages were paid in these ventures. Wages were also available to privateersmen in the Channel Islands, but only on the sale of their allotted shares to the *armateurs* of the vessel, at a pre-determined rate.[87] This system of share commutation sometimes applied on the mainland; for instance, the seafarers engaged in the *Duke* and *Dutchess* 'expedition', and those employed in the 'deep-water' undertaking of the *Adventure* of Portsmouth, could sell half of their share allocation for a monthly wage,[88] while a number of Plymouth ventures operated on this 'half purchase, half pay' basis in the Napoleonic War.[89]

Once the net prize receipts were split between the respective parties, further division took place, with the owners' portion distributed in line with the stake each individual held in the venture, and the men's allocation divided according to the number of shares each crew member was afforded in the agreement. Invariably, this was decided by rank; thus, if an able seaman was entitled to a single share, lesser ratings, such as boys, landmen or ordinary seamen, might own a quarter, a third, a half or three-quarters of a share, while specialist crew members like the carpenter, boatswain or gunner, and officers, could claim larger allocations, rising to 12 or 16 shares for the commander. Some captains, indeed, were granted a percentage of the men's portion of the fund; thus, James Vallenge, commander of the London 'deep-water' predator *Ranger* was to receive eight per cent of the crew's moiety,[90] while Samuel Barton of the *Brutus* of London fared slightly better, owning ten per cent of the men's half-share in the venture's net proceeds.[91]

In some ventures, however, the promoters were granted rights to part of the men's portion of the prize fund. In the articles governing the *Royal Family* privateers, for instance, it was agreed that the crew's moiety should be extended by six shares, which were to be allotted by the owners, on the Commodore's recommendation, to reward the valour of deserving individuals.[92] Similarly, the contract binding the owners and men of the *Surprize* of London stipulated that the crew's half of the net prize fund should be divided into 300 shares, with ten set aside to supply

> smart bounty money . . . to encourage the mariners and company of the said privateer in order to promote and advance the interest of the owners thereof.

The remaining 290 shares were to be divided amongst the 200 seafarers who were to comprise the ship's company, though if an insufficient number of men were recruited, the unsubscribed shares were to be used for the payment of the costs of the outfit and the encouragements and benefits offered to the crew.[93]

In these instances, the owners placed a direct levy on the crew's earnings by extending the number of shares, thereby diluting the value of each unit, and diverting the proceeds of the additional shares towards the defrayment of their own initial and incidental outgoings. Promoters encroached upon the crew's portion of the spoils by other means. Advance money, paid out by owners to persuade men to enlist, was deducted from each recipient's prize money before a dividend was made, while ill-equipped privateersmen, whose bedding and clothes were provided by the promoters on recruitment, were invariably obliged to surrender the cost of these necessaries out of their prize earnings. Another device, commonly employed in Bristol private men-of-war, was the allocation of a single share in the crew's half of the net prize fund for every carriage gun on board. These shares were generally divided equally between the owners and men, though in some cases all of the guns' shares went to the promoters; thus, in a 28-gun vessel such as the *Alexander* the owners were entitled to 14 shares in the men's moiety of the net profits,[94] while in the 32-gun *Tryall,* the promoters owned 32 parts of the crew's total income.[95] The men's earnings were eroded further by the payment of commission to the agent or agents that the law obliged each ship's company to appoint to represent their interest in prizes. As many agreements stipulated that one or more of the vessel's owners should act as the men's representative, the agent's charge on the general account was effectively a transfer of a percentage of the net proceeds from the crew to the promoters of the venture.

To earn his commission, the agent was obliged to organise the condemnation of prizes and to administer the general account. This could be an onerous occupation; while the Prize Court required evidence of the legality of the seizure, and the Navy Office required confirmation of condemnation and crew size for payment of bounties, sales of prize cargoes had to be implemented, the bills of creditors settled, payments of prize dividends organised and detailed accounts drawn up. On occasion, particularly when rich spoils were at stake, conflict arose over the distribution of funds, and the various disputants turned to the courts for a decision. Protracted legal battles might ensue, delaying the payment of rewards for many years; as Richard Taunton, a reluctant litigant in the dispute over the *Royal Family*'s prize fund, put it:

> Chancery suits is no wayes agreeable to my inclinations. I would almost as soon loose my right as to have ye Plague (long & tedious delays) of that Equitable Court.[96]

Clearly, even the most fortunate of outcomes might involve expense and risk for the privateering venturer.

Notes

1. DRO, Seale Papers. Draft of Agreement made between John Seale and Peter Ougier, 1781.
2. P. L. Wickens, 'The Economics of Privateering: Capital Dispersal in the American War of Independence' *Journal of European Economic History*, 13 (1984), 378.
3. LRO, Account Books of the *Enterprize*, 387 MD 45. The fitting out costs included £41 17s 4d spent on the procurement of letters of marque against France and Spain.
4. PRO, C 104/36(2).
5. PRO, C 103/130. Richard Taunton to Thomas Hall, 2 August 1746.
6. *Newcastle Chronicle*, 17 Februray 1781.
7. PRO, ADM 43/21(1).
8. *Exeter Flying Post*, 13 August 1779.
9. PRO, ADM 43/5(2). Seafarers signing the articles and receiving advance money were legally obliged to serve in the vessel. Thus, the men of the *Lion* were warned to return their advance money and obtain a discharge if they chose not to resume a cruise interrupted by the need for repairs; otherwise, threatened the owners, 'they will be treated with according to the Law for their non-performance of the cruise'. Quoted in Damer Powell, *Bristol Privateers*, 272.
10. PRO, ADM 43/21.
11. PRO, ADM 43/18.
12. LRO, Account Books of the *Enterprize*, 387 MD 45.

13. *Penny London Post or Morning Advertiser*, 5 May 1746; Vaughan, *Voyages and Cruises*, xxxv-xxxvi.
14. PRO, C 108/318. Creagh & Fallet to Patrick Galloway, 23 January 1703.
15. ACL, Papers of the *Southwell* Privateer, 24651.
16. PRO, ADM 43/10. Articles of Agreement, *King William*, 17 April 1744.
17. PRO, ADM 43/4(2). Articles of Agreement, *Tryall*, 30 October 1744.
18. PRO, ADM 43/4(2). Articles of Agreement, *Blandford*, 14 April 1746.
19. PRO, ADM 43/18. Articles of Agreement, *Brittania*, 6 February 1762.
20. PRO, HCA 32/478.
21. PRO, HCA 45/12.
22. PRO, C 114/36. See Appendix 5.
23. DRO, Seale Papers. Peter Ougier to John Seale, 11 August 1781.
24. PRO, HCA 42/147; Starkey, 'Privateering Career of the *King George*', 10.
25. PRO, HCA 32/316.
26. PRO, C 114/36. See Appendix 5.
27. PRO, C 104/36(1).
28. PRO, ADM 43/3(1). Articles of Agreement, *Adventure*, 1744.
29. DRO, Seale Papers, Draft of Agreement made between John Seale and Peter Ougier, 1781.
30. PRO, C 104/36; ACL, Papers of the *Southwell* Privateer, 24651; PRO, C 114/36; Cornwall County Museum, Truro, Ledger Book of Zephaniah Job, 1778-1786, ZJ 7; PRO, C 103/130. Richard Taunton to Thomas Hall, 26 August 1747.
31. Williams, *Liverpool Privateers*, 99n.
32. Newman Papers. John Olive to Richard Newman, 8 August 1780. I am grateful to Mrs Ray Freeman for supplying me with this reference. The cargoes of 'letters of marque' were covered in the manner of normal trading vessels; thus, when the predatory option of the *Hector's* 'cruising voyage' was abandoned, her agent managed to secure insurance, albeit with difficulty, on the cargo she loaded in Jamaica for return to Liverpool. LRO, Tuohy Papers, 380/TUO.
33. See Rodger, *Wooden World*, 125. Naval seafarers were entitled to shares in the proceeds of prizes condemned, payable on top of their regular wages.
34. Jamieson, 'Return to Privateering', 165.
35. PRO, C 103/130. Richard Taunton to Thomas Hall, 9 October 1747, 30 October 1747.
36. PRO, C 104/36(2).
37. *Morning Chronicle and London Advertiser*, 16 November 1778.
38. The examples cited in this paragraph, unless otherwise referenced, are drawn from PRO, HCA 26/1-70.
39. *Exeter Flying Post*, 25 September 1778.
40. *London Chronicle*, 3 November 1778.
41. *Exeter Flying Post*, 2, 9 and 23 July 1779.
42. *Exeter Flying Post*, 10 April 1778.

43. *Exeter Flying Post,* 25 June 1779.
44. *Morning Chronicle and London Advertiser,* 1 and 18 September, 22 October 1778, 15 January 1779.
45. *Exeter Flying Post,* 23 April 1779.
46. PRO, C 104/36.
47. PRO, ADM 43/10.
48. PRO, ADM 43/3(2).
49. PRO, ADM 43/3(1). Articles of Agreement, *Carlisle,* 1745.
50. Damer Powell, *Bristol Privateers,* 274.
51. PRO, C 104/36(2).
52. PRO, C 108/318. Creagh & Fallet to Patrick Galloway, 1 January 1703.
53. ACL, Papers of the *Southwell* Privateer, 24651.
54. PRO, ADM 43/5(2). Articles of Agreement, *Dursley Gally,* 1745.
55. PRO, ADM 43/16. Articles of Agreement, *Defiance,* 1759.
56. PRO, ADM 43/3(1). Articles of Agreement, *Boscawen,* 2 April 1745.
57. PRO, ADM 43/5(1). Articles of Agreement, *Tygress,* 4 March 1744.
58. PRO, ADM 43/4(2). Articles of Agreement, *Blandford,* 14 April 1746.
59. PRO, ADM 43/5(2). Articles of Agreement, *Dursley Gally,* 1745.
60. PRO, HCA 25/210(2). Articles of Agreement, *Tartar,* 1780.
61. PRO, ADM 43/3(2).
62. PRO, ADM 43/3(1).
63. PRO, ADM 43/6(2).
64. PRO, ADM 43/15(1).
65. PRO, ADM 43/24.
66. PRO, ADM 43/24.
67. PRO, ADM 43/5(1).
68. PRO, C 103/130. Richard Taunton to Thomas Hall, 15 January 1746.
69. PRO, HCA 30/210(2).
70. For instance, see PRO, ADM 43/4(2). Articles of Agreement, *Blandford;* and PRO, ADM 43/22(2). Articles of Agreement, *King George.*
71. PRO, C 114/36.
72. PRO, ADM 43/5(1).
73. PRO, ADM 43/4(1). Articles of Agreement, *Tryall,* 27 August 1745.
74. PRO, ADM 43/3(1). Articles of Agreement, *Boscawen,* 2 April 1745.
75. PRO, ADM 43/3(2).
76. PRO, ADM 43/3(2).
77. PRO, ADM 43/6(1).
78. PRO, ADM 43/3(1).
79. PRO, C 105/38(1), 39(1); ADM 43/1.
80. PRO, ADM 43/9.
81. PRO, HCA 30/663.
82. PRO, ADM/16, 18, 21.
83. PRO, ADM 43/3(1).
84. PRO, ADM 43/15(1).

85. PRO, C 114/36.
86. LRO, Account Books of the *Enterprize*, 387 MD 45.
87. For instance, PRO, ADM 43/6(2), 12, 16, 21. Articles of Agreement, *Success, Defiance, Prince William* and *Admiral Durell.*
88. PRO, C 104/36; ADM 43/3(2).
89. PRO, HCA 25/210.
90. PRO, ADM 43/14(2). See Appendix 4.
91. PRO, ADM 43/24. See Appendix 4.
92. PRO, ADM 43/13(2).
93. PRO, ADM 43/3(1). In the event, only 157 men were on board the *Surprize* at the capture of the *corsaire Appollo*, indicating that a considerable number of shares were unsubscribed.
94. PRO, ADM 43/5(2).
95. PRO, ADM 43/4(1).
96. PRO, C 103/130. Richard Taunton to Thomas Hall, 30 October 1747.

Part Two

SCALE

Four

1702–1712

'Their Privateers will be Lords and Ours will be Beggars'

The indecisive battle fought off Malaga in 1704 proved to be the last major fleet confrontation of the War of the Spanish Succession. Thereafter, as embittered London merchants pointed out, the French

> totally altered their methods of carrying on their naval war: And instead of sending forth great fleets, they fill the sea with privateers, and with squadrons of their nimble ships, and by that means watch all opportunities of seizing upon our trade.[1]

While Louis XIV's battle fleet was allowed to decay, naval resources were diverted into *guerre de course*, a concerted privateering attack on Anglo-Dutch commerce designed to cut the 'sinews of trade' which supported the allied war effort. This 'covert and indirect form of war' had been deployed with some success in the latter stages of the Nine Years' War when Jean Bart and his colleagues had played havoc with English and Dutch shipping. Conducted by private *armateurs*, with the financial and material backing of the state, *guerre de course* was born out of financial stringency as well as naval strategy, being

> the method of conducting war which is most feasible, simple, cheap, and safe and which will cost least to the state, the more so since any losses will not be felt by the King, who risks virtually nothing.[2]

The adoption of this policy by the French had a far-reaching effect on the war at sea. Strategically, *guerre de course* was a failure, for it never really impaired the ability of the allies to fund the war, while it surrendered the naval initiative to the Anglo-Dutch fleets, permitting them to maintain lines of communication, support land operations and protect, to some degree, trans-oceanic trade. Nevertheless, it inflicted serious damage on allied commerce, with nearly 7,000 prizes, the majority British owned, condemned to, or ransomed by, French *corsaires*. Dunkirk alone, a port specially built and fortified by Vauban for the use of privateers, accounted for a total of 1,685 condemnations—959 prizes and 726 ransoms[3]— realising a gross sales value of at least £1,666,000.[4] St Malo, Brest and Toulon were the other leading ports in this state-subsidised privateering onslaught which severely disrupted the flow of allied trade, enriched fortunate *armateurs* and made national heroes out of commanders such as the Chevalier de Forbin and duGuay Trouin.[5]

In the face of such losses, the British mercantile community complained bitterly that its sea-borne property was afforded inadequate protection by the Admiralty. Its sense of grievance reached a peak during the autumn of 1707 as the *guerre de course* intensified in home waters. The Russia convoy was captured by a combined squadron of *corsaires* and naval frigates under the command of de Forbin, the Lisbon and Virginia convoys were routed and the West Indies fleet was forced to sail out of season. These disasters were catalogued in the mercantile press, the 'Countryman' exclaiming that

> our ships have been taken by our Enemies as the Dutch take our Herrings by Shoals upon our own coasts . . . Our merchants are beggared; our Commerce broke; our Trade gone; our Staple and Manufacture ruined.[6]

The merchants' complaints were laid before the House of Lords on 25 February 1708. French *corsaires*, it was claimed, cruised unchallenged within sight of the English coast, while convoys were ill-timed, liable to costly delay and frequently attacked by superior French squadrons.[7] Parliament responded by passing two Acts designed to provide a regular protective force for home trade, and to invigorate the commerce-raiding activities of both naval and privateering vessels to quell the enemy's *guerre de course*. Thus, the Admiralty was to ensure that 'at least 43 ships of war be employed as cruisers in proper stations for . . . securing of the merchants' ships in their going out and returning home.' Moreover, for 'the better and more effectual encouragement' of the naval service and privateers, the Crown's ancient right to a share in prize proceeds was abolished, the sole interest in prizes being vested in the captor, while a bounty was instituted to stimulate the seizure of enemy men-of-war and *corsaires*, payable at the rate of £5 for every man on board the captured vessel at the commencement of the action.[8] To further encourage commerce-raiding activity, the means by which prizes were condemned, and the profits distributed, were regularised in a series of provisions aimed at clarifying the legal process, and expediting the payment of rewards.[9]

In taking such steps, Parliament clearly bowed to mercantile pressure, for privateering had been advanced as a means of countering the threat to home trade since the start of the war. Mr *Observator*, a keen proponent of the privateering business, in considering 'the management of the late war at sea' identified a number of difficulties encompassing 'the affairs of privateers'. Chief among these was the 'small prospect of advantage by letters of mart and reprisal', a disincentive that might be removed if 'Her Majesty quit her tenths of the Capture'. A further 'encouragement to privateers would be by easing the Captors in the Condemnation of their ships' by bringing to an end the 'oppression of Doctors' Commons'—the cumbersome legal process—which had frustrated privateering venturers seeking their reward in the Nine Years' War. It was also proposed that the contraband laws be clarified, and that men injured in private men-of-war should have access to hospital treatment,[10] while it was noted that the Dutch 'Placaert for the Encouragement of Privateers' provided financial incentives for the capture of hostile ships-of-war.[11]

That such demands were met, to a large degree, in the 1708 legisaltion testifies to the vision of Mr *Observator*, and to the power of the merchant community he represented. The effectiveness of the French *guerre de course* in the trade war presented the ideal opportunity for those interested in privateering to press the case for the 'encouragement' of their business. State support, it was argued, fostered the French commerce-raiding campaign—and the Dutch *commissievaart*[12]—and if similar incentives were offered to British venturers, a means of curbing 'their privateers with ours'[13] would naturally arise. At the same time, economic interests would be served; thus, the argument continued,

> we must take the length of our weapon from that of our enemies. If they get all and we get little their privateers will be lords and ours will be beggars.[14]

In such a context, a watershed in the history of British privateering enterprise was reached; 1708 not only marked the end of the Crown's interest in maritime prize, it also saw the establishment of an administrative apparatus within which the business was to operate throughout the eighteenth century.

I

War was declared on 4 May 1702, though letters of marque were not issued until five weeks later when the Royal Proclamation granting the right of reprisal to private individuals was published. From 11 June 1702 reprisals against the seaborne property of the subjects of 'Their Catholic Majesties, the Kings of France and Spain' were permissible, the designated enemy changing to 'France and others of Her Majesty's enemies' on 17 July 1707. This alteration had only a nominal effect on the privateering war, for the Bourbon powers remained the principal maritime adversaries until the end of hostilities. A total of 1,607 letters of marque were issued under the jurisdiction of the High Court of Admiralty in the Spanish Succession War; however, some 256 of these were 're-commissions', taken out by the new commander or owner of a previously commissioned vessel, leaving a figure of 1,343 privately-owned vessels licensed to seize enemy shipping and goods. As Table 1 indicates, 51 British ports and overseas bases were involved in the privateering business during the course of the conflict.

The 'input' into the privateering business in the 1702–1712 conflict, measured in terms of the number of vessels commissioned, was considerably greater than that evident in the Nine Years' War when 406 vessels had carried letters of marque.[15] This growth was mirrored in the total tonnage commissioned, though the increase—from 75,441 to 232,906 tons burthen—was slightly less marked, as average vessel size declined from 186 to 173.4 tons burthen. In tandem with this threefold rise in the level of activity, a much broader regional distribution was apparent in the later conflict. Whereas London investors had dominated the business in King William's War, owning or sharing in 68 per cent of the vessels set out with letters of marque, their pre-eminence was eroded in the 1702–1712 conflict, as they accounted for only 50 per cent of the national total despite an absolute increase in their interest from 237 to 671 commissioned vessels. The other principal base of the 1689–1697 war, the Channel Islands, expanded its stake in the activity from 14 per cent to 15.4 per cent of the national aggregate over the two wars, while Bristol remained the leading mainland outport, though the city's 'input' of seven vessels in the earlier conflict increased dramatically to 157 in the Spanish Succession War. Expansion also took place elsewhere, as Liverpool, the ports of south-east and south-west England, east coast bases and Scottish ports all developed their interests in privateering, with a number of ports —Minehead, Scarborough and Whitehaven, for instance—engaging in such enterprise for the first time.[16]

Table 1

Commissioned Vessels by Region, 1702-1712

Region	Number of commissions	Actual vessels	Average tonnage
London	814	671	217.2
Bristol	205	157	186
Liverpool	39	31	181.9
Channel Is — Guernsey (143) Jersey (64)	255	207	42.2
E England — Colchester (1) Hull (1) Newcastle (3) Scarborough (1) Yarmouth (5)	12	11	240
SE England — Deal (2) Dover (7) Folkestone (3) Hastings (1) New Romney (9) Portsmouth (8) Rye (2) Sandwich (2) Southampton (2)	37	36	93.2
SW England — Barnstaple (5) Bideford (13) Bridgwater (1) Dartmouth (9) Exeter (5) Falmouth (7) Minehead (5) Plymouth (9) Poole (1) Topsham (4)	65	59	159.8
Wales & NW England — Chester (2) Swansea (1) Whitehaven (6)	10	9	162.8
W Scotland — Glasgow (6)	6	6	135.8
E Scotland — Aberdeen (2) Bo'ness (2) Edinburgh (3) Leith (4)	11	11	114.3
Ireland — Belfast (2) Cork (8) Dublin (15) Waterford (3)	29	28	133.9
Overseas Bases — Africa (1) Antigua (1) Barbados (2) Gibraltar (4) Hamburg (1) Jamaica (5) Leghorn (14) Lisbon (4) Monserrat (1) Oporto (1)	36	34	171.8
*Port Unknown**	88	83	181.1
	1607	1343	173.4

* In the declarations made by commanders of these vessels no indication is given as to the home port of their owners. Fifty-seven of the *'port unknown'* vessels were commissioned in 1702.

Figures in brackets denote actual vessels.
Source: PRO, HCA 25/14-25; HCA 26/13-21.

A number of factors can be advanced to explain the overall growth in the scale of privateering activity and its changing regional pattern between the two wars. To a limited degree, such developments reflect inconsistencies in the sources utilised, and deficiencies in the measures adopted. The letter of marque declarations tend to understate the level of activity in the Nine Years' War, for Scottish vessels were commissioned by the Scottish Privy Council until the Act of Union in 1707, and are thus excluded; moreover, 'letters of marque' were subject to restriction in the last three years of the war, as the Admiralty sought to reserve manpower for the Navy, and this may have deterred investors from taking out commissions for their trading vessels. Such understatement is marginal, however, for only 14 Scottish vessels were commissioned between 1689 and 1707,[17] while 104 out of the 155 licences issued after 1695 were granted for armed merchantmen, even though they were valid only for a single, specified voyage.[18]

Wider factors were largely responsible for the expansion of privateering enterprise in the 1702–1712 war. Commerce-raiding opportunities were more extensive, in that reprisals were permissible for a longer period of time in Queen Anne's War, commissions being available in eleven as opposed to just nine years in the preceding campaign. Moreover, the war was global in scope, for the hostility of Spain added a significant colonial, as well as European, dimension to the range of potential prey, while the concurrent Northern War implicated the Baltic powers in a complex diplomatic web in which neutrals and belligerents, free goods and contraband of war, were determined by a confusing series of alliances and bi-lateral commercial agreements.

At the same time, these factors, together with the French *guerre de course,* rendered overseas commerce more unstable and hazardous. Thus, the closure of the Spanish market in Europe and South America, the uncertainties surrounding trade with the Baltic and the growing menace of French *corsaires* combined to curtail commercial activity in certain areas, and privateering emerged as one of the few viable options for investors with resources to spare. The mercantile communities of Bristol and the South West, for instance, were forced to adapt in these circumstances, as the region's principal export trades—grain, woollens and cod-fish—were highly dependent on Spanish markets, both in metropolitan Spain and in her Italian territories. While Exeter was able to divert its trade in serges via the Rotterdam entrepot,[19] other south-western ports were less successful in adapting to the adverse market conditions of wartime, an inflexibility which particularly afflicted those engaged in the Newfoundland cod fisheries. This long-distance trade was also highly vulnerable to enemy attack, for not only did the French destroy West Country settlements and fishing 'rooms' on the island of New-foundland, but their *corsaires* also preyed on fishing ships on the Grand Banks, in European waters and off the Devon coast; indeed, Barnstaple Bay proved so productive of prizes that it was dubbed the 'Golden Bay' by French privateersmen.[20] With the virtual collapse of this staple trade, together with the contraction in wool and grain exports, the privateering business represented a relatively important investment opportunity, explaining, in part, the growing interest exhibited in the activity by the merchants and shipowners of Bristol and cod-fishing ports such as Barnstaple, Bideford and Dartmouth.

While the extensive range of potential prizes, and the temporary demise of alternative trades, served to stimulate privateering investment, a further incentive was provided by the state. The legislation of 1708 sought to encourage naval and private commerce-raiding activity by improving the financial prospects facing men-of-warsmen and privateering venturers. In abolishing the Crown's right to a share in prizes, providing bounty money and regularising the distribution of rewards, it was envisaged that a means of countering the enemy's *guerre de course* would be effected. While these provisions were significant in the long run, their short-term impact on the scale of activity in the 1702–1712 war is less easy to perceive, though they certainly failed to revolutionise the business. The legislation seems to have had some effect, however; in national terms, Appendix 2 indicates that the level of predatory activity, notably in the 'Channel' sector, increased in March and remained relatively buoyant throughout the summer of 1708; in London, 1708 was a trough year in terms of the number of commissions issued, the entry of 'new' vessels into the private war-at-sea and the condemnation of prizes, a year which divided two, more active, phases of the war;[21] in the Channel Islands, a marked revival occurred in the issue of letters of marque after March 1708,[22] while the legislation coincided with an increase in vessel size and a decline in the number of shareholders per venture;[23] and in Bristol, it was perhaps more than coincidence that the *Duke* and the *Dutchess* were commissioned in April 1708, Woodes Rogers being provided with copies of the 'two Acts to encourage privateers', and reminded that

> all purchase that shall be taken, is to be ye sole use and benefitt of ye owners & men; and not liable to pay tenths.[24]

Such a consideration may have helped trigger the revival of privateering activity apparent in London and the Channel Islands after 1708, though other factors—the resuscitation of the French war effort in 1709, and the marked sensitivity of Channel Island *armateurs* to news of recent prizes[25]—were also at work. Further evidence is lacking, the silence of the records suggesting, perhaps, that the 1708 legislation proved less of a stimulant than its framers had anticipated.

Nevertheless, by increasing the incentives for venturers, the government added momentum to wider factors like the growing range of prey and the restriction of trading opportunities which nurtured the privateering business. Such expansionist forces acted upon a broad spectrum of enterprise, with private men-of-war and 'letters of marque' of various kinds comprising the 1,343 vessels licensed in the Spanish Succession War. The letter of marque declarations indicate that the 'Channel' branch of the privateering business was relatively extensive during the 1702-1712 conflict. As Table 2 shows, 259 licensed vessels fell within the tonnage and manning criteria laid down for 'small ships, vessels

Table 2

'Channel' Privateers by Region, 1702-1712

Region	Vessels of 2.5 tons per man or less		Regional Total	% 'Channel'
	- 49 tons	50-99 tons		
London	17	25	671	6.3
Bristol	0	5	157	3.2
Channel Is (2)	135	38	207	83.6
SE England (8)	22	0	36	61.1
SW England (2)	0	2	59	3.4
W Scotland (1)	1	0	6	16.7
E Scotland (1)	1	0	11	9.1
Ireland (2)	0	4	28	14.3
Overseas Bases (2)	0	3	34	8.8
Port Unknown	4	2	83	7.2
	180	79		

Figures in brackets denote number of ports.
Source: PRO, HCA 25/14-25; HCA 26/13-21.

and boats' in the legislation of 1759. By this broad measure, 'Channel' privateers constituted almost one-fifth of the craft licensed during Queen Anne's War, a proportion that was not to be surpassed until the American Revolutionary War.

Guernsey and Jersey were important centres of 'Channel' commerce-raiding activity throughout the 'long' eighteenth century. In the Spanish Succession War, these island bases were pre-dominant, setting forth 135 of the 180 heavily-manned vessels of under 49 tons burthen, together with a further 38 craft declared as measuring between 50 and 99 tons. The significance of this form of predatory enterprise to the Islanders is readily apparent in that these small-scale ventures represented over 80 per cent of the privateering 'input' of the shipowners of Guernsey and Jersey. Their interest in the commerce-raiding business was a comparatively recent phenomenon, however, for it was only in 1689 that the customary neutrality of the Islands had ceased; thereafter, the granting of reprisals against France invariably precipitated a flurry of predatory activity as the Islanders sought to exploit their locational advantages and their positive allegiance to the English crown. Proximity to the enemy's coast, detailed knowledge of his inshore waters and port approaches, together with the fact that capital and labour requirements were relatively limited, dictated that the main thrust of the Islanders' privateering response should be directed against French coastal trade, and embodied in small vessels adept at negotiating the shallow waters off the Breton, Norman and Biscay shore.[26] Accordingly, it was in this theatre that the smallest units of the British commissioned fleet were deployed, with picaroons such as the *Spreadeagle*, of 8 tons burthen, and the 6-ton *Swallow*,[27] set forth to cruise in the bays, and off the headlands, of the French coast.

On the mainland, 'Channel' privateering was largely conducted from the ports of south-east England. Here, 22 locally-owned vessels of less than 50 tons burthen were set forth 'to cruise upon the enemy in the Channel only', as the declarations of the *Greyhound Sloop*, of 20 tons burthen and 25 men, and the 10-ton, 24-man *Swallow*, both of Dover, indicate so precisely.[28] Folkestone, Rye and Sandwich venturers were also engaged in this form of activity, though 'Mascall's privateers', nine commerce-raiders fitted out by John Mascall, rendered New Romney the most significant of the South East's privateering bases.[29] Many of the 42 diminutive craft owned by London investors cruised in the Narrows, with predators such as the *Diligence*, the *Good Luck*, the *Neptune* and the *Swift*—all burthen between 30 and 40 tons, and worked by up to 40 men[30]—particularly active in these waters. Operating from the ports of

Kent and Sussex, these small-scale private men-of-war were equipped to prey upon enemy small fry and neutrals passing within easy reach of their adopted bases; at least one, however, appears to have preferred the safety of her haven, the *Sarah Gally*'s commander being warned by his owners that 'youl never doe anything all the time youl stay in Dover . . . but to put us to Charges.'[31]

'Channel' privateering activity was fairly evenly dispersed over the course of the 1702–1712 conflict. The letter of marque declarations suggest that at least two of these predators were 'in commission' in each of the 123 months in which reprisals were permissible, though, at its height in February 1709, this facet of the privateering business only engaged 25 craft requiring the services of 891 seafarers (see Appendix 2). Thus, the marked peaks and troughs—closely associated with the fluctuating complexion of enemy trade liable to confiscation—which typified 'Channel' rates of activity in later wars, were much less evident in Queen Anne's War.

A similar pattern was apparent in the 'deep-water' branch of the predatory business. While at least one such venture was victualled and presumably active at each stage of the conflict, the peak monthly rate for the war as a whole was a mere 21 private men-of-war in April 1703. Moreover, it was not until the closing stages of the war, from January 1710 onwards, that average manning levels consistently exceeded 100 seafarers, reflecting the increase in the scale of individual ventures—as indicated by the experience of Guernsey—consequent upon the re-deployment of large prize vessels.[32] In spite of this stimulus, it is clear from Table 3 that large-scale commerce-raiding enterprise remained largely undeveloped in the early eighteenth century, with only 92 ventures exhibiting 'deep-water' characteristics in the Spanish Succession War. London was the most significant port, with investors from 14 outports engaging in this form of activity. Nearly half of the vessels concerned carried fewer than 100 men, while only one, the 500-ton *Surprize Gally* of London was declared to be recruiting as many as 200 men.[33] Clearly, the conditions which fostered such 'privateers of force' had yet to emerge by the opening decade of the century. In particular, the prey which stimulated and sustained large-scale predatory operations was less abundant at this juncture, for the rapid expansion of sugar production in the French Caribbean, notably in St Domingue, did not commence until the 1720s;[34] accordingly, the valuable 'Martinicomen' and 'St Domingomen'—homeward-bound and vulnerable in the north-eastern Atlantic—had yet to fill the dreams of privateering venturers, and commerce-raiders operating in the archetypal 'deep-water' fashion were relatively few in number and limited in scale.

Table 3

'Deep-Water' Private Ships-of-War by Region, 1702–1712

Region	Crew Size				Regional Total	% 'Deep-Water'
	40-99*	100-149	150-199	200+		
London	16	17	6	1	671	6
Bristol	5	4	2	0	157	7
Channel Is (2)	7	5	1	0	207	6.3
SE England (3)	1	2	1	0	36	11.1
SW England (4)	3	4	0	0	59	11.9
Wales & NW England (1)	1	0	0	0	9	11.1
W Scotland (1)	1	0	0	0	6	16.7
Ireland (1)	1	0	0	0	28	3.6
Overseas Bases (1)	2	2	0	0	34	11.8
Port Unknown	7	3	0	0	83	12
	44	37	10	1		

*Vessels exceeding 99 tons burthen manned in the ratio of 2.5 tons per man or less.
Figures in brackets denote number of ports.
Source: PRO, HCA 25/14-25; HCA 26/13-21.

Instead, the ambitious commerce-raiding entrepreneur looked to other theatres for the rich prizes and windfall profits that his speculative investments promised. At least two 'grand schemes' to seize Spanish treasure in the South Seas were implemented during the Spanish Succession War, with William Dampier's voyage of 1703–1706 emulated and surpassed by the 'cruising voyage round the world' undertaken by Woodes Rogers and the crews of the *Duke* and the *Dutchess* between 1708 and 1711. Involving four of the commissioned vessels declared to be enlisting at least 100 men, both 'expeditions' set out to round the Horn, to seek out and seize the Acapulco-Manila register-ship and to plunder Spanish American settlements if the opportunity arose. Though the attempt of the *St George* and the *Cinque Ports Gally* ended in ignominious and acrimonious failure, this was not due to the impracticability of the plan, for Dampier's worm-infested, under-manned squadron reached and encountered its targets, to be denied by the incompetence, malice or misfortune—a matter of some dispute—of the personnel involved.[35] The promoters of Rogers' expedition, whose number included Thomas Eastney, an investor in the *St George*, learned from this experience and determined to adopt the scheme of their predecessors, though to prosecute it with rather more efficiency and vigour. Accordingly, lessons from the previous voyage were heeded; decisions were to be made by a properly constituted council of war, not in a 'hugger-mugger' of senior officers; owners' representatives were to sail with the vessels; while William Dampier was enlisted not as commander, but as pilot, for his 'knowledge in these parts we do mainly depend upon for satisfactory success'. Such measures paid off as the *Duke* and the *Dutchess,* together with the *Batchelor* prize vessel, returned in 1711 laden with captured goods worth some £148,000.[36] In the course of their circumnavigation, the two newly-built Bristol vessels, of 350 and 250 tons burthen, took the Acapulco treasure ship, sacked Guayaquil and rescued Alexander Selkirk from his solitary sojourn on the island of Juan Fernandez, where he had been marooned four years and four months earlier during Dampier's voyage.

While such stirring deeds have formed the basis of many an adventure story, most notably Defoe's *Robinson Crusoe*, the heavy capital investment required, the uncertainty and delay in the payment of rewards and the danger associated with such ventures meant that forays into the Pacific were rare. Lesser risks—and rewards—attended the operations of various relatively large commissioned craft despatched to the Mediterranean and the waters off Newfoundland in the quest for prizes. In these stations, the 'cruising voyage' form of predatory enterprise appears to have been favoured, with vessels such as the *Ambuscade* of Portsmouth instructed to steer for Lisbon, 'and from Lisbon a Cruising or upon Trade'. That the 28 officers and the 87 'sailers' comprising her complement agreed to serve aboard this powerful vessel—of 400 tons burthen and 30 carriage guns—for just one-sixth of any prize fund generated, further implies the 'letter of marque' nature of the venture, with wages probably paid to compensate the men for the limited prospects offered by such a division of spoil.[37] Vessels of a similar strength departed for specified destinations, an indication in itself that trading formed at least part of their purpose;

thus, the 450-ton *Camberwell Gally* of London, with a company of 85 men, was destined 'upon a voyage to Newfoundland',[38] the *Upton Gally*, a Dartmouth vessel of 140 tons burthen and 100 men, was bound 'for Lisbon, Newfoundland & back to London',[39] Guernseymen such as *La Chasse*, of 200 tons burthen and 130 men, and the 200-ton *Guernsey Frigat*, with a complement of 160 men, operated off the Newfoundland Banks,[40] while the *Diligence*, of 330 tons burthen and 140 men, and owned, like the *Ambuscade*, by Thomas Blakely, Thomas Missing and Thomas Ridge— 'three substantial entrepreneurs of Portsmouth'—embarked for the Straits in 1710.[41]

Such 'cruise and voyage' ventures accounted for much of the large-scale predatory enterprise undertaken in the 1702–1712 conflict. 'Letters of marque' of a more commercial disposition constituted a greater proportion of the commissioned fleet, however, despite the concerted activities of enemy *corsaires*. 'Armed trading vessels' had already become a regular aspect of the privateering business by the 1700s. In the Nine Years' War, the official distinction briefly drawn between 'letters of marque' and private ships-of-war revealed that two-thirds—104 out of 155—of the vessels commissioned after 1695 were licensed merchantmen, the majority belonging to London.[42] Though the letter of marque declarations made in the 1702–1712 conflict will not permit of such exactitude, it seems feasible that similar proportions applied in the later war, certainly with regard to the major overseas trading bases of London, Bristol and the emergent port of Liverpool. The relatively high average tonnage of commissioned vessels belonging to these ports suggests the presence of a significant number of 'armed traders', for these vessels, as the 1695–1697 data testify, were generally larger than specialist commerce-raiders in this era. In London, for instance, substantial commissioned merchantmen were engaged in a variety of trades; the *Ann of London* was bound from the capital to Virginia and back; the *Union Frigat* was destined for Jamaica; the *Blessing of London* was heading for the Baltic;[43] and the *Dutchess* and the *Sea Nimph*, having been 'fitted out for trade', were to proceed from the Thames to the Straits and 'from thence to such other ports or places as the Owners shall direct untill [their] return to London'.[44] Ranging in size from 230 to 400 tons burthen, and in crew strength from 24 to 73 men, these were typical 'armed trading vessels', embarking for specified destinations, loaded with cargo, but armed and commissioned to facilitate opportunist seizures of enemy property.

'Specialist vessels', operated by the chartered trading companies, also belonged to the port of London. Thus, the *Royal Affrica*, of 350 tons burthen, 30 guns and a crew of 70 men, was owned by the 'Royal Affrican Company of England',[45] while a single vessel, the *Hudson's Bay Frigat,* burthen 150 tons, with 16 guns and 36 men, was equipped with a letter of marque by the 'Honourable the Governor and Company of Merchant Venturers trading to Hudson's Bay'.[46] The East India Company was the third, and most significant of the commercial institutions to commission its vessels, though it is recorded as owning only two of London's licensed fleet in the Spanish Succession War. In fact, the *Bombay Frigat* and the *Indian Frigat* were auxiliary vessels owned by the Company to service its settlements in the East and to tender to its commercial fleet. At 130 and 140 tons burthen,[47] they were too small to participate directly in the eastern trade, which was conducted in large, purpose-built Indiamen hired from the 'shipping interest', an elite group of City merchants holding the monopoly right to supply the Company's shipping requirement. Sixty-three of these vessels embarked for Asia in the war years—'bound for the East Indies not in the way of the Algeraine cruisers'[48]—though only 36 were issued with letters of marque.[49] While they ranged in tonnage from the 600-ton *London* to the *Toddington,* of 230 tons burthen,[50] the majority of the Company's ships were between 300 and 500 tons burthen, and nearly all carried crews in the ratio of one man per five tons; thus, the 350-ton *Edward & Dudley* was navigated by 70 men, the *Dutchesse,* of 450 tons burthen, carried 90 men, while 100 men shipped aboard the *Grantham Frigott,* of 500 tons.[51] Indiamen were invariably armed with at least 20 carriage guns, and victualled for between 16 and 36 months for the arduous return voyage to India or China.

Numerically, therefore, the fleet commissioned in the Spanish Succession War was dominated by commercially-oriented craft, with 'armed traders' and 'specialist vessels'—as in the Nine Years' War —constituting perhaps two-thirds of the overall 'input' into the privateering business. Yet the operations of the private men-of-war which formed the remaining third of the fleet were by no means insignificant; indeed, with regard to predation, the 'Channel' privateers formed the most dynamic element of the commissioned fleet.

II

The aggregate 'output' of the various forms of privateering enterprise is compared to that of the Navy in Table 4.

Table 4

Prizes Condemned at Doctors' Commons, 1702-1714

Year	Privateers	Navy*	Total
1702	16	197	213
1703	95	253	348
1704	90	109	199
1705	116	86	202
1706	89	72	161
1707	111	66	177
1708	61	82	143
1709	78	133	211
1710	79	114	193
1711	87	64	151
1712	106	66	172
1713	27	19	46
1714	1	5	6
	956	1266	2222

* Including 'droits and perquisites' of the Admiralty.
Source: PRO, HCA 34/23-30, 58.

The data presented in Table 4 are derived from the sentences of common condemnation passed by the Prize Court in London between 1702 and 1714. They provide sparse details of the Court's decision to condemn captured property as lawful prize; yet they offer sufficient information to distinguish naval prizes from those taken by private commissioned vessels, and, in conjunction with the letter of marque declarations, the sentences permit analysis of the privateering 'catch' by port and region. Other sources have been used for such purposes, notably the lists of prizes prepared for the Customs Commissioners in 1697, 1712 and 1748.[52] Naturally, there are advantages and disadvantages in using these various series, and the results gleaned from them often differ. However, a very similar overall pattern of prize condemnation emerges from each of the analyses. Thus, it is clear that British commerce-raiding activity was much less successful than that of the French, in terms of the number of condemnations; using the same measure, it is evident that the return of British privateers compared favourably with that of the Navy, and that the Channel Islands were the most significant privateering bases; moreover, it is apparent that London remained the leading mainland prize-taking centre, though its predominant position was eroded as the outports increased their interests in the privateering business.

The detail within this broad picture reveals that 2,222 properties taken during Queen Anne's War were subject to common condemnation at Doctors' Commons, though some 2,239 prizes were entered on the Customs list.[53] Either way, this return pales in comparison with the enemy's commerce-raiding effort, for French *corsaires* alone were responsible for nearly 7,000 condemnations,[54] over three times the combined product of Britain's private and naval forces. This contrast explains, in part, the demands of the British mercantile class for the more efficient protection of its trading vessels, and the greater encouragement of its own commerce-destroyers. It also suggests that such a stimulus, when it came in 1708, failed to stem the tide of French success in the trade war, though the relative abundance of prospective prey—the number of commercial vessels each belligerent set out—was a significant contributory factor.

The Prize Court sentences indicate that 956 condemnations were made to private commissioned vessels in the 1702–1712 conflict, with a further 1,266 prizes, 57 per cent of the total, falling to naval vessels, or condemned as perquisites of the Admiralty. In this respect, the sentences and the Customs list diverge somewhat, for the Commissioners recorded that privateers accounted for 1,176 captures, 52.5 per cent of the prize total, while the state's force was responsible for 1,063 condemnations.[55] Nevertheless, both measures suggest the significance of privateers relative to the Navy in the prize war, while, at the same time, they affirm the ineffectiveness of the British privateering effort relative to the French *guerre de course*, which produced roughly seven times as many prizes. It was only in limited areas that the *corsaires* were rivalled by their British counterparts; in addressing the 'insolence' of French privateersmen, Mr *Observator* recognised this fact, asserting that

> 'tis impossible to curb their privateers with ours, for I know none we have, except a few belonging to the Islands of Jersey and Guernsey.[56]

Notwithstanding his exaggerated pessimism, Mr *Observator* afforded the

Channel Islands an importance which is reflected in the distribution of privateering prizes by port group, as presented in Table 5.

Table 5

Prizes Condemned to Commissioned Vessels by Region, 1702–1714

Region		Number of prizes
London		208
Bristol		85
Liverpool		4
Channel Is	—Guernsey (427) Jersey (97) Guernsey/Jersey (6)	530
E England	—Newcastle (1)	1
SE England	—Dover (9) Folkestone (5) New Romey (40) Portsmouth (11) Sandwich (3) Southampton (2) Folkestone/ New Romney (4)	74
SW England	—Falmouth (3) Plymouth (1) Poole (1)	5
Wales & NW England	—Swansea (1) Whitehaven (3)	4
Ireland	—Belfast (1) Cork (6) Dublin (1) Waterford (1)	9
Overseas Bases	—Leghorn (8) Oporto (2)	10
In consort	—London/Bristol (3) London/Guernsey (1) London/Leghorn(1) London/Bristol/ Guernsey (1) London/New Romney/ Folkestone (1) London/Port Unknown (1) Bristol/Guernsey (3) Bristol/Jersey (1) Bristol/Whitehaven (1) Bristol/Exeter/ Massachusetts (2)	15
Port Unknown		11
		956

Source: PRO, HCA 25/14-25; HCA 26/13-21; HCA 34/23-30, 58.

In absolute terms, the Islanders accounted for 530 of the sentences passed in the Prize Court, 55.4 per cent of the British privateering total, with another six prizes taken by Island vessels operating in consort with predators from other ports. London was chief amongst the mainland ports in terms of prize condemnations, with 208 enemy properties, 21.8 per cent of the national aggregate, falling to the capital's commissioned vessels, while Bristol's status as the leading outport of the day was apparent in the city's contribution of 85 condemnations to the prize total, 8.9 per cent of the whole. A further 18 provincial ports participated in prize-taking activity, with the bases of south-east England responsible for 74 condemnations, 7.7 per cent of the national total; in addition, commissioned vessels owned by British merchants resident in Leghorn, Massachusetts and Oporto accounted for 13 prize sentences, including three shared with British-based vessels, passed in the Prize Court in London.

This national pattern, which is also evident in the Customs list, requires some qualification. In the first place, London's significance as a prize-taking centre was less marked in the 1702–1712 conflict than it had been in the Nine Years' War. The Customs lists for the two wars indicate that London's pre-eminence declined as the Channel Islands and Bristol increased their share of the prize 'catch',[57] and vessels belonging to a wide array of outports—from Newcastle to Falmouth to Whitehaven—engaged in the prize war. Secondly, if the 'output' of the various bases, in terms of their prize return, is related to their 'input' into the privateering business, the number of vessels commissioned, the performance of the Channel Islands and, to a lesser degree, the ports of south-east England appears more impressive. Thus, the 530 Channel Island prizes were taken by a fleet of 207 licensed vessels, a rate of 2.6 prizes per predator, while the equivalent figure for south-east England was just over two, as the region equipped 36 vessels with letters of marque, and recorded 74 condemnations. Such ratios compare with that of 0.7 for the British privateering fleet as a whole, and 0.3 prizes per commissioned vessel if the Channel Islands and the south-eastern bases are excluded from the calculation. Similarly, London's importance to the prize war appears in a different light when the number of potential captors is related to the prizes condemned. Accordingly, the capital recorded a meagre rate of return of just 0.3 prizes per licensed vessel, rendering London a much less active prize-taking centre, in proportionate terms, than the Channel Islands, south-east England, or even Bristol, where a rate of return of 0.5 was achieved by the port's 157 authorised craft.

The regional distribution of prizes, and the varying rates of return, reflect the composition of the British privateering force in the Spanish Succession War. Thus, the great majority of commissioned vessels fitted out in the Channel Islands, and in the ports of south-east England, were 'Channel' privateers, small-scale ventures requiring relatively little capital to equip a sloop or fishing shallop for a short cruise in adjacent waters. In the ports of Kent and Sussex, this meant a brief foray into the Channel Narrows to intercept neutral vessels carrying contraband goods, or perhaps to the French coast to prey on enemy small fry. Island vessels, on the other hand, concentrated their attentions on French coastal and fishing vessels operating in the waters off Brittany and Normandy, or, more particularly, in the Bay of Biscay. In both of its guises, the 'Channel' privateer's ambitions were necessarily limited, for the size and range of the average predator from these bases rendered the seizure of a 'capital' prize a highly unlikely occurrence. Indeed, this was borne out in the 1702–1712 conflict, for the average worth of the Islanders' prizes was approximately £200,[58] while the 45 enemy properties condemned to 'Mascall's privateers' of New Romney had a mean appraised value of £500, ranging from the French wine and brandy, reckoned to be worth £1,250, found in the Dutch merchantman *Anna Petronella*, to the *Mary de Royan*, which had an estimated value of £29.[59] Two prizes taken by the *Neptune*, a 'Channel' privateer belonging to London, were less valuable still; thus, the *St Isabelle de Neuport*, a smack seized fishing in the Strait of Dover, had an appraised value of just £22 17s, of which the hull, masts and rigging comprised £12,[60] while the *Hope de Roan*, of 15 tons burthen, was judged to be worth some £26 4s.[61]

Given the restricted value of the typical prey, profitable operation of the 'Channel' privateer depended upon the apprehension of a number of prizes. Multiple successes were therefore a regular feature of this form of commerce-raiding activity, and the prize sentences offer a number of notable examples. The Guernseyman *Flying Dragon*, of 50 tons burthen, eight guns and 50 men, had 28 prizes, including a joint capture, condemned between 1704 and 1711, while the *Churchill Gally*, of 60 tons, eight guns and 50 men, took 20 prizes without assistance, and three in consort, during a number of cruises undertaken between 1708 and 1710. The *Hope* and the *Victory* were other Guernsey vessels which accounted for more than 20 prizes during the war, though a Jersey predator, Andrew de St Croix's command, the *Society*, of 20 tons burthen, with four guns and a complement of 25 men, was the most productive single private man-of-war in the 1702-1712 conflict, having 41 prizes, including eight joint captures, sentenced after 1704. In the eastern reaches of the Channel, multiple captures were recorded by a number of private men-of-war; the nine vessels owned by John Mascall of New Romney, for instance, were responsible for 4; condemnations, mainly contraband goods found in neutral holds, while the *Devereux Gally* of Folkestone recorded seven condemnations, including four in league with New Romney predators, and the *Greyhound Sloop*, the archetypal 'Channel' privateer at 20 tons burthen, four guns and 25 men, had six prizes condemned.[62] London vessels operating in these waters produced similar results, with Samuel Shapman's vessel, the *Neptune*, taking 14 prizes, 12 of which were carried into Dover, the *Swift Sloop* landing seven prizes at Cowes and Rye, and the *Good Luck*, of 30 tons burthen and 30 men, carrying four prizes into Channel ports.[63]

The activities of these and other London vessels in the English Channel affirm that the main thrust of the British privateering effort occurred in this theatre. Though this business comprised small-scale units, and individual prizes were generally of low value, its cumulative effect was significant, and felt in two main areas; while the harassment of neutral shipping in the Narrows interrupted the flow of contraband goods between the Bourbon powers and north-west Europe, the offensive mounted by the Channel Island privateers on the French coasting trade had a demoralising effect on the coastal populations of Brittany and Normandy for not only did it damage their trading and fishing fleets, but it also disrupted the sea-borne supply of commodities upon which these isolated communities depended.[64] Moreover, the diversion of prize goods—whether contraband wines and brandies lifted out of neutral carriers, or coal, grain or salt taken from French coasters—into the hands of Kentish or Channel Island venturers, made this form of commerce-raiding a lucrative business for many local merchants and seafarers. Hence, such activity, which involved but small risks, remained an important feature of the British privateering business throughout the eighteenth century.

It was not the only facet of the commerce-raiding business to return prizes, however, as 'cruising voyages' to the Mediterranean and Newfoundland, 'deep-water' operations in the north-eastern Atlantic, and 'expeditons' to the Pacific achieved varying degrees of success. Bristol, the leading outport of the day, was heavily involved in all aspects of this ocean-going enterprise, with the Newfoundland Banks a particularly fruitful cruising station for the town's ventures. Only 12 of the 85 prizes condemned to the city's privateers were conveyed back to the Avon, with five taken to ports in south-west England and eight landed at bases in the Mediterranean. Of the remainder, 13 were carried into St John's, Newfoundland, and no less than 47 were ransomed, an indication that the prize was apprehended in distant waters and of insufficient value to warrant an escort to port. Many of these ransoms took place in the fishing grounds of the North Atlantic where the *Eugene Gally* and the *Whetstone Gally*, Bristol's most productive commerce-raiders, accounted for 25 prizes, carrying four into St John's, and ransoming the others.

London venturers also ranged widely in the search for prize. They competed with Bristolians on the Grand Banks, carrying some 28 prizes into the island of Newfoundland, with 26 landed at St John's and another two at Ferryland. Most of these prizes were French vessels exploiting the abundant cod shoals found in the island's offshore grounds. Thus, the *St Hillaron de Nantes* was fishing on the Grand Banks when persuaded by two broadsides from the *Camberwell Gally* to strike her colours. The prize, of 100 tons burthen, was carrying 80 hogsheads of salt, six hogsheads of blubber, and 400 quintals of codfish, and was worth an estimated £208.[65] Nicholas Fleury's vessel, the *Jolie Gallere,* was fishing the same waters when seized by the *Herbert Gally* and carried to St John's, where the ship, its fishing equipment and cargo of salt were examined in July 1710.[66] These French deep-sea fishermen were also vulnerable to British privateering attack during their return voyage from the fishing grounds. The *St John Baptist,* an English-built vessel belonging to St Jean de Luz, was bound for Bilbao with a cargo of dried fish when seized by the *Albion* of London and carried into Lisbon.[67] Another French fishing vessel intercepted *en route* to the Iberian market with a cargo of fish was the *St Anthony de Padua*; engaged by the *Trumball* 30 leagues off Cape Finisterre, she succumbed after an hour's resistance, to be ransomed for 20,000 livres.[68]

Such captures suggest that a number of London predators were operating in the Western Approaches, preying on the enemy's colonial trade as it approached or departed the western seaboard of Europe. Though fishing vessels bound for the Catholic markets of southern Europe were taken in these waters, the real objects of this 'deep-water' enterprise were the cargoes of tropical produce bound from the Caribbean to the Atlantic ports of France and Spain. The seizure of the *Incomparable de Bordeaux* typified this form of activity; sailing from Martinique for Bordeaux with cocoa, indigo and sugar, this 125-ton merchantman was escorted to Plymouth by the *Leghorne Gally*, of 260 tons burthen and 60 men, after an engagement 20 leagues off Cape Ortegal during which some 70 shot of cannon were fired in her defence.[69] Outward-bound West

Indiamen were also vulnerable in this station, with vessels like the *Vigilant de Nantes* captured by the *Martha* in latitude 45°N, 60 leagues off Cape Finisterre, and taken thence to Kinsale.[70] That a further 18 London prizes were conveyed to ports in the West Country, with 14 carried to Lisbon—convenient landing places for craft apprehended in the north-eastern Atlantic—suggests that the Western Approaches was emerging as a productive cruising ground in the 1702–1712 war, a foretaste of what was to occur in subsequent conflicts.

The sentences of the Prize Court further indicate that London's commissioned vessels penetrated the Mediterranean to some effect during Queen Anne's War. Indeed, this was probably the most fruitful theatre for the capital's 'ocean-going' vessels, with 54 prizes, a quarter of the London total, landed at bases in the Mediterranean. Leghorn was particularly significant, receiving 23 captured vessels, an indication that British privateers found it as convenient a prize market and re-fitting base as did their Zeeland rivals.[71] It was also an opportune base from which to prey on the trade of Marseilles; thus, prizes such as the *Virgin de la Deliverance*, bound from Malta to Marseilles with wool and linen,[72] and the *Jesus, Maria and St Anne*, departing Marseilles with a cargo of cochineal,[73] were seized by London predators and carried into the free port of Leghorn. Eleven other Mediterranean bases were used by London captors as ports of landing during the course of the war, the most significant being Zant, in the Ionian Sea, with eight, Tunis with five, and the island of Malta, where four prizes were conveyed.

Substantial vessels were responsible for the majority of these captures. Thus, the 350-ton *Selby Frigat*, with 30 guns and a 60-strong company, accounted for nine condemnations, carrying seven into Mediterranean harbours; the *Pompey*, also of 350 tons burthen and 60 men, captured seven enemy vessels in the Mediterranean during 1712, in addition to two prizes conveyed to Newfoundland during an earlier cruise; and the *Adriatick Gally*, of 300 tons, 26 guns and 70 men,[74] landed prizes at Candia, Sardinia and Zant in 1711. These captors were probably engaged in 'cruising voyages', for their complements, though large for trading purposes, were much smaller than the crews normally carried by 'deep-water' private men-of-war. Moreover, they were similar in tonnage and manning to ventures such as the *Ambuscade* of Portsmouth which clearly displayed the characteristics of the predatory 'letter of marque'. Charged to proceed from Lisbon 'a Cruising or upon trade',[75] Captain William Thompson obviously chose the former option, for his vessel accounted for 11 prizes—Portsmouth's entire return—with two carried into Lisbon, and the remainder landed in the Mediterranean ports of Alicante, Barcelona, Naples and Nice.

While there is no evidence to suggest that 'letters of marque' of a more commercial temper, or the commissioned vessels operated by the chartered trading companies, participated in prize-taking activity to any significant degree, the most speculative arm of the British privateering business, the 'expeditionary forces', achieved a number of captures. Though Dampier's ill-fated 'expedition' to the South Seas, largely financed by London capitalists,[76] returned no prizes for adjudication in England, it was widely believed that the *St George* and the *Cinque Ports Gally* did seize Spanish property in the Pacific, the plunder being consumed *en route* or embezzled by the crew.[77] In contrast, the incursion of the *Duke* and the *Dutchess* into the Pacific was a relatively orderly affair, with over 20 Spanish properties taken during the vessels' circumnavigation. Most of these prize vessels were ransomed or disposed of during the voyage, with only two, the Acapulco treasure ship *Nostra Senora de la Encarnation yel Desengario*, and the *Havre de Grace*, formally sentenced in London. However, the detailed financial report of the expedition presented to the Master in Chancery suggests that the bulk of the booty was properly accounted for, and the net proceeds divided amongst the venturers, albeit some years after the return of the vessels.[78]

The gross income of this single Bristol venture, in comparison with the returns earned by the 200 or so private men-of-war set forth from the Channel Islands, indicates the range of enterprise and reward apparent in the British privateering business in the Spanish Succession War. While Woodes Rogers' expedition produced a gross prize fund of some £148,000, the total return accruing to the Channel Islanders from their persistent attacks on enemy trade in French coastal waters has been estimated at between £300,000 and £350,000.[79] Such a comparison suggests, quite clearly, that reward varied directly with risk.

Notes

1. 'The Lords' Address relating to the Merchants' Complaint on Account of Losses for Want of Cruisers and Convoys' *Cobbett's Parliamentary History of England* (1810), VI, 646.
2. Vauban's Memorandum on Privateering, 30 November 1695. Reprinted in

G. Symcox, ed., *War, Diplomacy and Imperialism, 1618–1713* (New York: Harper & Row, 1973) 239-42.

3. J. S. Bromley, 'The Importance of Dunkirk (1688–1713) Re-considered' in M. Mollet, ed., *Course et Piraterie* (Paris: Commission Internationale d'Histoire Maritime, 1975), I, 233-5.

4. J. S. Bromley, 'The French Privateering War, 1702–1713' in H. E. Bell and R. L. Ollard, eds, *Historical Essays, 1600-1750, presented to David Ogg* (Black, 1963) 217.

5. See E. H. Jenkins, *A History of the French Navy from its Beginnings to the Present Day* (MacDonald & Janes, 1973) 93-105.

6. *Observator*, 22 November 1707.

7. 'Lords' Address', *Cobbett's Parliamentary History*, 618-62.

8. 6 Anne c.65. 'An Act for the Better Securing the Trade of this Kingdom by Cruisers and Convoys'.

9. 6 Anne c.37. 'An Act for the Encouragement of Trade to America'.

10. *Observator*, 6 May 1702.

11. *Observator*, 10 June 1702.

12. Dutch privateering enjoyed a 'golden age' in the 1702-1712 conflict. See J. S. Bromley, 'Some Zeeland Privateering Instructions: Jacob Sautijn to Captain Saloman Reynders, 1707' in R. Hatton and J. S. Bromley, eds, *William III and Louis XIV. Essays by and for Mark A. Thomson* (Liverpool UP, 1968) 162-89.

13. *Observator*, 18 June 1707.

14. *Observator*, 27 January 1703.

15. W. R. Meyer, 'English Privateering in the War of 1688 to 1697' *Mariner's Mirror*, 67 (1981), 261.

16. The figures for the Nine Years' War are taken from W. R. Meyer, 'The Scale of English Privateering in the Wars of William and Anne' (Unpublished MA dissertation, University of Exeter, 1979) 28-33.

17. E. J. Graham, 'Privateering. The Scottish Experience, 1660-1808' (Unpublished MA dissertation, University of Exeter, 1979) 10.

18. Meyer, 'English Privateering, 1688 to 1697', 262.

19. E. A. G. Clark, *The Ports of the Exe Estuary, 1660-1860. A Study in Historical Geography* (Exeter UP, 1960) 107-08.

20. K. Matthews, 'A History of the West Country-Newfoundland Fishery' (Unpublished D.Phil thesis, University of Oxford, 1968) 283-304.

21. D. J. Starkey, 'British Privateering, 1702-1783, with particular reference to London' (Unpublished PhD thesis, University of Exeter, 1985) 93-4, 110.

22. Bromley, 'New Vocation', 118-9.

23. Bromley, 'Channel Island Privateers', 454-5.

24. PRO, C 104/36(2).

25. Bromley, 'New Vocation', 119.

26. In particular, see Bromley, 'Channel Island Privateers' and 'New Vocation'.

27. Declarations 7 March 1705, 20 July 1702. PRO, HCA 26/20, 17.

28. Declarations 20 March 1712, 7 April 1709. PRO, HCA 26/16, 25/22.
29. See Meyer, 'Mascall's Privateers'.
30. Declarations 14 December 1702, 19 October 1702, 5 December 1704, 22 September 1702. PRO, HCA 26/18, 17, 21, 17.
31. PRO, C 108/318. Creagh & Fallet to Patrick Galloway, 4 March 1703.
32. Bromley, 'New Vocation', 125-6.
33. Declaration 24 July 1711. PRO, HCA 26/15.
34. R. Davis, *The Rise of the Atlantic Economies* (Weidenfeld & Nicolson, 1973) 250-63.
35. See Rogers, 'Dampier's Voyage'; and Lee, 'Alexander Selkirk'.
36. PRO, C 104/36. See also B. M. H. Rogers, 'Woodes Rogers's Privateering Voyage of 1708–11' *Mariner's Mirror*, XIX (1933), 196-200.
37. PRO, ADM 43/1.
38. Declaration 5 May 1710. PRO, HCA 26/14.
39. Declaration 28 February 1709. PRO, HCA 26/14.
40. See Bromley, 'Channel Island Privateers', 445; and 'New Vocation', 125-6. These were prize vessels; both the scale and area of operation of these ventures were exceptional in the privateering experience of the Channel Islands during the early eighteenth century.
41. Bromley, 'Prize Office', 177.
42. Meyer, 'English Privateering, 1688 to 1697', 261-2.
43. Declarations 12 January 1709, 29 March 1709, 4 March 1712. PRO, HCA 26/13, 14, 16.
44. PRO, C 105/38(1), 39(1).
45. Declaration 29 August 1702. PRO, HCA 26/17.
46. Declaration 12 June 1702. PRO, HCA 26/17.
47. Declarations 21 March 1706, 3 April 1706. PRO, HCA 26/21, 21.
48. Declaration of Edmund Godfrey, master of the *Katherine*, 6 April 1710. PRO, HCA 26/14.
49. C. Hardy, *Register of Ships Employed in the Service of the Honourable United East India Company* (1799), I. For the years 1702 to 1707 the index of Captain's Logs was consulted. India Office Library, L/MAR/B.
50. Declarations 4 January 1706, 24 January 1711. PRO, HCA 26/21, 15.
51. Declarations 13 December 1705, 27 November 1702, 15 February 1712. PRO, HCA 26/21, 18, 16.
52. PRO, HCA 30/774, 775. These lists have been used extensively by Bromley and Meyer.
53. W. R. Meyer, 'English Privateering in the War of the Spanish Succession 1702–1713' *Mariner's Mirror*, 69 (1983), 436.
54. Bromley, 'French Privateering War', 219.
55. Meyer, 'English Privateering, 1702–1713', 436.
56. *Observator*, 18 June 1707.
57. Meyer, 'English Privateering, 1702–1713', 437.
58. Bromley, 'Channel Island Privateers', 448.

59. Meyer, 'Mascall's Privateers', 219.
60. PRO, HCA 32/67.
61. PRO, HCA 32/63.
62. The data relating to prize condemnations in this chapter are based on the sentences of the Prize Court. PRO, HCA 34/23-30, 58.
63. See Starkey, thesis, 115-17.
64. See Bromley, 'Channel Island Privateers', for a detailed discussion of the impact of Channel Island privateering on the French coastal population.
65. PRO, HCA 32/63.
66. PRO, HCA 32/67.
67. PRO, HCA 32/67.
68. PRO, HCA 32/50.
69. PRO, HCA 32/67.
70. PRO, HCA 32/85.
71. Bromley, 'Zeeland Privateering Instructions', 163-4.
72. PRO, HCA 32/85. Condemned to the *Neptune*, April 1708.
73. PRO, HCA 32/67. Condemned to the *Tuscan*, December 1711.
74. Declarations 16 April 1705, 10 December 1708, 9 November 1711. PRO, HCA 26/20, 13, 16.
75. PRO, ADM 43/1.
76. John Mascall of New Romney invested in the *Cinque Ports Galley*, his sole speculation in an 'ocean-going' privateer. Meyer, 'Mascall's Privateers', 217-18.
77. See Rogers, 'Dampier's Voyage', and Lee, 'Alexander Selkirk', for further details of this venture. For contemporary accounts, see William Funnell, *A Voyage Round the World* (1707); William Dampier, *A Vindication* (1707); and John Welbe, *Answer to Captain Dampier's Vindication* (1707).
78. The exhibits presented to the Master in Chancery, and his reports, are contained in PRO, C 104/36-40.
79. Bromley, 'New Vocation', 123.

Five

1718–1720

'To Cruise on the Spaniards under His Majesty's Commission'

In the quarter century following the Utrecht peace settlement of 1714, British privateering enterprise was severely restricted by the pacific foreign policy adopted by successive administrations. The accord reached with France in 1716 lasted into the 1730s, representing something of a calm hiatus amidst the storms of the Anglo-French relationship of the 'long' eighteenth century. An important feature of this agreement was the concern of both powers to restrain Spain's territorial ambitions in Europe while, at the same time, encroaching upon the Spaniards' faltering colonial monopoly in the New World. Though diplomatic tensions were high on the continent, and imperial rivalries were strong and intensifying in the Americas, these issues led to open, declared warfare on only one occasion during the 1714-1739 era.[1] This crisis was precipitated in 1717 by the occupation of Sardinia and Sicily by Spanish armies, an expansionist move that was swiftly checked by the combined forces of the Quadruple Alliance—Britain, France, the United Provinces and the Empire. By dint of this resort to arms, the disputed territories were restored to the Emperor in 1720 and the Mediterranean balance of power established at Utrecht was reasserted.

In the brief conflict of 1718-1720, Britain played a largely maritime role. Byng's destruction of the Spanish fleet off Cape Passaro in August 1718 was crucial to the allied cause, for it effectively cut Spain's line of communications with her invasion armies and facilitated the supply of the Imperial land forces in the decisive Messina and Milazzo campaigns.[2] In seeking to augment its naval forces, the British government authorised shipowners and seafarers to exact general reprisals upon Spanish commerce from 18 December 1718. Though only 98 letters of marque were taken out during the 14 months in which they were available, the privateering business this constituted was notable in two respects. In the first place, the 1718–1720 commissioned fleet was in some ways a microcosm of eighteenth-century British privateering enterprise, for each of the principal forms of venture was evident during the conflict. Secondly, this war of reprisal was unique in the 1689–1815 period in that private commerce-raiding against France was not authorised at any stage in the campaign; instead, venturers were permitted 'to cruise on the Spaniards under His Majesty's Commission',[3] a limitation which clearly conditioned the scale and form of privateering enterprise.

I

As no ventures were re-commissioned in the High Court of Admiralty during the War of the Quadruple Alliance, each of the 98 letters of marque issued at Doctors' Commons sanctioned the predatory activities of a single enterprise. As Table 6 shows, the vessels so licensed belonged to 11 ports and overseas bases, with London investors owning 62.2 per cent of the commissioned fleet. Provincial interest in the activity was limited, with Bristol's 'input' of 17 ventures eclipsing the contributions of a handful of lesser outports. Indeed, Penzance was the only other port in metropolitan Britain to witness the outfit of more than one licensed vessel, though two craft were despatched from Gibraltar by Stanhope Cotton, the base's Lieutenant-Governor,[4] and another two were set forth by British merchants resident in Port Mahon.

The regional distribution of the commissioned fleet was closely related to the character of the privateering response. Thus, the concentration of activity in London and Bristol, and the virtual disregard for the business of reprisal evident in the Channel Islands and the Cinque Ports, signalled the preponderance of 'letters of marque' in the commissioned fleet. In a situation that was to recur in the Anglo-Spanish war of 1739–1743, private men-of-war were few and far between as Spain's trade failed to evince more than a modicum of predatory enthusiasm from the British mercantile class. Only nine archetypal 'Channel' craft were licensed during the hostilities of 1718–1720, and six of these belonged to merchants resident overseas, including five from Oporto, Gibraltar and Port Mahon—bases

Table 6

Commissioned Vessels by Region, 1718–1720

Region	Number of Vessels	Average Tonnage
London	61	271.6
Bristol	17	198.8
Channel Is — Jersey (1)	1	60
SE England — Portsmouth (1)	1	300
SW England — Penzance (2) Topsham (1)	3	90
E Scotland — Dunbar (1)	1	200
Overseas Bases — Gibraltar (2) Jamaica (1) Oporto (1) Port Mahon (2)	6	85.8
Port Unknown	8	187.5
	98	232.6

Source: PRO, HCA 26/29.

in close proximity to Spanish coastal and short-sea trading routes. In contrast, the distance of this prey from the British Isles largely explains the outset of just two 'Channel' privateers— the *Friendship Sloop* of Bristol, and the *George Gally* of Penzance— from mainland Britain, and a single predator from the Channel Islands, the 60-ton, 60-man *Enterprize Gally*, set forth on a cruise of one month's duration in November 1719.[5]

The 'deep-water' arm of the commerce-raiding business extended to a mere four vessels, all belonging to London promoters. Commissioned on the same day, and owned by Benjamin Hooper and William Smith, it is likely that the *Greenwich* and the *King George*, both of 150 tons burthen and 80 men,[6] operated in company, reflecting, perhaps, the scale and value of the typical unit of Spanish colonial commerce. This consideration certainly governed the outfit of the remaining large-scale predators, the *Speedwell* and the *Success*, a consortship of some 600 tons burthen, 58 guns and 250 men.[7] An heir to the ventures of Dampier and Rogers, this 'expedition' was designed to round the Horn and attack the treasure ships and settlements of Spanish America. It bore all the hallmarks of the most ambitious strain of the privateering business; thus, it was constituted an expensive, high-risk attempt to locate and apprehend particularly valuable targets—either the Peruvian silver ships, the transhipment base of

Guayaquil, or the Manila-Acapulco galleon—deemed to be vulnerable to privateering attack; its motivation was private profit, the procurement of Imperial as well as British letters of marque giving lie to any notions of selfless service to the nation; its prosecution was marked by discord, violence and improvisation as Captains Clipperton and Shelvocke quarrelled bitterly, many of their men perished and the survivors struggled home by a variety of tortuous routes; and it was a truly epic adventure, a circumnavigation spiced by mutiny, daring attacks on the enemy and the assassination of a lone albatross—romantic images which have remained with privateering enterprise ever since.[8]

Though 'letters of marque' never assumed—nor ever aspired to—such a high profile, they accounted for a major proportion of Britain's privateering 'inputs' in the 1718–1720 conflict. With only 13 vessels displaying the features of the private man-of-war, it is probable that at least 80 commissioned vessels embarked on voyages rather than cruises, with the carriage of cargo an important, often primary, objective of the operation. Signs of all forms of this activity are evident, especially in the commissioned fleet set forth from London. Thus, five licensed Indiamen left the Thames for India and China during the war;[9] ranging in size from the 400-ton *Cardoga* to the *Fordwithe* and the *Marlborough*, both of 480 tons burthen,[10] these 'specialist' vessels were all manned in the ratio of 5 tons per man, equipped with 30 to 34 guns and victualled for 20 months. It would appear that 'cruising voyages' were also undertaken, with companies of 70 and 80 seafarers recruited for 400-ton vessels such as the *Holmead Frigate* and the *Pearle Gally*,[11] and numerous 50-strong complements shipped aboard lesser craft. Meanwhile, there were the ubiquitous 'armed traders', the merchantmen which relied on their own resources for protection, their crews being provided with an pecuniary incentive to resist assailants and attempt occasional seizures by virtue of the letter of marque carried; given the Spanish foe, and the incidence of ship names such as the *Leghorne Frigat*, *Portugal Gally*, *Tuscan Gally* and *Venetian Gally*, it may be presumed that the southern European and Mediterranean theatres were the likely scenes of any such activity.

This supposition is substantiated to some degree by the Prize Court sentences.[12] Seven properties seized during the war were condemned to privateering venturers—compared to the Navy's return of 30 condemnations—at Doctors' Commons; relatively insignificant, this 'catch' reflected not only the predominantly commercial character of the privateering fleet, but also its principal area of operation. Thus, three of the seven prizes were taken by 'armed trading vessels' from London and landed in Oporto, Gibraltar and Leghorn; two were apprehended by a brace of 'Channel' predators cruising in company, the *Prince Frederick Gally* and the *St Philip Castle*, and conveyed to the captors' home port of Port Mahon; while the other two prizes were taken back to Penzance by the *George Gally*, a craft of 70 tons burthen, with a declared complement of 14 seamen.[13]

However, no trace of the prizes taken during the course of George Shelvocke's 'expedition' to the South Seas is to be found in the records of the London Prize Court. As in other such ventures, much of the property seized in distant oceans was consumed *en route* or embezzled—a matter of opinion—and therefore rarely the subject of formal Admiralty Court adjudication. Invariably, this was the source of bitter disputes between promoters and seafarers; in Shelvocke's case, a charge of piracy and a committal to prison greeted his return to London in August 1722. At stake was at least £7,000, the sum that Edward Hughes, managing director of the venture, claimed that his captain had accumulated by means of piracy, pillage and fraud.[14] Such claims were never proven, Shelvocke was freed to enjoy the fruits of his endeavours, and the last of the great privateering 'expeditions' to the Pacific was remembered in the partial accounts of apologists and critics eager to vindicate their actions—and to describe their travels—to an inquisitive, impressionistic reading public.[15]

Extraordinary in terms of the 1718–1720 war, Shelvocke's 'Voyage Round the World' belonged to a tradition of commerce-raiding in the South Seas dating back through the 'expeditions' of Dampier and Rogers to the days of Drake and Elizabeth. These high-risk ventures were essentially the products of Anglo-Spanish conflict; as such, they looked to the past, for it was the inexorable intensification of the Anglo-French struggle that was to mark British foreign policy—and condition the privateering business—for the remainder of the century. In subsequent wars, therefore, it was mainly in the Channel and the Bay of Biscay that the predatory elements of Britain's commissioned fleet would find their quarry.

Notes

1. Anglo-Spanish relations were strained to the point of war in 1727. Amidst reports that Spanish privateers were at sea, there was news from Bristol that 'three Privateers are fitting out here, with the utmost Expedition, in order

to Cruize on the Spaniards. They are to carry from 24 to 30 guns. Their names are the *Levant, Crossley,* and *Queen Mary.*' *Brice's Weekly Journal,* 24 March 1727. However, there is no record of any letter of marque being issued in the High Court of Admiralty during the 1727 crisis. I am grateful to Stephen Fisher for this reference.

2. For the political and diplomatic background to the war, see W. Michael, *The Quadruple Alliance* (Macmillan, 1939); for the naval campaign, see W. Laird Clowes, *The Royal Navy. A History from the Earliest Times to the Death of Queen Victoria* (Sampson, Low, Marston & Co, 1897-1903), III, 33-8.

3. Owners' instructions to George Shelvocke, 1719. Perrin, *Voyage Round the World,* xii.

4. Declarations 13 May 1719. PRO, HCA 26/29.

5. Declaration 26 November 1719. PRO, HCA 26/29.

6. Declarations 10 June 1719. PRO, HCA 26/29.

7. Declarations 1 January 1719. PRO, HCA 26/29.

8. See Perrin's introduction to *Voyage Round the World.*

9. Hardy, *Register of Ships,* I.

10. Declarations 21 November, 28 January 1719, 23 December 1718. PRO, HCA 26/29.

11. Declarations 27 December 1718, 26 February 1719. PRO, HCA 26/29.

12. PRO, HCA 34/30.

13. Declaration 27 June 1719. PRO, HCA 26/29.

14. See Perrin's introduction to *Voyage Round the World.*

15. Shelvocke justified his conduct in *Voyage Round the World,* published in 1726. William Betagh, a lieutenant in the *Speedwell,* and no friend of Shelvocke's, was highly critical of his captain's conduct in an account of the 'expedition' published in 1728.

1739-1748

'Good Pickings for Privateers of Force'

The grant of 'general reprisals' against Spanish sea-borne commerce in July 1739 marked the onset of the War of Jenkins' Ear.[1] Superficially, this was a war of revenge, justified on the grounds that

> many and repeated depredations have been committed and many unjust seizures have been made in the West Indies and elsewhere by Spanish *guarda-costas* and ships acting under the Commission of the King of Spain.[2]

There were much deeper undercurrents, however. In essence, the issue of the *guarda-costas* was symptomatic of a profound Anglo-Spanish discord, as the aggressive, expansionist and increasingly voluble British mercantile class sought further incursions into—and ultimately the destruction of—the monopoly claimed by Spain to the trade of her American colonies. In seeking to undermine this ailing, anachronistic and restrictive structure, Britain threatened to demolish the balance established in the Utrecht Treaty of 1713, a prospect which inevitably jeopardised relations with France, her principal colonial and commercial rival, and Spain's ally. Anglo-French friction intensified, particularly in the Caribbean where Vernon's force seized Portobello and attacked Cartagena while d'Antin's fleet stood by to protect French interests and limit British gains. Formal war with France was not declared until March 1744, however, when the struggle for colonial ascendancy was subsumed into the European dynastic and territorial contest surrounding the Austrian succession.

The war for trade continued to dominate the maritime facet of the conflict after France's official intervention.[3] Fleet engagements were rare, with the indecisive battle fought off Toulon in February 1744 the only major action of the war. Trade-protection and commerce-destruction were the main priorities of the opposing navies, a reflection of the growing value of trans-oceanic cargoes and of the strategic importance afforded to the maintenance of trading links with the colonies. This was especially so in the West India trade, for in the years since Queen Anne's War the quantity of sugar shipped across the Atlantic had risen by over 250 per cent, with British production doubling and the output of the French islands of Guadeloupe, Martinique and St Domingue expanding by an estimated 365 per cent.[4] With concomitant increases in the supply of cocoa, coffee and indigo, particularly from the larger and more fertile French colonies, the trade in tropical staples was both rich and extensive by the 1740s; in addition, the sugar islands remained heavily dependent upon Europe for supplies of manufactured goods, provisions and slave labour. Meanwhile, in the Spanish Empire, the principal commercial arteries ran from periphery to core, the spices and treasure of the East being conveyed from Manila to Acapulco, and shipped from thence, with the silver of Mexico and Peru, in the *flotas* bound for Cadiz or Seville.

Various means were deployed to protect these lucrative overseas trades in the 1739–1748 war. Britain established naval bases in Jamaica and the Leeward Islands to safeguard her Caribbean interests,[5] while men-of-war escorted merchant vessels across the Atlantic and cruisers were stationed at strategic points in home waters. Though no attempt was made to found naval stations in the French West Indies—a source of some strategic weakness as the war progressed—convoys were an essential feature of France's defensive policy. Inefficiency, due largely to a lack of resources, bedevilled this protective system, however, and 'Martinicomen'[6] were regularly permitted to sail for Europe in small squadrons without naval escort; a shortage of tonnage, moreover, persuaded the French authorities to open their colonial trade to neutral shippers in 1745, a device which frustrated British predators leading to the adoption, in the Seven Years' War, of the controversial 'Rule of the War of 1756'. Spain, for her part, preferred to disperse her trade, transporting the specie of the Indies in register-ships sailing individually or in small flotillas at irregular intervals, rather than in the vast, predictable *flotas* utilised in peacetime.

The character of the belligerents' trade, and the defensive measures each implemented, naturally conditioned the form and scale of enemy attack. In the Anglo-Spanish phase of the war, Britain's offensive movements were aimed at the foci of Spanish American trade, with direct assaults mounted upon Portobello and Cartegena. To further 'humble

Spain in the Indies', Anson's squadron sailed into the Pacific—very much in the tradition of Drake, Rogers and Shelvocke—with a general brief to plunder Spanish possessions, seize the Manila galleon and set up a British base in the South Seas. Commerce-raiding activity in European waters was limited to the Navy's vain attempts to locate the *flota* perennially, and falsely, reported to be heading for home, and its more fruitful efforts to seize the register-ships which increasingly carried the produce of the Empire.

Such vessels were few and far between and too improbable a prospect, in themselves, to stimulate a concerted privateering response, while Spain's home trade was limited and distant from the centres of British predatory enterprise; privateering investment, therefore, extended only as far as the outfit of a relatively few 'letters of marque'. In contrast, Spanish private men-of-war represented a serious threat to British trade in many quarters. In 1739, for instance, a British captain reported from the Mediterranean that 'we have been continually pestered by privateers, the sea, to our shame, being covered with them';[7] over a year later, news came from New York that the 'Spaniards had got a great many privateers at sea, particularly in the Windward Passage, the way of ships from the continent to Jamaica';[8] in home waters, 'Spanish privateers hovered near every English port', a ploy which 'proved very calamitous to the English mercantile marine.'[9] Though losses were heavy, with 107 vessels taken by the Spaniards in 1741 alone,[10] the Navy's protective efficiency gradually improved and British commerce was able to proceed in growing safety as the war progressed.

This remained the case even after the commencement of hostilities with France in 1744. Failure to defeat the British fleet at Toulon and the subsequent concentration of resources on the land war meant that France's naval offensive was restricted to a series of unsuccessful 'missions'.[11] Moreover, the policy of *guerre de course* adopted after the naval disappointment at Malaga in 1704 was not revived in 1744. French *corsaires*, therefore, were much less of a threat to British trade than they had been in Louis XIV's wars, and the French privateering business suffered an appreciable decline, except in Bayonne and other Basque ports where commerce-raiding was seen as a means of reviving flagging commercial fortunes.[12] Increasingly, it was the British Navy that assumed the initiative in the trade war, intensifying the pressure on the defective, under-funded French convoy system. Though a number of remarkable defensive actions were fought by naval escorts, France's colonial trade began to suffer extensively as British naval supremacy became ever more apparent. Yet this advantage was by no means as complete and decisive as it was to become in the Seven Years' War, and the enemy's overseas commerce continued despite the inadequate protection it received. In these circumstances, there emerged an unprecedented opportunity for British privateering entrepreneurs. Accordingly, 'stout' private ships-of-war were fitted out to cruise in the north-eastern Atlantic to intercept the West Indiamen and register-ships sailing for Europe unescorted; or else, to await the 'fleet expected home from Martinico, & a Spanish fleet from Havannah', anticipating that

> one of His Majesty's squadrons will meet them, & beat their Convoys, which will make good pickings for Privateers of Force.[13]

Such prospects dictated that the 'deep-water' branch of the privateering business should emerge as the most significant form of British commerce-raiding enterprise in the 1739-1748 war.

I

Although Britain did not formally declare war until 19 October 1739, letters of marque were issued from July when the government authorised general reprisals against Spanish trade. Some 26 commissions were granted before the official declaration of war, 19 of which were issued to commanders of London vessels. When the French entered the war in March 1744 the Admiralty continued to grant letters of marque against Spain, while issuing separate commissions against France; thus, for a short time, commanders were required to take out two licences to fully authorise their vessels, a precursor of the system employed after 1777. From 28 June 1744 until the cessation of hostilities in 1748, letters of marque were issued against the trade of 'France and Spain', though two applicants, Peter Frankling, master of the *Dolphin Frigate* of Lynn, and James Barrett, captain of the London vessel *Montagu*, received commissions specifically designating the Spaniards as sole enemy.[14] In all, 1,582 letters of marque were issued during the course of the 1739–1748 conflict, authorising 1,191 vessels to engage in privateering activity. This force was distributed by port and region as presented in Table 7.

Table 7

Commissioned Vessels by Region, 1739–1748

Region	Number of commissions	Actual vessels	Average tonnage
London	841	614	294.9
Bristol	189	132	210.8
Liverpool	114	79	200.1
Channel Is — Alderney (1) Guernsey (55) Jersey (29)	105	85	61.5
E England — Boston (1) Bridlington (1) Donyland (1), Harwich (1), Hull (6) Lynn (2) Newcastle (2) North Shields (2) Scarborough (2) Sunderland (4) Whitby (7) Yarmouth (15)	51	44	260.1
SE England — Cowes (1) Deal (3) Deptford (1) Dover (31) Folkestone (1) Hastings (4) Portsmouth (3) Rye (8) Sandwich (3) Shoreham (1) Southampton (5)	72	61	75
SW England — Barnstaple (1) Bideford (8) Bridgwater (1) Dartmouth (16) Exeter (10) Exmouth (2) Falmouth (3) Fowey (4) Lyme (3) Plymouth (9) Poole (7) St Ives (1) Topsham (8) Weymouth (1)	99	74	165.3
Wales & NW England — Pembroke (2) Whitehaven (6)	8	8	196.3
W Scotland — Glasgow (8)	10	8	185
Ireland — Cork (8) Dublin (7)	17	15	238.7
Overseas Bases — Antigua (3) Barbados (3) Bermuda (2) Jamaica (3) Leghorn (9) Lisbon (1) New York (2) Oporto (1) St Christopher (3)	30	27	212.2
Port Unknown	46	44	234.1
	1582	1191	235.8

Figures in brackets denote actual vessels.

Source: PRO, HCA 25/26-37; HCA 26/4, 22-26, 29-32.

In comparison with Queen Annes's War, a decline of 152 vessels was apparent in the size of the British privateering fleet in the 1739–1748 conflict, despite the growth of the shipping industry in the intervening years. London remained the leading privateering base, though its stake diminished from 671 to 614 vessels, while Bristol's significant investment in the business continued notwithstanding a reduction of some 25 vessels in the city's 'input' between the two wars. A waning interest in the activity was also apparent in Ireland and Scotland, though it was in the Channel Islands that the most dramatic decline occurred, the Islanders' commissioned force shrinking from 207 to 85 vessels over the two wars. This falling trend was partially offset by expansion in other ports, with Liverpool's commissioned fleet increasing from 31 to 79 vessels, Dover's 'input' growing from seven to 31 ventures, and bases such as Dartmouth, Exeter, Hull and Yarmouth all exhibiting a greater interest in commerce-raiding. A further expansive factor was the involvement of more ports in the 1739–1748 privateering war—57 as opposed to 51—with Boston, Bridlington, Cowes, Fowey and Pembroke engaging in the activity for the first time in the century.

This net fall in privateering activity was due largely to differences in the length and scope of the respective conflicts. Letters of marque were available for almost a year longer in Queen Anne's War; significantly, they authorised commerce-raiding activity against both Bourbon powers for the duration of hostilities, while in the later conflict reprisals against France were only granted from March 1744. This inhibited the privateering business, for it was the extent and proximity of enemy commerce which invariably conditioned the level of activity, and Spanish trade was at once more distant and less valuable than that of France. Accordingly, the prospects facing British privateering entrepreneurs were relatively poor in the Anglo-Spanish phase of the conflict, a factor clearly apparent in the rate of issue of letters of marque. While 430 commissions were granted against Spain prior to the French intervention in March 1744, a total of 1,152 letters of marque were issued thereafter, with 139 taken out against France, 59 against Spain, and 954 authorising attacks on the seaborne property of both Bourbon powers.[15]

If the level of privateering activity suffered due to the comparative brevity of the Anglo-French war, the scale of the average enterprise in the Austrian Succession War clearly expanded. A total of 280,875 tons of British shipping was commissioned in the 1739–1748 war, an increase of 47,969 tons, or 20.6 per cent, on the equivalent figure for Queen Anne's War.[16] At 235.8 tons burthen, the average commissioned vessel was 62.4

tons larger than its predecessor had been in the 1702–1712 war, with each port group, excepting south-east England, exhibiting a growth in the mean burthen of its licensed vessels. In part, this was due to developments in the shipping industry as a whole, for it was during the second quarter of the eighteenth century that many British shipowners began to employ larger vessels, seeking to benefit from the economies of scale apparent in the utilisation of ships with greater capacity and proportionately lower costs.[17] More importantly, however, the increase in mean vessel size —together with the rise in average manning levels apparent in ports such as Liverpool and London[18]—reflected the changing composition of Britain's commissioned fleet as the larger, ocean-going craft employed as 'deep-water' private ships-of-war and 'letters of marque' assumed a more prominent role in the privateering business.

'Channel' privateering, in contrast, experienced an overall decline; indeed, during the 1739–1748 conflict, this form of commerce-raiding activity was probably less significant than in any of the other major eighteenth-century wars. Whereas 259 of the vessels commissioned in the 1702–1712 conflict had displayed the characteristics of the 'Channel' privateer—less than 100 tons burthen, with at least one crew member per 2.5 tons—the equivalent figure for the Austrian Succession War was just 160 craft; in proportionate terms, this represented 13.4 per cent of the total privateering fleet, compared to nearly 20 per cent in the earlier war. As Table 8 shows, these diminutive predators were set forth from some 23 ports; though still the most important centre of 'Channel' enterprise, the preponderance of the Channel Islands was eroded as a growing number of small-scale ventures were launched from the bases of south-east England, the West Country and Bristol.

In fitting out 58 archetypal 'Channel' privateers, and 85 commissioned vessels in all, the 'input' of the Channel Islanders into the privateering business reached its nadir for the 1702-1783 period. An uneven pattern was evident in south-east England, the other focal point of this enterprise, as Dover venturers extended their privateering investments, while a limited interest in commerce-raiding was displayed by merchants and shipowners in the other ports of the region. Thus, 31 licensed craft were fitted out in Dover, an outset which accounted for over half of the South East's commissioned fleet, and for much of the growth apparent in the regional 'input' since Queen Anne's War.

Table 8

'Channel' Privateers by Region, 1739-1748

Region	Vessels of 2.5 tons per man or less		Regional Total	% 'Channel'
	- 49 tons	50-99 tons		
London	7	13	614	3.3
Bristol	1	11	132	9.1
Liverpool	0	1	79	1.3
Channel Is (3)	40	18	85	68.2
SE England (8)	28	17	61	73.8
SW England (7)	8	9	74	23
Ireland (1)	0	1	15	6.7
Overseas Bases (1)	0	1	27	3.7
Port Unknown	1	4	44	11.4
	85	75		

Figures in brackets denote number of ports.
Source: PRO, HCA 25/26-37; HCA 26/4, 22-6, 29-32.

The factors which conditioned Dover's investments, however, were similar to those which operated on the 'Channel' arm of the business as a whole. It is clear, for instance, that the prospect of an abundant French prey in home waters was the principal stimulus to this form of activity, for it was not until the grant of general reprisals against France that the customary centres of 'Channel' enterprise, including Dover, developed a real interest in commerce-raiding. Previously, during the Anglo-Spanish phase of the war, only four commissions were taken out by Channel Island *armateurs*, and each of these had sanctioned an 'armed trading vessel', while in the South East, the *Walker* of Deal, of 70 tons burthen, with 28 men,[19] had been the only licensed vessel to exhibit the hallmarks of the 'Channel' predator. From March 1744, this picture altered considerably as the opportunity to cruise against French trade encouraged investors from Hastings and Rye, from Deal and Alderney, but especially from Dover, Guernsey and Jersey, to speculate in small-scale privateering operations in home waters.

The rate of 'Channel' activity was by no means constant during the Anglo-French war of reprisal. Indeed, as Appendix 2 shows, it varied widely from the trough of November 1746 when this form of predation appears to have abated entirely, to the peak reached in October 1747 in which 36 vessels, declared to be worked by an aggregate of 1,507 seafarers, were 'in commission'. Over the course of the conflict, the initial surge of interest in 1744 gave way to relatively modest levels of activity in 1745 and 1746 before a marked resurgence occurred in the final 12 months of warfare. Within this overview, however, a clear seasonal influence is evident in the number of predators and privateersmen operational, with the summer and autumnal months witnessing an appreciably higher rate of activity than the relatively dormant winter season.

The simple fact that venturers had less than five years in which to cruise against the French helps to explain the unusually muted response of the 'Channel' branch of the privateering business in the Austrian Succession War. More importantly, the 1740s witnessed a general shift towards investment in the 'deep-water' branch of the activity, a development apparent in the centres of 'Channel' enterprise as well as in the major overseas trading ports. Dover's fleet, for example, included 16 vessels burthen between 20 and 60 tons, with complements ranging from 20 to 50 men; yet, alongside these conventional 'Channel' predators, a number of relatively large-scale enterprises were mounted, as local merchants such as James Gravener and Isaac Samson combined with London investors, notably the ships' broker Robert Alston, to fit out the *Carlisle*, of 150 tons burthen, 63 men and four boys, the 150-ton *Dover*, manned by 94 seafarers, and the *York*, a vessel of 140 tons burthen and 72 men subsequently 'taken into His Majesty's pay at the rate of £4 a Man per Month'.[20]

Similar diversification was apparent in the Channel Islands as *armateurs* grew in ambition and set forth comparatively 'stout' vessels to cruise in the Bay of Biscay and off the northern coast of Spain. The Islanders' privateering enterprise was therefore embodied in 'deep-water' ventures such as the 400-ton *Lightning Privateer* of Guernsey, with a declared company of 200 men,[21] the *Charming Nancy* of Jersey, of 150 tons burthen and 97 men, and the 150-ton, 85-man Guernsey ship *Defiance*,[22] as well as in the diminutive predators—the 4-ton *Hazard* of Alderney, and the Jersey shallop *Expedition*, of 5 tons burthen,[23] being the smallest craft commissioned in the 1739–1748 war—customarily despatched to cruise against French small fry and, on occasion, to gather intelligence of enemy shipping movements.[24]

The letter of marque declarations indicate that this growing interest in 'deep-water' commerce-raiding enterprise was widespread, with promoters from 23 ports setting forth a total of 217 relatively powerful private ships-of-war, as Table 9 shows. Compared to the 1702–1712 conflict, an upsurge in 'deep-water' privateering activity clearly took place in the Austrian Succession War. This expansion was due entirely to the increase in the number of crews declared to exceed 99 men; accordingly, no less than 51 complements matched or eclipsed the largest privateering crew—stated as 200 strong—recruited in Queen Anne's War, while the fleet of vessels declared to be seeking between 100 and 199 seafarers rose by 95 between the two wars.

Table 9

'Deep-Water' Private Ships-of-War by Region, 1739–1748

Region	Crew Size				Regional Total	% 'Deep-Water'
	40-99*	100-149	150-199	200 +		
London	8	44	22	29	614	16.8
Bristol	3	16	14	14	132	35.6
Liverpool	1	2	3	2	79	10.1
Channel Is (2)	3	4	2	1	85	11.8
E England (2)	2	0	0	0	44	4.5
SE England (3)	2	6	0	0	61	13.1
SW England (8)	3	15	3	3	74	32.4
Wales & NW England (1)	0	2	0	0	8	25
Ireland (1)	1	1	0	2	15	26.7
Overseas Bases (3)	0	4	0	0	27	14.8
Port Unknown	1	4	0	0	44	11.4
	24	98	44	51		

* Vessels exceeding 99 tons burthen manned in the ratio of 2.5 tons per man or less.

Figures in brackets denote number of ports
Source: PRO, HCA 25/26-37; HCA 26/4, 22-6, 29-32.

London and Bristol clearly dominated this large-scale arm of the privateering business in the 1740s, accounting for 150, or 69.1 per cent of the ventures comprising Table 9; with 103 of these vessels, London was the leading centre in absolute terms, though Bristol's interest in 'deep-water' commerce-raiding was greater relative to the port's privateering 'input', with over one in three of the commissioned vessels departing Kingroad displaying 'deep-water' characteristics. A similar percentage of the South West's 74 licensed craft was of this ilk, with seven fitted out in the Exe, and a further seven set forth from Dartmouth, where the town's merchants collaborated with London speculators to invest in large-scale commerce-raiding enterprise for the first, and last, time. Elsewhere, investment in this form of activity was sporadic, with 'deep-water' ventures launched at bases as diverse as Dublin, Liverpool, Lynn and Pembroke.

Substantial amounts of capital were required to purchase, arm and provision these predators. Furthermore, they were essentially labour-intensive vessels worked by men who generally agreed to serve for a share in the profits rather than a monthly wage. Clearly, promoters would only consider making such large-scale *ex-ante* investments, and seafarers would only forego the regular pay of competing maritime occupations, at times when the prospects of earning a healthy return on their speculations were favourable. During the 1739–1748 conflict—though only after France's entry in March 1744—a number of factors coincided to render 'deep-water' privateering a particularly promising form of commerce-raiding enterprise. The balance of power in the naval struggle had yet to tip decisively in Britain's favour; accordingly, enemy trade, the object of privateering activity, was able to proceed throughout the war, albeit in increasingly difficult circumstances. This trade, moreover, was both extensive and valuable. While the Spaniards continued to despatch rich consignments of American bullion to Europe, the tropical produce of the French Caribbean was conveyed across the Atlantic in ever-growing quantities. In the three decades since the Utrecht settlement, the production of sugar in the French West Indies had more than trebled, with the output of St Domingue rising spectacularly from an estimated 138,000 cwt in 1714 to 848,000 cwt in 1742.[25] By the 1730s, over 600 vessels were employed each year to carry sugar to the refineries of Bordeaux, La Rochelle, Marseilles and Rouen, with cocoa, coffee and indigo adding to the diversity and value of their cargoes.[26]

Measures were taken to defend these richly-laden vessels in wartime, though the protective devices deployed by the Bourbon powers tended to stimulate, rather than deter, British privateering venturers. Thus, in conveying bullion in register-ships sailing individually or in small squadrons to elude the British naval fleets awaiting the ever-anticipated *flota*, the Spaniards dispersed their trade into smaller units, at once more difficult to detect and less valuable but also susceptible to the attentions of less powerful predators.[27] The French, on the other hand, preferred to concentrate their rich trans-Atlantic trade—rendered richer still by a marked secular upswing in the price of sugar[28]—into fleets escorted by naval convoys. Deficiencies in the funding and organisation of this 'system' were soon apparent, however, and costly delays ensued before vast assemblies of over 200 merchantmen sailed in the charge of a handful of convoys. Moreover, to circumvent such problems, shipowners could opt to despatch their vessels for Europe in small detachments relying on their own resources for defence.[29]

In these circumstances, with inadequate protection provided for France's trans-Atlantic commerce, and register-ships and 'Martinicomen' sailing unescorted, a significant portion of the enemy's colonial trade fell within the range of British 'deep-water' private men-of-war. Naturally, the more valuable craft, particularly the Spanish treasure ships and French West Indiamen 'running' without convoy, were well-armed and heavily manned to protect their valuable cargoes. This was well understood by seasoned privateersmen like George Walker who, on sighting eight hostile vessels, used their apparent strength to urge his men to greater efforts; the enemy, he observed,

> being armed they have something on board worth defending, for I take them to be merchantmen with letters of marque, and homeward-bound.[30]

Some considerable force was therefore necessary to transform the more valuable Bourbon cargoes into viable targets. If this explains the proliferation of heavily-armed predators with upwards of 100 men in the 1744–1748 commissioned fleet, it also accounts for the propensity of promoters to set forth consortships or squadrons of such craft. This was the heyday of the combination; for example, London venturers fitted out the *Duke*, *Prince Frederick* and *Prince George*,[31] the *Lowestoff* and *Shoreham's Revenge*,[32] the *Saltash* and *Warren Gally*,[33] and, most impressively, the *Royal Family* squadron, specifically to operate in unison; from Portsmouth, the *Adventure* and *Norton* embarked to cruise together; and in Bristol, the *Tyger* and the *Tygress* were fitted out to operate in tandem.[34]

It was in the north-eastern Atlantic that British 'deep-water' private ships-of-war sought to intercept fully-laden vessels bound for the western seaboard of France and Spain. Various stations were favoured in this broad theatre; 'deep-water' predators such as the *Alexander*, the *Southwell* and the consortship of the *Saltash* and *Warren Gally* preferred to operate in the approaches to French Biscay ports;[35] the *Fame* and the *Winchelsea*— ultimately bound on an 'expedition' to the East Indies—embarked to 'cruise 6 weeks in the Soundings for the homeward-bound Martinico ships that did not know of the war';[36] further to the south west, in 'latitude forty-six and forty-seven, longitude fourteen and fifty west of the Lizard', the *Boscawen* and the *Sheerness* met and agreed to combine forces;[37] meanwhile, in and around these various points, many other 'stout' privateers sought to apprehend the rich prizes that would

> not only distress the enemy & defend our trade, but will also make a good return to the owners for their large outsett.[38]

This is not to suggest that these 'deep-water' commerce-raiders were active simultaneously and continuously, erecting a series of impenetrable cordons across the Western Approaches, the Bay of Biscay and the enemy's roadsteads. It is quite clear from Appendix 2 that the level of 'deep-water' commerce-raiding activity fluctuated widely during the course of the war. Like its 'Channel' sister, this form of predation was obviously insignificant prior to the issue of letters of marque against France on 2 April 1744; with reprisals against both Bourbon powers now permissible, the monthly rate of activity increased rapidly, reaching a peak in September 1744 when 64 large-scale predators were 'in commission', engaging the services of a declared workforce of 9,978 seafarers. Thereafter, the level of 'deep-water' operations remained relatively high, averaging 44 ventures, and 7,354 men per month in 1745; a steadily declining trend was nevertheless evident until an upturn occurred in the summer of 1747, mirroring the rise in the rate of 'Channel' privateering activity.

An extraordinary feature of the 'deep-water' sector in the 1739–1748 conflict was the heavy and persistent involvement of a particular group of privateer owners—William Belchier, John Casamajor, Edward Ironside, Israel Jalabert, Parnell Nevill and James Talbot. Whether operating as a syndicate, acting individually or in partnership with other merchants, these London capitalists displayed an exceptional commitment to the commerce-raiding business, specialising in the outset of 'privateers of force'—the most powerful vessels of the commissioned fleet—in a series of ventures linking the financial resources of the capital with the predatory enterprise of Dartmouth and Bristol. At the centre of this activity were Israel Jalabert and Parnell Nevill; as early as November 1740, these City entrepreneurs combined with Arthur Holdsworth, Nathaniel Terry and other leading Dartmouth merchants to set forth the *Dartmouth Gally*, of 180 tons burthen and 140 men. A second cruise was undertaken in 1741,[39] though it was not until the outbreak of the Anglo-French war that this consortium renewed its interest in commerce-raiding. In May 1744, the *Young Ceres* of Dartmouth joined the *Dartmouth Gally* in the quest for Bourbon prizes, with the *Boscawen*, of 600 tons burthen and 300 men, the *Fortune* and the *Mars* adding to the predatory investments of the Dartmouth-London group by the end of the year.[40] Meanwhile, the London vessels *Bacchus*, *Dursley Gally* and *Hunter*, manned by an aggregate of 650 men, and variously owned by Jalabert, Belchier and Ironside, were operational at this time,[41] though it was not until the spring of 1745 that the outset of the squadron comprising the *Duke*, the *Prince Frederick* and the *Prince George* brought together the full London group[42]—their combined interests stretching to nine 'deep-water' craft, mustering a declared total of 1,780 seafarers in March and April 1745.

The extravagent successes which attended these cruises—particularly the endeavours of the *Boscawen*, the *Dartmouth Gally* and the combined effort of the *Duke* and the *Prince Frederick*[43]—appear to have encouraged Jalabert, Nevill and company to intensify their predatory investments. Accordingly, their attention, and part of their labour force—notably Commodore George Walker and the 'old Boscawens'—switched to Bristol where the *Royal Family* fleet was fitted out in the spring of 1746.[44] Though this was by no means the last commerce-raiding venture launched by the group,[45] it was clearly the most significant of their speculations, comprising four 'stout' vessels with an aggregate strength of 1,550 tons burthen, 92 guns and 850 men.[46] With George Walker in command, the *Royal Family* squadron departed Bristol in April 1746 to cruise for eight months in a southerly station between Cape St Vincent and the coast of North Africa. After five barren months,[47] the fleet met with some considerable success, and in the following year Messrs Belchier, Jalabert, Nevill *et al* determined to refit the vessels in Lisbon for a second sortie of eight months, and to extend their investment by supplementing the four 'stout' ships with a tender, the *Prince George*, of 70 tons burthen and 60 men.[48]

In the Articles of Agreement pertaining to this cruise, the large-scale, co-ordinated character of the enterprise is clearly evident. The *Royal Family* vessels were to operate as a fleet with the individual commanders subservient to the Commodore whose flag was raised in the *King George*. In this venture, British 'deep-water' privateering enterprise was expressed in its most extreme form, a concentration of capital and labour—five vessels burthen over 1,500 tons in total, and served by 853 men[49]—that was not to be witnessed again. It typified the aims and means of this strand of the commerce-raiding business in the 1740s; thus, the valuable cargoes returning to Europe from French and Spanish territories in the Americas were its principal targets; the relatively large, heavily-armed vessel, manned in quasi-naval fashion to fight for its reward, was the form that it took; its main area of operation was the north-eastern Atlantic, cruising in the Bay of Biscay, off the Iberian peninsula, and as far west as the Azores; the stimulus to this activity came from the knowledge that enemy trans-Atlantic trade was extensive, valuable and poorly protected relative to the scale of the attack; moreover, in the *Royal Family*'s attack on the Spanish '74' *Glorioso,* the correlation between risk and reward which conditioned all privateering activity was perfectly epitomised, as the assailants chanced life, limb and vessel in the belief that bullion worth £3 million was in the hold of the man-of-war.

Though a contemporary correspondent erroneously reported that the *Royal Family* privateers were 'all going in concert on an Eight Months cruize to the South Seas',[50] only one privateering 'expedition' was mounted in the 1739-1748 conflict, and even this differed from earlier schemes in many important respects. While Dampier, Rogers and Shelvocke had rounded the Horn and headed north along the South American coast, the *Fame* and the *Winchelsea*—mustering 1,550 tons, 88 guns and 600 men—set out to cruise in the Western Approaches and thence off Buenos Ayres before steering for the East Indies via the Cape of Good Hope. Here, in 'the Streights of Sunda or Banda' the intended prey was the homeward-bound French East Indiamen rather than the Spanish treasure ships from Manila or Peru. Such targets proved elusive, however, and the 'best cruise on the globe' disintegrated as Commodore Phillips Comyn and his senior officers decided to lodge their letters of marque with the Dutch authorities in Batavia and lease their vessels as trading ships. The London promoters of the venture, whose number included Valens Comyn, Thomas Hall, Richard Taunton and other investors in the *Royal Family* squadron, were outraged at this action, unable to comprehend

> what has induced our Commanders and officers to disobey every order
> they did receive from the directors and to break the articles entered

into with the people, which was to cruise against the enemy, not to
make a truce with them and enter into a contract of trade to be couriers
as well as convoys to the Dutch merchants in the East Indies.

Fear was deemed to be the principal explanation for the behaviour of
this 'sett of fools, knaves and Cowards'. Accordingly, there was some
satisfaction in London—'a just reward for men of no honour'—as news
of the failure of Comyn's trading enterprise reached home. There was
also considerable sympathy for 'ye poor, honest, brave tars' who suffered
most from the Commodore's treachery; such feelings quickly evaporated,
however, when the 186 survivors of the expedition arrived in London
and angrily confronted the owners with their demands for recompense.
Indeed, it was only the timely intervention of a press gang that saved the
promoters of the venture from the violence of the 'wild men [who] would
not be govern'd by reason and justice'.[51]

If the operations of 'letters of marque' failed to excite the heady
emotions, or to generate the documentary evidence, associated with the
'deep-water' and 'expeditionary' ventures of the 1740s, this reflects the
comparative normality, rather than the insignificance, of their endeavour.
Indeed, as in all the eighteenth-century conflicts, a substantial portion of
British privateering enterprise was embodied in various forms of 'letter
of marque' activity during the 1739–1748 war. Though it is clear that a
considerable number of commissioned vessels sailed for the Caribbean,
Newfoundland waters or the Mediterranean, the available source material
rarely indicates the balance between trading and predation in the purpose
of these ventures. The circumstantial evidence, however, suggests that
most embarked with predominantly commercial ambitions, for commerce-
raiding in the Western Hemisphere was largely the domain of venturers
from the West Indian and North American colonies,[52] while British
overseas trade could proceed in growing safety and in more favourable
market conditions as the French naval effort faltered. Large-scale investments were accordingly concentrated in ventures of an overtly
'deep-water' or commercial disposition, though a number did display the
characteristics of the 'cruising voyage'. For instance, in April 1744, the
150-ton *King William* of Bristol, 'now being on an Outward voyage . . .
to Newfoundland and to any port or ports in the Mediterranean', was
served by 87 seafarers, including a doctor, a gunner, a master-at-arms and
others whose specialist skills concerned fighting the ship. This large
company, furthermore, agreed to serve for monthly wages as well as a
share in one-sixth of the proceeds of any prizes taken during the voyage.

Significantly, on her return to Bristol in the following month, the *King William* was re-fitted as a private man-of-war and 51 extra men were enlisted.[53] The *Benson Gally* of Bideford appears to have persevered longer with her 'cruising voyage' to the Newfoundland Banks. Owned by Thomas Benson, this predator was 300 tons burthen, with 26 guns and 100 men, and apparently cruised in conjunction with a number of fishing vessels belonging to the same owner. Thus, during the 1744 season, the *Benson Gally* apprehended four French vessels fishing for cod on the Grand Banks, despatching each to Placentia in Newfoundland where a prize master and crew were recruited from the *Britannia* and the *New Key*, two of the Benson fishing fleet, and ordered to navigate the prizes back to North Devon.[54] Presumably, this unusual arrangement was designed to give a degree of flexibility to the *Benson Gally*'s operations, in true 'cruising voyage' fashion; thus, should her commerce-raiding efforts prove unfruitful, privateersmen might easily become fishermen or shore-based labourers, while the vessel herself might be utilised to carry cod, men and equipment back to Europe at the end of the season.

In other theatres, glimpses of the 'cruising voyage' mode of operation can be seen in the exploits of the *Constantine*, a Bristol vessel which captured eight prizes in the Mediterranean in the course of a number of voyages undertaken between 1741 and 1748.[55] Vessels such as the *Golden Lyon* of Liverpool, a 250-ton ship fitted out for Virginia with a company of 100 men, the 300-ton *Hawke*, bound from Liverpool to Jamaica with 70 men aboard, and the *Royal George*, of 350 tons burthen and 100 men, and destined for 'Leghorn, Naples, Gallipoly and back to London',[56] bore the hallmarks of the relatively powerful 'cruise and voyage' ventures which were to feature more prominently in the 1756–1762 and 1777–1783 wars.

However, in the 1740s, it would appear that the 'armed trading vessel' was the predominant form of 'letter of marque' enterprise. Such craft set forth from a variety of bases: eight Channel Island merchantmen, variously engaged in the Carolina, Newfoundland, southern European and West India trades, were commissioned during the course of the war;[57] most, if not all, of the licensed ships sailing from east coast ports were 'armed traders', with vessels such as the *Spencer* of Whitby, of 300 tons burthen with 20 men, and the 500-ton *Two Brothers* of Yarmouth, also with a 20-strong company, typifying the large bulk-carriers built in the shipyards of the North East and employed in the coal and timber trades;[58] in the West Country, vessels belonging to Dartmouth, Exeter and Poole were commissioned for their voyages to Newfoundland, while Glasgow tobacco ships and Whitehaven slavers were afforded a supplementary prize-taking function by the carriage of a letter of marque; above all, 'armed trading vessels' were fitted out in the major overseas trading ports of Bristol, Liverpool and, most especially, London, and despatched to the Caribbean, North America, Africa or southern Europe.

The significance of this licensed trading activity, relative to privateering enterprise as a whole, varied with the political complexion of the war. In general, 'armed traders' constituted the most important element of the commissioned fleet during the Anglo-Spanish phase of the conflict, a primacy which dissipated after March 1744 when the intervention of France quickened the commerce-raiding pulse of the maritime community and the overtly predatory 'deep-water' ventures proceeded to dominate the privateering business (see Appendix 2). This is apparent in the manning of commissioned vessels. Thus, in overall terms, the letter of marque declarations indicate that only eight crews exceeded 100 men prior to the French entry, whereas nearly 200 companies of this strength were recruited thereafter; in terms of the individual unit, the shift from trade to predation is illustrated by the improvement in the *Warren Gally*'s complement from 40 men in 1740 to 120 men in 1744,[59] and in the enlistment of an additional 60 hands between the 1741 voyage of the *Gibraltar Gally* and her cruise of 1744;[60] it can also be seen in terms of personnel, with George Walker employed in the *Neopolitan* 'letter of marque' in 1740 before assuming command of the *Mars* private ship-of-war in 1744, the *Boscawen* in 1745 and the *Royal Family* squadron in 1746.[61]

The variable impact of enemy commerce-raiding activity also influenced the scale and distribution of commissioned trading ventures. Bristol, for instance, suffered especially from the attentions of Spanish privateers,[62] a factor explaining, in part, the city's pronounced interest in 'deep-water' private ships-of-war, and the concomitant outfit of a mere 20 or so 'armed trading vessels' in a fleet of 132 commissioned craft.[63] In Liverpool, on the other hand,

> in the last war, 1739 to 1748, trade flourished and spread her golden wings so extensively that, if they had possessed it seven years longer, it would have enlarged the size and riches of the town to a prodigious degree. The harbour being situated so near the mouth of the North Channel between Ireland and Scotland (a passage very little known to or frequented by the enemy) afforded many conveniences to the merchants here, untasted by those of other ports.[64]

Consequently, barely half-a-dozen of Liverpool's commissioned vessels embarked on 'deep-water' cruises, with some 37 'armed trading vessels' departing the Mersey for Africa and the trade in slaves, 15 heading directly for the West Indies, 14 for the North American colonies, and a single commissioned vessel, the *Johnson*, sailing for Naples and Leghorn in November 1743.[65]

The composition of London's commissioned fleet is less clear, though it is certain that 'armed trading vessels' constituted a large proportion of the capital's privateering ventures. This was particularly so in the 1739–1743 phase of the war when the great majority of the 257 vessels licensed displayed the traits of the commissioned merchantman. Thereafter, in line with the national trend, private men-of-war assumed a high profile in London's privateering business, though stereotype 'armed traders' such as the 220-ton, 41-man *George Dogger* and the *St George*, of 250 tons burthen and 20 men, continued to operate.[66] In addition, London was the home port of the 'specialist' vessels which frequently carried letters of marque in wartime. Indeed, apart from the *Princess Mary*, a customs cutter based at East Donyland, Essex, and the revenue sloop *Amelia* of Rye,[67] all the 'specialist letters of marque' identified in the Austrian Succession War sailed from the Thames. These ships—either owned by the Hudson's Bay Company, or leased to the East India Company—accounted for 92 of the 614 London vessels commissioned during the conflict.

Four 'specialist' craft belonged to the Hudson's Bay Company. Thus, on 27 April 1744, the captains of the *Hudson's Bay Pink*, the *Mary Frigat*, the *Prince Rupert* and the *Seahorse Pink* were each granted two letters of marque to sanction commerce-raiding activity against France and Spain. While the *Hudson's Bay Pink* and the *Mary Frigat* were each of 130 tons burthen, with a crew of 30 men, the other two Company ships were both 180 tons burthen, with companies of 40 and 50 men.[68] That four vessels were commissioned in the 1744 season, compared to just one in the entire 1702–1712 conflict, reflects the increase in the Company's trade that had occurred in the intervening years. From 1715 onwards, the 'Honourable Governors' generally despatched at least three vessels a year to their North American settlements[69] and in wartime there was always the possibility that a prize might enliven the arduous journey to the Bay and back. Thus, in 1744, the crew of the *Prince Rupert* 'were full of expectation that the voyage would bring them a prize of some sort or another'. Their hopes remained unfulfilled, however, as the 18-gun vessel only reached the Bay after evading what appeared to Captain

George Spurrell to be French men-of-war in the Davis Straits.[70]

Similar dangers faced the East India Company's vessels in the long voyage to India or China, although they were well equipped for defensive and, if need be, aggressive purposes. During the 1739–1748 conflict, 181 voyages were undertaken on the Company's account by some 91 ships, the majority hired from the 'shipping interest'. Only three of these Indiamen were not equipped with letters of marque; the *Normanton* and the *Richmond* departed for India in 1739 without commissions, while the *Swift*, a Company-owned packet of 128 tons burthen, made a number of voyages to the sub-continent during the war, unlicensed each time.[71] The other 88 Indiamen were issued with a total of 152 letters of marque during the war years, 64 of which were 're-commissions'. Most of these vessels conformed to the building pattern established by the 'shipping interest' and the Company in the mid-eighteenth century, with 74 having a declared tonnage of between 490 and 500 tons burthen, an armament of 30 guns and crews of 99 men.[72] Four of the other vessels, ranging in tonnage from the *Dolphin*, of 360 tons burthen, to the 180-ton *Swallow*, were formally owned by the Company and utilised as 'packets'.[73]

These 'specialist vessels' constituted 7.9 per cent of the craft licensed in the Austrian Succession War, a high proportion compared to other eighteenth-century conflicts. However, the total 'input' into the privateering business was relatively small as fewer vessels operated with letters of marque than in any of the major wars of the era. Yet the evident decline in the 'Channel' form of the activity and the upsurge in 'deep-water' enterprise, particularly the emergence of the large-scale 'privateer of force', served to raise the gross tonnage commissioned above the equivalent figure for Queen Anne's War, while the mean burthen of the fleet reached a peak for the century as a whole. Aggregate investment in privateering enterprise was therefore at a relatively high level, though the form that it took fluctuated over the course of the war, as the predominantly commercial operations of the Anglo-Spanish War gave way to the overtly predatory activities of a range of private men-of-war after March 1744.

II

The 'output' of the privateering business, in terms of the number of prizes condemned, is compared to that of the Navy in Table 10.

Table 10

Prizes Condemned at Doctors' Commons, 1739–1751

Year	Privateers	Navy*	Total
1739	0	8	8
1740	0	11	11
1741	3	14	17
1742	3	32	35
1743	0	32	32
1744	105	42	147
1745	121	48	169
1746	67	60	127
1747	57	145	202
1748	51	53	104
1749	0	3	3
1750	1	0	1
1751	0	1	1
	408	449	857

* Including 'droits and perquisites' of the Admiralty.
Source: PRO, HCA 34/31-36.

The 857 sentences of common condemnation passed in the London Prize Court during the 1739–1748 conflict represented a substantially lower aggregate than that recorded in the Spanish Succession War when 2,222 enemy properties were successfully prosecuted. As in the earlier war, this is just one of the measures that have been adopted to gauge the 'output' of commerce-raiding activity and, once more, various sources have yielded differing results.[74] Another record, for instance, the lists of prizes compiled for the Commissioner of Customs, indicates that some 1,246 enemy properties were condemned between 13 December 1739 and 1 December 1749, with 574 falling to the Navy, 669 taken by private commissioned vessels, and three taken by naval and privateering craft acting in consort.[75] While these figures deviate from the analysis derived from the Prize Court sentences, both in aggregate terms and in the respective contributions of the state and private forces, the broad chronological pattern of the prize war is similar in the two series. Thus, it is clear that the Anglo-Spanish phase of the war was relatively unproductive of prizes, particularly for the privateering business, compared to the period after March 1744 when reprisals against French trade were authorised. Moreover, it was in 1744 and 1745 that British privateering activity was at its most effective in terms of the number of prizes condemned, though the Customs Lists suggest that a secondary peak occurred in 1747; naval prize-taking activity, in contrast, was relatively limited in the early stages of the Anglo-French war, reaching a peak in 1747 when 184 condemnations to the Navy were entered in the Customs Lists, and 145 sentences were passed in the Prize Court.

The comparatively barren character of the Anglo-Spanish War for British privateering vessels is reflected in the Prize Court's condemnation of just six properties to private commissioned vessels before 1744. Although this perhaps understates the impact of privateering activity by neglecting prizes condemned in the colonial Vice-Admiralty Courts,[76] it clearly suggests that commerce-raiding was afforded a relatively low priority by the 400 or so British vessels commissioned in this phase of the conflict. Accordingly, five of the prizes were condemned to 'letters of marque', with the Bristol merchantman *Constantine* taking the *San Caetano* into Gibraltar in 1741,[77] and the *Frances* of London, burthen 150 tons with 30 men, claiming the Spanish specie discovered in the captain's cabin of the Dutch vessel *Lady Elizabeth Gally*.[78] Another London ship, the *Warren Gally*, was operating as an 'armed trading vessel' when she encountered the French merchantman *Mary of Bilboa* five or six leagues SSW of the Isle of Wight and found her laden with 411 bags of Spanish wool worth some £9,753 0s 1d.[79] Two further Spanish prizes were condemned to 'specialist vessels'; thus, the *Princess Mary*, a Customs cutter of 73 tons burthen and 25 men, achieved the remarkable feat of seizing the *Guipuscoa*, a privateer served by a complement of 110 men,[80] while the Indiaman *Duke of Dorset* apprehended the *Nuestra Senora del Rosario* 12 leagues from Batavia and carried her into Marro.[81] The remaining prize, the 20-ton passenger ship *Nuestra Senora de Candelarios,* carrying 60 men, women and children from Tenerife to Port Teston in the Canaries, fell prey to the *Dartmouth Gally*—at 180 tons burthen, with a company of 130 men, the only private man-of-war to return a prize in Anglo-Spanish War.[82]

The Navy enjoyed much greater success in the Spanish phase of the war, having 97 prizes condemned prior to the end of 1743. Thereafter, the 'output' of the privateering business expanded considerably as 'deep-water' private ships-of-war and 'Channel' privateers were enticed into the trade war, stimulated by the prospect of French prizes. Such was the impact of these commerce-raiders that their return, in terms of the number of prizes condemned, exceeded that of the Navy after March 1744, most especially in the first 20 months of the French war when 226 prizes were sentenced to privateering venturers, and 90 fell to the state force. This imbalance was probably corrected in qualitative terms, however, for naval prizes were generally more valuable than the properties condemned to commissioned vessels.[83] Furthermore, it is clear from the payment of head money that the King's ships exacted a much greater toll on enemy ships-of-war and *corsaires* than did the British privateering force, an indication that the burden of trade protection rested principally upon the shoulders of the Navy. The award of these bounties, at the rate of £5 for each man-of-warsman or privateersman serving in the captured vessel, had been established in 1708 and applied equally to naval and private captors; in the 1739-1748 conflict, as Table 11 shows, naval seafarers were in receipt of the great bulk of head money granted.

Table 11

Head Money Paid to Naval Seamen and Privateering Venturers, 1739–1755 *

| | Payments | | Bounty Paid | | Average size of |
	No**	%	£	%	captured crew
Privateers	47.33	14.9	19295	8.7	81.5
Navy	269.67	85.1	202160	91.3	149.9
	317	100	221455	100	139.7

* Claims were not lodged, or are lacking, in respect of a number of eligible privateering prizes. See Appendix 1.

** The *Glorioso* was captured jointly by the *Royal Family* privateers, and the *Russell* and *Dartmouth* men-of-war; the Prize Court awarded one-third of the head money, £1,275, to the private men-of-war.

Source: PRO, ADM 43/2-13.

Evidently the role of the British privateering force was subsidiary to that of the Navy in the military struggle against the Franco-Spanish fleets, and in the sphere of commerce protection. The Navy accounted for 85.1 per cent of the captures warranting payment of head money, while men-of-warsmen received 91.3 per cent of the £221,455 paid out, their prizes being significantly better manned, on average, than the vessels-of-war taken by British privateers. Of the 317 bounties paid by the Navy Office,[84] 65 were in respect of enemy naval vessels, with 62.67, or 96.4 per cent, of these being awarded to naval captors; the residual 3.6 per cent—namely the *Solebay*, the *San Joseph* and the *Royal Family*'s third share in the *Glorioso*—fell to private men-of-war. In the war against French and Spanish *corsaires*, Britain's commissioned vessels were more effective, accounting for 45, or 17.9 per cent, of the bounty payments made for captured enemy predators, a source of some £16,850 for privateering venturers. Again, however, it was the Navy that inflicted the greater damage, taking 207 enemy commerce-raiders, manned by an average of 94.7 seafarers compared with a mean crew size of 74.9 men exhibited by the *corsaires* captured by British privateers.

These figures reflect the priorities of the state and the private naval forces. The King's ships were primarily concerned with fleet operations and trade protection, with the apprehension of enemy merchantmen necessarily, if reluctantly, afforded a relatively low priority; accordingly, 270, or 60.1 per cent of the 449 prizes condemned to naval vessels in the 1739–1748 war qualified for the payment of bounty money. Private licensed vessels, on the other hand, were specifically set forth to prey on enemy commerce and generally instructed to steer clear of enemy men-of-war and *corsaires*, for physical and financial damage might result from encounters with such vessels, while profits lay in condemned cargo rather than in head money. Hence, ships-of-war constituted just 11.8 per cent of the prizes condemned to commissioned vessels in the Austrian Succession War, with 360 commercial properties forming the bulk of the privateering 'catch'. These 408 prizes were taken by vessels from 19 British ports as Table 12 indicates.

Table 12

Prizes Condemned to Commissioned Vessels by Region, 1739–1751

Region		Number of prizes
London		107
Bristol		82
Liverpool		8
Channel Is	—Guernsey (78) Jersey (46)	124
E England	—Donyland (2)	2
SE England	—Dover (34) Folkestone (3) Portsmouth (6) Rye (2) Sandwich (5)	50
SW England	—Bideford (4), Dartmouth (12) Exeter (3) Falmouth (2) Plymouth (1) Poole (2) Topsham (2)	26
Ireland	—Dublin (1)	1
In consort	—London/Bristol (1) London/Jersey (1) London/Bristol/Portsmouth (1) Bristol/Dartmouth (5)	8
		408

Source: PRO, HCA 25/26-37; HCA 26/4, 22-26, 29-32; HCA 34/31-36.

The Channel Islands emerged as the leading prize-taking centre in the 1739–1748 conflict. This was true in absolute terms as the privateers of Guernsey and Jersey recorded 124 condemnations; it was also the case in a relative sense, for these prizes were returned by a fleet of 85 licensed vessels at a rate of 1.5 successes per predator. London venturers accounted for 107 enemy properties, though this substantial 'catch' was taken by a predatory force of over 600 vessels. In relation to 'input', therefore, Bristol's return of 82 prizes, together with seven more shared with venturers from elsewhere, was more impressive, as a crude 'productivity rate' of 0.6 condemnations per vessel resulted from the activities of the port's 132 commissioned craft. Apart from the lone success of the *Boyne* of Dublin,[85] the privateers of southern England accounted for the remaining condemned properties, with 50 prosecuted by the South East's 61 commerce-raiding ventures, and 26 taken by the West Country's fleet of 74 commissioned vessels. In contrast, the 'letters of marque' and private men-of-war despatched from west coast ports, from eastern England and from Scotland barely featured in prize-taking activity, though Liverpool venturers benefited by dint of eight condemnations; even this return was meagre relative to the scale of their investment, for 79 commissioned vessels were fitted out in the Mersey.

Thus, in its broad outline, the regional distribution of prizes in the Austrian Succession War resembled the picture drawn in the 1702–1712 conflict, though most returns were at significantly lower levels in the 1740s. As in the earlier war, the dispersal of condemnations can be largely attributed to the structure of the privateering fleet as 'Channel' privateers —sustained by a diet of multiple, low-value seizures—continued to dominate the commerce-raiding business of the Channel Islands, while commercially-oriented 'letters of marque' bulked large in the commissioned fleets set forth from London, Liverpool, eastern England and Scotland. There were clear signs of change, however. In quantitative terms, the contribution of the Channel Islands to the national prize return fell from 55.4 per cent of the 1702–1712 total to just 30 per cent of the 1739–1748 aggregate. Though this sharp fall was partially corrected by an increase in the share of south-east England—the other customary centre of 'Channel' privateering—from 7.7 to 12.3 per cent of the respective totals, this expansion was largely achieved by comparatively large-scale ventures. Therefore, it is clear that the 'Channel' branch of the privateering business suffered a relative decline in the 1740s. In contrast, London and Bristol, the principal seats of large-scale, 'deep-water' commerce-raiding enterprise, claimed a larger proportion of the prize aggregate, with the capital's share rising from 21.8 to 26.2 per cent between the two wars and Bristol's return amounting to 20.1 per cent of the 1739–1748 total, more than double the share recorded by the port in Queen Anne's War.

Such figures clearly suggest that the shift from 'Channel' to 'deep-water' privateering enterprise evident in the composition of the commissioned fleet was also reflected in the 'output' of the business. A substantial body of qualitative evidence serves to confirm this supposition. For instance, in the South East and the Channel Islands, the enemy's small fry, together with contraband cargoes found in neutral or British holds, still constituted the bulk of the prize 'catch'.[86] Yet a significant number of these seizures were conducted by relatively large-scale ventures. Thus, the head money vouchers indicate that three Channel Island privateers captured French *corsaires*; while the *Success* of Jersey, of 50 tons burthen and 34 men, exhibited the characteristics of the typical Island predator, the *Charming Nancy* and the *Defiance*—both of 150 tons burthen, with 97- and 85-strong crews respectively—were among the most most powerful craft set forth by Island *armateurs*.[87] Since the *Charming Nancy* was one of the most successful Jersey predators, taking at least eight prizes, including one seized during an 'armed trading' venture,[88] it would seem that indigenous 'deep-water' enterprise played a growing part in the Islanders' commerce-raiding efforts during the 1740s.

In south-eastern England, the more substantial ventures dominated the regional prize return, with Dover vessels such as the *Carlisle*, the *Dover*, the *Eagle* and the *York*, and the *Swift* of Sandwich—all exceeding 100 tons burthen with crews of at least 60 men[89]—cruising to great effect in the Channel Narrows. The prize sentences relate that this quintet of comparatively powerful predators accounted for some 31 individual condemnations, with the *Carlisle* returning 11 prizes to Dover, the *Eagle* registering 10 successes, and the *Swift* seizing five enemy vessels, conveying them variously to Deal, Dover, Ostend and Sandwich. Nine enemy *corsaires* formed part of this 'catch', generating a total of £1,940 in head money for the owners and privateersmen involved.[90] The *Eagle* and the *York*, moreover, combined forces to take five galliot hoys bound from Le Havre to Rouen, the French crews escaping to the shore at Boulogne with much of their ships' documentation.[91] As well as this standard fare, the *York* took the *Thunderbolt*, a smuggling cutter of 14 tons and eight men belonging to Rye, two leagues off Dungeness shortly after midnight on 24 November 1745. Bound for France with 'money to purchase brandy' the smuggler was condemned to the *York* as lawful prize in 1746.[92] The *Eagle* engaged in similar activity; thus,

> the *Royal Ranger*, Tort, Bird, or Grayling, Master, a smuggler of 8 carriage guns, and 18 swivel guns, and two chests of fine small arms, is taken by the *New Eagle* Privateer, Capt Bazely, and brought into Dover. She is reckoned to be the finest vessel belonging to the Smugglers, who when the *Eagle* came up, seemed determined to defend themselves; but seeing Capt Bazely preparing to board them, they made sail, and ran the vessel ashore; and instantly carried off a considerable Quantity of Money and valuable Goods: but Bird, and several noted Smugglers are secured.[93]

If these relatively powerful craft tended to supplant the archetypal

'Channel' privateers in the Narrow Seas, 'deep-water' private men-of-war from other ports also preyed upon French coastal trade in the Channel. The *Saltash* and the *Warren Gally* of London were particularly successful in this respect, deploying their combined force of 400 tons, 48 guns and 240 men[94] in the waters off the Breton peninsula. Cruising in the vicinity of the 'Isle of Bass and Ushant', occasionally 'exchanging several shot with the fort' on the Isle,[95] this substantial consortship harassed the coasting traffic of Brest in the spring and summer of 1746. On 13 March, nine miles from L'Orient, the two London predators encountered a fleet of 30 to 40 merchantmen under the convoy of three small French warships. The escorts deserted their charges, four of which were captured and another burned; in addition, the *Ceres,* one of the convoys, carrying 10 guns and 50 men, was seized by the assailants who, on boarding their prize, found that the entire crew, excepting Cloath Marton and Jean le Ffloathe, had escaped to the shore.[96] After taking a 'bark' laden with 'wines, pruins & Slosom', Charles Wilson, commander of the *Warren Gally*, decided to quit this station and 'goe off to sea as they may hear of me at Brest.'[97]

In so doing, Wilson effectively reverted to type, for it was further to the south and to the west that such comparatively large-scale ventures generally operated. Here, the *Warren Gally* had spent her 1744 cruise, taking *Les Deux Freres et la Souer*, homeward-bound from St Domingue with sugar and indigo, 100 miles from the Lizard;[98] and it was in this broad theatre that she and the *Saltash* were to cruise in 1747, apprehending the *corsaire Kouli Kan* seven leagues to the south of Scilly.[99] Such actions were characteristic of the 'deep-water' branch of the privateering business, as large-scale ventures sought to intercept the enemy's colonial trade, able, if not always willing, to engage his vessels-of-war. The effectiveness of this form of predation in the 1740s is indicated by the Prize Court sentences. London's return of 107 condemnations was achieved by 56 separate captors, 42 of which were manned by at least 100 seafarers, including 19 of the 29 vessels declared to be worked by 200 men or more. In Bristol, the well-armed, heavily-manned craft proved to be the most prolific captors, with 11 of the 14 ventures served by crews exceeding 199 men successfully prosecuting a seizure, and a further eight with companies ranging from 150 to 199 men participating in prize-taking activity. Elsewhere, the more powerful units of the commissioned fleet were the most potent in the prize war; thus, the 180-ton, 200-man *Dartmouth Gally*, and the *Boscawen,* of 600 tons burthen and 300 men,[100] accounted for 14 of Dartmouth's 17 individual and shared condemnations;

in Liverpool, the *Old Noll Privateer*, of 360 tons burthen and 160 men,[101] was responsible for four of the port's eight prizes, with 'deep-water' vessels worked by 100 men or more taking the remainder; similarly, the *Adventure*, of 100 tons burthen and 100 men, sometimes in unison with her consort, the *Norton*, accounted for all six of Portsmouth's prizes,[102] while captors such as the *George* and the *Godolphin* of Exeter, the *Postillion Privateer* of Topsham, and the *Boyne* of Dublin, were each declared as shipping at least 100 men aboard.[103]

The quality and value of the prizes taken by 'deep-water' commerce-raiders—and the impact that this predation had upon the enemy—are difficult to determine with any precision. However, sufficient evidence exists to provide a good impression of the character and significance of this enterprise. It is clear, for instance, that the trans-Atlantic trade of the Bourbon powers—the very extent, value and perceived vulnerability of which excited this privateering response—did, in fact, yield most of the prizes taken by the large-scale predators. Vessels engaged in various branches of the enemy's overseas commerce were taken, the value of their cargoes generally conditioning the amount of force required to effect their seizure. Merchantmen outward-bound for French Canadian settlements, the Caribbean or Spanish America occasionally fell prey to 'deep-water' private ships-of-war as they proceeded through home waters and the north-eastern Atlantic. Laden with provisions, manufactures, wines and sundry commodities for the colonies, such craft were among the least valuable of prizes for their bulk, low-cost cargoes were in ready supply in the British market.

Moreover, convoys normally protected this traffic until it reached mid-ocean,[104] and predatory opportunities were accordingly limited to vessels detached from their escorts. Such stragglers were generally poorly-defended and rarely able to offer much resistance to arrest, particularly against the more powerful assailants. *La Catherine*, for example, a snow of 80 tons burthen, with 15 crew members, four passengers and a cargo of flour, oil and iron, bound from Bayonne to Havana, did not attempt to ward off the 300-man *Boscawen*, especially as the London private man-of-war *Garland*, of 400 tons burthen and 250 men, was within sight.[105] Similarly, *La Trompeuse*, bound from Bordeaux to America with provisions and wine, struck without firing a gun at the *Duke of Beaufort* whose crew was over four times the size of the Frenchman's 24-strong company.[106] Resistance might be offered, however, if there were a genuine chance of escape; thus, the Martinique-bound *Les Six Souers* fought the *Postillion Privateer* of Topsham for over an hour as the Frenchman 'proceeded towards the Island of Aix in order to go under the shelter of a convoy'.[107]

In essence, these relatively low-value outward-bound merchantmen were incidental targets of the 'deep-water' private ships-of-war, for vessels returning fully laden to metropolitan France and Spain were invariably more valuable and often more vulnerable as they approached their destinations. 'Bankers' heading for the fish marts of southern Europe from the Newfoundland fishing grounds and merchantmen sailing from Canada to France were frequently taken by British predators in European waters;[108] yet it was not the cod, fur or timber of the temperate regions, but the cargoes of sugar, coffee and indigo despatched from the tropical colonies which most interested 'deep-water' venturers. Seizures of 'rich Martinicomen' were avidly reported in the mercantile press of the 1740s,[109] much to the satisfaction, no doubt, of the British West India merchants whose profits had increasingly suffered as a consequence of French competition. Though the newspapers may well have exaggerated the frequency and value of these captures, it is clear from other evidence that cargoes of tropical produce, often yielded with little or no resistance, sustained many of the large-scale ventures. The *Dartmouth Gally*, for instance, 'did take from His Majesty's enemies several rich & valuable prizes'[110] in two cruises in 1744 and 1745, the richest being the *Ceres* from 'Martinico to Nantz', and the *St Armand of Bordeaux* and *Le St Jean Baptiste* heading from Guadeloupe for Bordeaux. These prizes, which ranged from 100 to 150 tons burthen with between 16 and 26 men, were apprehended in separate encounters in the Channel Soundings; in each instance, the French crews decided against defending their cargoes of sugar, coffee, cotton, sweetmeats and indigo against the 24 guns and 200 men of the Dartmouth vessel.[111]

Discretion also persuaded Antoine Lavaisser, master of the 140-ton, 15-man *Les Deux Freres*, bound from St Domingue with sugar, and crowns to the value of £1,000, to lower his colours to the *Dursley* of London, a predator of 350 tons burthen and a declared complement of 250 men.[112] In similar instances, *La Galere de Languedoc*, of 140 tons burthen, 14 guns and 27 men, surrendered her cargo of sugar and coffee to the vastly superior *Garland* 100 leagues west of Cape Finisterre,[113] while further inshore, off Ferrol, *L'Impreveu* fired a single shot at the *George* of Exeter before her captain realised that she 'was not of force or strength sufficient to make resistance to any effect and therefore he soon struck his colours to the captors'; the Quebec-built prize of 170 tons burthen and 21 men was thence conveyed to Exeter where her lading of sugar, coffee, cocoa and copper was examined pending condemnation.[114] Even the larger West Indiamen might succumb without resistance, the depleted crew of *La Vestale* for instance, swimming for the nearby Spanish shore as the *Tygress* of Dartmouth approached, leaving their 300-ton vessel and its cargo of 518 hogsheads of sugar in the charge of Samuel Desportte, who was soundly asleep when the boarding party alighted.[115]

If such vessels had neither the power nor the good fortune to resist or elude their captors, the more valuable elements of the Bourbon mercantile marine were usually provided with the means to defend themselves against assailants. Private ships-of-war had to be ready, therefore, to take considerable risks to earn the vast profits which 'deep-water' commerce-raiding enterprise promised. In the 1740s, it would seem that British privateering venturers were prepared as never before to chance their vessels and their lives in the quest for instant wealth. This gamble did not always pay off. The *Leviathan*, for example, in company with the *Dublin, Duke of Bedford* and *Townshend* private men-of-war, attempted to 'get in amongst' a French fleet of 120 sail convoyed by eight men-of-war, only to be chased away empty-handed after two days.[116] Frustration also resulted from the *Prince Charles'* engagement with six 'Martinicomen' 30 leagues west of Ushant. Having induced two of the enemy fleet to strike, the British predator and her prizes were distracted by the arrival of what appeared to be the Brest squadron; sadly for both parties, the naval vessels were British and it was Sir John Balchen's men who benefited as the fleet of French West Indiamen escaped from the privateer into the arms of a stronger adversary.[117] Though thwarted by friend and foe alike, these 'deep-water' private ships-of-war were more fortunate than the *Bristol,* whose captain mistook a French 64-gun man-of-war for an Indiaman and boldly proceeded to engage her with the predictable result that the 600-ton, 400-man aggressor was soon obliged to concede to the superior firepower of her intended prey.[118] Other predators were to be disappointed at the outcome of their belligerent exertions; the *Boscawen's* men, for instance, laboured for three hours to overcome *Les Deux Amis,* with both sides suffering heavy casualties, only to find that the sugar, coffee and 60,000 pieces of eight conveyed from the West Indies had been previously discharged at Corunna,[119] while similar news deflated the crews of the *Royal Family* privateers on the surrender of the *Glorioso.*[120]

On other occasions, however, the aggression of 'deep-water' privateers-men was more generously rewarded. Thus, the *Blandford* seized a West Indiaman worth an estimated £30,000 despite an injury to Captain Stonehouse, whose leg was shattered by a cannonball and subsequently subjected to a fatal amputation;[121] *Le Triton*, a 450-ton vessel laden with gum from Senegal fell to the *Saltash* after a four-hour engagement in which four Frenchmen perished;[122] the demise of a priest, killed by a shot which penetrated the side of the *Fiere*, persuaded this valuable East Indiaman to strike to the *Sheerness;*[123] while the *Royal Family*'s first cruise generated an estimated gross return of £220,000 as four prizes were taken with the loss of just a single seafarer.[124]

Yet the real essence of 'deep-water' enterprise—the search for the 'glittering', seemingly vulnerable prizes, the violence which such high stakes precipitated, and the audacity and scale of the attack—was perhaps best illustrated in two of the more famous incidents of the 1739–1748 trade war. In attacking a fleet of eight armed merchant vessels on 24 May 1745, the companies of the *Boscawen* and the *Sheerness* were motivated by the prospect of the rich colonial cargoes presumed to fill the Frenchmen's holds. They operated in quasi-naval fashion, seeking to break the enemy's line of battle in a 'warm' engagement which saw five of the merchant fleet taken, one sunk and 113 French lives lost. As all six prizes held *lettres de marque*, a bounty of £1,400 was paid in respect of the 280 men they carried prior to the action, though the principal returns of at least £40,000 accrued from the 1,650 hogsheads of fine sugar and the 100 tons of coffee discovered aboard the captured 'Martinicomen'.[125]

Two months later, in July 1745, the *Duke* and the *Prince Frederick*, mustering a combined force of 48 guns and 399 men, encountered three large merchantmen sailing without escort to the westward of St Mary's in the Azores. When the 'white rag' was hoisted and the three vessels formed a line of battle, the British commerce-raiders attacked on the assumption that the Bourbon ships were homeward bound from Martinique. After 'entertaining each other for three hours' with a series of broadsides and pistol shot, during which Lieutenant Curtis of the *Prince Frederick* was 'shot thro' the head with a cannon-ball', two of the enemy vessels succumbed, and Captain James Talbot was 'agreeably surprized' to learn that his prizes were register-ships bound from Callao in Peru to Spain. In all, 13 privateersmen were killed and 33 more wounded in the apprehension of the *Marquis D'Antin* and the *Lewis Erasmus*, while nine Spaniards died and 12 were injured in the vain attempt to safeguard their cargo of bullion and cocoa, estimated to be worth between £700,000 and £1,000,000. The incapacitated prizes were towed to Kinsale, and thence to Bristol where the captured gold and silver was discharged and despatched to London in an armed convoy of 45 wagons.[126]

While 'deep-water' privateersmen were frequently obliged to fight for the more worthwhile prizes, their military skills were sometimes deployed in combat with the enemy's vessels-of-war. Such encounters rarely yielded the 'capital' prizes sought by the large-scale commerce-raiding undertakings; moreover, they might well result in physical and financial loss should the adversary's weight of shot, seamanship or tactics prove superior. Yet these engagements were a regular feature of the private ship-of-war's operations. Many were unavoidable, of course, as the would-be predator was forced to defend herself against enemy attack; others were initiated by privateering commanders eager to protect or enhance their reputations, or aware that their target was guarding some particularly precious cargo. Commanders who surrendered without resistance to vessels of a similar force, and those who shied away from well-defended merchantmen, were regularly denounced as cowards by their fellow venturers—the owners of the project and the men who served aboard the vessel. Vilification of the faint-hearted captain was often very public. William Foy, for instance, felt obliged to publish a rebuttal of the 'scandalous aspersions . . . maliciously and industriously reported' that he went down below during an engagement.[127] A commander's abilities might also be judged in private; thus, the 'ill-conduct' of Captain Halliburton of the *Centurion* in spending much of his cruise in the Cattewater, Plymouth, was blamed by his owners for the venture's failure, while his cowardly decision not to pursue an action bred resentment among the ship's people who apparently 'swore like madmen' as their captain's behaviour denied them 'Hatsfull of money'.

Whereas Halliburton's diffidence—'disappointing for a man of his education'—led to his discharge,[128] commanders might found their reputations, and secure their future employment, on brave, perhaps reckless, attacks on enemy vessels of force. Samuel Phillips did just this as he persuaded the 142 men of the 28-gun *Alexander* to surprise and recapture the *Solebay* as she lay in St Martin's Road, off Bordeaux, on 21 April 1746. On approaching the French man-of-war, Phillips

> ordered the men to grapple and board her on the bow, and threw in 50 men armed each with a Pistol, Pole-Ax, and Cutlass, and at the same time gave them two vollies of small arms from the *Alexander's* crew on board which put the Enemy into Great Confusion.

As the French men-of-warsmen retired below decks, five carriage guns were discharged into the *Solebay's* sides inducing 'terror and surrender' amongst her crew. Upon examination, it was discovered that the prize had a complement of 202 men, ten of whom had perished in the action, while she was laden with a valuable quantity of bale goods and 'was intended as Convoy for some Ships bound to Martinico'. Accordingly, £1,010 was paid in bounty money to the venturers engaged in the *Alexander*, and the captured vessel of 436 40/94 tons burthen was surveyed, together with her tackle and ordnance, and resold to the Navy for £4,880 11 2d. Phillips, moreover, was introduced to George II, permitted to kiss the sovereign's hand and presented with a reward of 500 guineas and a gold medal.[129]

The *Royal Family* squadron—acting under the impression that bullion worth £3 million was at stake—earned more head money, £1,275, and a more lasting fame, from the capture of the *Glorioso*, of 74 guns and 765 men, on 18 October 1747. This was but one-third of the total bounty, however, for the remainder was paid to the men of the *Russell* and the *Dartmouth*, two naval vessels which joined the commerce-raiders in the engagement with the Spanish man-of-war and finally obliged her to submit. Such a division was probably resented by the privateering venturers, for George Walker's 'flagship', the *King George*, of 26 guns and 282 men, had first chased the Spaniard for five hours and then engaged her for two and a half hours before the rest of the private fleet came up and pursued the *Glorioso* into the path of the British men-of-war. 'I really think we are justly entitled to half of the value of that prize', opined Richard Taunton, a shareholder in the *Royal Family*,

> because the *Russell* could not have taken or man'd that ship or returned the prisoners (double the number of her crew) without our help & besides we engaged her the day before the *Russell* & followed the Chace till taken.[130]

The Admiralty Court disagreed, for only a quarter of the proceeds were awarded to the *King George* and her consorts, worth a mere £3,025, while the lion's share fell to the *Russell's* men, the *Dartmouth* having blown up during the action with the loss of all but ten of her company.[131]

The assaults upon the *Glorioso* and the *Solebay* were isolated instances of the participation of 'deep-water' predators in successful actions against enemy men-of-war. Indeed, the head money vouchers indicate that only one other bounty was claimed by privateering venturers in respect of the seizure of a naval vessel, and this amounted to just £160, paid to the owners and men of the *Princess Augusta* for the capture of a small Spanish naval vessel of 32 men.[132] A further 45 bounties, however, rewarded privateersmen for their achievements in reducing the French commissioned fleet by 41 *corsaires,* and the Spanish predatory force by some four privateers. This 'catch' was not to be superseded in any of the subsequent eighteenth-century conflicts; moreover, the average size of captured crews, and the aggregate income of £16,850 they generated for privateering venturers in the 1739–1748 conflict also remained unsurpassed. Thus, a mean company of 74.9 men served aboard these commissioned Bourbon craft, ranging from the 23-strong crew of the French 'letter of marque' *La Victoire* to the complement of the Spanish private man-of-war *El Venzidor,* which numbered 222 at the commencement of her bloody engagement with the *Tyger* of Bristol, and 193 at its conclusion.[133]

The *Tyger,* of 560 tons burthen and 300 men,[134] was one of the most substantial of the 'deep-water' predators set out in the Austrian Succession War. No less than 29 of the 45 payments made to privateering venturers for the capture of *corsaires* rewarded those engaged in enterprises of a similar kind based in Bristol, Dartmouth and London, while a further 13 bounties were claimed by relatively powerful undertakings mounted from Dover, Portsmouth, Sandwich and the Channel Islands. If this further reflects the dominant role of 'deep-water' craft in the 1739–1748 prize war, it does not present the full story, for commissioned vessels of a different hue also participated in the seizure and condemnation of enemy property. 'Channel' privateers accounted for the bulk of the Channel Islanders' prizes, while small-scale ventures promoted in mainland ports —like the 50-ton, 50-man *Rochester Sloop* of London, and the Bristol predator *Fly,* of 40 tons burthen and 50 men—returned a dozen prizes.[135] The 'expeditionary force' of the *Fame* and the *Winchelsea,* despite its eventual failure, carried three French West Indiamen into Lisbon during the early stages of its voyage to the Philippines.[136]

Meanwhile, a number of 'letters of marque' executed their right to profit from the condemnation of seized vessels and goods. The *George Dogger,* for instance, was operating as an 'armed trading vessel' when she drove *L'Ensor* ashore on the Isle of Wight to earn £90 in head money for her owners and crew. Typically, monthly wages were paid to the 41 officers and men serving in the captor; they were also entitled to one-fifth of the net proceeds of any prizes taken, the residual 80 per cent belonging to the vessel's owner, William Belchier, a Lombard Street banker[137] and a leading investor in London 'privateers of force'. The exact contribution of other such 'armed traders' is unclear, though the *Charming Nancy* of Jersey prosecuted a joint capture,[138] while the declared characteristics of mainland captors such as the *St George* of Bristol, of 250 tons burthen and 40 men, and the 150-ton, 30-man *Frances* of

London,[139] were indicative of the predominantly commercial nature of their voyages.

At least four 'specialist vessels' took prizes in the pursuit of their particular occupations. The *Falmouth*, named after her home port, was engaged in government service as an 'advice boat' and charged to proceed 'from Plymouth with the trade to Portsmouth'. In the course of this 12 months' appointment, the Cornish vessel, of 320 tons burthen and 120 men, apprehended *Le Consolant* and *Le Subtil*, two French privateers of 37 and 64 men respectively, with one-third of the bounty money thereby generated distributed amongst the crew.[140] Two prizes fell to the Customs cutter *Princess Mary*; in 1741, this 73-ton craft carried a Spanish privateer into her home base of East Donyland, Essex, and five years later, still under the command of Robert Martin, she captured *La Petite Fortune* and conveyed the prize to Colchester.[141] East Indiamen, the most substantial of 'specialist letters of marque', were responsible for two condemnations during the 1739–1748 conflict. While the *Duke of Dorset* accounted for one of the few prizes taken during the Anglo-Spanish phase of the war, the *Mahajoub* was seized by the *Bombay Castle* off the coast of Coromandel on 22 August 1747 and landed at Fort St Davids, though a final sentence of condemnation was delayed until 27 June 1750 owing to doubts about the prize's nationality.[142]

Such captures were adjudicated in London, for Prize Courts had yet to be established in the Far East. However, seized property carried into British colonies in the Caribbean, mainland North America and New-foundland, and, nearer home, into Gibraltar and Minorca, were liable to common condemnation in the various Vice-Admiralty Courts constituted to deal with such business in the early eighteenth century.[143] While this practice occasionally served to exclude prizes taken by 'deep-water' captors from the London Prize Court records—for example, *L'Aigle*, a *corsaire* of 28 guns and 175 men captured by the *Tygress* and sentenced at Gibraltar,[144] and the 16 prizes allegedly worth £400,000, taken by Fortunatus Wright of the *Fame* in the Mediterranean[145]—it seriously obscured the prize return of the 'cruise and voyage' ventures set forth to prey and trade in the more distant stations.

Nevertheless, the material generated at Doctors' Commons suggests that this form of 'letter of marque' activity achieved some notable successes. In the North Atlantic, for instance, the predatory efforts of the *Benson Gally* produced four prizes; these captures added 47,000 cod, 24 hogsheads of blubber and five barrels of train oil to the output of Thomas Benson's fishermen, while his fleet was augmented by 360 tons of French shipping, and 74 men from Grandville and La Rochelle were forcibly removed from the competitive cod-fishing industry of the Newfoundland Banks.[146] The Bristol vessel *Mediterranean,* of 200 tons burthen and 60 men, also found her passage to Newfoundland productive, taking a 'rich St Domingo ship' in the Western Approaches and thereafter a 'Banker' and a Greenlandman further to the north.[147] Successful 'cruising voyages' to the Mediterranean were mounted by vessels such as the *Constantine* of Bristol, captor of eight prizes ranging in value from the 200 dollars fetched by a Spanish settee to the £30,000 worth of silk and linen taken out of two French merchantmen bound from the Levant to Marseilles.[148] The *Ruby,* owned by merchants resident in Messina, Naples and London, also operated to some effect in this theatre, carrying three prizes into Malta, Rhodes and Zant in 1744; of 350 tons burthen, with a complement of 80 men, she exhibited the hallmarks of the 'cruising voyage' mode of commerce-raiding undertaking.[149]

Ventures of similar proportions departed Bristol and Liverpool for the West Indies in the 1740s. Though the 300-ton *Eagle* and the 350-ton *Salisbury,* both bound for Jamaica from Bristol with companies of 60 men, had prizes adjudicated at Doctors' Commons,[150] evidence of the apprehension of prizes during these Caribbean 'cruising voyages' is generally sparse. This may reflect the dominance of colonial private men-of-war in this theatre; however, it would seem that investment in the 'cruise and voyage' form of predatory activity was relatively limited in the 1740s as speculators perceived that prize-taking prospects were much brighter in European waters. An abundance of prey, the enemy's defective 'system' of trade protection, and a naval balance of power that was turning, though not yet comprehensively so, in Britain's favour, were the factors which interacted to stimulate an unprecedented interest in 'deep-water' privateering enterprise. In subsequent wars, the changing mix of these ingredients tended to favour other sectors of the privateering business.

Notes

1. The war was so named after Captain Jenkins, the master of a merchant brig arrested by a *guarda-costa* in 1731. A Spanish officer allegedly cut off his ear, an atrocity which caused an outcry when it was related to Parliament in 1738, signalling a further deterioration in Anglo-Spanish relations.

2. *London Gazette*, 10 July 1739.

3. This outline of the 1739-1748 maritime conflict is based largely on R. Pares, *War and Trade in the West Indies, 1739–1763* (Oxford: Clarendon Press, 1936).

4. R. B. Sheridan, *Sugar and Slavery. An Economic History of the British West Indies* (Caribbean UP, 1974) 416-17.

5. D. Baugh, *British Naval Administration in the Age of Walpole* (Princeton UP, 1965) 341-55.

6. Martinique was the entrepot and administrative centre of the French West Indies. British privateering venturers seem to have used the term 'Martinicomen' as a generalisation to describe French merchant vessels sailing from the Caribbean, though the term 'St Domingomen' was also used.

7. *Daily Post*, 19 October 1739.

8. *Champion, or Evening Advertiser*, 3 January 1741.

9. J. Alban Fraser, *Spain and the West Country* (Burn, Oates and Washbourne, 1935) 244.

10. A. Cameron and R. Farndon, *Scenes from Sea and City. Lloyd's List, 1734–1984* (Lloyd's List, 1984) 35.

11. Jenkins, *History of the French Navy*, 114-15.

12. For instance, St Malo's *corsaires* accounted for 858 prizes and ransoms in the 1695–1713 wars, compared with just 72 in the 1744–1748 conflict, while Brest's 'output' declined from 918 to 54 prizes over the same period. See R. P. Crowhurst, *The Defence of British Trade, 1689–1815* (Folkestone: Dawson, 1977) 28; for Bayonne, see R. P. Crowhurst, 'Bayonne Privateering, 1744–1763' in Mollet, ed., *Course et Piraterie*, I, 453-68.

13. PRO, C 103/130. Richard Taunton to Thomas Hall, 8 November 1746.

14. Declarations 28 February 1745, 9 June 1748. PRO, HCA 26/32, 32. James Barrett's declaration was originally entered in HCA 26/26, against 'France and Spain', but then crossed out and noted 'entered in the Spanish letter of marque book, taken only against the Spaniards'. The declaration duly appears in HCA 26/32 against Spain, the last commission of the war.

15. PRO, HCA 26/29-32 against Spain; HCA 26/4 against France; HCA 26/22-26 against France and Spain.

16. Starkey, thesis, 73, 153, 338.

17. Davis, *Shipping Industry*, 73; C. J. French, 'The Trade and Shipping of the Port of London, 1700–1776' (Unpublished PhD thesis, University of Exeter, 1980), 381.

18. Starkey, thesis, 179; D. J. Starkey, 'Liverpool Privateering, 1702-1783' (Unpublished MA dissertation, University of Exeter, 1979) 62.

19. Declaration 16 June 1741. PRO, HCA 25/28. Though the *Amelia* of Rye, at 70 tons and 30 men, was of a similar strength, she was probably in the service of the Customs Commissioners. Declaration 23 April 1742. PRO, HCA 25/28; see the petition of her captain, Nathaniel Pigram, to the

Treasury. *Calendar of Treasury Books and Papers* (HMSO, 1903), V (1742–5), 489.
20. The tonnage figures are derived from declarations made on 23 July 1745, 12 May 1744, 26 August 1745. PRO, HCA 26/23, 4, 24. Crew sizes are taken from the head money vouchers. PRO, ADM 43/3(1), 3(1), 5(1). The *York's* company exceeded 72 men, 'the rest being put on board prizes or sick on shore'.
21. Declaration 15 October 1747. PRO, HCA 26/25.
22. PRO, ADM 43/10, 12.
23. Declarations 15 May 1746, 29 January 1747. PRO, HCA 25/28, 28.
24. The reconnaissance function of Channel Island privateers is discussed by P. Raban, 'War and Trade in the Mid-Eighteenth Century' *Société Guernesiaise Report and Transactions*, (1986), 135-9.
25. Sheridan, *Sugar and Slavery*, 416-17.
26. H. I. Priestley, *France Overseas through the Old Regime. A Study of European Expansion* (New York: Appleton-Century, 1939) 260.
27. Pares, *War and Trade*, 109-14.
28. The price of sugar on the London market rose from a peak of 24s 9d per cwt between 1735 and 1738, to 42s 9½d per cwt in 1747. Sheridan, *Sugar and Slavery*, 417-18.
29. The shortcomings in the 'convoy system' devised by the French Minister of Marine, Maurepas, are discussed by Pares, *War and Trade*, 311-25.
30. Vaughan, *Voyages and Cruises*, 49.
31. See *Gentleman's Magazine*, XV (1745), 418.
32. The Articles of Agreement stipulated that the proceeds of all prizes taken jointly or separately by either ship were to be divided into five ports, with four belonging to the *Lowestoff's* men, and one to the crew of the *Shoreham's Revenge*. PRO, ADM 43/6(1)
33. See Starkey, thesis, 189-90.
34. PRO, ADM 43/3(2), 6(1).
35. For the *Alexander*, see PRO, ADM 43/5(2) and Powell, *Bristol Privateers*, 137-9; for the *Southwell*, see ACL, Papers of the *Southwell* Privateer, 24651; for the *Saltash* and *Warren Gally* see Starkey, thesis, 189-90.
36. PRO, C 103/130. Richard Taunton to Thomas Hall, 27 October 1746.
37. Vaughan, *Voyages and Cruises*, 49.
38. PRO, C 103/130. Richard Taunton to Thomas Hall, 2 August 1746.
39. Declarations 8 November 1740, 25 September 1741. PRO, HCA 26/30, 31.
40. Declarations 29 June, 11 July, 16 October, 17 November 1744. PRO, HCA 26/22.
41. Declarations 25 September, 2 November, 18 September 1744. PRO, HCA 26/22.
42. Declarations 6 April, 23 March 1745. PRO, HCA 26/23.
43. The third vessel of the squadron, the *Prince George*, was lost in the early stages of the cruise. Having called in at Dartmouth in an unsuccessful search

for seamen 'the most melancholy accident' befell her, as, 'with double reif top-sails, no wind of consequence', she 'overset', and all but 20 of the 134 men on board were drowned. *Gentleman's Magazine*, XV (1745), 418.

44. For a contemporary narrative account of the *Royal Family* venture, see Vaughan, *Voyages and Cruises*.

45. In 1748, the *Duke of Beaufort*, of 130 tons burthen and 100 men, and the 450-ton, 250-man *Princess of Orange* were set forth by the group. Declarations 8, 29 February 1748. PRO HCA 26/26.

46. Declarations 15 March 1746. PRO, HCA 26/24. William Belchier, John Casamajor, Valens Comyn, Edward Ironside, Israel Jalabert, Parnell Nevill and James Talbot were the 'sole owners' of the squadron, and agents for the project, according to the head money claim for the *Glorioso*. PRO, ADM 43/13(2). However, Richard Taunton's correspondence with Thomas Hall makes it clear that there were other owners, whose interests were represented by these seven 'directors' of the venture. PRO, C 103/130.

47. PRO, C 103/130. Richard Taunton to Thomas Hall, 8 November 1746.

48. Declaration 3 March 1747. PRO, HCA 26/25.

49. The 'Book of Rates' for the *Royal Family*'s second cruise, together with the Articles of Agreement, are to be found in PRO, ADM 43/13(2). See Appendix 6.

50. *Penny London Post, or Morning Advertiser*, 2 April 1746.

51. The details in this section are derived from Richard Taunton's correspondence with Thomas Hall, 1745–1747. PRO, C 103/130.

52. Swanson, 'Profitability of Privateering', and 'Privateering and Imperial Warfare'.

53. Declarations 18 April 1744. PRO, HCA 25/30, 31. The Articles of Agreement dated 17 April and 21 May 1744 are to be found in PRO, ADM 43/10.

54. PRO, HCA 32/102(1), 113(1), 127(1), 143(1).

55. Damer Powell, *Bristol Privateers*, 143-4. That the *Constantine* took prizes on 'her trading voyages, without cruising' suggests that she may have operated as an 'armed trading vessel' in 1747 and 1748.

56. Declarations 28 March 1745, 27 January 1748, 23 February 1747. PRO, HCA 26/23, 26, 25. I am indebted to Maurice Schofield for providing me with details of the voyages of these vessels, drawn from the Naval Office Shipping Lists and the Liverpool Plantation Registers.

57. Raban, 'War and Trade', 145-8.

58. Declarations 19 August 1747, 9 July 1745. PRO, HCA 26/25, 23. See Davis, *Shipping Industry*, 63.

59. Declarations 31 August 1739, 14 June 1744. PRO, HCA 26/29, 4.

60. Declarations 5 January 1741, 19 October 1744. PRO, HCA 26/30, 22.

61. Vaughan, *Voyages and Cruises*.

62. Alban Fraser, *Spain and the West Country*, 244.

63. Only 14 'letters of marque' are identified by Damer Powell, *Bristol Privateers*, 135-83.
64. *Williamson's Liverpool Memorandum Book* (1753), quoted in Williams, *Liverpool Privateers*, 37-8.
65. Maurice Schofield kindly provided this information, which is derived from the Naval Office Shipping Lists and the Liverpool Plantation Registers. The destination of a number of vessels is uncertain; moreover, some of those cited may have been engaged in 'cruising voyages'.
66. Declarations 25 April 1747, 27 November 1746. PRO, HCA 26/25, 24. For the *George Dogger* see also PRO, ADM 43/9.
67. Declaration 18 April 1744. PRO, HCA 26/4. The bail for this venture was provided by the Customs Commissioners. See PRO, HCA 25/31. The *Princess Mary* was commissioned against Spain in 1741. Declaration 4 June 1741. PRO, HCA 26/31. For the *Amelia*, see note 19.
68. PRO, HCA 26/4, 32.
69. Davies, *Letters from Hudson's Bay*, 335-41.
70. Wilson, *Great Company*, I, 326-7.
71. Hardy, *Register of Ships*, I. At this time, a typical Indiaman would have a lifespan of four voyages.
72. See Sutherland, *London Merchant*, 111-12.
73. Declarations 4 December 1744, 2 July 1747. PRO, HCA 26/22, 25.
74. Figures published in the *Whitehall Evening Post* in April 1748 suggest that 2,528 prizes were taken between 1745 and 1748, with 1,462 falling to the King's ships and 1,066 seized by privateers. See Damer Powell, *Bristol Privateers*, 137.
75. PRO, HCA 30/774, 775. These lists have been analysed by Meyer, dissertation, 271-96.
76. British colonial privateers enjoyed more success in the Anglo-Spanish War, engaging in 144 prize actions in the Caribbean and North American waters during the 1739-1743 phase of the conflict. See Swanson, 'Privateering and Imperial Warfare', 374.
77. PRO, HCA 34/31. See Damer Powell, *Bristol Privateers*, 143-4.
78. Declaration 8 May 1741. PRO, HCA 26/30. PRO, HCA 34/31.
79. The *Mary of Bilboa* was 140 tons burthen with an 11-strong crew; her hull had an appraised value of £599 14s, while her tackle was worth £114 5s 2d. PRO, HCA 32/160(3).
80. Declaration 4 June 1741. PRO, HCA 25/28. PRO, HCA 32/113(1).
81. PRO, HCA 32/138.
82. Declaration 25 September 1741. PRO, HCA 26/31. PRO, HCA 32/138.
83. Meyer, dissertation, 295-6.
84. In addition, bounty payments totalling £5,150 were made to privateering venturers in the North American colonies in respect of 17 enemy *corsaires* taken by colonial privateers. PRO, ADM 43/2-13.
85. PRO, HCA 34/37.

86. For more detail on Channel Island captors and their prizes, see Jamieson, 'Return to Privateering', 148-51, and Raban, 'War and Trade'.

87. The tonnage figures are taken from declarations dated 25 February 1746, 28 November 1744, 29 September 1747. PRO, HCA 26/24, 22, 26. Crew sizes are derived from the head money vouchers. PRO, ADM 43/6(2), 10, 12.

88. PRO, HCA 34/33, 35. See also Raban, 'War and Trade', 147.

89. See note 20. The *Eagle's* declaration was dated 7 May 1744, and the *Swift's* 4 April 1744. See PRO, HCA 25/31, 26/4, and ADM 43/9, 10, 3(1).

90. PRO, ADM 43/3(1), 5(1), 9, 10. The profits of four of these ventures were to be divided into two parts, one owned by the promoters with the other belonging to the ship's company. In the case of the *Dover*, however, the crew owned five-eighths of the net proceeds.

91. PRO, HCA 32/139.

92. PRO, HCA 32/154.

93. *Penny London Post, or Morning Advertiser*, 21 January 1745. Apparently, the rewards accruing from smuggling prizes were somewhat limited. Thus, in July 1745, Bazely petitioned the Lords of the Treasury, setting forth 'his services in taking several notorious smuggling vessels going to France'; on learning that he was 'entitled to only a third of the said services' he pleaded for the 'King's share and other encouragement to provide sufficient recompense for himself and owners'. *Calendar of Treasury Books and Papers* (HMSO, 1903), V (1742-1745), 704.

94. Declarations 27 April, 14 June 1744. PRO, HCA 26/4, 4. The *Warren Gally* had been commissioned as an 'armed trading vessel' on 31 August 1739, PRO, HCA 26/29. In July 1745, both vessels were re-commissioned under the same ownership of 'Christopher and John Huddy, and Banks & Co'. PRO, HCA 26/23.

95. PRO, HCA 32/116(1).

96. The *Ceres* was originally the *Young Ceres* privateer of Dartmouth, seized by the French man-of-war *Mercury*. She was declared a re-capture and restored to her 'real, true & sole proprietors'—Israel Jalabert, Parnell Nevill, Arthur Holdsworth, Nathaniel Terry, William Cowell and Robert Sparke—in May 1746. PRO, HCA 32/100(1).

97. PRO, HCA 32/116(1).

98. PRO, HCA 32/104(2).

99. PRO, HCA 32/155.

100. Declarations 2 April, 11 July 1744. PRO, HCA 26/4, 22.

101. Declarations 18 May 1744. PRO, HCA 26/4, 32.

102. Declarations 30 April 1744. PRO, HCA 26/4, 32. The 'Conditions, Articles & Rules to be observed on board the *Adventure*' also applied to the *Norton*. PRO, ADM 43/3(2).

103. Declarations 4 October 1744, 9 July 1744, 16 July 1746, 26 September 1744. PRO, HCA 26/22, [25/31], 24, 22.

104. J. G. Clark, *La Rochelle and the Atlantic Economy during the Eighteenth Century* (Johns Hopkins UP, 1981) 154.
105. PRO, HCA 32/102(1).
106. PRO, HCA 32/154.
107. PRO, HCA 32/151(1).
108. For instance, see PRO, HCA 32/127(1), 127(2), 130(1).
109. For instance, the pages of the *Country Journal, or the Craftsman* and the *Penny London Post, or the Morning Advertiser* are peppered with news of the seizures of valuable West Indiamen. Damer Powell's account, based largely upon the *Bristol Oracle and County Advertiser*, contains numerous references to rich 'Martinico' prizes. *Bristol Privateers*, 135-83.
110. DRO, 1032 F/Z 7. Deposition of Arthur Holdsworth in relation to a Chancery suit brought by Mary Southcote in 1750.
111. PRO, HCA 32/103(3), 95(1), 124. The *Ceres* was worth an estimated £30,000 according to the *Country Journal, or Craftsman*, 19 May 1744.
112. Declaration 2 November 1744. PRO, HCA 26/22. The prize papers are to be found in PRO, HCA 32/104(1).
113. PRO, HCA 32/130(2).
114. PRO, HCA 32/18(1).
115. PRO, HCA 32/156.
116. Damer Powell, *Bristol Privateers*, 153.
117. Damer Powell, *Bristol Privateers*, 157.
118. Declaration 6 May 1745. PRO, HCA 25/34. Damer Powell, *Bristol Privateers*, 143.
119. PRO, HCA 32/105(1); ADM 43/3(2).
120. Vaughan, *Voyages and Cruises*, xlii-xliv.
121. Damer Powell, *Bristol Privateers*, 140.
122. PRO, HCA 32/154.
123. *Penny London Post, or Morning Chronicle*, 6 March 1745; Damer Powell, *Bristol Privateers*, 163.
124. Vaughan, *Voyages and Cruises*, 136.
125. PRO, ADM 43/3(1); PRO, HCA 32/94(1), 97(2), 98(3), 106, 157(1); Vaughan, *Voyages and Cruises*, xxviii-xxxi, 48-54; and Powell, *Bristol Privateers*, 163-4.
126. *Gentleman's Magazine*, XV (1745), 418-9 and 428-9; Vaughan, *Voyages and Cruises*, xxxiv-xxxv; see P. L. Ford, 'List of some Briefs in Appeal Causes' *Massachusetts Historical Society Proceedings*, V (1888-89), 90-1, for brief details of the appeal case heard in respect of the *Marquis D'Antin*.
127. *Bristol Oracle*, 10 August 1745, quoted in Damer Powell, *Bristol Privateers*, 165.
128. PRO, C 103/130. Richard Taunton to Thomas Hall, 13 October 1744, 28 January 1745, 26 August 1747.
129. PRO, ADM 43/5(2); *Penny London Post, or Morning Advertiser* 25, 28 April 1746; Damer Powell, *Bristol Privateers*, 137-9.

130. PRO, C 103/130. Richard Taunton to Thomas Hall, 9 January 1748.

131. PRO, ADM 43/13(2); Vaughan, *Voyages and Cruises*, xlii-xliv, 150-97; see E. C. Thomas, 'Captain Buckle and the Capture of the *Glorioso' Mariner's Mirror*, 68 (1982), 49-56, for an account of the action from a naval perspective.

132. PRO, ADM 43/5(1). It is clear from different sources that other men-of-war were taken, though no claim was lodged for head money. The *Ceres*, for instance, was re-captured by the *Saltash* and the *Warren Gally*, whose agent neglected to submit a claim. See PRO, HCA 32/139. Similarly, the *Nuestra Senora de Gratia Dindester*, a Spanish frigate, did not generate bounty money for the venturers engaged in her captor, the *Garland*. See PRO, HCA 32/139.

133. PRO, ADM 43/3(1), 6(1). For the *Tyger's* battle with *El Venzidor*, and her joint-capture of the 217-man *Nuestra Senora Vegonia* of Bilbao, with the *Tygress*, see Damer Powell, *Bristol Privateers*, 168.

134. Declaration 30 June 1747. PRO, HCA 26/25.

135. Declarations 20 April 1744, 21 August 1746. PRO, HCA 26/4, 24.

136. PRO, HCA 34/32.

137. PRO, ADM 43/9.

138. Raban, 'War and Trade', 147.

139. Declarations 22 December 1744, 8 May 1741. PRO, HCA 26/22, 30.

140. PRO, ADM 43/11(2).

141. PRO, HCA 32/113(1), 34/34.

142. PRO, HCA 32/133.

143. Andrews, *Colonial Period*, IV, 222-71.

144. PRO, ADM 43/5(1).

145. Williams, *Liverpool Privateers*, 48-9.

146. PRO, HCA 32/102(1), 113(1), 127(1), 143(1).

147. Declaration 29 May 1744. PRO, HCA 26/4, 32. Damer Powell, *Bristol Privateers*, 154-5.

148. Damer Powell, *Bristol Privateers*, 143-4.

149. Declaration 15 June 1742. PRO, HCA 26/31. The *Ruby* was commissioned against France in April 1744, Captain Robert Saunders declaring that his company was to be 240 strong. PRO, HCA 26/4. Prizes sentences. PRO, HCA 34/32.

150. Declarations 27 August 1744, 25 November 1743. PRO, HCA 25/31, 26/31. Damer Powell, *Bristol Privateers*, 147, 161-2. Prize sentences. PRO, HCA 34/32

Plate 2

'Good Success to the King William Privateer'

Motif drawn on the Articles of Agreement pertaining to the *King William* of Bristol, 21 May 1744

(PRO, ADM 41/10. Reproduced by permission of the Public Record Office)

Plate 3

Views of the *Duke of Bedford* Privateer

Launched at Bristol in April 1741, the *Duke of Bedford* was a purpose-built private ship-of-war of 300 tons burthen, 28 guns and 200 men (Reproduced by permission of the City of Bristol Museum and Art Gallery)

Plate 5

The Capture of the *Glorioso*, 1747

Charles Brooking's painting depicts the engagement of the Spanish man-of-war *Glorioso*, 74 guns, with HMS *Russell*, HMS *Dartmouth*, and the *Royal Family*, private ships-of-war. In the foreground, the *Glorioso* (right) fires at the *Russell*, while, to the rear, the *Dartmouth* has exploded and is about to sink. To the left, the private man-of-war *King George* lies shattered after chasing and engaging the Spaniard for over seven hours, with the assistance of her consorts, seen here in the background.

A new advantageous Plan of PRIVATEERING.

For a SIX MONTHS CRUIZE.

All Gentlemen *Seamen* and Able *Landmen,*

WHO delight in the Music of Great-Guns, and distressing the Enemies of Great-Britain, have now a fine Opportunity of making their Fortunes, by entering on Board The MARS PRIVATEER, Just built for that Purpose, and now lying in the Harbour of TEINGMOUTH, allowed to be one of the finest Vessels in England, she measures 300 Tons, mounts 20 Guns, 12-pounders, and Two 6-pounders, on one Deck; Twelve Brass Guns, 4-pounders, on the Gunnels, on Carriages, Two Brass 3-pounders in each Top, besides Swivels, Cohorns, and every necessary Implement of War, with excellent Accommodations for 140 Men, who will be entirely sheltered, her Sides being filled on the Stocks in such a Manner as to be shot-proof.

Commanded by WILLIAM SCOTT, Who has already been remarkably successful in the last Privateer he commanded; and for Encouragement, every Seaman shall have Eight Shares of Prize Money, with Liberty to sell Four Shares, at Forty Shillings per Month, to the Proprietors of the Privateer, so that every Seaman will have Forty Shillings per Month paid Monthly, and Four Shares of Prize Money good during the Six Months; Ordinary Seamen and Able Landmen, and Scout Boys, Thirty Shillings per Month, and Three Shares good; Small Boys in Proportion, with one Month's Advance, and Two Shillings per Day for their Work before sailing, and no Deduction out of their Prize Money for Outfits. Apply to Captain SCOTT, on Board the Vessel; Mr ANDREW CAUSE, at the London Inn, in Newton-Bushel; or Mr. MANNING, Sail-maker, Teingmouth.

。 This Vessel is Cutter built, Brig rigg'd, and will sail for Guernsey in Three Weeks; Such Able Seamen, &c. as are willing to make their Fortunes, are requested to make Application to Capt. SCOTT, on board the Vessel, on or before that Time, where they will meet Encouragement.

Exeter, Feb. 16, 1780.

Wanted,—TWO FRENCH HORNS.

Plate 6
'A New Advantageous Plan of Privateering'
Recruitment Notice for the *Mars*, a private ship-of-war belonging to Guernsey, but fitted out at Teignmouth. The share commutation system typical of Channel Island commerce-raiding enterprise applied in this venture.
(*Exeter Flying Post*, 18 February 1780. Reproduced by permission of the West Country Studies Library, Exeter)

WHEREAS an Act of Mutiny and Piracy was committed on the High Seas in Latitude 43° : 00', and Longitude 33° : 00' West, on the 20th Day of March last, by Part of the Crew of the King George Private Ship of War, Joseph Clapp, Commander, by feizing of the Arms, confining the Captain and moft of the Officers in Irons, and taking on themfelves the Command of faid Veffel, with which they proceeded to the North Weft Coaft of Ireland, where, on the 2d Day of April Inft. the undermentioned Perfons being the chief Ringleaders of the Mutiny and Piracy aforefaid, hoifted out the Cutter, in which they made their Efcape to the Shore, taking with them eight Pair of Piftols, four Mufquets, and three Cutlaffes, with feveral Cartouch Boxes filled with Ammunition. ——In Order to the apprehending the faid attrocious Offenders, and bringing them to public Juftice, the Committee of the Reprifal Affociation do hereby offer a Reward of TEN GUINEAS to be paid on the apprehending of John Rollins, Mafter of faid Veffel, and FIVE GUINEAS for each of the other undermentioned Perfons, being Able Seamen, which Reward will be paid by Jofeph Squire, Merchant, in Plymouth, and Agent for the faid Affociation; or by applying to Robert Wells, Efq; at the Reprifal Affociation Office, London.

DESCRIPTIONS.

JOHN ROLLINS, aged 50, 5 Feet 6 Inches high, wears his own Hair very fhort, his Eyes much funk in his Head, a bad Set of Teeth, chews much Tobacco, and greatly given to Liquor; the Middle Finger of his Right Hand fwelled and ftiff, and ftoops as he walks; Had on when he left the Ship an old Sky-blue Coat, dark-blue Waiftcoat, Black ftriped Breeches, and Naval Uniform Hat.

JAMES ANDERSON, alias WRIGHT, aged 30, 5 Feet 3 Inches high, a round-fhouldered thick-fet Man, wears his own fhort Hair, weak watry Eyes, fhort Neck, chubby, and his Dialect rather Scotch.

JOHN SCOTT, aged 30, 5 Feet 7 Inches high, wears his own Black Hair curled, a fallow Complexion, Black Eyes, a good Set of Teeth, ftoops as he walks, but a well made, ftout, active Man.

JAMES M'LAUGHLAN, aged 26, 5 Feet 6 Inches high, wears his fhort Black Hair, a fwarthy Complexion, and a confined follen Countenance, his Nofe a little awry, and his Face freckled.

JOHN JOHNSON, aged 22, 5 Feet 9 Inches high, wears his own brown Hair, his Face pock-marked and wreckled, chews much Tobacco, and addicted greatly to Liquor; is a ftout well-made Man, and was born at Warrington, in Lancafhire.

WILLIAM DAVIS, aged 23, 5 Feet 8 Inches high, wears his own brown Hair tied behind, has a large chubby Head, and fullen Countenance; very round-fhouldered, and was born at Clovelly, Devon.

WALTER DOYLE, aged 21, 5 Feet 5 Inches high, wears his own light-brown Hair, fair Complexion, thin in the Face, flightly made, and born in North Shields.

JOHN FIN, a Negroe, born at Barbadoes, aged 25, 5 Feet 6 Inches high, bad Legs and Feet, and knock-kneed; fpeaks good Englifh, Portuguefe, and fome French, carried away by the aforementioned People againft his Inclination.

Plate 7

'Wanted!'

Rewards offered for the apprehension of Mutineers from the *King George*, a private ship-of-war belonging to the 'Reprisal Association' of London.

(*Exeter Flying Post*, 23 April 1779. Reproduced by permission of the West Country Studies Library, Exeter)

Plate 8

The *Pearl* taking the *Don Carlos*, 1782

Nicholas Pocock's sketch of the seizure of the *Don Carlos*, a Spanish privateer of 16 guns and 120 men, by the Bristol private ship-of-war *Pearl* in March 1782.

(Reproduced by permission of the City of Bristol Museum and Art Gallery)

Seven

1756–1762

'Small Ships, Vessels, or Boats, being, or pretending to be, English Privateers'

British maritime power was of paramount importance in the Seven Years' War. In true Mahanian fashion, control of the sea was instrumental to the decisive victories secured in North America, the West Indies and the Indian sub-continent. Such an outcome appeared unlikely at first as the loss of Minorca brought disgrace to the Navy; thereafter, the imposition of an increasingly effective blockade on France's Atlantic ports restricted the enemy's fleets, laying the foundations for the triumphant actions at Lagos and Quiberon Bay. In the colonies, the Navy's ascendancy manifested itself in the amphibious success at Quebec and in the seizure of the sugar islands of Guadeloupe and Martinique, while the humiliation of Spain at Florida and Manila confirmed Britain's emergence as the dominant imperial power.[1]

In a marked and unprecedented way, the course of the 1756–1763 naval war conditioned the scale and character of the British privateering business. As the Navy's initial uncertainty gave way to a growing authority in 1757 and 1758, and complete domination with the 'year of victories' in 1759, so the shipping and trade of France, the target of commerce-raiding activity, was progressively swept from the seas. In accordance with these broad contours, British privateering enterprise flourished in the opening stages of the war, with large numbers of private men-of-war set forth to feed on a relatively abundant prey; this, in itself, reduced the long-term prospects for the predatory force, and incentives diminished further as the close naval blockade and colonial losses further inhibited French overseas trade. In such unfavourable circumstances, privateering entrepreneurs tended to divert their resources into trading operations, a shift signalled by the preponderance of 'letters of marque' in the much reduced commissioned fleet of the 1759–1761 period, a trend that was only partially reversed by the entry of Spain into the war in January 1762. Though such a clear inverse relationship between naval strength and privateering activity was evident at other times in the century, it was expressed in its most extreme form in the Seven Years' War.

The nature of privateering enterprise, and commerce-raiding activity in general, was further influenced by the diplomatic course of the 1756–1763 conflict as Britain adopted an increasingly aggressive attitude to the question of neutral trade with belligerent powers. This issue was nominally governed by a series of bi-lateral treaties entered into by the European maritime states in the mid-seventeenth century. However, the passing of a century witnessed the expansion of international trade and shipping, together with marked colonial development, factors which altered the fundamental power relations upon which these agreements were based, rendering them inadequate and inappropriate. In particular, the concept of 'free ships, free goods', embodied in the 1674 Anglo-Dutch Marine Treaty, and implied in English pacts with Denmark, Spain and Sweden, proved wholly incompatible with the commercial and military realities of the mid-eighteenth century. Whereas a neutral's right to carry belligerents' cargoes—excluding contraband goods—had been indisputable and relatively insignificant in the 1660s and 1670s, it was viewed quite differently in the 1740s and 1750s as the lucrative trade of the French Caribbean, which was restricted to French bottoms in peacetime, was increasingly conveyed in neutral holds during wartime. The process of re-defining this right began in the Austrian Succession War with a broader and more subjective interpretation of contraband goods; in the Seven Years' War, Britain took matters a stage further, dictating that neutrals might not engage legitimately in any trade with a belligerent that was normally closed to them by the operation of Navigation Laws.[2]

Essentially, the adoption of this 'Rule of the War of 1756' exposed French colonial goods shipped under a neutral flag to arrest and condemnation. Naturally, it acted as a stimulus to commerce-raiding activity—naval and private—in greatly broadening the range of prize-taking opportunities. It held significant ramifications for the privateering business in particular, for neutral shipping tended to rely on documentary rather than military defences, and with this paper immunity to seizure torn up, such vessels were vulnerable to the attentions of the most diminutive assailant. Thus, 'Channel' privateering was given fresh impetus by the legal and diplomatic developments of 1756, though restrictions were placed on this form of enterprise as the war proceeded. Inevitably, the neutral powers were incensed at Britain's hostile attitude to their lucrative wartime carrying trade, and further alienated by the blind eye which the British law courts apparently turned to the depredations allegedly committed in the search for prize. In a situation of growing diplomatic tension, with the Dutch threatening to form an anti-British coalition of neutrals, Pitt's administration felt obliged to limit the activities of the private ships-of-war it had tacitly encouraged—via the law courts— in the early stages of the war.[3] Accordingly, the Privateers' Act of June 1759 imposed restrictions on the issue of letters of marque; thus, owners of commissioned vessels could no longer offer themselves as guarantors of the conduct of their own ventures, commanders were required to provide more detailed declarations in the Prize Court as to the characteristics of their vessels, and, most significantly, commissions granted for vessels of less than 100 tons burthen, with fewer than twelve four-pound guns and 40 men, were deemed null and void from 1 June 1759, while the future issue of letters of marque for such vessels was to be obligatory no longer, but at the discretion of the Lords of the Admiralty.[4]

In focusing upon the 'small ships, Vessels, or Boats, being, or pretending to be, English privateers', the legislation implicitly recognised the value of the 'Channel' arm of the privateering business, but it also inferred that an element of this enterprise was undertaken by unlicensed vessels acting as private men-of-war. This concurs with the 'repeated complaints of . . . divers outrageous Acts of Piracy and Robbery' lodged by the neutral states in the early stages of the war, as their vessels were harassed by all manner of craft—from row-boats and fishing shallops to men-of-war—particularly in the English Channel.[5] Thus, in stimulating the attack on neutral trade, the government effectively encouraged irregular commerce-raiding activity; the 1759 Act, therefore, was a corrective measure designed to placate the neutral powers by restricting the unbridled assault on their shipping. Its timing, however, suggests that it was little more than a gesture, for the vitality of the prize war was rapidly dissipating by mid-1759. Moreover, in addressing the captors and not the courts, the administration was treating the symptoms rather than the cause of a problem that was to surface again in the American Revolutionary War.

Commerce-raiding thus assumed a central position in the Seven Years' War. As an expression of Britain's growing sea power, it jeopardised her relations with the neutral maritime states as well as sapping the enemy's commercial strength. The British privateering business was both a feature and a function of this naval ascendancy, adding to the damage inflicted upon Franco-Spanish trade, yet dependent ultimately for its viability on the abundance of prospective targets, a stimulus which varied with the naval and diplomatic course of the conflict. The scale and character of this private enterprise was therefore inextricably linked with the fluctuating fortunes of the public war.

I

The Royal Proclamation and Declaration of 17 May 1756 marked the formal commencement of the Anglo-French conflict, although hostilities had already begun at sea and in the North American colonies. Reprisals against French trade and shipping were authorised by Act of Parliament which laid down procedures for the issue of letters of marque and the adjudication of captured property. Essentially, this re-iterated the provisions of the 1744 Prize Act, though additional clauses relating to the powers of prize agents and shipboard discipline were included.[6] On 8 June, the Admiralty Office gave notice that warrants for the granting of letters of marque were available,[7] and on 10 June the first commissions were issued in the High Court of Admiralty. The declaration of war against Spain on 1 January 1762 obliged Parliament to pass a further Prize Act,[8] and from 9 January to 15 November 1762 letters of marque permitting reprisals against the sea-borne property of 'France and Spain' were issued. A total of 2,105 licences were granted in the High Court of Admiralty during the war, authorising the commerce-raiding activities of some 1,679 vessels. These ventures were mounted from 75 British ports and overseas bases, as indicated in Table 13.

Table 13

Commissioned Vessels by Region, 1756-1762

Region	Number of commissions	Actual vessels	Average tonnage
London	811	648	312.5
Bristol	344	253	187.5
Liverpool	331	246	190.2
Channel Is — Alderney (6) Guernsey (76) Jersey (46)	158	128	77.1
E England — Boston (1) Bridlington (1) Gainsborough (1) Hull (12) Ipswich (2) Leeds (1) Lynn (7) Newcastle (6) Scarborough (19) South Shields (1) Stockton (1) Sunderland (3) Whitby (6) Yarmouth (11) York (1)	76	73	286
SE England — Chichester (1) Cowes (5) Deal (1) Dover (32) Earl Brown (2) Folkestone (35) Gosport (1) Hastings (20) Portsmouth (3) Rochester (1) Rye (4) Sandwich (9) Shoreham (2)	144	116	82.7
SW England — Appledore (1) Barnstaple (1) Bideford (2) Dartmouth (3) Exeter (20) Falmouth (2) Lyme (1) Marazion (1) Mount's Bay (1) Plymouth (4) Poole (18) St Olave (1) Teignmouth (3) Topsham (1) Upwey (1) Weymouth (2)	72	62	115.6
Wales & NW England — Chester (1) Lancaster (13) Whitehaven (14)	31	28	180.4
W Scotland — Glasgow (21) Greenock (1)	29	22	161.4
E Scotland — Aberdeen (1) Dundee (1) Edinburgh (5) Leith (2)	9	9	211.1
Ireland — Belfast (2) Cork (14) Dublin (21) Limerick (1) Londonderry (1) Newry (1)	44	40	174.8
Overseas Bases — Antigua (5) Barbados (2) Bermuda (4) Gibraltar (4) Jamaica (3) Leghorn (5) New York (3) Philadelphia (1) Quebec (1) St Christopher (2)	32	30	201.3
Port Unknown	24	24	205.5
	2105	1679	221.7

Figures in brackets denote actual vessels.
Source: PRO, HCA 25/38-55; HCA 26/5-12, 27-28.

Growth was apparent in the British privateering business in the Seven Years' War, with 1,679 vessels commissioned during the conflict, an increase of 488 on the 'input' into the 1739–1748 war. This was reflected in the expansion of total tonnage commissioned by some 91,000 tons over the two wars, despite a fall in mean vessel size from 235.8 to 221.7 tons burthen. That commissions were available for a shorter span of time in the later conflict, seven as opposed to nine years, serves to amplify the overall rise in privateering investment. Various factors explain this trend. France was the sole adversary for much of the war and, as the 1739–1748 conflict had illustrated, venturers perceived that prospects of gain were brighter when the target was French, rather than Spanish, sea-borne property; the spectacular successes of the previous conflict remained fresh in the memory of the mercantile community, encouraging further investment in commerce-raiding activity; the adoption of the 'Rule of the War of 1756' added to the range of targets, for neutral vessels carrying French produce were now liable to condemnation; and the renewed growth of British overseas trade in the 1740s and 1750s greatly stimulated the shipping industry,[9] increasing the supply of capital, vessels and seafarers for possible deployment in the privateering business.

This mid-century expansion in the commercial sector involved a marked regional diffusion in activity, as an increasing proportion of the rising volume of trade was handled in the outports.[10] Such de-centralisation was reflected in the distribution of the commissioned fleet in the Seven Years' War, with London's relative significance as a privateering base diminishing, despite an absolute growth in the capital's 'input', and a greater number of provincial ports engaging in the business. Thus, London's 648 licensed vessels represented 38.6 per cent of the national total, compared with an equivalent figure of nearly 50 per cent in the 1739-1748 war, while all the the regional groupings, excepting south-west England, expanded their privateering interests. Growth occurred in the major outports, as Liverpool venturers sent out 246 commissioned vessels, three times the port's 'input' in the Austrian Successsion War, Bristol nearly doubled its stake from 132 to 253 vessels over the two wars, and the Channel Islands—a 'major' outport in privateering terms—increased their interest from 85 to 128 vessels; it was also evident in the smaller harbours, as entrepreneurs from ports such as Cork, Folkestone and Scarborough, who had previously exhibited a minor involvement in the activity, expanded their privateering investments markedly in the Seven Years' War; and expansion was further apparent in that an unprecedented total of 75 ports engaged in the activity, with vessels belonging to bases such as Greenock, Lancaster and Marazion equipped with letters of marque for the first time.

If expansion and de-centralisation characterised the privateering business in the Seven Years' War, the intensity of commissioned activity varied considerably over the course of the conflict. This was clearly signalled by the uneven flow of letters of marque issued at Doctors' Commons. Thus, in the first 31 months of the war, down to the end of 1758, some 1,246 commissions were issued, a rate of 40.2 per month; over the next three years, however, a mere 514 licences were granted at an average of 14.3 per month, before a resurgence occurred in the final phase of the war with the issue of 345 commissions in 1762.

This pattern was related directly to the extent and perceived vulnerability of the prospective prey. Accordingly, privateering enterprise was at its most vigorous in the early stages of the war as venturers responded to the prize-taking potential afforded by a relatively extensive French mercantile fleet, and the perennial dream of encountering the valuable, unprotected vessels bound for home before hostilities had commenced; similarly, in 1762, the addition of Spanish commerce to the range of targets revived predatory ambitions, with investors predictably 'expecting great prizes in the beginning of the War'.[11] However, in the interim period from early in 1759 to the end of 1761, the incentive to fit out commissioned vessels was drastically reduced as French commerce was largely swept from the seas. In 1757 and 1758, for example, shipping activity virtually ceased at La Rochelle, while the 55 merchant ships fitted out at Nantes in 1756 had dwindled to just 11 by 1760 and six in 1761. Bordeaux's trade was similarly curtailed, the combined value of the port's colonial imports and exports declining from 30 million livres per year in 1753–1755 to under 8 million livres in 1758 and 1759, and less than 4 million livres in 1760; re-exports passing through Bordeaux fell even more precipitously, with less than 8,000 cwt of sugar handled annually from 1757 to 1761 compared with a yearly average of 300,000 cwt in the 1750–1756 period.[12]

Clearly, the ebb and flow of the war at sea was germane to the composition of the commissioned fleet in the 1756–1762 war. Thus, the sensitivity of privateering entrepreneurs to the vacillating scale of enemy commerce dictated that most commerce-raiding ventures were undertaken in the first three years of the conflict, prior to the collapse of French sea-borne trade, and in 1762, when Spanish commerce became liable to seizure. In these phases of the conflict, 'Channel' privateers and 'deep-water' private ships-of-war were the dominant forms of privateering enterprise, though 'letters of marque' were also set forth, mainly from the larger British ports. When prize-taking prospects declined with the demise of French shipping activity, trade emerged as the most promising option for the British mercantile community and, consequently, commissioned traders constituted the bulk of the much diminished privateering force from 1759 to 1761. This pattern of investment is plainly illustrated by Appendix 2, with 51 predatory ventures, requiring the labour of 3,731 privateersmen, launched in the opening month of the war, the rate of activity rising steadily to a peak of 96 vessels and 11,331 seafarers, in September 1757. From these heights— previously unscaled—the intensity of the commerce-raiding assault subsided fairly gently to the summer of 1759 when a precipitous decline set in. Throughout 1760 and 1761, interest in private men-of-war remained negligible, indicating that most of the 286 commissions issued in these years authorised the prize-taking endeavours of 'letters of marque'; a reversal of this trend was occasioned by the onset of the Anglo-Spanish war, with the level of commerce-raiding activity extending to 35 vessels and 3,641 privateersmen 'in commission' during April 1762.

Within the predatory arm of the privateering business, a resurgence was apparent in the 'Channel' form of enterprise. Relatively insignificant in the 1740s, small-scale ventures were set forth in increasing numbers in the Seven Years' War as speculators in various ports responded to the favourable conditions pertaining in the conflict, notably the prolonged enmity of France and the exposure to condemnation of all neutral-borne French property by the implementation of the 'Rule of the War of 1756'. The depth of this response is suggested by the letter of marque declarations; thus, as Table 14 shows, 256 commissioned vessels fell within the guidelines—under 100 tons burthen, with crews in the ratio of 2.5 tons per man or less—adopted in the 1759 Privateers' Act.

In absolute terms, the 'input' into the 'Channel' branch of the 1756–1762 privateering business exceeded the equivalent 1739–1748 measure by nearly 100 vessels. As in the 1740s, the Channel Islands and the ports of south-east England dominated this form of predatory enterprise, with venturers from London and Bristol, and a number of smaller bases, notably in the West Country, also investing in diminutive commerce-raiders. There was a changed order of significance, however, as the South East's stake in 'Channel' enterprise—embodied largely in vessels of 30 to 60 tons burthen, with crews of 25 to 50 men—superseded the Islanders' 'input' for the only time in the eighteenth century.

Table 14

'*Channel*' *Privateers by Region, 1756-1762*

Region	Vessels of 2.5 tons per man or less		Regional Total	% 'Channel'
	-49 tons	50-99 tons		
London	5	18	648	3.5
Bristol	4	16	253	7.9
Liverpool	2	3	246	2
Channel Is (3)	65	23	128	68.8
SE England (10)	69	31	116	86.2
SW England (8)	5	6	62	17.7
Ireland (3)	3	3	40	15
Overseas Bases (2)	1	2	30	10
	154	102		

Figures in brackets denote number of ports.
Source: PRO, HCA 25/38-55; HCA 26/5-12, 27-8.

Most of these craft, as Appendix 2 indicates, were operating during the first three years of the conflict when rates of activity were consistently higher, though average manning levels were somewhat lower, than those apparent in the 1744-1748 Anglo-French war. Again, some seasonality was evident as 'inputs' in 'Channel' enterprise climaxed in August 1758 at a level of 44 vessels and 1,435 seafarers, following upon a trough in the winter of 1757-1758. Yet in the summer of 1759 this pattern disintegrated, and 'Channel' privateering entered a prolonged slump; if this reflected the curtailment of enemy commercial activity evident at this juncture, it was also a consequence of the Privateers' Act which revoked letters of marque issued before 1 June 1759 for vessels of 99 tons burthen or less, manned by fewer than 40 seafarers, and made any future grant for such predators discretionary.[13]

In employing their discretion, the Lords of the Admiralty clearly sought to suppress the burgeoning commerce-raiding business of south-east ports such as Dover, Folkestone, Hastings and Rye. Not a single letter of marque was granted to 'Channel' venturers in this region after June 1759, inferring that it was they who had been responsible for the irregularities of which the Dutch and the other neutral states complained so bitterly. This may have been so, but the real focus of neutral anger was the 'tyranny' of the 'Rule of the War of 1756', and the proliferation of contentious commerce-raiding activity which it appears to have spawned. Neutral vessels, it was alleged, were subject to persistent visitation and search as they plied the English Channel; they were harassed by all manner of craft, including row-boats and fishing shallops carrying handfuls of men armed with clubs and pistols; frequently, ran the complaints, such searches resulted in the outright plunder of neutral property; moreover, even if the property was duly arrested and judged, it was subject to a highly partial process of law.[14]

Such indiscretions clearly reflected the British government's hardened attitude towards the rights of neutral traders. Precisely who perpetrated these depredations is rather obscure, however, due to the very nature of the alleged offences and the heated controversy they aroused. Yet in extending its control over the privateering forces already subject to regulation, it would seem that Pitt's administration was offering the 'Channel' privateering fleet as a sacrificial lamb to appease the Dutch and their neutral allies. Essentially, the prohibition of this form of enterprise was a convenient means of apportioning blame and appearing to take action without seriously undermining the 'Rule of the War of 1756' and the flotilla of uncommissioned plunderers it unleashed. In fact, the business activity most inhibited by the 1759 legislation was little different to that apparent in previous and subsequent conflicts. It comprised regularly organised and structured ventures, clearly distinct from the row-boats and other small craft 'pretending to be English privateers'; accordingly, owners and seafarers were related by properly engrossed articles of agreement, while extant muster rolls suggest that even relatively small privateering complements operated along orderly, hierarchical lines. For example, three typical 'Channel' privateers of Hastings and Rye were worked by the following companies:[15]

Eagle	Swallow	Two Henrys
(40 tons)	(45 tons)	(40 tons)
Captain	Captain	Captain
2 Lieutenants	Lieutenant	2 Lieutenants
Master	Master	Master
Gunner	Gunner	Gunner
Boatswain	Boatswain	Boatswain
9 Seamen	Surgeon	Doctor
	Carpenter	Linguister
	Master's mate	6 Seamen
	Linguister	
	16 Seamen	
15	25	14

Similar organisational traits were evident in the large 'Channel' component of the Channel Islands' commissioned fleet,[16] though in a peculiar local variation it was normally agreed that the seafarers could sell their allotted share in the prize fund to the *armateurs* in return for a monthly wage.[17] However, Their Lordships evidently viewed the predatory enterprise of the Islanders in a rather different light to the privateering endeavours of the men of Kent and Sussex. No less than 36 of the 50 discretionary letters of marque granted after June 1759 were taken out by Island *armateurs*,[18] suggesting, perhaps, that the reconnaissance function alluded to by local propagandists was deemed to be of some utility by the Admiralty.[19] The same conclusion was apparently reached in Paris, for in 1759 the French seriously considered invading and suppressing Jersey, though the scheme was never implemented.[20]

Channel Island venturers also engaged in more substantial undertakings during the Seven Years' War, setting forth 35 vessels of a 'deep-water' hue. While this represented over a quarter of the Islanders' commerce-raiding speculations, the centres of this branch of the privateering business remained London and Bristol. As Table 15 indicates, nearly two-thirds of the 222 'deep-water' craft commissioned at Doctors' Commons, including all but two of the 44 'privateers of force' recruiting 200 men or more, embarked from the Thames or Kingroad.[21]

Table 15

'Deep-Water' Private Ships-of-War by Region, 1756-1762

Region	Crew Size 40-99*	100-149	150-199	200+	Regional Total	% 'Deep-Water'
London	14	30	7	32	648	12.8
Bristol	10	36	6	10	253	24.5
Liverpool	0	8	4	0	246	4.9
Channel Is (2)	9	24	2	0	128	27.3
E England (2)	1	1	0	0	73	2.7
SE England (2)	2	0	0	0	116	1.7
SW England (6)	6	2	3	2	62	21
E Scotland (1)	0	1	0	0	9	11.1
Ireland (2)	1	3	4	0	40	20
Overseas Bases (1)	0	1	0	0	30	3.3
Port Unknown	1	2	0	0	24	12.5
	44	108	26	44		

* Vessels exceeding 99 tons burthen manned in the ratio of 2.5 tons per man or less.
Figures in brackets denote number of ports.
Source: PRO, HCA 25/38-55; HCA 26/5-12, 27-8.

Though the 'deep-water' branch of the commerce-raiding business was slightly more extensive than that commissioned in the 1740s, a clear decline in 'inputs' was evident in relative terms, for investment in privateering enterprise as a whole had increased considerably in the Seven Years' War. Within the sector, Bristol, Liverpool and the Channel Islands increased their stake, though Dartmouth's flirtation with large-scale predation was not repeated and Dover's privateering entrepreneurs concentrated their resources almost exclusively in 'Channel' privateers. A shift, moreover, was evident in the scale of ventures, with the number of crews of 150 men or more declining from 95 to 70 while lesser companies of 40 to 149 privateersmen were recruited for 152 vessels as against 122 in the Austrian Succession War. It would seem that 'deep-water' enterprise was increasingly manifesting itself in relatively small-scale units; accordingly, 'privateers of force'—the dynamic feature of the 1739-1748 commissioned fleet—were less prevalent, with major concentrations of privateering capital, in the fashion of the *Royal Family* squadron, not in evidence during the Seven Years' War.

Various factors contrived to produce this declining trend in the scale of operations. On the supply side, seafarers were relatively scarce in the 1756-1762 conflict, a manpower shortage caused by the increase in naval employment from 59,750 at the height of the 1739-1748 war to a peak of 84,797 in 1762, and signalled by the rise in the merchant seaman's wage to the unprecedented level of 70 shillings per month in the winter of 1757-1758.[22] If this rendered the enlistment of massive privateering crews ever more difficult, the character of their prospective prey also militated against the colossal ventures which had proved so effective in the 1740s. Spanish trade, for instance, was neutral until January 1762, and thus the valuable register-ships, which had helped stimulate the large-scale response of the previous war, were beyond the range of commerce-raiding speculators for much of the conflict. More significantly, incentives were further diminished by the decision of the French administration not to provide any direct protection, in the form of convoys, for the colonial trade. While this deterred shipowners from setting forth their vessels, passports were issued, permitting neutral shippers to participate in the carriage of supplies to the French Caribbean, and to return cargoes of sugar and other tropical goods to the European market.[23] At once less valuable and more difficult to prosecute, the neutral carrier was also susceptible to the attacks of less potent assailants; in these circumstances, the powerful combinations of predators—and large-scale ventures, in general—were becoming somewhat outmoded.

'Deep-water' enterprise was nevertheless a significant facet of the British privateering war. Indeed, as Appendix 2 suggests, this form of predation reached a new level of intensity in October 1757 when 70 ventures were 'in commission', engaging the services of 10,346 privateersmen. Activity rates declined during 1758 and 1759, however, as the Navy's preponderance in European waters and the seizure of Canada and Guadeloupe restricted France's trans-Atlantic commerce and severely curtailed the prize-taking opportunities facing 'deep-water' venturers. These fluctuating prospects were clearly reflected in Bristol's experience. Thus, in 1756, the 'zeal' of the city's merchants and shipowners 'produced a fleet of cruisers far exceeding anything attempted in previous wars';[24] yet by June 1759,

of 56 privateers fitted out at this port there is at this time but a single
one remaining at sea; the rest are either laid up or altering for
mercantile service.[25]

The diversion of investment away from commerce-raiding was widespread during the 1759–1761 stage of the war. In the privateering business,
this development resulted in the growing significance of 'letters of
marque' in these years; important in the opening phase of the conflict,
notwithstanding the extent of predatory operations, these merchantmen
constituted virtually the entire licensed fleet as prize-taking prospects
receded. Typically, various forms of 'war and trade' activity were
apparent, with the Mediterranean and the Caribbean the principal foci of
operations. Here, the essentially predatory 'cruise and voyage' ventures
were active, seeking prizes but also ready to load a cargo if conditions
favoured commerce. Indeed, the Mediterranean proved to be a most
productive station for the commissioned fleet, with London vessels such
as the *Deal Castle*, the *Reynolds* and the *Ruby* cruising to some effect in
the inland sea.[26] Epitomising this form of enterprise, the *Deal Castle* was
400 tons burthen, equipped with 22 carriage and swivel guns, and worked
by 108 seafarers—16 officers, 39 seamen, 43 landmen and 10 boys—in
her passage from London to Salerno, Naples and Leghorn. Monthly wages
were paid to the crew on a scale that ranged from the £8 received each
month by Captain Richard Harman to the 40 shillings earned by the
vessel's landmen. In agreeing 'to navigate and if need be fight the said
ship', the ship's company recognised the dual-purpose nature of the
venture; moreover, to encourage the predatory aspect of their bi-
employment the ship's articles laid down that the crew was entitled to a
quarter of the net proceeds of any prizes they might take.[27]

Similar ventures were launched from Bristol and Liverpool, though the
strong trans-Atlantic character of the trade of these west coast ports
dictated that the Americas, particularly the Caribbean, emerged as the
centre of their operations. Accordingly, the *Britannia* departed Kingroad
on a 'cruise and voyage' mission to Nevis and St Christopher in 1762
with 35 seamen, 15 part-seamen, 12 landmen, 5 boys and 21 officers and
specialists comprising her 88-strong crew. Fitted out as a 'deep-water'
private man-of-war with a declared complement of 280 men earlier in the
conflict,[28] this 450-ton vessel was clearly organised on 'war and trade'
lines, her crew being paid monthly wages—at rates some 25 per cent less
than the *Deal Castle*'s crew—and owning just one quarter of any prize
fund generated.[29] Such detail is lacking for other Bristol vessels, though

it is probable that craft like the *Constantine,* of 200 tons burthen and 80 men, and the 350-ton, 100-man *King George* were engaged in this dual-purpose form of commerce-raiding activity.[30] Liverpool's commissioned fleet also contained a number of vessels with declared tonnages and crew sizes—like the Jamaica-bound *Adventure,* of 270 tons burthen and 100 men and the 400-ton *Caesar,* also for Jamaica with 70 men aboard[31]—indicative of a 'cruise and voyage' intent.

'Armed trading vessels', however, appear to have formed a more important part of the commissioned enterprise of both ports. Bristol's licensed fleet included 62 vessels with 'deep-water' credentials, a further 20 archetypal 'Channel' privateers and a limited number of 'cruise and voyage' ventures; it would seem, therefore, that a residual of perhaps one half—quite possibly more—of the port's 253 commissioned vessels was principally concerned with trading operations. Certainly, as a proportion of the port's privateering 'input', these 'armed traders' became more important as the war progressed and commercial prospects improved, with vessels able to embark, like the *Jupiter,* for the seized territory of Guadeloupe as well as more familiar destinations like Africa, Jamaica, Maryland and Newfoundland.[32] 'Armed traders' represented a much larger element of Liverpool's interest in the privateering business. While 12 craft with crews of at least 100 men embarked from the Mersey on 'cruising voyages' and 'deep-water' cruises, and five exhibited the tonnage and manning characteristics of the 'Channel' predator, the remaining 235 Liverpool vessels embarked for specific destinations in the manner of the armed merchantman. Without doubt, a number of the more heavily manned of these vessels—70- and 60-strong crews were to be enlisted for 12 craft burthen between 200 and 400 tons—were despatched with more than a passing interest in commerce-raiding; yet, it is probable that over 200 of Liverpool's licensed ventures were predominantly concerned with the carriage of goods. Africa was the destination most commonly cited in the Liverpool Plantation Registers, as 129 of the port's commissioned vessels—generally of 100 to 150 tons burthen, with companies of 30 or 40 men—headed for the Guinea Coast during the course of the war. If this suggests the port's expanding interests in the slave trade—only 37 commissioned vessels had cleared for Africa in the 1739-1748 conflict—the despatch of 69 vessels for the Caribbean indicates the significance of the West India trade; though most sailed for Jamaica and Barbados, the departure of 15 vessels for Guadeloupe and, in 1762, the embarkation of the *Sarah* for Martinique and the *Liver* for Havana, reflects the commercial advantages accruing from territorial conquest. Liverpool's armed merchantmen also set forth for mainland North America, especially for Virginia, Maryland and South Carolina, while four departed for European destinations—Barcelona, Madeira, Riga and the 'Mediterranean'.

Trade was the primary function of vessels commissioned by merchants resident in other outports in the Seven Years' War. In the North West, 10 of Lancaster's licensed vessels were engaged in the slave trade, and another four were West Indiamen; Whitehaven's vessels were largely deployed in the Virginia trade, though five were slavers and the *Richmond*, of 250 tons burthen and 60 men, was set out on a nine months' cruise in 1756;[33] meanwhile, the *Black Prince*, the only Chester ship to sail with a letter of marque, was taken by two French men-of-war as she sought a cargo of slaves in Angola. West Country vessels were engaged in more temperate trades, as Bideford, Dartmouth and Plymouth venturers took out commissions for their Newfoundlandmen and the Exeter Whale Fishery Company considered licensing the *Exeter* for her 1759 voyage to the Davis Straits.[34] Merchants in the ports of eastern England were similarly preoccupied with commerce, though the focus of their enterprise was London and the carriage thereto of bulk cargoes of coal and timber coastwise and across the North Sea in commissioned vessels of 300 to 500 tons burthen and crews which rarely exceeded 40 men. 'Armed traders' were predominant in the commissioned fleets of Scottish ports,[35] while even the Channel Islanders took out letters of marque for eight vessels despatched on commercial voyages to America, the West Indies and Oporto.[36]

The precise extent of London's interest in 'armed trading vessels' is uncertain, though it may be presumed—only 104 of the capital's 648 licensed vessels fell within the 'Channel' or 'deep-water' parameters—that a greater proportion of the port's shipping and maritime labour was deployed in 'letters of marque' than in private men-of-war, particularly as the conflict proceeded and the enemy's trade diminished. Characteristically, some of these resources were invested in the 'specialist vessels' operated from the Thames by the chartered trading companies. In the Seven Years' War, 87 of these craft sailed with letters of marque; thus, when commissions became available in June 1756, Charles Hay appeared at the Admiralty Court to offer bail and make declarations regarding four vessels owned by the Hudson's Bay Company—the *Hudson's Bay, Old Prince Rupert, Prince Rupert* and *Seahorse*—then at sea bound from London to the Bay.[37] A further eight letters of marque were taken out for these and two other Company-owned vessels, the *New Prince Rupert* and the *King George*, during the course of the war, the Company's ships ranging in size from the *Hudson's Bay*, of 130 tons burthen and 34 men, to the *King George*, a 'brig-built ship with a Lyon's Head and black, yellow and red sides' of 220 tons burthen and a complement of 48 men.[38] Larger vessels were hired by the East India Company and employed in the trade with the Orient. All but four of the 91 ships so engaged during the 1756–1762 war sailed for India and China with letters of marque,[39] the majority conforming to the standard description of 499 tons and 99 men adopted in the mid-eighteenth century. A number, however, exceeded this chartered tonnage figure, a sign that the 'shipping interest' was supplying more substantial vessels for the Company's use. The *Shaftesbury*, of 600 tons burthen, and the 690-ton *Albion* exemplify this move,[40] while the deployment of the *Earl Temple* and the *Pitt*, prize vessels of 850 and 800 tons burthen,[41] further suggests that the Company was keen to expand the carrying capacity of its vessels.

Such vessels added to the diversity of the privateering business in the Seven Years' War. It is clear that the 'input' of ships, men and resources into this wide-ranging branch of the maritime economy reached an unprecedented eighteenth-century level, a reflection of the continued growth of the British shipping industry rather than an upsurge in commerce-raiding endeavour. Indeed, it was the commercially-oriented element of the licensed fleet which accounted for much of the 1756–1762 expansion as the complex, vacillating economic prospects thrown up by the war increasingly favoured trade rather predation. In the commerce-raiding sector, moreover, the scale of enterprise tended to decline as the complexion of the enemy's trade served to stimulate 'Channel' and the more modest 'deep-water' private ships-of-war rather than the 'privateers of force'.

II

The Prize Court sentences indicate that the aggregate rise in privateering 'inputs' was not matched by a concomitant increase in the 'output' of the activity. Instead, the prize return of the Seven Years' War fell in comparison with the privateering 'catch' of the smaller fleet commissioned in the 1740s; with naval power the dominant factor in Britain's military triumph, moreover, the King's ships accounted for the majority of prizes condemned, as Table 16 clearly illustrates.

Table 16

Prizes Condemned at Doctors' Commons, 1756-1763

Year	Privateers	Navy*	Total
1756	42	89	131
1757	113	286	399
1758	87	66	153
1759	50	48	98
1760	34	69	103
1761	15	94	109
1762	33	95	128
1763	8	47	55
	382	794	1176

* Including 'droits and perquisites' of the Admiralty.
Source: PRO, HCA 34/37-42.

A total of 1,176 common condemnations were made in the Prize Court during the Seven Years' War. Although this figure undoubtedly under-states the level of prize-taking activity in excluding the disputed properties upon which the Court reserved judgement, it is comparable with the totals of 2,222 and 857 sentences passed respectively in the 1702–1712 and 1739–1748 wars. The condemnation of an additional 319 prizes indicates that commerce-raiding activity was more effective in the Seven Years' War than it had been in the previous conflict, though the return was barely half of that recorded in Queen Anne's War. Moreover, this revival was due entirely to the improved performance of the Navy, as the return of the British privateering business, which had plummeted from 956 to 408 condemnations between the two previous conflicts, declined even further, with just 382 condemnations recorded by commissioned vessels between 1756 and 1763. This fall took place even though the fleet equipped with letters of marque was nearly 500 vessels stronger than it had been in the 1739–1748 conflict, indicating that a precipitous decline in the overall 'productivity rate' of the privateering business occurred in the Seven Years' War.

However, such a conclusion is tempered by the distribution of prize sentences over the war years. The first 18 months of the conflict were the most productive for both the Navy and the commissioned force, with an annual peak of 399 condemnations reached in 1757. This was the highest yearly aggregate yet recorded in the century; furthermore, the total of 113 prizes condemned to licensed venturers in 1757 had only been surpassed twice in previous conflicts—in 1705 and 1745—an indication of the relative intensity of privateering activity in the early stages of the conflict. The condemnation rate tended to subside thereafter, with a mere 15 prizes sentenced to commissioned vessels in 1761 before the entry of Spain precipitated a slight upswing in 1762. Such a prize-taking chronology conformed to the pattern of the wider maritime struggle, and followed the fluctuating scale and character of 'inputs' into the privateering business. Thus, just as the existence of a substantial French sea-borne commerce stimulated predatory activity in the first 30 months of hostilities, so its evident demise from 1759 onwards placed a ceiling on commerce-raiding ambitions, and entrepreneurs turned to more promising trades.

The role of the Navy in curtailing French shipping operations was reflected in the condemnation of 794 prizes to the King's ships, 67.5 per cent of the total. A further measure of the Navy's significance in the prize war was afforded by the payment of head money to captors of enemy *corsaires* and men-of-war. As in the previous conflict, men-of-warsmen were in receipt of the bulk of bounty money awarded by the Navy Office in the Seven Years' War; the division of these spoils between the state and private naval forces is presented in Table 17.

Table 17

Head Money Paid to Naval Seamen and Privateering Venturers, 1756–1763

	Payments		Bounty Paid		Average size of captured crew
	No	%	£	%	
Privateers	23	9.8	9085	6.3	79
Navy	212	90.2	134012.5	93.7	126.4
	235	100	143097.5	100	121.8

* Claims were not lodged, or are lacking, in respect of a number of eligible privateering prizes. See Appendix 1.
Source: PRO, ADM 43/14-22.

The award of nine out of ten head money payments to men-of-warsmen indicates the dominant part played by the Navy in the limitation of the Franco-Spanish naval and commerce-raiding threat. While His Majesty's ships accounted for 36 enemy men-of-war and 176 *corsaires*, British private men-of-war and 'letters of marque' were rewarded with just 23 bounties, paid for 20 hostile privateers, and three men-of-war. This dominance was further reflected in the size of payments, for the average complement serving in the Navy's prizes was stronger by some 47 men than the mean crews shipped aboard the vessels-of-war taken by privateers. However, in contrast to the 1739–1748 conflict, naval and privateering captures did not represent the greater part of the Navy's prize-taking effort; whereas 269.67 enemy ships-of-war and *corsaires* had constituted 60.1 per cent of naval condemnations in the previous conflict, in the Seven Years' War the equivalent figure had dropped to 212 condemnations, just 26.7 per cent of the 794 properties sentenced to His Majesty's ships. Thus, the overall improvement in the Navy's prize-taking performance was achieved at the expense of the enemy's commercial shipping, and not by the capture of his military vessels. This development did not escape the notice of critical privateersmen; thus, in 1757, a lieutenant detained aboard a French *corsaire* found it remarkable that his captors, sailing between 48°N and 51°N, encountered 30 fellow predators but no English cruisers; by this, he deduced that

> our Men-of-War generally cruize in the Bay, or from Ushent to Cape Finisterre, that being a station more probable to meet with French merchantmen than Privateers, who are cruizing to the Northward on our Trade that are making for the Chops of the Channel.[42]

Such a policy held clear ramifications for the privateering business as the Navy's commerce-raiding success inevitably depleted enemy trade, the principal object of privateering activity. Opportunities for prize-taking were therefore limited, a further factor contributing to the relatively poor condemnation rate achieved by the privateering fleet. The regional distribution of this 'output' is presented in Table 18.

Table 18

Prizes Condemned to Commissioned Vessels by Region, 1756–1763

Region		Number of prizes
London		73
Bristol		81
Liverpool		14
Channel Is	—Guernsey (74) Jersey (78)	152
SE England	—Dover (11) Hastings (4) Hastings/Rye (1)	16
SW England	—Bideford (1) Falmouth (2) Poole (3) Teignmouth (1) Topsham (2) Weymouth (1)	10
Ireland	—Cork (1)	1
Overseas Bases	—Leghorn (12) Quebec (1)	13
In consort	—London/Bristol (2) London/ Liverpool (1) Bristol/Bideford (7), Bristol/Jersey (3) Liverpool/ Guernsey (3)	16
Port Unknown		6
		382

Source: PRO, HCA 25/38-55; HCA 26/5-12, 27-28; HCA 34/37-42.

The expansion and dispersal of the British privateering force apparent in the Seven Years' War was not reflected in the distribution of prize condemnations by port. Indeed, a familiar scene is drawn in Table 18, with London, Bristol and the Channel Islands emerging as the leading prize-taking centres, supported by Liverpool, and the ports of south-east and south-west England. Developments were apparent in the Seven Years' War, however: London was less significant than previously, accounting for 73 prizes, a fall of 34 condemnations on the return of the 1740s; Bristol emerged as the leading mainland port, with a dozen shared captures adding to the city's contribution of 81 condemnations; the Channel Islanders improved their prize return from 124 to 152 condemnations over the two wars, with Jersey matching Guernsey for the first time; moreover, the rate of return—prizes per privateer—declined locally as well as nationally, with ratios of one prize condemned for every nine London privateers, one for every three licensed Bristol vessels, and 1.2 prizes per potential predator in the Channel Islands, against comparable figures of 1:6, 1:1.6, and 1.5:1 for the Austrian Succession War.

Private men-of-war accounted for the majority of common condemnations made to privateering venturers at Doctors' Commons, notwithstanding the expansive character of 'letter of marque' enterprise during the 1756–1762 war. In terms of the number of properties condemned, 'Channel' privateering was the most successful arm of the commerce-raiding business, with small-scale predators responsible for nearly half of the total prize return. The Channel Islanders dominated this activity, preying in customary fashion upon the French coasting trade and thereby diverting significant quantities of wine, brandy, grain, salt and timber from the coastal communities of Brittany and Normandy to the warehouses and markets of Guernsey and Jersey.[43] Such prizes were taken throughout the war as the Islanders' immunity from the 1759 Privateers' Act resulted in their prosecution of over 60 of the 99 condemnations effected during the relatively barren years of 1759, 1760 and 1761.[44] Success on this scale appears to have eluded venturers in south-east England, the other principal seat of 'Channel' enterprise; here, in the war as a whole, just 17 common condemnations benefited the privateersmen of Dover, Hastings and Rye—a return too meagre, in itself, to have provoked the heated controversy surrounding commerce-raiding activity in the Channel Narrows. While the omission of disputed properties from the sentences of the Prize Court might explain the apparent ineffectiveness of the South East's predators, it is also feasible that the properly authorised privateers of this region expended their energies in the illicit harassment and plunder of neutral vessels—an occupation fuelled by the 'Rule of the War of 1756' and largely unseen by the official eye.

It was only in rare instances that the excesses of 'Channel' privateersmen were brought before the High Court of Admiralty. In one such case, the Portuguese owners of *La Notre Dame de la Conception* appealed against the condemnation of their ship and its cargo to the promoters and men of the *Lockhart* on the grounds that their property was neutral and not engaged in trade with France. As well as the conflicting interpretations of international law normally submitted in such disputes—the 1654 Anglo-Portuguese Treaty versus the 'Rule of the War of 1756' on this occasion—the Court of Prize Appeals also heard of a series of misdemeanours allegedly perpetrated by the captors. Thus, the provisions of the prize were dissipated by the 'excessive waste of Captain Vye's people'; casks were broken open and the cabin rummaged for evidence; bribes were offered to prisoners to persuade them to alter their testimony; the privateersmen, moreover, refused to release the sea chests and clothes seized during the capture. This irregular behaviour may have influenced the Appeals Court in finding against the captors and awarding £1,317 11s 1d to the appellants in respect of the value of their ship and cargo, together with costs and damages;[45] it also suggests the impunity with which British privateersmen might treat the rights of neutrals, an attitude encouraged by the administration's decision to discard the 'free ships, free goods' philosophy of the seventeenth-century bi-lateral treaties in favour of a more rigorous interpretation of the trade a neutral might legitimately conduct with a belligerent.

Belonging to Bristol, the *Lockhart*, of 50 tons burthen and 50 men,[46] was one of a number of 'Channel' captors belonging to the major trading ports. London venturers profited from the condemnation of a prize, *Name Unknown*, carried into Weymouth by the *Favourite*, of 80 tons burthen and 60 men, and the *St Julien*, a French vessel conveyed to Margate by the 70-ton, 60-man *Prince Bevern*.[47] Two Liverpool wherries, the *Mandrin* and the *Revenge*, also participated in prize-taking activity; departing the Mersey on 1 July 1756 to cruise in consort, these predators, both declared as 40 tons burthen with 40 men, effected a number of seizures despite a well-publicised disagreement between their respective commanders.[48] The 90-ton *Blakeney* of Liverpool, with a company of 70 men, was also active in the early stages of the war as she combined forces with the 130-ton, 80-man *Hawke* of Exeter to attack the *Robuste, Le Juste* and two snows from St Domingue for La Rochelle. After a damaging, two-hour engagement, the French West Indiamen, of 350 and 450 tons burthen, yielded their valuable cargoes of sugar, coffee and indigo to Captains Day and Harrison;[49] though no record of condemnation is contained in the prize sentences, it seems that the *Robuste* arrived in the Exe on 19 October 1756, for customs officials reported that upwards of 120 hogsheads of coffee had been taken out of her and landed at Topsham, 'the first importation of coffee at this Port'.[50]

If, in form, these Liverpool captors resembled the archetypal 'Channel' privateer, they were much more akin to the 'deep-water' commerce-raider in their cruising stations and mode of operation. The *Revenge*, for instance, seized *La Marie Esther*, outward-bound from La Rochelle for America with sundry provisions and manufactures, in the Bay of Biscay, while she later combined with the *Mandrin* to cut two Dutch vessels out of the Bordeaux river.[51] Furthermore, it was 25 leagues off Cape Finisterre that the *Blakeney* and the *Hawke* encountered their prize 'St Domingomen', firing a number of broadsides at the small French fleet which had formed itself into a line of battle.[52] More conventional large-scale predators also exploited the propitious conditions implied by these seizures—an abundance of French colonial vessels homeward-bound in the north-eastern Atlantic. Thus, from June 1756 to the end of 1757, 'deep-water' private men-of-war accounted for at least 80 prizes, just over 50 per cent of the total condemned in this 18-month period—generally conveying them to home bases or to convenient ports of landing such as Falmouth or Plymouth, Cork or Kinsale.

The 200-ton, 150-man *Anson*, for instance, the first private man-of-war to depart Bristol, had three West Indiamen—*La Promethe* of Bordeaux, *La Marie Esther* and *L'Aimable Julie*—condemned in September 1756.[53] In October, the *Tyger*, of 570 tons burthen and 300 men, recalled her efforts of 1747-1748 in successfully prosecuting three prizes, including the homeward-bound 'Martinicomen' *Le Comte de Noailles* and the *Nestor*. Sailing in company, having lost their convoys, the West Indiamen were obliged to strike their colours after the *Tyger's* opening broadside had killed the captain, first lieutenant, and seven seamen aboard the *Nestor*.[54] Seizures of French Caribbean produce also brought swift returns to Liverpool investors; indeed, George Campbell, owner of the successful *Anson* of Liverpool, as well as the *Blakeney,* acknowledged the source of his wealth in bestowing the title 'St Domingo' upon the large estate he purchased with his commerce-raiding profits.[55]

London's more extensive investment in this form of predation yielded dividends as the *Prince Edward* and the *Royal George* captured French West Indiamen during the summer of 1756, while in October, the *Antigallican* apprehended the 250-ton *La Marie Therese*, a 'Martinicoman' bound for Le Havre with sugar and cotton, 80 leagues WSW of Cape Finisterre.[56] In December, the *Charming Nancy,* of 250 tons burthen and 117 men, had four prizes condemned;[57] one of the most substantial Channel Island ventures, this captor reflected the growing interest of *armateurs* in relatively large-scale operations in the Bay of Biscay, a development which added exotic cargoes of sugar, coffee, cotton and indigo to the more mundane prize goods brought in by the 'Channel' privateersmen. In 1757, this 'deep-water' assault reached a climax as some 30 ventures registered 62 common condemnations during the year, with combinations of captors like the *Antelope, Defiance* and *Tartar,* the *Tygress* of Bideford and her consorts the *Caesar, Lyon* and *Phoenix* of Bristol, and the *Isaac of Liverpool*'s co-operative effort with four London predators, suggesting the intensity of the assault.

In their search for French colonial traffic, these and other such 'stout' private ships-of-war adopted various stations in the north-eastern Atlantic. In 1756 and 1757, however, the waters off Capes Finisterre and Ortegal emerged as the focal point of predatory operations as the enemy's trade, poorly defended in home waters and increasingly frustrated in its attempts to breach the naval blockade of France's Atlantic ports, frequently sought refuge in the harbours of north-west Spain. Here, goods might be transhipped into Dutch or Spanish bottoms and discreetly conveyed to France under the protection of neutral colours and false documentation; alternatively, French vessels might slip anchor and try to reach Bayonne, St Jean de Luz or Bordeaux by closely following the Biscay coast beyond the range of the blockading force. Naturally, the convergence of homeward-bound merchantmen and collusive neutrals attracted private men-of-war to this locality;[58] thus, it was off Cape Finisterre that the *Antelope* seized *L'Olimpiard* in March 1757,[59] while five months later and 30 leagues to the west, *Le Prince de Conti*, an outward-bound French East Indiaman of 600 tons burthen, 30 guns and 194 men, was 'taken in fight' by five British predators after discharging 1,000 rounds of great shot in resistance.[60]

Further inshore, the *Antigallican* apprehended *Le Duc de Penthievre*, a returning East Indiaman, in the 'channel that forms the entry of the ports of Ferrol and Corunna'. A considerable diplomatic controversy ensued as the French demanded restitution of their property on the grounds that the seizure had taken place in a neutral roadstead; despite the protestations of the *Antigallican*'s managers, both in the press and in the House of Commons, the Spanish Court determined that its territory had been violated, and ordered that the prize should be seized and restored to its owners. 'An Impartial and true Account' of this affair suggests that disregard for neutral rights was not confined to the 'Channel' arm of the privateering business; thus, after condemning the 'rough behaviour' of William Foster, commander of the *Antigallican*, and the 'connivance' of the British consul at Corunna, the anonymous observer disclosed that

> there is actually more than one instance of English Privateers being so insolent and paying so little regard to the Territory of a Prince in friendship with their master, as to carry away French ships at Anchor in Spanish ports.[61]

As the naval blockade intensified—assisted, it seems, by privateers operating close inshore[62]—so enemy vessels found it ever more difficult to reach or leave French Atlantic ports. *Le Provost*, for instance, a *corsaire* of 300 tons burthen, 24 guns and a sickly crew of 320 men, was taken by three London private ships-of-war as she headed for Bayonne or Bordeaux, hugging the Spanish coast 'to avoid the English fleet' which had previously thwarted her attempts to reach Brittany.[63] In the same month of October 1757, *L'Oriflame*, a *corsaire* of 250 tons burthen and 94 men, was seized by the 700-ton, 300-man *Victory* 150 leagues north of the Azores; however, as her captain related to the Prize Court, *L'Oriflame* had left Bordeaux with a cargo for Louisbourg, only to be turned back by the British fleet, her owners then deciding to re-fit her as a commerce-raider.[64] This option was taken up by growing numbers of *armateurs* as the tide turned against French commerce; others, cowed by losses and painfully aware of the limited protective qualities of the French Navy, simply laid up their vessels for the duration of the war and raised only token objections to the temporary relaxation of the Navigation Laws and the permissible encroachment of neutrals into a business normally monopolised by Frenchmen.[65]

The consequent dearth of 'Martinicomen' and other French colonial craft necessarily restricted the opportunities facing 'deep-water' venturers towards the close of 1757 and, thereafter, successes in the customary stations of the large-scale predator were relatively scarce. Condemnations declined, with only 31 properties sentenced to archetypal 'deep-water' venturers in 1758, followed by three in 1759, two in 1760 and four in 1761. Private ships-of-war such as the *Resolution* and the *Spy* encountered only Dutch carriers and French *corsaires* during their cruises in the Western Approaches,[66] while the fading prospects of prize-taking off the capes of north-west Spain provoked a mutiny amongst the 200-strong crew of the *King George* of Bristol in May 1761. Having almost cut off Captain Read's nose and confined his officers, the mutineers

> intended to hoist Jolly Robin and the Cross Bones at the mast head
> and go a-pirating in the East Indies.

In the event, 'upwards of 100' of the ship's people escaped to Camarinas in Spain, while the *King George* proceeded on her cruise, managing to apprehend the East Indiaman *Le Beaumont* after a bloody engagement in which 20 of the captor's loyal seafarers perished.[67]

As the appeal of the Atlantic station diminished with the demise of France's colonial trade, so British commerce-raiding enterprise gravitated towards the Mediterranean. During the course of 1758, bases such as Leghorn, Malta, Messina and Zant began to replace Falmouth, Kinsale and Plymouth as the main landing places cited in the prize sentences; in 1759 and 1760, 20 properties were condemned to captors operating in the Mediterranean, four times the 'catch' taken in the Bay of Biscay and the Western Approaches. Predators like the *Enterprize,* the *Liverpool* and the *Tyger,* which had previously cruised to some effect in the north-eastern Atlantic, operated further afield in 1758, the former two commerce-raiders carrying seven prizes into Leghorn,[68] and the *Tyger* succumbing to the French man-of-war *Rose* off Malta.[69] It was in the Mediterranean, moreover, that the redoubtable Fortunatus Wright, commander of the *St George* of Liverpool, played such havoc with French shipping that three vessels were fitted out in Marseilles specifically to seek him out and 'give him no quarter, but burn him on board'.[70] Meanwhile, John Patrick, captain of the *Leopard,* and then of the *Fame,* earned a darker reputation in this station for his somewhat cavalier approach to the laws of maritime war, though seven of his captures were duly condemned at Doctors' Commons.[71]

'Cruise and voyage' ventures accounted for a number of prizes carried into Mediterranean ports and subsequently condemned in London. The *Deal Castle,* for instance, took four prizes during her 'cruising voyage', including *Le Bellette,*[72] a French *corsaire* of 85 men, and *Le St Matheau,* a 60-ton vessel captured 10 leagues east of Cape Bona in her passage from Alexandria to Marseilles.[73] Another small, Marseilles-owned merchantman, *Le St Joseph,* bound for Constantinople with cloth and paper in her hold, was seized seven leagues off Cape St Angello by the *Prince Edward,* a London 'letter of marque' of 350 tons burthen and 80 men returning from Smyrna with a cargo of raisins.[74] Similar characteristics were displayed by various other London captors—the 280-ton, 60-man *Diamond Gally* and the *Greyhound,* of 210 tons burthen and 70 men, for instance[75]—despatched to the Mediterranean in search of prizes, with the further aim of securing a cargo should conditions so dictate. The Caribbean was also the focus of such enterprise, though evidence of prize-taking in this theatre is scant due to the condemnation of seized property in the Vice-Admiralty courts. Newspaper accounts suggest that enemy goods were occasionally taken in the West Indies, while the *Brittannia,* outward bound on a 'cruising voyage' to St Kitts, not only repulsed her Spanish assailant, the *Nuestra Senora del Mar,* but proceeded to board and take the privateer, an exploit which generated £565 in head money for the owners and men of the Bristol vessel.[76]

'Letters of marque' of a more commercial disposition were also successful in turning adversity into profit during the Seven Years' War. Thus, after 'an obstinate engagement of 9 hours', the captain, mate, five foremastmen and four boys of the *Endeavour* of Yarmouth repelled boarders from *L'Esperance,* a *corsaire* she encountered a few miles off the Portuguese coast; indeed, so stiff was the resistance offered that the French vessel sank with the loss of her captain and nine men, while the *Endeavour*'s people were 'much wounded' and therefore unable to work the ship and guard their 14 prisoners, who were consequently transferred to HMS *Spy.*[77] In a similar vein, the men of the *Sarah,* an 'armed trading vessel' of Liverpool generated £390 in head money by their seizure of the French hospital ship *Sampson,* 15 leagues west of St Vincent. The supplemental character of this predation is clear, however, in the agreement signed by these seafarers; thus, the terms upon which they agreed to sail to Barbados were laid down in a printed contract, a series of clauses concerning the proposed distribution of prize goods, discipline and encouragement being added on the reverse in longhand. Accordingly, the 32 crew members of the *Sarah*—eight officers and specialists, 20 seamen, three landmen and one boy—stood to gain a share in one-quarter of the net proceeds of their capture.[78]

'Armed trading vessels' and 'specialist vessels'—only one prize was condemned to an Indiaman, the *Royal George,* during the Seven Years' War[79]—generally sought to steer clear of enemy shipping and rarely participated in prize-taking activity. The proliferation of this form of privateering enterprise, particularly after 1757, reflected the demise of the enemy's trans-Atlantic trade and, with it, the evaporation of commerce-raiding prospects. Resources were accordingly diverted into trading operations or else invested in predatory ventures to the Mediterranean or the West Indies. Under these influences, expansion and declining productivity characterised the British privateering business in the Seven Years' War.

Notes

1. See J. S. Corbett, *England in the Seven Years' War. A Study in Combined Strategy* (1907), 2 vols; Mahan, *Sea Power,* 281-329; Clowes, *Royal Navy,* III, 146-309; Kennedy, *British Naval Mastery,* 98-107; and Jenkins, *History of the French Navy,* 118-41.

2. See Pares, *Colonial Blockade*, for a full treatment of the question of neutral rights, and the diplomatic controversies it provoked.

3. The Anglo-Dutch diplomatic crisis is discussed in detail by A. C. Carter, *The Dutch Republic in Europe in the Seven Years' War* (1971), 103-28; and 'How to Revise Treaties without Negotiating: Commonsense, Mutual Fears, and the Anglo-Dutch Trade Disputes of 1759', in R. Hatton and M. S. Anderson, eds, *Studies in Diplomatic History. Essays in Memory of David Baynes Horn* (1970).

4. 32 George II, c.25. 'An Act for the Encouragement of Seamen and the Prevention of Piracies by Private Ships-of-War'. This legislation was also designed to release privateersmen for service in the Royal Navy according to S. F. Gradish, *The Manning of the British Navy during the Seven Years' War* (1980), 48-9.

5. As early as 10 July 1756, *Felix Farley's Bristol Journal* reported that the Dutch had lodged complaints about the detention of ten vessels. Further neutral protests were made at regular intervals in the opening years of the war. See Stark, *Abolition of Privateering*, 72-4, for details of these complaints and examples of the harassment endured by neutral merchantmen.

6. 29 George II, c.34. 'An Act for the Encouragement of Seamen and the more Speedy and Effectual Manning of His Majesty's Navy'.

7. *London Gazette*, 8 June 1756.

8. 2 George III, c.16. 'An Act for the Encouragement of Seamen and the more Speedy and Effectual Manning of His Majesty's Navy'.

9. Davis, 'Foreign Trade, 1700-1774'.

10. Minchinton, ed., *Overseas Trade*, 33-6; French, thesis.

11. *Public Advertiser*, 5 January 1762.

12. Clark, *La Rochelle*, 155-7; Crowhurst, *Defence of British Trade*, 29; Pares, *War and Trade*, 390-1.

13. The revocation of commissions issued prior to 1 June 1759 is not considered in Appendix 2; therefore, the decline in activity rates was probably more precipitous than the figures suggest.

14. See Pares, *Colonial Blockade*, for a thorough analysis of these issues. The printed case books of the Prize Appeals Court, PRO, HCA 45/1-3, indicate the conflicting stances of British captors and neutral claimants, with the 'Rule of the War of 1756' repeatedly pitted against one or other of the seventeenth-century bi-lateral treaties.

15. PRO, ADM 43/15(1). According to their declarants, these vessels had companies of 20, 30 and 25 men respectively. Declarations 27 July 1756, 19 August, 13 July 1757. PRO, HCA 26/5, 8, 8.

16. See Raban, 'War and Trade', 140, for an analysis of the Channel Islanders' commissioned fleet.

17. See PRO, ADM 43/16, 21. Articles of Agreement, *Admiral Durel*, *Defiance* and *Prince William*. In fact, most privateersmen chose to reduce the financial risk inherent in their occupation, preferring to commute their stake in the

profits for a guaranteed income, at a rate which varied from four to six livres tournois per share per month.

18. PRO, HCA 25/48-55, HCA 26/11-12, 27-8.

19. For more detail on this and other aspects of Channel Island privateering in the Seven Years' War, see Jamieson, 'Return to Privateering', 151-7; and Raban, 'War and Trade', 135-9.

20. Corbett, *England in the Seven Years' War*, II, 10-12.

21. The two exceptions were the *Dorset*, of 400 tons burthen and 200 men, and the 200-ton, 200-man *Hawke*, both fitted out by Poole venturers. Declarations 13 April, 2 September 1757. PRO, HCA 25/42, 26/8. The *Resolution*, of 400 tons burthen and 250 men, was fitted out in Liverpool, though owned by 'John Parke & Co, London merchants' and registered in London on 12 February 1757. Declaration 9 February 1757. PRO, HCA 26/7. Registration information kindly provided by Maurice Schofield. The *Resolution* cruised with the *Spy* of Liverpool. See Williams, *Liverpool Privateers*, 88, 118-20.

22. C. C. Lloyd, *The British Seaman, 1200-1860. A Social Survey* (Collins, 1968) 286-90; Davis, *Shipping Industry*, 137.

23. The debate surrounding this issue and the reaction of French shipowners, as reflected in the meetings of the various Chambers of Commerce in the maritime districts, is discussed by Pares, *War and Trade*, 359-75.

24. Damer Powell, *Bristol Privateers*, 184.

25. *Felix Farley's Bristol Journal*, 9 June 1759.

26. Starkey, thesis, 245, 249.

27. Declaration 8 July 1756. PRO, HCA 26/5. Articles of Agreement, 21 July 1756. PRO, ADM 43/16.

28. Declaration 12 May 1757. PRO, HCA 25/43. See Damer Powell, *Bristol Privateers*, 191-3.

29. Articles of Agreement, 6 February 1762. PRO, ADM 43/18.

30. Declarations 7 August 1756, 7 July 1757. PRO, HCA 25/38, 43.

31. Declarations 26 August 1758, 9 September 1757. PRO, HCA 26/10, 25/44.

32. Damer Powell, *Bristol Privateers*, 184-245, gives the destinations of 15 of Bristol 'letters of marque', information derived from contemporary news-papers.

33. A protection was granted for the *Richmond's* crew on 16 December 1756. Maurice Schofield kindly provided this detail and also the information on the destinations of Liverpool, Chester, Lancaster and Whitehaven vessels.

34. C. Dixon, 'The Exeter Whale Fishery Company, 1754-1787' *Mariner's Mirror*, 62 (1976), 225-31.

35. Graham, dissertation, 79.

36. Raban, 'War and Trade', 146-8.

37. PRO, HCA 26/5.

38. Declaration 2 May 1761. PRO, HCA 26/12.

39. Hardy, *Register of Ships*, I and II.

40. Declarations 26 October 1757, 3 April 1762. PRO, HCA 26/8, 28.

41. French, thesis, 201.
42. *London Chronicle*, 28 June 1757.
43. Raban, 'War and Trade', 134.
44. PRO, HCA 34/40-1.
45. PRO, HCA 42/84.
46. Declaration 1 April 1758. PRO, HCA 26/9.
47. Declarations 3 April 1759, 3 June 1757. PRO, HCA 26/11, 7. Prize sentences, PRO, HCA 34/40.
48. Declarations 17 June 1756. PRO, HCA 26/5. Williams, *Liverpool Privateers*, 96-7.
49. Declarations 19, 7 August 1756, PRO, HCA 26/5, 5. Williams, *Liverpool Privateers*, 90-2.
50. PRO, CUST 64/4. Collector, Exeter to Board of Customs, 23 October, 24 November 1756. I am indebted to Stephen Fisher for this reference.
51. Williams, *Liverpool Privateers*, 96-7.
52. Williams, *Liverpool Privateers*, 90-2.
53. Declaration 17 June 1756. PRO, HCA 26/5. Prize sentences,PRO, HCA 34/37. See Damer Powell, *Bristol Privateers*, 187-8.
54. Declaration 17 June 1756. PRO, HCA 25/38. Prize Sentences, PRO, HCA 34/37. See Damer Powell, *Bristol Privateers*, 235-7.
55. The 'St Domingo' estate was situated in Everton. In 1869, St Domingo methodist church was established, and in 1879 the football club associated with the church was reformed into Everton Football Club. See J. Roberts, *Everton. The Official Centenary History* (Granada, 1978) 14-5; and Williams, *Liverpool Privateers*, 92-3.
56. PRO, HCA 32/224(3).
57. Declaration 10 June 1756. PRO, HCA 26/5. Prizes sentences, PRO, HCA 34/37. See also PRO, ADM 43/16.
58. Pares, *War and Trade*, 360.
59. PRO, HCA 32/229.
60. PRO, HCA 32/233.
61. *London Chronicle*, 19 March, 5, 21, 26 April, 28 May 1756. See the petitions of the proprietors of the *Antigallican* in the *Journals of the House of Commons*, 28 (1757-1761), 80; 29 (1761-1764), 469-70; 33 (1770-1772), 520-1, 667. The House eventually divided as to whether it should refer the matter to a Committee; the motion was soundly defeated the tellers counting one Aye and 147 Noes.
62. Pares, *War and Trade*, 360, suggests that privateers and men-of-war formed a 'chain' which French merchantmen found difficult to penetrate.
63. PRO, HCA 32/233.
64. PRO, HCA 32/229.
65. Pares, *War and Trade*, 359-75.
66. Williams, *Liverpool Privateers*, 118-22.
67. Damer Powell, *Bristol Privateers*, 219-21. Some 107 seafarers were on

board the *King George* at the commencement of this action. PRO, ADM 43/22(2).

68. PRO, HCA 34/40.
69. Damer Powell, *Bristol Privateers*, 236-7. The *Tyger* was subsequently retaken by the *King George* private ship-of-war of Bristol. See PRO, ADM 43/18(1).
70. Williams, *Liverpool Privateers*, 62-8.
71. Damer Powell, *Bristol Privateers*, 207-13.
72. PRO, ADM 43/16.
73. PRO, HCA 32/224(2).
74. PRO, HCA 32/206.
75. Declarations 10 February 1757, 11 June 1756. PRO, HCA 26/7, 5.
76. PRO, ADM 43/18. Damer Powell, *Bristol Privateers*, 193.
77. PRO, ADM 43/15(2).
78. PRO, ADM 43/21.
79. *Le Favory* was taken by the *Royal George* and carried into Fort St George. PRO, HCA 34/41.

Eight

1777–1783

'Additional Forces'

If sea power had been at the basis of Britain's triumph in the Seven Years' War, a different story was to unfold in the American Revolutionary War as the Bourbon powers exploited the colonial rebellion in North America to exact a measure of revenge for the humiliations of 1756–1763. The foundations for this retribution were laid in the years of peace as France and, to a lesser extent, Spain replenished and developed their naval resources, while successive British administrations preferred to reduce expenditure on the Navy.

At the outbreak of the American revolt in 1775, therefore, Britain was in a potentially vulnerable position for she faced the prospect of quelling an insurrection in a distant continent with her mastery of European waters threatened by the growing naval strength of her principal rivals. This strategic weakness became more apparent as policy towards the rebels vacillated between appeasement and punishment, and revolt developed into revolution. Obliged to fight a major land war in North America, Britain was confronted with the immense logistical difficulties of conveying and supplying her armies across 3,000 miles of ocean.[1] Moreover, she was increasingly isolated as the hostile neutrality of France, Spain and the United Provinces was translated successively into declared enmity. In these adverse circumstances the Navy was forced on to the defensive in the attempt to protect British interests in North America, the Caribbean, the Mediterranean and the Far East; accordingly, its resources were so stretched that the decisive superiority it had assumed during the Seven Years' War was just a dim and distant memory in the late 1770s.[2]

The merchant shipping industry encountered both difficulties and opportunities in this complex, global struggle. While the Atlantic staple trades were depressed by the closure of colonial markets, demand for tonnage and seafarers increased as the government hired merchantmen to transport the tools of war and the Admiralty sought great numbers of men for naval service; the wide range of adversaries rendered sea-borne commerce more vulnerable, though it also widened the target and improved the prospects for British commerce-raiders; furthermore, the absence of a 'close' blockade increased the risk to home trade in affording the Franco-Spanish fleets a greater degree of freedom, yet it also encouraged enemy trade to proceed, thereby adding to the opportunities for predatory gains. In such a context, with incentives increased and commercial options generally limited, the British privateering business flourished in the American Revolutionary War, reaching its *apogee*, by most measures, for the 'long' eighteenth century as a whole.[3]

The impact of this burgeoning enterprise varied regionally, however. In localities depressed by the unfavourable commercial circumstances of the war, the privateering business served to stimulate shipping activity, while in other areas it added to the competition for the human and material resources rendered scarce by the demands of the other maritime sectors. Moreover, expansion in the business was spread unevenly over the war years. Indeed, it was not until April 1777, two years after the skirmish at Lexington, and long after the rebel colonists had despatched their own commerce-raiders,[4] that privateer commissions were granted to British venturers. This delay was due to the uncertain status of the enemy, for in granting reprisals against the rebels' trade Parliament would have implicitly recognised the independence of the very colonies it sought to retain. Thus, it was not until the revolution was clearly established that privateer commissions—rather than letters of marque, which could only authorise reprisals against the subjects of a sovereign state—were issued, permitting the licensee to make prize of ships and goods belonging to the inhabitants of the 'colonies now in rebellion', as well as any British ship 'found trading to or from the said colonies contrary to the provisions' of the 1775 Prohibition of Trade Act.[5] That a large segment of the American mercantile marine was deployed in privateering by this time meant that such targets were too meagre to provoke much specialist commerce-raiding activity from the British Isles, though a considerable number of 'letters of marque' set forth in 1777 and 1778. Predictably, it was the authorisation of general reprisals against French commerce in August 1778 that encouraged entrepreneurs to fit out private men-of-war in significant numbers, while the private war-at-sea assumed an even more conventional eighteenth-century guise in June 1779 when letters of marque permitting the seizure of Spanish sea-borne property became available.

Rather less typical, however, was the onset of war with the United Provinces in December 1780, a development which presented British commerce-raiders with the first opportunity to cruise specifically against Dutch trade since the Third Dutch War of 1672–1674. This chance was eagerly embraced, and from 26 December 1780 there occurred a veritable 'mania' in privateering investment[6] as venturers urgently fitted out all manner of craft 'from the full conviction of filling their pockets and revenging their country's cause against that treacherous and self interested nation.'[7] Such righteous indignation pervaded the mercantile press at this time as the finger of blame for the Anglo-Dutch rift was pointed at the 'False Grotten Heers'[8] whose 'treacherous behaviour'[9] in supplying the enemy and carrying his trade ran counter to the 1674 and 1678 treaties between the two nations.

In essence, this was a hyperbolic re-iteration of Britain's interpretation of the question of neutral trading rights, an issue which had threatened war in 1759 and which remained unresolved at the outbreak of the American Revolution.[10] The neutral powers, on the other hand, continued to adhere to the principle of 'free ships, free goods', and in March 1780 an anti-British coalition of states formed the Armed Neutrality to defend this right. Instigated by the Russians,[11] the alliance represented a further threat to Britain's naval supremacy, a challenge that intensified when the United Provinces, the leading neutral power, joined the Armed Neutrality in December 1780. In the face of the overtly hostile Dutch stance, the British administration 'acted with spirit'[12] and declared war upon the Republic.

Thus, the American Revolutionary War developed into a many-faceted conflict in which conditions were ripe for the expansion of various elements of the privateering business. Reprisals were ultimately permissible against the merchant shipping of four adversaries, including three of the largest European fleets; the Navy was unable to re-establish the maritime hegemony which had stifled enemy trade in 1759–1761, while its pre-occupation with a surfeit of strategic duties impaired its ability to compete with the private forces in the prize war; the demands of a further competitor, the merchant service, were reduced by the curtailment of trading activity in a number of ports; moreover, the government, requiring all the maritime strength it could muster, was reluctant to inhibit privateering enterprise and a return to the restrictive measures of 1759, imposed in the interests of diplomacy, was never contemplated. In such circumstances, the privateering business was one of the few aspects of British maritime endeavour to thrive in the 1777–1783 conflict.

I

In April 1777 the French ambassador to Britain, the Marquis de Noailles, was

> completely convinced of the importance at this time of keeping abreast
> of the additional forces England can procure through the issuance of
> letters of marque.[13]

His concern was justified as the High Court of Admiralty issued 7,352 privateer commissions and letters of marque between 3 April 1777 and 20 January 1783, three times the total granted in the Seven Years' War, and more than four times the issue of the 1702–1712 and 1739–1748 conflicts. Such comparisons require qualification, however, for licences were issued separately against each of the four adversaries engaged in the American Revolutionary War, a procedure unknown in earlier conflicts, save for a brief spell in 1744 when reprisals against France and Spain required distinct authorisation. While this bureaucratic device served to increase the incidence of duplication, and to exaggerate the true level of privateering activity, it also provided a rough measure of the relative significance of the various enemies and a guide to the overall course of the private war-at-sea. In Table 19, the gross issue of licences is broken down by designated enemy, suggesting that French commerce was the most attractive target for British privateering venturers, with 31.7 per cent of all commissions taken out against the Bourbon power; the American colonies stimulated marginally less activity, while Spain and the United Provinces accounted for just 20.5 and 16.8 per cent of the gross issue respectively. A different order of precedence emerges, however, if the figures are related to the length of time each adversary was formally engaged in the private war-at-sea. Thus, it was Dutch trade which precipitated the most intensive privateering activity as venturers took out an average of 47.4 letters of marque against the Republic in each of the 26 months in which they were available. The significance that French sea-borne property held for British privateering enterprise is confirmed

Table 19

Privateer Commissions and Letters of Marque Granted at Doctors' Commons,
1777-1783

Enemy	Number of Commissions	Dates of Issue	Reference
American Colonies	2285	3 April 1777- 20 January 1783	HCA 25/56-75, 26/60-70
France	2328	17 August 1778- 20 January 1783	HCA 25/76-95, 26/33-44
Spain	1506	29 June 1779- 20 January 1783	HCA 25/109-122, 26/45-52
United Provinces	1233	26 December 1780- 20 January 1783	HCA 25/96-108, 26/53-59
	7352		

by such a relative measure, with a monthly average of 43.1 French commissions taken out from August 1778. On the other hand, colonial commerce provoked a relatively subdued interest, for just 32.6 commissions per month issued over almost six years of conflict, while the response to Spanish enmity was only slightly more enthusiastic at 34.2 letters of marque per month.

The monthly averages conceal the fluctuations which occurred in the rate of issue. In Figure 1, the licences issued during the American Revolutionary War are presented by month as well as by designated enemy. A staggered profile is revealed, with surges in the rate of issue apparent at the outbreak of hostilities with each adversary. Thus, 97 privateer commissions were granted against the 'colonies now in rebellion' in April 1777, clearly the largest monthly issue prior to the intervention of France; 268 licences were processed at Doctors' Commons in August 1778, including 202 letters of marque taken out against France in the last two weeks of the month; a new peak was reached in the summer of 1779 as 100 Spanish letters of marque were issued on 29 and 30 June, with a further 186 taken out in July; this was surpassed in the

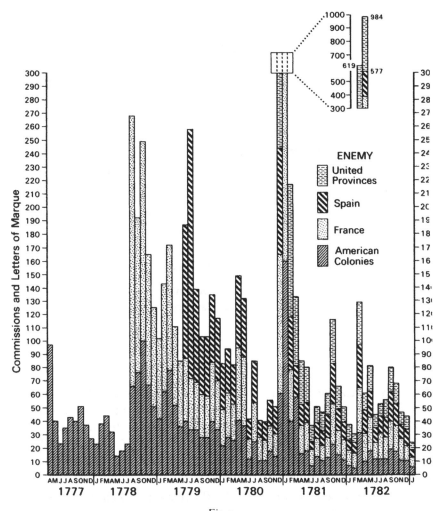

Fig. 1
Monthly Issue of Privateer Commissions and Letters of Marque by Enemy, 1777–1783

opening stages of the Dutch War as 379 licences against the United Provinces were dispensed by the Admiralty's hard-pressed officials from 26 to 30 December 1780, including 200 before noon on the first day of issue,[14] and some 383 Dutch commissions, and 577 authorisations against the other adversaries, were issued in January 1781. As these peaks were separated by periods in which the rate of issue tended to decline in a gradual, if uneven, manner, it would seem that privateering enterprise was at its height in the early stages of each successive phase of the 1777–1783 war.

If the gross issue of licences suggests, in broad outline, the course of the private war-at-sea, it clearly overstates the scale of the British privateering business in the American Revolutionary War, for nearly two-thirds of the commissions granted were either duplicates or re-commissions. Nevertheless, an 'additional force' of some 2,676 vessels, stronger by nearly a thousand vessels than its counterpart in the Seven Years' War, was despatched from 111 British ports and overseas bases during the course of the 1777–1783 privateering war. The regional distribution of this considerable commissioned fleet is presented in Table 20. Clearly, the growth and regional diffusion of privateering enterprise that had been evident in the 1756–1762 conflict continued apace in the American Revolutionary War. Some 550,989 tons of British shipping was commissioned from April 1777 to January 1783, an increase of 178,795 tons on the Seven Years' War, though average vessel size declined from 221.7 to 205.9 tons burthen between the two conflicts. The growing influence of the outports largely explained this fall in mean tonnage, with ventures mounted from 102 ports in the British Isles, and nine overseas bases, a spatial dispersal of activity unrivalled in the entire 1689–1815 period. Indeed, London, the home of the largest licensed craft, accounted for only 26.9 per cent of the fleet commissioned at Doctors' Commons, compared with 37.8 per cent in the Seven Years' War and roughly 50 per cent in previous wars. While this may have reflected the accelerating de-centralisation of the merchant shipping industry apparent in the third quarter of the century,[15] the fact that the capital's stake in the privateering fleet was to rise again—to 32.3 per cent in the French Revolutionary War, and 33.1 per cent in the Napoleonic War (see Appendices 7 and 8) —suggests that exceptional forces were at work in the American Revolutionary War.

Table 20

Commissioned Vessels by Region, 1777–1783

Region	Number of commissions	Actual vessels	Average tonnage
London	2032	719	328.2
Bristol	665	203	178.2
Liverpool	1384	390	197.1
Channel Is — Alderney (26) Guernsey (90) Jersey (107)	715	223	95.2
E England — Berwick (3) Bridlington (1) Harwich (4) Hull (30) Ipswich (1) Lynn (4) Newcastle (24) North Shields (7) Scarborough (10) South Shields (4) Stockton (2) Sunderland (3) Tynemouth (1) Wells (1) Whitby (22) Yarmouth (18)	268	135	293.4
SE England — Brighton (2) Chatham (1) Chichester (4) Cowes (9) Deal (6) Dover (48) Folkestone (102) Gosport (5) Gravesend (1) Hastings (21) Margate (2) Newhaven (1) Portsmouth (10) Ramsgate (6) Rochester (1) Ryde (2) Rye (8) Sandgate (1) Shoreham (4) Southampton (9)	482	243	117.3
SW England — Bideford (1) Bridport (2) Brixham (4) Dartmouth (68) Exeter (20) Exmouth (1) Falmouth (26) Fowey (4) Gweek (4) Helford (2) Ilfracombe (5) Looe (3) Lyme (5) Padstow (2), Penryn (3) Penzance (23) Plymouth (42) Poole (26) Scilly Isles (1) St Ives (12) St Austell (1) Teignmouth (4) Topsham (2) Totnes (1) Truro (2) West Lulworth (1) Weymouth (18)	685	283	103.2
Wales & NW England — Chester (9) Douglas (3) Haverfordwest (2) Lancaster (30) Milford (3) Pembroke (1) Swansea (1) Whitehaven (29) Workington (2)	189	80	187.7
W Scotland — Ayr (4) Clyde (4) Glasgow (123) Greenock (84) Irvine (1)	549	216	179.5

Region	Number of commissions	Actual vessels	Average tonnage
E Scotland — Aberdeen (2) Bo'ness (2) Carron (7) Dunbar (3) Dundee (1) Edinburgh (5) Leith (11) Perth (1)	77	32	173.6
Ireland — Belfast (7) Cork (20) Down Patrick (2) Drogheda (1) Dublin (30) Kinsale (1) Londonderry (5) Newry (7) Rush (1) Strangford (1) Waterford (6)	204	81	151.9
Overseas Bases — Antigua (2) Barbados (2) Bermuda (3) Gibraltar (7) Jamaica (2) Leghorn (5) New York (8) Port Mahon (4) Quebec (2)	65	35	204.3
Port Unknown	37	36	127.7
	7352	2676	205.9

Figures in brackets denote actual vessels.
Source: PRO, HCA 25/56-122; HCA 26/33-70.

Two influences, in particular, seem to have had an extraordinary impact upon the spatial dispersal of privateering activity in the 1777–1783 conflict. Firstly, the war caused severe difficulties for British merchants and shipowners engaged in the North American and West Indian trades, as the rebels closed markets to British goods, and set forth a considerable force of commerce-raiders to prey on the ships of their erstwhile trading partners in the Caribbean, the North Atlantic and in European waters. Accordingly, ports with major interests in the Atlantic staple trades exhibited a marked growth in privateering investment as merchants equipped their vessels with commissions to operate as 'letters of marque' or private men-of-war. Thus, Liverpool's licensed fleet comprised 390 vessels, an increase of over 50 per cent on the Seven Years' War, while Lancaster and Whitehaven doubled their stake in the business and the Clydeside ports of Glasgow and Greenock extended their interest in privateering from 22 to 207 commissioned vessels over the same period. Bristol, however, a port with long-held, if declining, interests in the colonial trades, failed to respond in like manner to the adverse wartime circumstances, a decline of 50 commissioned vessels on the 1756–1762 fleet indicating, perhaps, the extent of the port's demise in the face of growing competition from other west coast bases.

In the second place, the enmity of the United Provinces, unprecedented in the eighteenth-century, served to stimulate privateering enterprise in general, and that of the lesser outports in particular. While entrepreneurs in London and other major ports responded very positively to the predatory opportunities thrown up by the Dutch War, it was in the harbours and havens of southern England that the 'spirit of privateering' was invoked most dramatically. This was reflected in the issue of privateer commissions; thus, 39 ports in the regional groupings of south-east and south-west England took out 338, or 27.4 per cent, of the letters of marque granted against the Dutch, while they accounted for just 825, or 13.5 per cent, of the licences issued against the other three adversaries. Venturers from small bases such as Fowey, Padstow, Penryn, and Ryde first engaged in the privateering business on the advent of the Dutch War, while Dartmouth, Dover, Exeter and Folkestone, long accustomed to setting forth commerce-raiders against French and Spanish trade, fitted out a large proportion of their commissioned fleets after 26 December 1780.[16] If the knowledge that 'the Channel is at this moment full of Dutchmen'[17] stirred merchants in these bases to employ 'every vessel that can swim upon the water for 24 hours . . . for a cruise against the Dutch',[18] interest in cruising against the Republic's trade was scarcely less enthusiastic elsewhere. Thus, locational advantages persuaded venturers in east coast ports—from Aberdeen south to Harwich—to fit out predators in the quest for Dutch prizes in the North Sea, while the commerce-raiding impulse was also felt in Irish bases and in the coastal communities of western Scotland.[19]

The rebellion of the American colonies and the formal hostility of the United Provinces also affected the composition of the fleet commissioned in the High Court of Admiralty. In broad terms, the marked trans-Atlantic character of the conflict stimulated all forms of 'letter of marque' enterprise. Accordingly, an unprecedented number of 'cruising voyages' to the Caribbean were instigated as venturers sought to exploit the predatory void created in that station by the changed allegiance of American commerce-raiders; 'specialist vessels', in the form of transports, victuallers and ordnance ships hired by the government and commissioned by their owners, were increasingly important as the needs of war in a distant theatre escalated; while 'armed trading vessels', as in all the eighteenth-century privateering conflicts, 'ran' for a variety of destinations, their operations dominating the business prior to the commencement of the Anglo-French War in August 1778. For its part, the war against Dutch trade fostered a marked expansion in the 'Channel' branch of the licensed fleet; though private men-of-war of more substantial proportions were active in this phase of the war, the nature of the prey determined that the small-scale predator should dominate the privateering response of 1780–1781.

This is not to suggest that 'Channel' commerce-raiding venturers had lain dormant until the grant of reprisals against the United Provinces. Indeed, their diminutive commerce-raiders had been in evidence as early as the spring of 1778, and continued to feature in privateering operations throughout the war—to the extent that this branch of the business reached its peak for the century as a whole in the 1777–1783 conflict. Thus, as Table 21 indicates, 517 'Channel' privateers were set forth during the war,[20] a fleet nearly twice as large as that commissioned in the 1756–1762 contest.

Table 21

'Channel' Privateers by Region, 1777–1783

Region	Vessels of 2.5 tons per man or less		Regional Total	% 'Channel'
	-49 tons	50-99 tons		
London	6	37	719	6
Bristol	8	13	203	10.3
Liverpool	5	15	390	5.1
Channel Is (3)	65	67	223	59.2
E England (7)	6	10	135	11.9
SE England (17)	49	33	243	33.7
SW England (24)	78	65	283	50.5
Wales &				
NW England (4)	3	6	80	11.3
W Scotland (3)	2	6	216	3.7
E Scotland (5)	1	4	32	15.6
Ireland (7)	5	17	81	27.2
Overseas Bases (3)	3	3	35	17.1
Port Unknown	6	4	36	27.8
	237	280		

Figures in brackets denote number of ports.
Source: PRO, HCA 25/56-122; HCA 26/33-70.

Though the Channel Islands and the bases of south-east England remained important, the West Country emerged as the leading centre of 'Channel' activity in the 1777–1783 war. Small-scale predators belonging to 24 south-western ports—20 on the Channel shore, as well as Bideford, Ilfracombe, Padstow and St Ives on the north coast—embarked during the conflict. While Plymouth, Dartmouth and Falmouth venturers were at the forefront of this burst of privateering activity, investors from small havens such as Brixham, Gweek and Penryn were also tempted into the commerce-raiding business. Elsewhere, interest in this form of predation was widely apparent, both in the major overseas trading ports and in bases such as Hull, Lancaster, Newcastle and Swansea which had hitherto remained aloof from 'Channel' operations; moreover, news that 'the spirit of privateering seems to prevail in every seaport town in Scotland'[21] was vindicated by the rare involvement of eight Scottish ports in the outfit of archetypal 'Channel' craft.

The fluctuating level of activity within the the 'Channel' sector—as charted in Appendix 2—suggests that seasonal factors were at play, with peaks evident in the summers of 1779, 1780 and 1782. Overriding the influence of the season, however, was the impact of the extent and character of the target, for 'Channel' operations were clearly conditioned by fluctuations in the 'state of the war'. In 1777 and the early months of 1778, therefore, such enterprise was limited to a handful of predators, a reflection of the distance and relative poverty of rebel commerce. As American trade with France developed—and Anglo-French relations deteriorated accordingly—during the course of 1778, so the interest of 'Channel' venturers was awakened; thus, a number of Channel Island craft set forth on cruises anticipating the outbreak of the increasingly inevitable conflict with France, while Dover's merchants were alert to the diplomatic situation, with correspondence dated 11 July 1778 suggesting that

> our people here, who had such great success with their privateers last war, are determined not to be idle spectators if a Rupture commences with France; we have several vessels ready to be converted into Privateers ... when we are sure of having employment for them.[22]

When the time came, in August 1778, six Dover vessels were duly commissioned, while 'Channel' predators were also set forth from Hastings, Rye and Southampton. Folkestone, however, emerged as the South East's leading commerce-raiding port, with the town's shipowners despatching 25 'Channel' and relatively small 'deep-water' craft in the autumn of 1778. Newspaper readers were informed that some of these vessels possessed particular handling qualities; thus,

> a number of Folkestone cutters are to be commissioned and fitted out as privateers. The utility of these vessels is well known to most seamen, as they can lie half a point nearer to the wind than a square-rigged vessel.[23]

In the Channel Islands, the pace of privateering activity inevitably quickened with the formal outbreak of hostilities with France. Letters of marque against French trade were acquired for those vessels which had set forth on anticipatory cruises, while a further 52 ventures were mounted from the Islands—nine from Alderney, 19 from Guernsey, and 25 from Jersey—before the end of 1778. Predictably, this enterprise was largely undertaken in relatively small vessels, with the *Jersey*, of 45 tons burthen and 30 men, and the 80-ton *Tyger*, with a 60-strong crew, typical of the scale of operations.[24] The principal object of such vessels, and their peacetime occupation, was indicated by a correspondent from Plymouth; thus,

> all the vessels from the islands of Jersey and Guernsey, which before the disturbances were employed in the smuggling trade, are now converted into privateers, of which there are a great number, who annoy the French home trade exceedingly.[25]

'Channel' ventures were launched in various other ports in the wake of the grant of general reprisals against France. Venturers set forth some 20 or so small-scale predators from harbours in Cornwall, Devon and Dorset, with Penzance the most notable Cornish port, and Dartmouth and Poole—the focal points of the Newfoundland trade—particularly prominent. Further north, the onset of the French War precipitated widespread interest in 'Channel' commerce-raiders, with small, heavily-manned vessels setting forth from Chester and Whitehaven, from Belfast and Dublin, and from Clydeside and Edinburgh. Moreover, a handful of Bristol and Liverpool vessels were deployed in this business, while London merchants invested in craft such as the *Swallow* and the *Tartar*—sent out on anticipatory cruises in the summer of 1778—and the *Chance*, *Favourite* and *Fly*, all of which displayed the characteristics of the 'Channel' predator. In sum, this widespread interest in small-scale predatory ventures amounted to a veritable boom in the business, with the peak of 74 vessels and 2,597 men 'in commission' during October

1778 substantially eclipsing levels of 'Channel' activity achieved in previous conflicts.

Investment in 'Channel' privateers tended to wane during 1779 and 1780, though the intervention of Spain led to a slight resurgence, with 43 predators, requiring the services of 1,729 seafarers, operational in July 1779. However, it was the outbreak of the Dutch War in December 1780 which elevated 'Channel' enterprise to remarkable and unprecedented heights. Thus, in January and February 1781, at least 10,000 seafarers were engaged in over 300 small-scale private men-of-war set forth on short cruises of up to six months' duration. The Channel Islands, south-east England and, most significantly, the West Country were the main centres of this commerce-raiding assault, though the 'spirit of privateering' was by no means restricted to the ports fringing the English Channel. Indeed, the prospect of Dutch prizes stimulated activity in scores of ports, and was largely responsible for the diffusion of 'Channel' enterprise into maritime districts like Scotland and north-east England which had previously exhibited little concern for such endeavours.

Without question, it was the extent, proximity and vulnerability of Dutch trade which conditioned the scale and form of the British privateering response of 1780–1781. 'Before the Dutch can possibly put themselves on the defensive', ran one report, 'their trade must be nearly ruined; they now have full 16,000 traders employed, a very considerable part of which must of necessity fall into our hands'.[26] Another correspondent predicted that

> the present moment is a fine harvest for privateers, the trade of the Dutch being now very great and several homeward bound fleets are shortly expected, which from their imaginary security must fall an easy conquest to our ships of war.[27]

News that valuable Dutch merchantmen, in 'their imaginary security', had innocently put into Dover and the Thames, to be taken by boatmen and watermen 'without noise or difficulty',[28] apparently bore out these opinions and added further to the excitement. Haste was of the essence, for the enemy would not remain so ignorant for long, while competition from other predators would naturally intensify as the favourable prospects for commerce-raiding became apparent to one and all. Accordingly, hectic activity was seen at Doctors' Commons as agents sought commissions for ventures already launched; provincial newspapers, from the *Exeter Flying Post*, the *Sherborne and Yeovil Mercury* and *Felix Farley's Bristol Journal* in the West Country, to the *Glasgow Mercury* and the *Newcastle Chronicle* in the north, abounded with advertisements of ships for sale under the heading 'Dutch War', and recruitment notices for commerce-raiders—for 'now's the time to make your fortunes my lads, and drub the Dutch!';[29] in London, the shipping market was buoyant as

> almost every ship that lay for sale, or lay idle in the Thames, was bought up yesterday and men instantly employed to fit it out and make it ready with all possible dispatch, to act as a letter of marque or privateer against . . . the United Provinces.[30]

Such was the demand that London investors travelled to the outports to procure shipping; thus, in Portsmouth,

> we are mad with joy at the prospect of a Dutch War: the town is full of people from London come down to buy ships for privateers: they give any price, let the vessel be ever so small.[31]

This privateering 'mania' had burned itself out by mid-1781 as the aggression of British privateers and naval vessels resulted in the loss or withdrawal of much of the Dutch mercantile fleet. Thus, the clamour to obtain letters of marque against the Dutch had abated by March, while the rate of activity in the 'Channel' sector had fallen to 41 vessels and 1,270 seafarers by July, and the turn-of-the-year reports of frenetic purchasing activity in the shipping market had given way to advertisements of privateers for sale in the summer months.[32] Within a short period, therefore, the speculative cycle had run its course, and the cutters, luggers and sloops hastily fitted out as 'Channel' private ships-of-war at the height of the boom had returned to the commercial sector; in the meantime, they had played the leading role in the most intensive bout of British privateering activity witnessed in the 'long' eighteenth century.

'Deep-water' enterprise also reached a climax during the privateering 'mania', with 111 ventures declared to be enlisting an aggregate of 8,947 seafarers in February 1781 (see Appendix 2). This peak was much less pronounced than that evident in the 'Channel' sector, however, for it only marginally exceeded the levels of activity apparent in the months following the grant of reprisals against France and Spain. It was less dramatic in a long-term context, moreover, for employment levels in the 'deep-water' branch of the privateering business declined during the 1777–1783 conflict, despite the rise in the number of ventures undertaken. The explanation for this seemingly contradictory pattern is quite clear; while an average crew size of 148 privateersmen had prevailed in the peak month of the Seven Years' War, the mean complement serving aboard the much larger 'deep-water' fleet of February 1781 was just over 80 strong; as Table 22 indicates, relatively small-scale predatory units, engaging the services of less than 100 men, dominated this form of enterprise in the American Revolutionary War.

Table 22

'Deep-Water' Private Ships-of-War by Region, 1777–1783

Region	Crew Size				Regional Total	% 'Deep-Water'
	49-99*	100-149	150-199	200 +		
London	38	19	5	6	719	9.5
Bristol	20	18	3	0	203	20.2
Liverpool	14	5	0	0	390	4.9
Channel Is (3)	46	11	0	0	223	25.6
E England (2)	0	3	0	0	135	2.2
SE England (6)	22	9	1	0	243	13.2
SW England (10)	20	6	2	0	283	9.9
Wales & NW England (3)	6	1	0	0	80	8.8
W Scotland (3)	11	1	1	0	216	6
E Scotland (4)	4	0	0	0	32	12.5
Ireland (3)	6	3	1	0	81	12.3
Overseas Bases (2)	2	4	0	0	35	17.1
	189	80	13	6		

* Vessels exceeding 99 tons burthen manned in the ratio of 2.5 tons per man or less.

Figures in brackets denote number of ports.

Source: PRO, HCA 25/56-122; HCA 26/33-70.

In terms of the number of ventures launched, 'deep-water' commerce-raiding reached its eighteenth-century zenith in the 1777–1783 war, though, in relative terms, the 288 large-scale predators set forth constituted a much smaller proportion of Britain's privateering enterprise than had been the case in the mid-century conflicts. Regionally, this element of the fleet was broadly based, with every maritime district participating in the activity, and London and Bristol much less predominant than previously. Nevertheless, echoes of the 1740s and the 1750s were still evident; thus, London remained the most important base, with 68 'deep-water' vessels fitted out in the Thames, including all six of the private ships-of-war declared to be enlisting at least 200 seafarers. Typically, 'stout' vessels such as the 480-ton *Queen Charlotte*, owned by the 'Reprisal Association' and equipped with 28 nine- and four-pound guns, and the *Terrible*, of 400 tons burthen, 26 nine- and four-pounders and 12 swivels, were the craft in which these complements sought their fortunes.[33] Amongst their number was the *Tartar*, the only semblance of an 'expedition' mounted in the war; of 600 tons burthen and 220 men, she was set forth by a group of London and Channel Island merchants to cruise in the East Indies.[34] However, the *Enterprize*, reputedly 'the finest ship of war yet fitted out by the merchants of the City of London',[35] was probably the most powerful of these 'privateers of force'. Captain Thomas Eden's declaration stated that she was 700 tons burthen, with 32 carriage guns of nine, six and four pounds weight of shot, 24 swivels and a crew of 200 men, while newspaper reports indicated that formerly she had been the *Aquilon*, a naval frigate purchased by a syndicate of commerce-raiding entrepreneurs headed by Sir John and Sir Robert Eden, brothers of the commander.[36]

Bristol merchants also persevered with large-scale operations, to the extent that one-fifth of the port's licensed fleet bore the hallmarks of the 'deep-water' venture. Though the vast companies of 200 or more privateersmen no longer departed from Kingroad, the scale of Bristol's predatory operations still drew contemporary comment; thus, in the autumn of 1778, one observer noted that

> privateering goes on with the utmost alacrity at this port. Our cruisers now exceed 30 sail, several of them stout ships, mounting upwards of 30 guns, nine- and six-pounders, and carrying near 200 men.[37]

Despite the persistent, if waning, interest of London and Bristol in particularly large-scale operations—and the outfit of vessels requiring 150 or more privateersmen in such bases as Exeter, Hastings and Glasgow—the trend towards the deployment of less powerful predators which had surfaced in the Seven Years' War accelerated in the 1777–1783 conflict. Clearly, the day of the 'privateer of force' had all but passed, as 'deep-water' privateering enterprise was increasingly embodied in craft of 100 to 250 tons burthen, worked by companies of 40 to 99 seafarers. As in the previous war, factors of supply and demand contrived to fashion this shift. Accordingly, labour was relatively scarce, as naval employment continued to rise, peaking at 107,446 men early in 1783;[38] meanwhile, the Bourbon powers and the Americans increasingly used neutral ships for the carriage of their trans-Atlantic commerce, and neutral entrepots in the West Indies for the transshipment of contraband cargoes. Substantial concentrations of manpower were therefore difficult and expensive to assemble, and somewhat unnecessary for the apprehension of a prey that relied upon diplomatic immunity rather than carriage guns and cutlasses for its safe passage.

Under such influences, 'deep-water' activity tended to meld with other forms of predatory enterprise. In the Channel Islands and the ports of south-east and south-west England, commerce-raiders of over 100 tons burthen were more abundant than in earlier wars. Yet their crews rarely exceeded 60 to 70 men, an indication that shipowners in these centres of 'Channel' enterprise were able and willing to employ larger vessels in their customary form of predatory pursuit rather than a sign of a wholesale shift in their investment strategy. In the ports with major interests in the West Indies trade, 'deep-water' resources were deployed in the outset of 'cruising voyages' to a Caribbean theatre that was awash with both prey and cargo, and, unusually, was devoid of rival predators from the North American colonies. Bristol's largest privateering crew, for instance, was engaged in the 300-ton *Minerva*, 'a vessel intended to cruise in consort with the ship *Byron*, on a cruising voyage to Jamaica', a venture in which her projected complement of 180 men was to receive 'the customary Monthly Wages, besides their share of Prize Money.'[39] In the event, the *Minerva* returned to her home port with 193 men in her company, while the *Byron* was worked by 155 and 156 seafarers in two separate 'cruising voyages' to the West Indies.[40] Such complements were abnormally large, however, for the payment of wages encouraged shipowners to limit the size of their crews; thus, companies engaged in 'cruise and voyage' ventures usually ranged in strength from 60 to 150 men as the muster rolls submitted by Bristol captains between 1778 and 1782 make clear.[41]

Crews of this size were also common in Liverpool's commissioned fleet. Here, surviving muster rolls suggest that the port's commerce-raiding complements were generally larger than those quoted in the letter of marque declarations, that Liverpool's interest in 'deep-water' privateering was more intense than is indicated in Table 22.[42] At least 40 of the crew lists submitted to the Sixpenny Office by Liverpool masters related to vessels engaged in predatory activity, though there were probably many others as contemporary accounts indicate that over 100 commerce-raiders embarked from the Mersey in the winter of 1778–1779 alone.[43] 'Cruise and voyage' ventures formed an important part of this fleet, with the *Mentor*, advertised as sailing for Jamaica 'with all commissions against the Americans, French and Spaniards', and the *Bess*—'intended to sail upon a Cruize from Liverpool for 6 months, then to proceed to St Vincent' - typifing the 'dualism' of this type of activity.[44] Moreover, Liverpool venturers, with no real tradition of 'deep-water' commerce-raiding, appear to have deployed the organisational structure utilised in 'cruising voyages' in a number of their private ships-of-war. The *Ellis* and the *Gregson*, for instance, cruised upon French colonial trade in the Western Approaches in the classic fashion of the 'deep-water' predator, yet their crews owned just one quarter of the prize fund thereby generated—a division of spoils current in 'letters of marque' (see Appendix 5); similarly, the *Enterprize*'s men were paid wages—a further trait of the 'letter of marque'—even though the owners' instructions to the captain made it abundantly clear that the seizure of prizes, and not the carriage of cargo, was the venture's sole purpose.[45]

While 'cruise and voyage' ventures added a Caribbean dimension to 'deep-water' enterprise in the 1777–1783 conflict, more conventional, commercially-oriented forms of 'letter of marque' were an important feature of the commissioned fleet. 'Armed traders' were in evidence throughout the conflict; prior to France's formal intervention, these licensed merchantmen outnumbered private men-of-war by a considerable margin, and even at the height of the commerce-raiding 'mania' of 1780–1781 over one-third of the vessels commissioned were principally engaged in the carriage of goods.[46] An exceptional view of the range of trades in which these licensed merchant vessels were employed can be gained from the cargo and destination details demanded of declarants seeking privateer commissions against the rebel colonists.[47] The strong trans-Atlantic flavour of much of this enterprise is clearly apparent, with vessels sailing for a variety of locations in the western hemisphere. Canada was the destination of a number of privately-operated vessels; thus, the *Amazon* and the *Jenny* departed London for Quebec loaded with bale goods, hardware and refined sugar, the *St Lawrence* headed for Montreal with linens, woollens and wine, and various other craft, principally from Liverpool and London, were bound for Halifax with cargoes of bricks, rum, salt and woollens. Greenlandmen such as the *Achilles* and the *Marianne* of London, and the *Cove, Dolphin, John's Margaret, Marlborough* and *Priscilla* of Newcastle, were fitted out in the Tyne and despatched to the whale fishery in the Davis Straits.[48]

The Newfoundland trade was well represented in the declarations with vessels such as the *Molly* of Dartmouth, the *Friendship* of Exeter, the *Earl of Sandwich* of Poole and the Teignmouth-based *Racehorse*—laden with plantation stores, provisions, and 'materials for the Newfoundland fishery' —reflecting the West Country's strong interest in the cod-fishing business. Bristol merchants also engaged in the trade, with John Noble taking out commissions for the *Charlotte*, of 180 tons burthen and 15 men, and the 150-ton *Hope,* with a crew of 20 men, both bound for Newfoundland with salt, iron and 'divers merchandises' in 1778; similarly, Jersey entrepreneurs equipped their deep-sea fishing vessels with privateering licences, while the Liverpool merchantmen *Bellona* and *Quaker,* the *Joseph* and *Katty* of Greenock, and London vessels such as the 90-ton lugger *Intrepid,* supplied the 'oldest colony' with coals, provisions and dry goods. In many cases, this voyage across the North Atlantic to Canada or Newfoundland was merely the first leg of a 'triangular' route, the Halifax and Quebec ships frequently sailing to the West Indies before returning to the British Isles, and the Newfoundland fishing craft carrying their cargoes of cod and train oil, in time-honoured fashion, to a market in Catholic Europe, variously specified in the declarations as the 'Streights', 'Leghorn' or 'Spain, Portugal or Italy'.

'Armed trading vessels' destined for loyal ports on North America's eastern seaboard were fitted out at a number of bases. Cargoes of cheese, flour, porter, salt and the ubiquitous 'provisions' were despatched to New York from Glasgow and Greenock, Whitehaven and Workington, as well as from the Mersey and the Thames; in 1780 and 1781, the *Antigallican, Bassil* and *Hope* of Liverpool, and the *Hercules* and *Lady Georgiana* of London, conveyed provisions to Charlestown, South Carolina, while the London vessel *Alert* and the *Tonyn* of Liverpool headed for Georgia; further south, St Augustine, in East Florida, was an intended port of call for Glasgow ships such as the *Alexander* and the *Glasgow,* and the *Patowmack* of London, in their respective voyages to the Caribbean; moreover, commissioned traders occasionally embarked from London for mainland bases in the Gulf of Mexico, steering a course for West Florida, Pensacola, the Musquito Shore or the Bay of Honduras.

The Caribbean, however, was the principal focus of Britain's trans-Atlantic 'letter of marque' activity, as 'armed trading vessels' as well as 'cruise and voyage' ventures headed for this critical theatre. Armed merchantmen cleared for a variety of West Indian destinations with Antigua, Barbados, Grenada, Jamaica, Nevis, St Christopher, St Kitts, St Vincent and Tobago all cited in the declarations. London and Liverpool dominated this trade, though Bristol and the Clydeside ports fitted out numerous West Indiamen, and vessels also sailed for the Caribbean from bases as diverse as Ayr, Cork, Dublin, Hastings, the Isle of Man, Lancaster and Whitehaven. Such craft ranged from 60 to 400 tons burthen, with crews of between 10 and 50 seafarers enlisted to load and defend cargoes of provisions and supplies of all kinds—from bricks, coal and wrought iron to beef, butter, beer and candles, to linens, woollens and osnabrigs.

Cargoes were also picked up *en route* to the West Indies; it was common for trading vessels to call in at Cork or Waterford to take in 'Irish provisions' to convey across the Atlantic; other licensed vessels called at Halifax or Newfoundland to load fish and timber for consumption on the sugar plantations; yet more headed for the coast of Africa with calicoes, muslins or 'East India goods for the purchase of slaves', thence proceeding to the Caribbean with the human cargoes exchanged for these goods. In this latter trade, Liverpool was predominant by the 1770s, and at least 41 of the port's commissioned fleet embarked on this triangular route, despite the adverse conditions which had brought such traffic to a virtual standstill by 1779.[49] London's interest in slaving was reflected in the outset of licensed ships such as the *Adventure, London* and *Winchcomb,* while Bristol's merchants obtained privateering licences for a handful of slavers, and Channel Island entrepreneurs occasionally speculated in such commerce, the 70-ton *Tartar* of Guernsey, for instance, heading for 'the coast of Africa and Barbados' in June 1778.

Vessels engaged in a variety of European trades were also commissioned against the rebel colonists. Thus, the declarations indicate that the 400-ton *Active* was due to sail from her home port of Yarmouth to London with provisions, while the *Carpenter* of Liverpool, a 600-ton vessel laden with salt, was similarly commissioned for a short voyage to the capital and back in 1781. In September 1777, the Glasgow ships *Cunningham* and *Neptune* were commissioned for their voyages to Cette in southern France with cargoes of tobacco. Northern European destinations were cited in a number of declarations, with the *King of Spain* of Borrowstoness sailing for St Petersburg, the *George* and the *William* of Liverpool, and the *William* of London, bound for Riga with salt and provisions, the *Albion* leaving the Thames in ballast for Stettin to pick up a cargo of staves, and the *Aurora* and *Ceres* clearing the Mersey for Archangel with salt; in addition, ships such as the *Empress of Russia,* owned by Chester merchants, and various London-based vessels were destined simply for the 'Baltick'. Generally, such craft were capacious, burthen between 250 and 500 tons, with relatively small crews to load and protect their cargoes of grain and timber in the return passage across the North Sea. Ships of a similar size were engaged in the Mediterranean trade, with declarants quoting destinations such as Genoa, Leghorn and Turkey in applying for their commissions. This route was more hazardous than the short voyage to Scandinavia, however, and larger crews were recruited, primarily for defensive purposes; thus, in July 1779, a correspondent from Leghorn related that

> yesterday sailed from hence, in company, the *Favourite*, *Saville*, *Italian Merchant*, and *Smyrna Gally*, all Turkeymen for England. They are all large ships, have letters of marque, and each of them mounts upwards of 20 guns. They are estimated to be worth over £200,000 sterling, and are exceedingly well manned and prepared for defence, should they be attacked, and no small force will be able to take them.[50]

Various types of 'specialist vessel' were also commissioned in the American Revolutionary War. Primarily concerned, like the 'armed trading vessel', with the carriage of goods, or with other particular duties, the licences carried by these craft added a prize-taking element to their operations. An important part of this enterprise was a direct consequence of the American orientation of the military struggle, for in attempting to solve the 'unprecedented administrative and logistical problems arising from the necessity of supporting a great army and a large naval force in the western hemisphere',[51] the government hired a large number of merchant ships to transport the tools of war across the Atlantic and to other theatres of war. In general, these were relatively large vessels, hired for their carrying capacity rather than their speed or fighting capabilities. Accordingly, it was to Liverpool, London and the bases of north-east England—where such bulk carriers were readily available—that the government's procurement agencies looked for the requisite tonnage. Thus, at least 11 of Liverpool's licensed vessels were leased to the state during the war, with five retained in the service of the Navy Board, and six more deployed by the 'Lords of the Treasury'. These vessels ranged in size from the *Jonathon*, of 180 tons burthen and 35 men, employed to carry coals to Jamaica, to the 749-ton *Robinson*, and the *Mersey*, a vessel of 751 tons burthen engaged to convey stores to North America in 1777.[52] In the North East, commissioned vessels such as the 350-ton, 60-man *Friendship* of Whitby, the *Aid*, of 340 tons burthen and 30 men, belonging to Scarborough, and the *Peggy* of Shields, of 240 tons burthen and 30 men, typified the craft enlisted to serve the war effort,[53] while vessels of similar dimensions were hired at Glasgow and Whitehaven.

London, however, was the principal source of the government's shipping requirement. This is reflected in the capital's commissioned fleet, for 106, or 14.7 per cent, of the 719 licenced vessels fitted out in the Thames were employed in 'His Majesty's service'. Varying in size from the 158-ton *Golden Fleece* to the *Denbigh*, and the *Juliana*, both of 800 tons burthen,[54] the cargoes of these vessels were as diverse as their intended voyages. Coals, naval stores, ordnance, provisions, troops and victualling goods were loaded into the holds of the capital's hired ships, with North America—Florida, Halifax, New York, Quebec, or, in desperation, 'any port in north or south America in His Majesty's troop's hands'[55]—the main destinations, though some were bound for Antigua, Barbados and Jamaica, and others for Gibraltar and Minorca. If this indicates the range of territories Britain was obliged to protect in the war, the complexity of the bureaucratic machinery which evolved to deal with the logistics of this defence is suggested by the fact that London shipowners leased their vessels to four separate government agencies. Thus, the 'Lords of the Treasury' and the Ordnance Board each hired 33 of London's commissioned vessels, while 25 were contracted to the Navy Board, two to the Victualling Board, and a further 13 commanders declared that their vessels were 'retained in His Majesty's service'. Though such a procurement system tended to drive up freight rates as the various agencies competed with each other for the available tonnage, the formidable task of conveying men and material to the principal areas of conflict was accomplished without seriously impeding the British war effort.

Nearer home, the servants of another government agency invested in the privateering business as the Commissioners of His Majesty's Customs noted the receipt of 'many applications . . . from the Commanders of the cruizers in the service of this Revenue desiring our leave to take out Letters of Marque'.[56] Such leave was granted on the clear understanding that the right of reprisal bestowed upon these craft by privateering licences was secondary to the vessel's normal employment and had no bearing on any illicit goods taken in the line of duty. Commissions were obtained at the captain's own expense and, 'as the Revenue will not be benefited by any of of the Captures that may be taken from the enemy', any damage sustained in the process of such seizures was to be borne by the licensee himself. Captains such as Richard Wallis, commander of the *Rose* of Southampton, were therefore granted a form of perquisite in that he and his crew of two mates and 17 mariners were permitted to use the 200-ton *Rose* against the enemy provided that such activity did not impede his regular duty, and that it was undertaken at his own risk.[57] Similar arrangements prevailed in the *Assistance* of Dover, a revenue vessel of 168 tons burthen, served by a captain, two lieutenants, a master, a gunner, and 16 able and ordinary seamen,[58] the *Brilliant* of St Ives,[59] and the *Eagle* and *Swallow*, two 'Customs House cutters' which brought a Dutch privateer into Shields on 1 April 1782.[60]

The ships of the chartered trading companies were the remaining type of 'specialist vessel' to be commissioned in the American Revolutionary War. As in previous conflicts, the Hudson's Bay Company equipped its vessels with licences, three ships leaving the Thames for the Bay in the May of each wartime year carrying cargoes of 'woollens and linens, powder, arms, ammunition and provisions.'[61] Typically, the East India Company was more active; thus, Hardy's *Register* indicates that 101 vessels left the Thames for India and China on behalf of the Honourable Company from 1777 to 1783.[62] Privateering licences were carried by 84 of these Indiamen, which ranged in size from the 606-ton *Blandford* to the *Locke*, London's largest commissioned vessel at 1,100 tons burthen.[63] Though generally larger than their predecessors, these ships were still navigated by crews of 99 men, armed with 26 carriage guns, and victualled for 12 to 24 months—characteristics which had applied in the mid-century wars. Their cargoes normally consisted of provisions, bale goods, iron and woollens, though troops were occasionally transported to the Orient, and vessels such as the *Bessborough* were loaded with 'naval and victualling stores for the use of His Majesty's ships in the East Indies', as well as 'goods on account of the East India Company'.[64]

While Indiamen and Hudson's Bay vessels were a regular facet of British privateering enterprise in the wars of the eighteenth century, the issue of licences for Customs cutters and government transports accentuated the size and diversity of the 'specialist' element of the commissioned fleet. With growth evident in other forms of 'letter of marque' enterprise, and intensive activity periodically apparent in the predatory sector— notwithstanding the demise of the 'privateers of force'—the 1777–1783 fleet represented the largest and most cosmopolitan of the 'additional forces' set out in the 1689–1815 era.

II

The Prize Court in London condemned 2,333 of the properties seized during the course of the American Revolutionary War. As Table 23 indicates, private commissioned vessels assumed the ascendancy in the prize war, having 1,312 properties condemned, 56.2 per cent of the total successfully prosecuted at Doctors' Commons, compared to the Navy's return of 1,021 prizes. These totals include the 'final and definitive' sentences, though not the interlocutory decrees, relating to disputed properties, along with the common condemnations which were considered alone in previous wars. In comparison with the returns of earlier wars, therefore, the 1777–1783 prize figures are inflated by approximately 10 per cent. If this is taken into account, it is evident that the prize-taking performance of the fleet commissioned during the American Revolutionary War, in terms of the number of condemnations effected,

Table 23

Prizes Condemned at Doctors' Commons, 1776-1785

Year	American		French		Spanish		Dutch		Total	
	P	N	P	N	P	N	P	N	P	N
1776	0	11	0	0	0	0	0	0	0	11
1777	14	62	0	0	0	0	0	0	14	62
1778	79	37	122	43	0	0	0	0	201	80
1779	28	32	235	128	29	36	0	0	292	196
1780	22	14	184	129	41	51	0	0	247	194
1781	14	14	184	97	35	15	116	160	349	286
1782	22	13	99	92	19	8	13	35	153	148
1783	4	10	46	23	2	5	0	0	52	38
1784	0	0	2	3	0	2	0	0	2	5
1785	0	0	0	1	2	0	0	0	2	1
	183	193	872	516	128	117	129	195	1312	1021

P = Privateers' prizes.
N = Naval prizes, including 'droits and perquisites' of the Admiralty.
Source: PRO, HCA 34/43-57, 59.

surpassed that of Queen Anne's War by approximately 200 condemnations, and represented a substantial improvement on the 'catch' taken in the mid-century conflicts. In relative terms, however, the privateering effort of the 1777–1783 conflict was less impressive, for it was achieved by the largest licensed fleet set forth in the era; accordingly, a 'productivity rate' of two privateers per prize was recorded by the 1777–1783 force, as against an equivalent rate of 1.4 in the 1702–1712 war.

The annual distribution of condemnations presents the prize-taking picture in a slightly different light. As Table 23 shows, the great majority of prizes were sentenced between 1778 and 1782, with over 400 condemned in each of the years 1779, 1780 and 1781, surpassing the previous annual peak of 399 condemnations recorded in 1757. Commissioned vessels featured prominently in this activity, the yearly return of the licensed fleet from 1778 to 1782 comfortably exceeding that of the hitherto unprecedented 1745 figure of 121 condemnations. This was the most intensive phase of prize-taking activity witnessed thus far in the eighteenth century, with the 1781 total of 635 successful prosecutions the largest annual aggregate of the 1689–1783 period.

That this peak should occur in the first complete year in which Britain faced all four adversaries was no coincidence, for the dispersal of condemnations over the war years tended to follow the course of the war, expanding as the range of trade liable to confiscation widened. Thus, in 1776 and 1777, the prize return was relatively modest, and dominated by the Navy, as the sea-borne property of the rebel American colonists remained the sole target; thereafter, the successive entry of the European powers served to stimulate prize-taking activity as British ships-of-war, especially privately-owned commerce-raiders, grasped the opportunity to feed off an increasingly abundant prey. This climaxed in the winter of 1780–1781 when the onset of the Dutch War provoked a widespread speculative 'mania' in the privateering business and encouraged predators of all types—naval as well as private—to engage in an intensive bout of commerce-raiding aggression. However, as Table 23 illustrates, it was the French mercantile marine which suffered the heaviest losses to Britain's maritime forces during 1781 despite the impetus given to predatory activity by the prospect of the extensive and vulnerable Dutch merchant marine. This was true of the war as a whole—indeed, it was true of all the eighteenth-century conflicts—as the Bourbon power yielded 1,388 prizes to British commerce-raiders, 59.5 per cent of the overall total. While the privateering force accounted for 872, or 62.8 per cent, of the French condemnations, and a narrow majority of Spanish sentences, the Navy was predominant in the seizure and condemnation of American and Dutch prizes.

The King's ships were also considerably more significant in the fight against enemy naval vessels and *corsaires*. As in previous wars, the lion's share of the head money awarded to captors of hostile ships-of-war was claimed by naval seafarers. Indeed, as Table 24 shows, over 96 per cent of the £248,930 paid out in bounties during the American Revolutionary War rewarded men-of-warsmen, while privateering venturers received just £9,355. Some 47,915 seafarers served in the 93 enemy ships-of-war and 288 *corsaires* which represented the Navy's best aggregate 'catch' of the century to date. However, the average complement working aboard the

Table 24

Head Money Paid to Naval Seamen and Privateering Venturers, 1777–1783*

	Payments		Bounty Paid		Average size of captured crew
	No	%	£	%	
Privateers	46.5**	10.9	9355	3.8	40.2
Navy	381	89.1	239575	96.2	125.8
	427.5	100	248930	100	116.5

* Claims were not lodged, or are lacking, in respect of a number of eligible privateering prizes. See Appendix 1.

** Naval seamen and privateering venturers shared three bounty payments, while a further award was shared by naval seamen and colonial privateering venturers.

Source: PRO, ADM 43/23-31.

captured vessels-of-war, at 125.8 men, was marginally smaller than the equivalent figure for the 1756–1763 war, and some 24 men per vessel lighter than the mean crew taken in the Austrian Succession War.

Privateering venturers claimed head money on five enemy ships-of-war and 41.5 *corsaires*,[65] twice the number returned in the Seven Years' War; yet a decline in average crew size, from 79 to 40.2 men per captured vessel, meant that the total bounty paid increased by only £270 between the two conflicts. In terms of trade protection, therefore, the commissioned fleet continued to play a decidedly secondary role to that of the Navy, accounting for roughly one-tenth of the enemy vessels-of-war taken, a tenth which comprised the least powerful of the belligerent craft yielded to Britain's maritime forces. Moreover, while 37.3 per cent of the 1,021 properties condemned to naval vessels qualified for the payment of head money, only 3.5 per cent of the 1,312 prizes taken by private commissioned vessels warranted such a reward. Commerce-destruction, quite clearly, was the principal concern of the large privateering force set forth from over 100 British ports during the 1777–1783 conflict. The regional distribution of the prizes condemned to this diverse fleet is presented in Table 25.

Commissioned vessels from 52 British ports and two overseas bases enjoyed some success in the 1777–1783 prize war. As befitting the most decentralised privateering fleet set forth in the eighteenth century, this was clearly the most broadly-based prize-taking effort of the era, eclipsing that of the Spanish Succession War, when 23 separate bases had fitted out successful ventures. Such a widespread distribution of condemnations served to weaken the dominance that London, Bristol and the Channel Islands had displayed in the prize sentences of earlier conflicts. While the combined contributions of these three bases had accounted for at least 77 per cent of previous prize totals, their share amounted to just 49.5 per cent despite absolute increases in the 'catch' each recorded. Many of the residual prizes fell to ventures mounted from ports of south-east and south-west England, which claimed a joint 'haul' of 363 condemned properties, 27.7 per cent of the national total, and from Liverpool, where the 'spirit of privateering' was felt to such a degree that 139 prizes were taken by the town's privateers, an eight-fold increase on the Seven Years' War. Elsewhere, successes were more limited, though still notable in bases such as Edinburgh and Glasgow, which had never before had prizes condemned in the High Court of Admiralty, and in the ports of eastern England, where private men-of-war were fitted out for the first time. A further unusual feature of the distribution of prizes in the 1777-1783 conflict was the relatively high incidence of condemnations made to predators acting in consort with vessels from other ports, and with naval vessels; indeed, 73 prizes were shared in this fashion, 5.6 per cent of the aggregate prize figure, a sign that *ad hoc* combinations effected at sea were much more prevalent than in earlier wars.

If decentralisation characterised the distribution of prizes in the American Revolutionary War, differing regional traits were evident in

Table 25

Prizes Condemned to Commissioned Vessels by Region, 1777-1785

Region	Number of prizes
London	126
Bristol	88
Liverpool	139
Channel Is — Alderney (22) Guernsey (167) Jersey (239) Alderney/Guernsey (1) Alderney/Jersey (5) Guernsey/Jersey (1)	435
E England — Berwick (1) Bridlington (2) Harwich (6) Hull (6) Newcastle (8) Scarborough (1), Yarmouth (5) Whitby/Yarmouth (1)	30
SE England — Brighton (1) Cowes (9) Dover (88) Folkestone (56) Hastings (14) Margate (4) Portsmouth (6) Rye (11) Southampton (1) Dover/Folkestone (2) Folkestone/Hastings (1)	193
SW England — Bridport (2) Dartmouth (35) Exeter (7) Falmouth (16) Fowey (3) Gweek (6) Looe (2) Lyme (3) Penryn (1) Penzance (33) Plymouth (23) Poole (12) St Ives (9) Teignmouth (1) Weymouth (10) Penzance/Falmouth (1) Penzance/Gweek (3) Penzance/Penryn (1) Penzance/St Ives (1) Plymouth/Falmouth (1)	170
Wales & NW England — Chester (4) Lancaster (4) Pembroke (1) Whitehaven (2)	11
W Scotland — Glasgow (1) Greenock (1) Glasgow/Greenock (1)	3
E Scotland — Carron (1) Edinburgh (3)	4
Ireland — Belfast (4) Cork (1) Dublin (11)	16
Overseas Bases — Leghorn (42) Port Mahon (1)	43
In consort — London/Bristol (7) London/Dartmouth (1) London/Falmouth (2) London/Guernsey (1) London/HM* (2) London/Ilfracombe/Padstow/Penzance/Plymouth/Scilly/St Ives (1) London/Liverpool (2) London/Penryn (1) London/Southampton (1) Bristol/Alderney/Dartmouth/Falmouth (1) Bristol/Exeter (1) Bristol/Jersey (1) Bristol/Liverpool (3) Liverpool/Hastings (2) Liverpool/Jersey (6) Liverpool/Lancaster (2) Alderney/Dartmouth (1) Guernsey/Falmouth (1) Guernsey/Folkestone (1) Guernsey/Lancaster (1) Guernsey/Penzance (6) Jersey/HM (1) Jersey/Penzance (1) Jersey/Teignmouth (1) Newcastle/HM (1) Newcastle/Poole (1) Dover/Folkestone/HM (1) Folkestone/HM (1) Hastings/Dartmouth (1) Falmouth/HM (1) Plymouth/HM (1)	54
	1312

* HM denotes naval vessel

Source: PRO, HCA 25/56-122; HCA 26/33-70; HCA 34/43-57, 59.

terms of 'productivity', the nationality of prizes and the dispersal of condemnations over the war years. Thus, the Channel Islands were the most productive British base in terms of the quantity of prizes taken—with an average of 0.5 predators per prize, or two condemnations for every commissioned vessel; taking south-east and south-west England together, a ratio of two potential captors per prize pertained as an 'input' of 526 licensed vessels returned an 'output' of 263 condemnations, the most impressive of the mainland rates of return; meanwhile, in London, Bristol and Liverpool, comparable ratios of 5.7, 2.3 and 2.8 licensed vessels per condemnation applied respectively, though in each instance the rate of return represented an appreciable improvement on the equivalent 1756–1762 figure.

In most localities, the majority of properties condemned were French-owned. This was especially the case in the Channel Islands where French vessels and goods constituted 71 per cent of the prizes taken, and in south-eastern bases like Dover, with 65 French prizes, 73.9 per cent of the port's 'catch', and Folkestone, where 46 of the 56 properties condemned belonged to French subjects. It was also true of the major ports, for French property formed 55.7, 61.1 and 64.7 per cent of the prizes taken by Bristol, London and Liverpool privateers respectively. However, in the West Country and in eastern England, a slightly different pattern emerged; here, Dutch ships and cargoes tended to dominate the prize returns of ports such as Harwich, Hull, Penzance and St Ives, though the sea-borne commerce of the other adversaries was an important facet of the 'catches' of centres like Dartmouth and Newcastle. Related strongly to this distribution of prizes by nationality was the dispersal of condemnations over time. Accordingly, the bases which accounted for a preponderance of French prizes tended to engage in prize-taking activity from 1778 onwards, whereas the ports which displayed a stronger interest in Dutch prizes generally concentrated their efforts in 1781 and 1782.

The regional distribution of condemnations reflected, to a certain extent, the vitality of the various branches of the privateering business. In particular, the combined return of 798 prizes to ventures mounted in the ports of south-east and south-west England, and in the Channel Islands, suggests that 'Channel' privateering—largely based in these regions—was the most productive form of commerce-raiding enterprise in the American Revolutionary War. Though by no means all of these successes were recorded by small-scale predators, the prize-taking contribution of the 'Channel' arm of the business was swollen by the endeavours of venturers from a variety of other bases who engaged in this form of activity to an unprecedented degree, particularly after the onset of the Dutch War.

The character and significance of this enterprise is indicated by a wide array of evidence. Channel Island privateersmen, for instance, cruised to such effect in the opening two months of the French War that one commentator predicted that 'the owners of privateers, in the islands of Guernsey and Jersey, will most undoubtedly be the richest people in these islands'.[66] Their 'little brigs, not much bigger than common sloops' continued to 'prodigiously annoy the French commerce'[67] throughout the war, exacting a heavy toll upon France's coastal traffic, particularly in the Bay of Biscay. Nearly three-quarters of the Islanders' prizes were taken in this station, suggesting that the focus of their predatory operations had shifted southwards over the course of the century. Salt, wine and brandy, naval stores, and provisions such as grain, flour and meat were the principal cargoes seized, though occasionally Island predators secured the exotic produce of the Caribbean, taking French West Indiamen laden with cocoa, coffee, cotton and sugar as they approached Bordeaux, Le Havre or Nantes.[68] Outward-bound vessels from such ports also fell prey to Island venturers, whose French 'catch' was supplemented by the condemnation of 90 American-owned cargoes and vessels—the majority destined for the French market—33 Spanish properties, and just three Dutch prizes.

Neutral vessels carrying enemy or contraband goods were sometimes apprehended and prosecuted by Channel Island privateersmen. In southeast England, this variety of prey formed a much more important part of the regional prize return, as it had done in earlier rounds of the Anglo-French contest. Rising to 193 condemnations, with small havens such as Brighton and Margate participating in prize-taking activity for the first time, the South East's contribution included a significant number of contraband cargoes found in neutral holds. Dover's privateersmen appear to have been particularly adept at making such discoveries, at least half of the port's 88 prizes—a prolific return for a force of 48 commissioned vessels—constituting consignments of naval stores carried in neutral bottoms. In February 1779, for example, 11 Dutch vessels, three Swedish merchantmen and the *Jonge Printz*, a Russian ship carrying hemp, were arrested and taken into Dover. The Prize Court, in each instance, condemned the naval stores on board as French prize and ordered the release of the neutral vessel.[69] Folkestone was the other principal fount of this activity in the South East, with typical 'Channel' predators such as the *Active*, of 70 tons burthen and 40 men, and larger craft like the

210-ton *Union*, with 90 men in her company,[70] bringing in vessels belonging to Denmark, Hamburg, Lubeck, Sweden and, above all, the Dutch. Though most of these merchantmen were restored to their neutral owners, at least 30 of the cargoes found therein were adjudged contraband and therefore condemned as lawful prize to Folkestone venturers.

'Channel' enterprise flourished in other regions during the American Revolutionary War. The ports of south-west England engaged as never before in this form of commerce-raiding, with relatively small, heavily-manned predators such as the *Dolphin* and the *Union* of Penzance, and the *Lighthorse* of Plymouth, accounting for a number of French prizes in 1779 and 1780. However, it was the grant of reprisals against Dutch commerce in December 1780—precipitated, in part, by the persistent harassment of neutral vessels in the Channel—that induced venturers in the West Country and further afield to set forth a considerable 'additional force', composed primarily of 'Channel' privateers. The operational focus of this activity was the western reaches of the English Channel; here, no less than 30 vessels were in sight as *De Juffrow Susanna* succumbed to six joint-captors—three naval vessels and three private men-of-war—off the Scillies;[71] a further eight predators—belonging to Ilfracombe, London, Padstow, Penzance, Plymouth, Scilly and St Ives—participated in the capture of the *Princess of Orange*;[72] meanwhile, the Lisbon packet was boarded or spoken by more than 40 British cruisers and privateers in the Soundings, indicating 'how closely the mouth of the Channel was patrolled and how keen was the search'.[73]

These waters, it appears, teemed with commerce-raiders, leading to a proliferation of contested cases at Doctors' Commons as would-be joint-captors claimed a share in prizes on the grounds that they had been 'in sight of' the seizure or had otherwise materially assisted in the engagement; indeed, in one rather optimistic appeal, Edward Plaine, commander of the *Lark* of Falmouth, alleged that he had informed the *Fox*'s captain, James Verco, of the outbreak of hostilities with the Dutch and was therefore entitled to a part of the prize subsequently taken by the *Fox*.[74] Though Plaine's claim was dismissed, the success of other claimants explains the high incidence of joint condemnations in the American Revolutionary War and signifies the intensity of the privateering assault in the Channel during the early months of 1781.

West Country ports were at the forefront of this activity, with archetypal 'Channel' predators such as the *Dolphin* and the *Grace* of Penzance, the *Good Intent* and the *Swallow* of Looe, the *Snap Dragon* and the *Spider* of Dartmouth, and the *Fox* of Plymouth, accounting for the majority of the 170 condemnations recorded by the South West's privateering fleet. It was to Falmouth, Penzance and Plymouth that many of these prizes were returned, and it was in the inns and auction houses of these towns that condemned goods and vessels were offered for sale.[75] If such trade added to local commercial activity, a further boost was provided by the utilisation of south-western ports as re-fitting bases and prize marts by private men-of-war from other regions. In the opening days of the Dutch War, for instance, the London 'privateers of force' *Enterprize* and *Resolution* were re-fitted at Falmouth and Mount's Bay 'with all possible expedition, to cruize in search of Dutch merchantmen'.[76] Small-scale ventures from elsewhere also operated in the South West; thus, in May 1781, there was news that the *Kidnapper* of Lancaster had landed 'three more prizes' at Falmouth,[77] while two months earlier it had been reported that the '*Look Out,* Capt Wright, of L'pool with 4 guns has taken & sent into Scilly, the *De Vleyt,* from Curacao to Amsterdam laden with 724 bags coffee, 77 casks indigo, 100 hogsheads sugar', though the *Prince of Orange* of Guernsey, 'with 10-12 men, hove in sight & of course claims part of the seizure'.[78]

The predatory activity of 'Channel' privateers was also visible in more unusual theatres during the Dutch War, as small-scale ventures launched in Berwick, Hull, Newcastle and Yarmouth met with some success in the North Sea. Thus, the *Jonge Daniel,* a 'Dutch fishing smack from Arundale to Amsterdam with Lobsters is sent into Hull by the *Dolphin* . . . of 8 carriage guns, 8 swivels and 30 men',[79] while the *Caroline* of Hull carried home the *Elizabeth-Catherine,* 'from Memel with flax and hemp worth an estimated £5,000'.[80] Berwick predators were active at this juncture, the *Elizabeth* carrying the timber-laden *Hay Fortune* of Emden into Harwich,[81] and the *Intrepid* returning to her home port with an American brig and her cargo of tobacco apprehended off the coast of Norway.[82] Further west, 20 leagues NW of Shetland, the *Lively* of Leith reportedly captured two American vessels in their passage from Amsterdam to Boston, prizes worth an estimated £28,000,[83] while to the south the Yarmouth privateer *Spy* arrested the *St Anna,* a neutral vessel from Stockholm for Brest with a contraband cargo of pitch, iron, planks and tar.[84]

If such instances suggest the widespread character of 'Channel' privateering during the 1777–1783 conflict, further testimony to the effectiveness of this branch of the commerce-raiding business is afforded by the head money vouchers. In the mid-century wars, 'deep-water' venturers had claimed the vast majority of the bounties paid for the apprehension of the enemy's vessels-of-war, with the 'privateers of force'

especially prominent in this aspect of the prize war. However, in line with
the decline in the scale of operations, a fall in the average size of captured
crews was evident, from 79 in the 1756–1762 war to just 40.2 men in the
American Revolutionary War, with at least 27 of the 46.5 head money
payments awarded to captors manned by less than 40 men.[85] These
diminutive predators belonged to various southern ports, from Dover,
Folkestone, Hastings and Rye in the South East, to Falmouth, Penzance
and Plymouth in the West Country. Their prizes were generally taken
close to home; thus, the 16-man *Stag* of Rye captured *Le Vautour* of 48
men nine leagues from Dieppe and the 20-man *L'Espeigle* three leagues
off-shore in Rye Bay,[86] while the *Phoenix* and the *Shaftesbury* of Penzance
seized the *Marquis de Morbecq*, of 12 carriage guns and 59 men, a few miles
south of Start Point,[87] and the 26-man *Hind* apprehended *La Nannette*, a
corsaire of St Malo despatched to cruise on the English coast with 20 men
in her company.[88]

While these and other similar captures added head money to the
commerce-raiding profits of 'Channel' venturers, they also helped to
reduce the threat posed by enemy *corsaires* in coastal waters—a threat that
was quite considerable judging by newspaper accounts of the depredations
of the *Black Prince* in the Bristol Channel, the loss of a fleet of colliers off
Yarmouth and the capture of two vessels within sight of Exmouth Bar.[89]
'Deep-water' private ships-of-war, in contrast, contributed relatively little
to the protection of home trade during the 1777–1783 conflict; indeed,
only four of the muster rolls submitted to the Navy Office by commerce-
raiding venturers comprised more than 100 names, though crews of 99,
96 and 92 men were recored as serving aboard the *Active,* the *Bellona* and
the *Brutus*.[90] A further sign that the decline evident in the extent of the
large-scale arm of the privateering business was matched by a fall in its
'output' was the diminished contribution of London and Bristol—the
customary centres of 'deep-water' enterprise—to the national prize return.
Taken together, ventures launched in the two ports accounted for just
16.3 per cent of the privateering 'catch', a proportion which compared
with equivalent figures of over 40 per cent for the mid-century wars and
which included the successes of other forms of enterprise—at least 10 of
London's 72 captors, for instance, displayed the hallmarks of the 'Channel'
privateer and a further 20 were fitted out as 'letter of marque'.[91]
Nevertheless, predation of a distinctly 'deep-water' character continued
to take place as a variety of commissioned craft sought to feed off the
enemy's colonial trade in the shipping lanes of the north-eastern Atlantic.

In these waters, the 'privateers of force'—somewhat depleted in number compared to earlier conflicts—experienced mixed fortunes in their predatory endeavours. Some large-scale ventures ended in acute disappointment; the 'expeditionary' aspirations of the *Tartar*'s men, for example, quickly succumbed to disease, though not before the French goods found aboard a Dutch vessel, *De Vrown Catherina Maria,* had been taken and condemned as lawful prize;[92] in another case, the first cruise of the Reprisal Association's vessel, the *King George,* clearly ended in mutinous disarray, notwithstanding conflicting accounts of the precise circumstances. One report from 'Foy, Cornwall' had it that the Captain had been put in chains by the officers due to his improper behaviour in

> that he put into the island of St Michael and staied there for six weeks successively, without one reasonable excuse, except drinking and whoring; and to compleat the scene, before he sailed, by some means or other ('tis said he forced open the Nunnery) brought off two Nuns, which are now on board the ship.[93]

A different story was related by the Committee of the Reprisal Association, which blamed the disturbances on 'part of the crew', particularly the 'chief ringleaders of the Mutiny and Piracy' who had confined the captain and his officers in irons and made their escape to Ireland; accordingly, a reward of 10 guineas was offered for the apprehension of John Rollins, a man possessed of 'a bad set of teeth . . . and greatly given to Liquor', and 5 guineas for the capture of his seven fellow mutineers.[94] Whatever the truth of the case, Joseph Clapp was shortly afterwards replaced by Francis Wherry as commander of the *King George,* and a single Spanish prize, *El Postillion de Mexico,* was returned to Fowey before the private ship-of-war was taken by the French frigate *Concorde,* of 36 eighteen-pounders, 'after a close engagement of three hours, and the loss of 49 men.'[95]

Other 'privateers of force' fared better. For instance, the *Terrible,* of 400 tons burthen and 200 men, carried an American prize into Falmouth in 1779,[96] while the Reprisal Association's second vessel, the *Queen Charlotte* accounted for three prizes, with *Le Franchon,* 'from Brest to America with Soldiers' cloathing, ammunition, etc' taken on 8 March 1779 and *La Louvrier,* bound for Bordeaux with tobacco and staves subsequently conveyed to Dover. Though 230 men were reported to be serving aboard the captor during these actions, she was manned by just 126 seafarers in June 1781 when the *Essex,* a rebel privateer of 134 men, was captured and carried into Kinsale.[97]

The *Enterprize,* however, was the most productive of the large-scale ventures, emerging as the leading London captor in the war as a whole.

Burthen 700 tons, with a company of 200 men, her predatory career extended from September 1778 when she 'fell down the river from Ratcliff Cross, having all her provisions and water on board', to the autumn of 1781 when the *Thomas*, bound from Boston for Cadiz with tobacco and staves, was apprehended and despatched to Limerick.[98] In the meantime, the *Enterprize* had taken a further 14 prizes during a number of cruises in the customary haunts of the 'deep-water' commerce-raider;[99] thus, at least four captures were effected within 27 miles of Cape Finisterre, while *Les Deux Souers* was captured in latitude 45° 48'N as she headed for Bordeaux, *El Altrevido* was seized to the south in latitude 41°N in her attempt to reach Cape Ortegal and thence Bilbao, and the Boston vessels *Betsey* and *Thomas* were taken in a more westerly station, close to the Azores, in their passage to Cadiz. Typically, most of these prizes were landed in western ports, with Falmouth, Limerick and Penzance favoured by the prize masters charged with their delivery, though two were escorted to London and another two were obliged by the weather to put into Portsmouth as they headed for the Thames.

The cargoes condemned to the *Enterprize* included the staple commodities which motivated 'deep-water' venturers throughout the eighteenth century. Thus, sugar and coffee were taken out of *Les Deux Souers*, bound from Guadeloupe to Bordeaux; cocoa, coffee, cotton and indigo, loaded at Cayenne and destined for Marseilles, was found in the hold of the *St Joachim*; silver coin for the purchase of slaves was carried by *El Altrevido*, a Spanish vessel belonging to the 'Factory of the Royal Company of the Slave Trade'; and tobacco was the principal lading of the predator's three American prizes. Significantly, however, no resistance was offered by these prizes, inferring that they were of relatively limited value compared to the richly-laden vessels which had engaged the 'privateers of force' so readily in the 1740s and 1750s.

As well as these colonial goods, the *Enterprize* made prize of the salt, wool, tar, pitch and naval stores discovered aboard six neutral vessels adjudged to be trading with enemy ports. Such captures were common in the 1777–1783 conflict, continuing the trend discernible in the Seven Years' War and explaining, in part, the demise of large-scale venturing as the century proceeded. Clearly, assailants of the *Enterprize*'s calibre—a 'vessel of very considerable force' according to one Dutch captain—were unlikely to encounter any resistance from neutral merchantmen like the *Vrouw Barbara and Hendrina*, armed with two swivels and navigated by 11 men, or *De Vrouw Anthonia Elizabeth*, of 150 lasts, six carriage guns and 12 men.[100] The increasing use of such craft for the supply of Bourbon shipping needs therefore acted as a disincentive, serving to marginalise the 'privateers of force' in the American Revolutionary War.

Accordingly, the growing number of 'deep-water' vessels of a more modest strength were increasingly significant in the 1777–1783 prize war. In London—the last bastion of the mammoth private ships-of-war—venturers concerned in the *Grand Trimmer*, of 280 tons burthen and 140 men, were rewarded by the return of eight prizes in 1780 and 1781, including four cargoes of ordnance and naval stores found in neutral holds, and two French West Indiamen with sugar, cotton and coffee worth an estimated £40,000 taken in consort with the 120-ton *Alligator* of London, and the *Ranger*, of 150 tons burthen and 110 men, belonging to Bristol.[101] The 200-ton, 50-man *Active* claimed a further 11 prizes, mostly French craft taken off the Breton peninsula, though the *Jonge Guilliam* of Hamburg was detained two miles off South Foreland and found to be carrying contraband copper and ironware to Rouen, and the Swedish merchantman *Concordia* was likewise intercepted in her voyage to an enemy port.[102] Various other of London's less powerful 'deep-water' vessels tasted success as enemy traders and neutral carriers succumbed to predators like the *Lady's Resolution*, of 250 tons burthen and 120 men, the 100-ton, 70-man *Revenge* and the *Shark*, a 180-ton vessel with 90 men in her company apparently bound, like many others, in ballast for southern Europe to pick up a cargo of wine.[103]

Predatory ventures of similar dimensions dominated the prize return of Bristol. Here, the companies of 200 or more privateersmen assembled in the 1740s and 1750s were generally supplanted by complements of 80 to 140 men as the city's interest in large-scale ventures—and in the privateering business as a whole—tended to wane. A number of notable successes were recorded, however; *La Ferme*, for instance, a French East Indiaman reputedly worth £100,000, was condemned in November 1778 to the *Alexander* and the *Tartar*, vessels of 200 and 240 tons burthen respectively, each with a 100-strong crew,[104] while the cargo of the *St Innis*, consisting of sugar, black pepper and a 'beautiful zebra, remarkably tame and quite young' was 'estimated at upwards of £200,000'. The *Ranger*, of 150 tons burthen and 70 men, in company with the Liverpool 'letter of marque' *Amazon*, captured this 700-ton Spanish ship in her passage from Manila to Cadiz, after a long engagement in which the Spaniards were driven from their guns by grape shot fired through the port holes, and subsequently obliged to surrender as an explosion on the quarter-deck killed 24 crew members and left the rest in confusion.[105]

West Indiamen formed a more substantial part of the 'catch' of Bristol's 'deep-water' craft, though newspaper reports suggest that they were generally of a relatively modest value;[106] typically, these captures were undertaken by predators such as the *Old England*, the *Rover* and the *Tyger*—burthen from 150 to 250 tons, with 100 or so mariners. Yet it was left to two of the port's most powerful vessels, the *Lion* and the *Vigilant*, both with 180 men, to engage in one of the most famous actions of the 1777–1783 conflict. Confronted by two French men-of-war of 64 and 74 guns, the two privateers put up a long and spirited resistance before the *Vigilant* was captured and the *Lion* obliged to sheer off and limp home to Bristol 'in a very shattered condition'; though it ended in utter defeat, this encounter raised echoes of the *Royal Family*'s battle with the *Glorioso* in 1747.[107]

The 'deep-water' enterprise of a range of other outports generated earnings for venturers in the 1777–1783 war. A Spanish ship, the *Havanneiro*, bound from Havana to Cadiz with 'hides, sugar, coffee, logwood and hard dollars' valued at £200,000 was one of a number of prizes taken by the *Antigallican* of Newcastle, another being the 41-man corsaire, *Le Bien Venu*, taken in company with HM Cutter *Resolution*.[108] The West Country's largest predator, the *King George* of Exeter, burthen 350 tons, with 150 men in her company, took two prizes in 1779, including *El Alesandro*, a Spanish merchantman which had departed New Orleans as a neutral in June 1779.[109] Relatively large-scale Dartmouth ventures were also active, the 100-ton, 60-man *Friendship* taking *La Fortune*, laden with sugar, coffee and indigo, and the *Lady Howe*, of 280 tons burthen and 85 men, capturing *De Negotie en Zeevaart*, a 280-ton Dutchman bound from Demerary to Middelburgh with just 16 men and eight carriage guns protecting her cargo of sugar, cotton and a valuable consignment of elephant's teeth.[110] While this arrest was conducted in latitude 44° 5'N, to the north of Tenerife, the 150-ton, 50-man *Plymouth Hero* of Plymouth accounted for a similar prize in latitude 49° 20'N in the form of *De Harmonie*, of 240 tons, one gun and 13 men, with a cargo of 220 barrels of sugar, 109 hogsheads of tobacco, 393 bags of coffee and 123 bags of cocoa bound from St Eustatius for Amsterdam;[111] valuable and vulnerable, these prizes were taken in March 1781, a sign that the optimistic predictions of British privateering venturers regarding the character of Dutch trade were being fulfilled.

Caribbean produce in French holds had fallen prey to Channel Island privateersmen much earlier in the conflict. By September 1778, these predators had 'already taken nine sail of West Indiamen, which reckoned at only £15,000 each, amount to £135,000'.[112] In the following month, there was 'agreeable news' from Guernsey that the *Beazley* privateer had taken three French West Indiamen in latitude 47°N; originally the rebel privateer *Lexington*, this 140-ton, 100-man venture was one of a number of Jersey's 'deep-water' craft set forth to cruise in the Bay of Biscay.[113] The Guernsey predator *Surprise*, of 150 tons burthen and 70 men, apparently ventured further afield, for she arrived in Dartmouth in October 1779, having taken two West Indiamen, the *St Joseph* in latitude 36°N, longitude 27°W, and *Le Comte de Neyon* in latitude 44°N, longitude 21°W, suggesting that she had ranged from the Bay as far west as the Azores.[114] While the sugar, coffee and cotton loaded into these holds at Martinique—valued at £20,000—represented a handsome prize for the captors, a more unusual and potentially more lucrative seizure was undertaken by the *Resolution* 25 leagues off Cape Finisterre. In this characteristic 'deep-water' station, the 250-ton, 100-man Guernsey privateer apprehended *La Duguesclin*, a French East Indiaman of 520 tons burthen, laden with China tea worth an estimated £120,000, though it later transpired that the cargo was in a perishing condition.[115]

The capture of *La Duguesclin*—and also *La Ferme* and the *St Innis*—suggests that French vessels from the East as well as the West Indies fell prey to British privateersmen in the American Revolutionary War. 'A correspondent from Liverpool' indicated that the port's privateering venturers profited spectacularly from this source, having taken the following six vessels by January 1779:[116]

Deux Amis taken by the	*Knight*,	Wilson	500,000
Iris	do	*Townside*, Watmough	280,000
Aquilon	do	*St Peter*, Holland	200,000
Epamindus	do	*Rockingham*, Batty	400,000
Carnatic	do	*Mentor*, Dawson	400,000
Gaston	do	*Brothers*, Fisher	200,000
Amounting together, to the sum of			£1,880,000

Exaggerated though these estimates might be—the gross proceeds of the *Carnatic*, for instance, amounted to just £114,000[117]—they infer the significance which the privateering business held for Liverpool during the 1777–1783 conflict. Whereas earlier wars had seen the port's venturers deploy their privateering resources in 'armed trading vessels', the dislocation of the Atlantic staple trades after 1775 led to the outfit of a growing number of private ships-of-war as merchants employed their idle capital in commerce-raiding enterprise. This counter-cyclical investment caused much contemporary comment; thus, on the eve of the French war, it was reported tҺat

> the merchan s of Liverpool are very busy in fitting out privateers; they have lost a number of ships during the American disputes and are therefore resolved to revenge themselves on their French allies.[118]

Various lists were published in late 1778 and early 1779 to indicate the extent and effectiveness of Liverpool's privateering response,[119] though the self-congratulatory tone of correspondence from the town in the early stages of the Anglo-French conflict gave way, in the summer of 1779, to

> a most dismal and contrasted picture of the maritime state of [Liverpool], compared with what it was in the autumn and the winter. The French have waged particular war against the privateers and letters of marque of that town. Nothing can be more strongly painted on the faces exhibited on the 'Change, than dejection, disappointment, and despair—not a tide sets in that is not the harbinger of some recent loss or defeat.[120]

The prize sentences reflect both the scale and the fluctuating pattern of Liverpool's prize-taking performance. A total of 154 enemy properties, including 15 taken in consort with vessels from elsewhere, was condemned to Liverpool venturers during the conflict; while this surpassed by a wide margin the town's return in previour wars, it also rendered Liverpool the leading prize-taking port on the British mainland. These seizures were effected throughout the war, with 16 Spanish and 14 Dutch prizes taken after June 1779, though in line with contemporary accounts it was in the opening nine months of the French War that the majority of Liverpool's condemnations were concentrated. During this phase, at least half of the port's 101 French prizes were sentenced in a flourish of predatory activity which served to mitigate the effects of the severe commercial depression experienced by Liverpool's maritime community from 1775 onwards.[121] 'Deep-water' private ships-of-war, albeit of a relatively modest strength and organised, perhaps, on 'letter of marque' lines, were responsible for most of these condemnations. Thus, predators like the *Ellis* and the *Gregson*, the *Enterprize*, the *Marchioness of Granby*, the *St Peter* and the *Wasp*—all burthen from 100 to 370 tons, with crews ranging from 90 to 140 men—apprehended a wide variety of cargoes bound to the French market from the East Indies, from the Newfoundland fisheries, from Spain and southern Europe, but above all, from the West Indies.[122]

Liverpool's 'letters of marque' were also active in the prize war, with various 'dual-purpose' and commercially-oriented craft adding to the flow of enemy property diverted to the Mersey. In this, the port was fairly typical, for 'letter of marque' enterprise in general yielded an unusually large return in the American Revolutionary War. 'Cruising voyages' to the West Indies were the most productive form of this endeavour, though the true extent of such predation is unclear due to the condemnation of prizes in West Indian Vice-Admiralty Courts. Vessels taken *en route* to the Caribbean were generally adjudicated in London, however; the *Carnatic*, for instance, probably the most valuable of all 'letter of marque' prizes, was escorted to the Thames in November 1778—'so large a ship and so deeply laden, that she cannot be brought up the river from Gravesend till part of her cargo is taken out'. An East Indiaman from Pondicherry, this famous prize was taken by the *Mentor* of Liverpool in latitude 30°N, longitude 24°W after a short engagement in which the assailants astutely detected that dummy carriage guns were fitted in the Frenchman's ports.[123] In a similar westerly location, the *Telemachus* and the *Ulysses*—owned, like the *Mentor*, by Baker and Dawson of Liverpool—seized the *Soledad*, a Spanish frigate of 600 tons burthen returning after three years in the South Seas and reputed to be worth approximately £1 million.[124]

London venturers also tasted success in the outward legs of trans-Atlantic 'cruising voyages'; thus, the *Active*, a 550-ton vessel bound for 'Cork, Limerick and the West Indies' with a wage-earning crew of 99 men, captured the *corsaire L'Audacieux* in April 1781 and returned her to the Thames,[125] while the *Quebec*, of 600 tons burthen and 80 men, accounted for the rebel privateer *Banter* during her voyage to Canada and despatched the prize back to London.[126] Likewise, 'cruising voyages' from Bristol were happily interrupted by prize-taking in European waters, with the '*Emperor*, letter of marque' returning two Spanish prizes back to Kingroad in the early stages of her Jamaican voyage,[127] though the *Comte d'Artois*, an Indiaman from Mauritius for Lorient, captured by the Jamaica-bound *Minerva*, in consort with the *Ranger*, was perhaps more lucrative.[128]

On reaching their stations, it is clear from newspaper accounts that many of these 'cruise and voyage' ventures actively pursued the predatory option of their bi-employment. In the Caribbean, for instance, the *Jackall* of Bristol sent two prizes into Antigua and Tortola before combining with four colonial privateers to take the island of St Bartholomew.[129] Two years later, on 24 February 1781, the Dutch colonies of Demerara and Essequibo were attacked by four Bristol predators—the *Bellona*, the *Hornet*, the *Mercury* and the *Porcupine*—in conjunction with two Barbadian privateers, and some 15 prizes, totalling 4,098 tons and 124 guns, were taken.[130] More conventional commerce-raiding activity produced further prizes for these ventures, while other archetypal 'cruise and voyage' enterprises mounted from Bristol, such as the *Byron* and the *Chambers*, were successful in apprehending prizes in the West Indies.[131] Liverpool venturers operated to some effect in this station, the Spanish privateer *Santa Engracia* being carried into Antigua by the *Ellen*,[132] the *Sarah Goulbourne* conveying a Dutch ship of 400 tons, with 400 hogsheads of sugar aboard, into Jamaica, and the *Stag* re-fitting at St Kitts after taking 'a ship of 18 guns & 65 men bound from Martinique to America with dry goods, etc, valued at £12,000'.[133] In the Mediterranean, 'cruising voyages' instigated by London venturers were productive of prizes, the *Tartar*, for example, 'a letter of marque for Smyrna and Constantinople' delivering one prize into Messina and another into Trieste,[134] while the *Maidstone* carried two vessels into Leghorn for examination in 1781, as well as returning prizes to Villa Franca and Zant.[135]

'Armed traders' and 'specialist vessels' added to the scale and diversity of 'letter of marque' predation in the American Revolutionary War. In the opening stages of the privateering war, prior to France's intervention, 'armed trading vessels' such as the *Molly* of Exeter and the *Swift* of Plymouth captured American prizes in their respective voyages to Oporto and Tenerife. Laden with woollens and other bale goods, the *Molly* recaptured the *Prince George* from the rebel privateer *Civil Usage* in July 1777,[136] while the *Swift* returned to Plymouth with a cargo of 'Genuine old Tenerife and Vidonia Wines' as well as the 'good schooner *Leopard* . . . lately taken from the rebels' and her prize lading of 'White Oak Pipe Staves . . . and 1,000 pounds of remarkably fine clean Bee's Wax'; both vessels, together with their cargoes, were offered 'for sale, by the Candle, at the Fountain Tavern, on Smart's Quay, Plymouth' in April 1778.[137]

As the war progressed, so similar opportunist seizures were undertaken by craft engaged in various trades. The *Blossom* and the *Winchcombe*, for instance, slavers registered in London but owned by Samuel Hartley of Liverpool, each had a prize condemned in 1779;[138] two Dutch privateers were taken by the *Marianne*, the 71-man *Neckar* succumbing after an abortive attack on the Tyne-bound whaling vessel in May 1781,[139] and *De Valck*, of 16 guns and 37 men, striking her colours to the *Marianne* and her fellow whaler, the *Achilles* of London, and two Customs cutters, the *Eagle* and the *Swallow* of Shields, in March 1782;[140] East Indiamen were active in the prize war, the *Locke* of 1,100 tons burthen and 99 men, returning to the Thames with a French prize,[141] the 756-ton, 99-man *Ganges* carrying the *Brugsche Vrye* into Portsmouth,[142] and the 'East India ketch-of-war' *Nancy* escorting a Spanish prize into Madras in 1780, though a final sentence was not passed until March 1788 as the captor had acted without a Spanish commission and the prize was consequently contested.[143] Further prizes fell to vessels employed by the Government. Thus, a number of ships 'retained in His Majesty's service' effected seizures of enemy property, with the 'armed victuallers' *Active, Carnatic, Castor* and *Tom* participating in the capture of a Spanish prize in their passage to the Caribbean,[144] and the *General Conway* taking the *Two Brothers* while in the employ of 'the Lords of the Treasury';[145] moreover, the masters of Customs cutters such as the *Assistance* of Dover and the *Rose* of Southampton, took advantage of their letters of marque and added small French *corsaires* to their normal 'catch' of smugglers and illicit traders.[146]

Thus, British privateering enterprise in all of its guises contributed to the prize return of the American Revolutionary War. Commissioned vessels of all denominations were active in the many theatres of this global conflict, seeking to prey upon a broad range of targets, or else intent on defending cargoes against an array of prospective assailants. By virtue of these operations the potential of the 'additional forces' which so concerned the French Ambassador in 1777 was realised to the extent that the largest private fleet commissioned in the 1689–1815 era also proved to be the most potent.

Notes

1. See Syrett, *Shipping and the American War*; and P. Mackesy, *The War for America, 1775-1783* (Longman, 1964) 65-9.
2. See Kennedy, *British Naval Mastery*, 107-22.
3. The number of vessels commissioned declined in the 1793-1815 wars. See Appendices 7 and 8.
4. For American privateering, see W. B. Clark, *Ben Franklin's Privateers. A Naval Epic of the American Revolution* (New York: Greenwood, 1956): G. W. Allen, *Massachusetts Privateers of the Revolution* (Cambridge, Mass., 1927); and W. J. Morgan, 'American Privateering in America's War for Independence, 1775-1783' in Mollet, ed., *Course et Piraterie*, II, 556-71.

5. 'Instructions to Privateers', 27 March 1777. PRO, HCA 26/60. 16 George III, c.5, 'An Act to Prohibit all Trade and Intercourse with the Colonies . . . in Rebellion'.

6. See D. J. Starkey, 'British Privateering against the Dutch in the American Revolutionary War, 1780-1783' in S. Fisher, ed., *Studies in British Privateering, Trading Enterprise and Seamen's Welfare, 1775-1900* (Exeter UP, 1987) 1-18.

7. *Glasgow Mercury*, 21 December 1780.

8. *Morning Chronicle and London Advertiser*, 3 January 1781.

9. *Morning Chronicle and London Advertiser*, 27 December 1780.

10. See D. A. Miller, *Sir Joseph Yorke and Anglo-Dutch Relations, 1774-1780* (The Hague: Mouton, 1970) and Carter, *Neutrality or Commitment*, 97-106.

11. See I. de Madariaga, *Britain, Russia and the Armed Neutrality of 1780* (Hollis & Carter, 1962).

12. *Morning Chronicle and London Advertiser*, 27 December 1780.

13. Cited in W. J. Morgan, ed., *Naval Documents of the American Revolution* (Washington, 1980), VIII, 762.

14. *Morning Chronicle and London Advertiser*, 27 December 1780.

15. See Minchinton, *Overseas Trade*, 34-5; and French, thesis.

16. Starkey, 'British Privateering against the Dutch', 11-13.

17. *Morning Chronicle and London Advertiser*, 27 December 1780.

18. *Glasgow Mercury*, 21 December 1780.

19. See L. Cullen, 'Ireland and Irishmen in Eighteenth-Century Privateering' in Mollet, ed., *Course et Piraterie*, I, 480; Graham, dissertation, 83-5.

20. Declarants applying for privateer commissions against the American colonists (PRO, HCA 25/56-75; HCA 26/60-70) were required to state the occupation, cargo and destination of their vessels. The majority of 'Channel' privateers were stated to be engaged 'in trade', laden with ballast or provisions, and heading for southern European destinations such as Cadiz, the Canaries, Fyal, Gibraltar, Lisbon, Madeira, Oporto and Portugal. As no commissioned vessel was cited as being engaged on 'a cruise', it would seem that such details were used—almost euphemistically—to denote the predatory intent of the venture, though it is quite possible that many of these vessels adopted cruising stations near their stated destinations. Moreover, some of the vessels purportedly sailing 'in ballast to pick up a cargo of wine or fruit' may well have done so, perhaps in a 'cruise and voyage' form of operation. Similar characteristics were regularly quoted by declarants for 'deep-water' private men-of-war.

21. *Exeter Flying Post*, 30 July 1779.

22. *Exeter Flying Post*, 17 August 1778.

23. *Exeter Flying Post*, 4 September 1778.

24. Declarations 18 August, 7 November 1778. PRO, HCA 26/33, 64. Reference is made to the American declarations in this chapter, though many were duplicated as applicants often took out licences against other current adversaries at the same Court session. When no American commission was

issued, declarations for letters of marque against the European powers are cited.

25. *Sherborne and Yeovil Mercury*, 28 September 1778.

26. *Morning Chronicle and London Advertiser*, 25 December 1780.

27. *Gazatteer and New Daily Advertiser*, 23 December 1780.

28. *Gazatteer and New Daily Advertiser*, 27 December 1780. *Morning Chronicle and London Advertiser*, 29 December 1780.

29. Recruitment notice for the *Dreadnought*. *Newcastle Chronicle*, 17 February 1781.

30. *Morning Chronicle and London Advertiser*, 21 December 1780.

31. *Morning Chronicle and London Advertiser*, 27 December 1780.

32. For instance, see the July and August editions of the *Sherborne and Yeovil Mercury* and the *Newcastle Chronicle*.

33. Declarations 5 January 1779, 5 December 1778. PRO, HCA 26/64, 64.

34. Declaration 20 January 1780. PRO, HCA 26/66. See Jamieson, 'Return to Privateering', 159-60. A total of 218 men signed the Articles of Agreement. PRO, HCA 25/210(2).

35. *Morning Chronicle and London Advertiser*, 18 September 1778.

36. Declaration 22 August 1778. PRO, HCA 26/63; *Morning Chronicle and London Advertiser*, 1 September 1778.

37. *London Chronicle*, 5 November 1778.

38. Lloyd, *British Seaman*, 288.

39. Declaration 22 February 1779. PRO, HCA 25/81; Damer Powell, *Bristol Privateers*, 277.

40. SMV, Muster Rolls, 1777-1783.

41. SMV, Muster Rolls, 1777-1783. See also the list of Bristol 'letters of marque' and private ships-of-war published in *Felix Farley's Bristol Journal*, 3 October 1778.

42. PRO, BT 98/38-40. The inexplicable understatement of manning figures apparent in the Liverpool declarations did not occur in other ports or for other conflicts. It conceals the strength of particularly large complements of 212, 162, and 135 men serving aboard the *Telemachus*, the *Bellona* and the *Stag* respectively, and at least 28 crews in the range of 70 to 120 seafarers.

43. LRO, List of Private Armed Ships fitted out at Liverpool, 942 HOL 10, 411.

44. PRO, C 114/36; Declaration 23 September 1778. PRO, HCA 25/78.

45. LRO, Account Books of the *Enterprize*, 387 MD 45.

46. Some 890 vessels were commissioned or re-commissioned against the Dutch between 26 December 1780 and 1 March 1781. At least 300 of these vessels were probably armed traders. PRO, HCA 26/53-6.

47. PRO, HCA 26/60-70. While details of the occupation, cargo and destination of private men-of-war were necessarily vague, declarants for 'letter of marque' ventures generally offered more precise information as to the proposed trade of their vessels. Unless otherwise stated, the

examples in this section are taken from the American letter of marque declarations.

48. I am grateful to Tony Barrow for this information. See PRO, ADM 43/25(1), 29, for details of head money paid to the owners and men of the *Achilles* and the *Marianne*.
49. Only 11 vessels left Liverpool for Africa in 1779, compared to 105 in 1773, and 85 in 1783. LRO, 942 HOL 10, 363.
50. *Exeter Flying Post*, 27 August 1779.
51. Syrett, *Shipping and the American War*, vii.
52. Declarations 12 September 1777, 10 July 1779, 12 April 1777. PRO, HCA 26/60, 65, 60.
53. The declarations for these and three other north-eastern vessels hired by the Government were made on 23 October 1778. PRO, HCA 26/63.
54. Declarations 15 August 1777, 6 March 1779, 8 May 1780. PRO, HCA 26/61, 65, 67.
55. Declaration of William Butterwick, commander of the *Favourite*, 10 December 1778. PRO, HCA 26/64.
56. Head money vouchers submitted in respect of the *Rose* of Southampton PRO, ADM 43/25(2).
57. PRO, ADM 43/25(2).
58. PRO, ADM 43/30.
59. PRO, ADM 43/29.
60. *Newcastle Courant*, 6 April 1782.
61. Declaration of Joseph Richards, commander of the *Prince Rupert*, 13 May 1777. PRO, HCA 26/60.
62. Hardy, *Register of Ships*, II.
63. Declarations 7 May, 26 January 1781. PRO, HCA 26/69.
64. Declaration 16 June 1777. PRO, HCA 26/60.
65. In addition, 16 head money payments were made to privateers belonging to the loyal American colonies.
66. *Exeter Flying Post*, 4 September 1778.
67. *Exeter Flying Post*, 9 October 1778.
68. Jamieson, 'Return to Privateering', 169-72.
69. PRO, HCA 34/46.
70. Declarations 7 November 1778, 26 March 1779. PRO, HCA 26/63, 65.
71. PRO, HCA 32/380.
72. PRO, HCA 34/52.
73. M. Oppenheim, *The Maritime History of Devon* (University of Exeter, 1968) 112.
74. PRO, HCA 32/380.
75. For instance, see the spring 1781 editions of the *Sherborne and Yeovil Mercury*.
76. *Morning Chronicle and London Advertiser*, 22, 30 December 1780.
77. *Newcastle Courant*, 19 May 1781.
78. *Newcastle Journal*, 24, 31 March 1781.

79. *Newcastle Chronicle*, 20 January 1781.
80. *Newcastle Chronicle*, 3 March 1781.
81. *Newcastle Chronicle*, 10 March 1781.
82. *Newcastle Journal*, 11 August 1781.
83. *Newcastle Chronicle*, 22 September 1781.
84. *Newcastle Journal*, 7 April 1781.
85. PRO, ADM 43/23-30. Crew lists are missing from a number of head money claims. At least six other captors were probably 'Channel' privateers.
86. PRO, ADM 43/28.
87. PRO, ADM 43/30.
88. PRO, ADM 43/30.
89. The *Black Prince* caused much comment in West Country newspapers in the summer and autumn of 1779. Variously described as 'of Boston', a 'smuggler with three commissions on board' and 'with many Englishmen' in her crew, she harassed the coal and coasting trade of the Bristol Channel, leading one Swansea correspondent to lament that 'tis a sad thing that no ship-of-war protects our trade'. See *Exeter Flying Post*, and *Sherborne and Yeovil Mercury*, August-October 1779. For the losses off Yarmouth, see *Exeter Flying Post*, 13 August 1779; and off Exmouth, see *Exeter Flying Post*, 1 January 1779.
90. The *Brutus* operated with her tender, the *Little Brutus*, adding 29 men to the complement of the venture. PRO, ADM 43/24.
91. Starkey, thesis, 313-28.
92. Jamieson, 'Return to Privateering', 159-60. Prize sentence PRO, HCA 34/53.
93. *Morning Chronicle and London Advertiser*, 13 April 1779.
94. *Exeter Flying Post*, 23 April 1779.
95. Declaration 6 May 1779. PRO, HCA 26/65. Prize sentence PRO, HCA 34/53.
96. Declaration 5 December 1778. PRO, HCA 26/64. Prize sentence PRO, HCA 34/44.
97. *Exeter Flying Post*, 23 April 1779. A further 38 seamen were recruited at Studland and Falmouth after the engagement with the *Essex*. PRO, ADM 43/25(1).
98. Declaration 22 August 1778. PRO, HCA 26/63. *Morning Chronicle and London Advertiser*, 18 September 1778. PRO, HCA 32/461.
99. This account of the *Enterprize*'s predatory career is largely based on the Prize Papers. PRO, HCA 32/273, 278, 280, 306, 369, 373, 395, 441, 461, 478.
100. These neutral victims sapped the strength of the *Enterprize* in the sense that prize crews were required to navigate them to a home port. The captor's company was so depleted by this necessity that at least one prize was lost because men could not be spared to man her; subsequently, a further 12 men were killed and 22 wounded in a damaging encounter with a

French 44-gun frigate. PRO, HCA 32/478; *Exeter Flying Post*, 26 February 1779.

101. Declaration 10 December 1779. PRO, HCA 26/66. Prize sentences PRO, HCA 34/49-53. Damer Powell, *Bristol Privateers*, 282.

102. Declaration 22 August 1778. PRO, HCA 25/78. William Watson testified before officials at Dover, the only London captain to make his declaration in an outport during the war. See PRO, HCA 32/306, 373, 398, 463, for prize details.

103. Declarations 12 November 1778, 8 January 1781, 12 March 1779. PRO, HCA 26/64, 68, 65.

104. Declarations 25 August, 2 September 1778. PRO, HCA 25/77. Prize sentence PRO, HCA 34/45. Damer Powell, *Bristol Privateers*, 246.

105. Declaration 19 July 1779. PRO, HCA 25/84. *Exeter Flying Post*, 17 September 1779. *Felix Farley's Bristol Journal*, 18 November 1779. Williams, *Liverpool Privateers*, 257-9.

106. See *Felix Farley's Bristol Journal* for the war years. See also Damer Powell, *Bristol Privateers*, 246-99.

107. Declarations 28, 15 December 1778. PRO, HCA 26/63. *Felix Farley's Bristol Journal*, 19 December 1778. Damer Powell, *Bristol Privateers*, 246, 271-3, 290-1.

108. *Exeter Flying Post*, 3 December 1779. PRO, ADM 43/28.

109. Declaration 1 July 1779. PRO, HCA 26/46. Prize Appeal Papers PRO, HCA 42/46.

110. Declarations 27 April, 28 December 1780. PRO, HCA 26/67, 54. Prize Papers PRO, HCA 32/333, HCA 42/140.

111. Declaration 9 January 1781. PRO, HCA 26/56. Prize Papers PRO, HCA 32/349.

112. *Exeter Flying Post*, 4 September 1778.

113. Declaration 17 August 1778. PRO, HCA 26/33. *Sherborne and Yeovil Mercury*, 19 October 1778.

114. Declaration 17 August 1778. PRO, HCA 26/33. *Exeter Flying Post*, 22 October 1779.

115. Declaration 27 May 1779. PRO, HCA 26/65. *Exeter Flying Post*, 10 September 1779. Jamieson, 'Return to Privateering', 169.

116. *Exeter Flying Post*, 22 January 1779.

117. PRO, C 114/36 (see Appendix 5). A contemporary 'List of Prizes' published in Liverpool includes four of these captures, offering the following valuations: *Le Gaston*, £110,000; the *Carnatic*, £170,000; *Les Deux Amis*, £115,000; *L'Iris*, £30,000. LRO, 942 HOL 10, 411.

118. *Gazatteer and New Daily Advertiser*, 12 August 1778.

119. See LRO, 942 HOL 10, 411, and *Exeter Flying Post*, 22 January 1779. These lists tend to differ in terms of detail, though the general upsurge in Liverpool's privateering investment and in the port's prize return is clearly apparent.

120. *Exeter Flying Post,* 6 August 1779.
121. See Parkinson, *Rise of the Port of Liverpool,* 136-7, for an account of the town's economy during the conflict.
122. See the 'List of Prizes' in LRO, 942 HOL 10, 411.
123. *Exeter Flying Post,* 13, 27 November 1778. See Williams, *Liverpool Privateers,* 239-40. For details of the sale of the *Carnatic's* cargo, see PRO, C 114/36 and Appendix 5.
124. *Exeter Flying Post,* 7, 28 January 1780. As no evidence exists to corroborate this newspaper report, it seems highly unlikely that the prize was worth this astonishing sum.
125. PRO, ADM 43/25(2).
126. Declaration 12 March 1782. PRO, HCA 26/70. Prize sentence PRO, HCA 34/44.
127. *Exeter Flying Post,* 6 August 1779. Damer Powell, *Bristol Privateers,* 200.
128. Damer Powell, *Bristol Privateers,* 277.
129. *Felix Farley's Bristol Journal,* 29 May 1779. Damer Powell, *Bristol Privateers,* 267-8.
130. These Bristol ventures acted without letters of marque against the Dutch, in the belief that the government would waive its right to the prizes. Damer Powell, *Bristol Privateers,* 252-3.
131. Damer Powell, *Bristol Privateers,* 254, 257.
132. PRO, ADM 43/25(1).
133. *Glasgow Mercury,* 13, 21 June 1781.
134. *Morning Chronicle and London Advertiser,* 14 August 1778. Prize sentences PRO, HCA 34/48.
135. Prize sentences PRO, HCA 34/52, 55.
136. W. W. Holman Wilson, 'Topsham Privateer', *Devon and Cornwall Notes and Queries,* VIII (1924-5), 17-8.
137. *Sherborne and Yeovil Mercury,* 30 March 1778.
138. Declaration 11 May 1779. PRO, HCA 26/65. Prize sentences PRO, HCA 34/47, 53.
139. PRO, ADM 43/25(1). *Newcastle Chronicle,* 5 May 1781.
140. PRO, ADM 43/29. *Newcastle Courant,* 6 April 1782.
141. Declaration 26 January 1781. PRO, HCA 26/69. Prize sentence PRO, HCA 34/59.
142. Declaration 26 October 1781. PRO, HCA 26/69. Prize sentence PRO, HCA 34/50.
143. PRO, HCA 32/415.
144. PRO, HCA 45/9. The *Carnatic* was the French East Indiaman taken by the *Mentor.* The prize at stake, *La Misercordia,* was originally condemned to HMS *Leviathan,* but awarded jointly to the commissioned vessels on appeal.
145. Declaration 12 April 1777. PRO, HCA 26/60. Prize sentence PRO, HCA 34/43.
146. PRO, ADM 43/24, 25(2).

Part Three

SIGNIFICANCE

Nine

Constraints and Determinants

The scale, form and regional distribution of privateering enterprise varied
widely during the course of the eighteenth century. An array of inter
related factors—short-term and long run, local as well as national and
international—acted upon each other to determine the level and nature
of activity sanctioned by letters of marque. At base, there were the
prerequisites. Clearly, given its place within the code of international
maritime law, the business of reprisal could only proceed at times when
the state deemed it meet to permit the seizure of foreign sea-borne
property. Such authorisation was generally, though not necessarily,
restricted to periods of declared war,[1] and directed against the subjects
of an enemy nation.[2] The state, moreover, might fashion the character of
'inputs' into the predatory business by reserving the issue of licences, as
in 1695 and 1759, to ventures of a particular quality, while it invariably
prescribed a code of conduct for venturers in the 'instructions' issued to
privateersmen and the procedures laid down for the adjudication of prize.
Ultimately, therefore, privateering enterprise was subject to the political
sentiments which existed within and between nations, a factor amply
illustrated in 1856 when the plenipotentiaries at the Congress of Paris
declared that 'privateering is and remains abolished'.[3]

A further basic constraint was the supply of capital and labour. As the
privateering business was essentially a transitory feature of the maritime
economy, it was largely sustained by vessels, equipment and seafarers
drawn from other branches of the mercantile marine, though venturers
might generate some of their own resources as a war proceeded and prize
vessels were re-armed, profits ploughed back and landmen attracted to
the business.[4] The capacity of the shipping industry was therefore a crucial
determinant of the scale and character of commerce-raiding enterprise.
That the privateering 'input' tended to increase, and to disperse spatially,
over the course of the eighteenth century reflected, to a certain extent,

the expansion and decentralisation of British overseas trade and shipping activity during the period.[5] Moreover, the composition and quality of the commissioned fleet was principally fashioned by the distribution of maritime capital and labour. Accordingly, large-scale ventures, whether primarily commercial or predatory in intent, were generally mounted in London and the larger outports where ships and manpower were available in some abundance; limitations in factor supply, on the other hand, dictated that the privateering endeavour of the Channel Islanders and venturers in the south-coast bases was generally embodied in small-scale units[6]—the brigs, cutters and sloops which typified 'Channel' enterprise.

Within these broad parameters of the law and the supply of productive resources, the scale and form of the privateering business fluctuated according to a variety of influences. Seasonal factors held some sway, particularly in the 'Channel' sector where activity was generally more intense in the summer months than at other times of the year. Of much greater significance, however, were the highly volatile commercial conditions of wartime. Venturers were sensitive to the prospects afforded by predatory enterprise, just as they were keenly aware of the prevailing state of the more conventional markets; accordingly, it was their perceptions as to the extent, value and vulnerability of enemy commerce—set against the profitable potential of competing maritime opportunities—which largely conditioned the character of the business.

Generally speaking, these considerations varied with the nationality of the target. War against France, for instance, usually elicited a strong privateering response; it was a broadly-based response, moreover, for the French mercantile marine was both large and widespread, furnishing small fry for 'Channel' privateers in home waters, 'Martinicomen' for 'deep-water' private ships-of-war in the north-eastern Atlantic, and a range of prey for 'letters of marque' in the Mediterranean, the Caribbean and the East Indies. A more intense reaction, however, followed the grant of reprisals against Dutch sea-borne property in 1780, albeit short-lived and concentrated in the 'Channel' branch of the business. Spanish trade, in contrast, normally provoked little interest in the centres of 'Channel' commerce-raiding and stimulated but a modicum of 'deep-water' activity, though 'letter of marque' ventures were frequently undertaken and 'expeditions' to the Pacific were invariably a function of Anglo-Spanish conflict.

Such generalisations, of course, did not apply to all regions or at all stages of the various wars of the eighteenth century. Locational factors had a strong bearing on the perceived extent of enemy trade and therefore the propensity of venturers to engage in privateering activity. Thus, Guernsey and Jersey were conveniently sited for predation upon the relatively abundant coastal commerce of Brittany, Normandy and the Bay of Biscay; similarly, privateersmen operating from the ports of Kent and Sussex were well-placed to feed upon French sea-borne property—often in neutral bottoms—as it passed through the Strait of Dover; even east-coast bases, though distant from Bourbon shipping routes, enjoyed some locational advantages when Dutch trade became liable to seizure and the North Sea emerged as a viable cruising ground; and, in a different sense, Liverpool's situation fashioned its privateering experience as the relatively safe passage to the Atlantic via the North Channel fostered the growth of overseas trade at a critical phase in the port's development. Seeking to exploit these advantages, privateering venturers in the Channel Islands and the bases of south-east England specialised in short-haul cruises in adjacent waters, but only in times of Anglo-French conflict, while east-coast investors remained aloof from the predatory arm of the business except during the Dutch War, and Liverpudlians concentrated their interests in 'letters of marque' rather than private men-of-war, particularly in the mid-century wars.

Short-term, local perceptions sometimes magnified the extent of the prospective target. Intelligence that prizes were there for the taking might convince a venturer to enter or remain in the privateering sector, with John du Grave's advice that contraband-laden neutrals were approaching the Channel Narrows in 1703, or the Channel Islanders' belief that 'Martinicomen' were in mid-Atlantic in 1779, typifying the kind of local knowledge and rumour upon which an investor might act.[7] Similarly, tangible proof of the profitibility of the business with the return of rich prizes to a home port could be influential; here, the arrival of the *Lewis Erasmus* and the *Marquis D'Antin* in Bristol, and the subsequent conveyance of bullion in 45 armed waggons to the Tower of London, provides the classic example, this celebrated event adding a considerable impetus to the boom in 'deep-water' investment in the 1740s.[8]

Privateering enterprise was also shaped by the value of the prospective prey. At the aggregate level, this can be seen in the limited response of venturers to the issue of commissions against a distant and poorly developed rebel trade in 1777. At the level of the individual venture, there was a close correlation between the value of the intended target and the scale of the would-be assailant; thus, the low-value cargoes of the French home trade attracted the attentions of diminutive 'Channel' predators, while the trans-oceanic consignments of bullion, spice and sugar were normally afforded some protection and therefore susceptible only to the heavy armaments and quasi-naval crews of the 'deep-water' private ships-of-war. Naturally, a similar relationship prevailed aboard 'letters of marque', though defensive considerations were paramount as the more valuable cargoes were generally conveyed and protected in the larger, well-manned vessels, often sailing in company; accordingly, the 99-strong company of the archetypal mid-century East Indiaman compared with the complements of 10 to 25 men shipped aboard the commissioned colliers and Baltic ships of the north-eastern ports.

Closely bound up with the intrinsic worth of enemy commerce was the question of its vulnerability. This was by no means constant, for shipowners and captains naturally adapted their procedures to enhance the security of their vessels as war progressed, while the fluctuating course of the naval struggle underlay the safety of trade, particularly overseas trade, serving variously to improve or diminish the predatory or commercial prospects facing investors and seafarers. Conventional wisdom, for example, had it that 'the beginning of the Dispute is always the time to make money by privateering'.[9] This was logical, for at such junctures foreign-going merchantmen were often acutely vulnerable; homeward-bound vessels had departed in peacetime with little regard for, and few precautions against, the possibility of seizure, while the protective measures afforded by the state—principally, the provision of naval convoys—took some time to organise and to implement. Accordingly, privateering activity—at least in its 'Channel' and 'deep-water' guises —was generally at its peak in the early stages of a conflict as venturers eagerly sought to beat their predatory rivals in the race to claim easy, but finite, pickings.

This was not the full story, however, for even at the height of a war when naval forces were fully mobilised, an adversary's shipping might prove susceptible to privateering assaults of a sufficient calibre or audacity. In this sense, the 'expeditionary' incursions into the Pacific were not despatched in haste to catch the Spanish galleons and settlements unawares; rather, they tended to proceed in a somewhat leisurely fashion, their main obstacle—and the Spaniard's principal line of defence—being the logistics of transporting a force of up to 500 men to a distant theatre and timing its arrival to coincide with the appearance of the treasure ships. Likewise, the scale and form of predatory activity in European waters tended to evolve over the course of a war as promoters modified their operations to meet the defensive measures employed by the enemy. In the 1740s, for instance, Maurepas' convoy system, and the Spaniards' deployment of register-ships, encouraged British commerce-raiding investors to increase the unit-scale of their ventures as the conflict proceeded and inadequacies in the protective measures of the Bourbon powers were demonstrated; similarly, the flexibility and persistence of venturers was clearly apparent in 1758 and 1759 as the focus of their operations shifted from the Western Approaches to the Mediterranean as France's trans-Atlantic trade disintegrated.

A key influence upon the abundance and conduct of enemy commerce and, with it, the British privateering response, was the balance of power in the naval war. To a certain degree, the contention that privateering was 'the resort of the losing side in a war'[10] was true, for a navy in retreat could hardly limit the enemy's trade as well as repulse his ships-of-war. Here, the experience of Britain's naval ascendancy in 1759–1761 stands in sharp relief to the difficult years of 1778–1782; while French commerce was swept from the seas and the British privateering business was depressed in the first instance, the American Revolutionary War witnessed the proliferation of enemy trade and consequently the *apogee* of privateering enterprise for the century as a whole. Reinforcing these trends, of course, was the tendency of Britain's wartime commerce to ebb and flow with the Navy's ability to control the seas; thus, in the Seven Years' War, shipping resources were consumed by a vibrant commercial sector, a trend reversed in the subsequent conflict when the contraction of the Atlantic staple trades meant that ample quantities of capital and labour were available for deployment in the privateering business.

However, a number of caveats should be inserted into this general view. Large-scale predatory units, for instance, were at their most effective in the 1740s when the Anglo-French naval struggle was evenly balanced and 'privateers of force' were able to exploit the 'good pickings' accruing from the mutual distraction of the state fleets. Other commissioned vessels, notably East Indiamen and the ships of the Hudson's Bay Company, operated despite the vacillating course of the naval war, though their sailing schedules were frequently amended for precautionary purposes. Naval success, moreover, influenced the quality of privateering 'inputs'. Accordingly, the gradual accretion of British sea power in the 1740s and 1750s persuaded French West India merchants to ship increasing quantities of goods in neutral vessels protected more by diplomatic rights than physical might; the 'privateers of force' of the 1740s, therefore, gave way to the more modest predatory units of the American Revolutionary War.

Whatever the state of the war, the privateering business was only one of a number of investment opportunities facing a maritime community. No matter how favourable the conditions for commerce-raiding might appear, the prospects current in a range of home and overseas trades might prove more attractive to investors in a particular locality. To some degree, such a preference was reflected in the proportion of 'armed trading vessels' in a port's licensed fleet; thus, the preponderance of slavers and West Indiamen in the commissioned enterprise of Liverpool in the 1740s and 1750s suggests that the town's merchants deemed commerce to be a more lucrative, or safer, source of profits than predation. In a negative sense, also, the limited involvement of a port or region in the privateering business implies that other activities consumed the bulk of local maritime resources; for instance, north-eastern shipping entrepreneurs appear to have concentrated their wartime investments, as in peacetime, on the expansive 'coal and coasting' trade, rendering the growing ports of Tyneside and Wearside relatively insignificant as privateering bases.[11] Commerce-raiding therefore assumed its place as a further option in the wartime economy of a port, and even at times and in places where the 'spirit of privateering' infected the maritime community there were always alternative employments for capital and labour.[12]

The British privateering experience of the eighteenth century was thus fashioned by a complex of interactive forces. Over this period, various broad contours in the scale and character of the business can be detected. 'Letters of marque' were a constant feature of the commissioned fleets of the era, as commerce generally proceeded despite the onset of hostilities. Predatory activity fluctuated more dramatically; in terms of operational levels, 1744–1745, 1756–1757 and 1778–1781 were the most vital phases of Britain's private war-at-sea; with regard to the nature of this activity, small-scale operations were predominant in the 1702–1712 conflict, with 'deep-water' enterprise emerging as the most dynamic form of predation in the mid-century wars, and a revitalised 'Channel' sector, together with an important corps of 'cruise and voyage' ventures, constituting the expansive elements of the 1777–1783 licensed force. Regardless of their designation, these various types of commissioned vessel were set forth to earn profits for the private individuals concerned in their outfit and operation. In this quest, they were authorised and encouraged to endamage the ships and cargoes of the enemy. Accordingly, and in many ways, these privateers contributed to Britain's economic and military effort in the wars of the eighteenth century.

Notes

1. In 1739, general reprisals against Spain were authorised before a declaration of war. The distinction between a grant of reprisals and a declaration of war was drawn by the High Court of Admiralty in the case of the *Pere Adam* in 1778; thus, a claim that the property should be restored, as it was seized in an English port before the commencement of hostilities, was rejected 'because a commission of general reprizals is stronger than even a declaration of war, authorizing [captors] to seize the goods of the foreign subjects everywhere, and immediately; whereas by treaty in case of declaration of war, there are six months allowed to remove their persons and properties.' *Exeter Flying Post*, 13 November 1778.

2. In the American Revolutionary War, reprisals were permissible against rebel trade on the grounds that it breached the 1775 Prohibition of Trade Act, not because it was enemy-owned.

3. A number of countries, notably Spain and the United States, declined to accede to the Declaration. See Stark, *Abolition of Privateering*, 139-60.

4. For example, in the later stages of Queen Anne's War, the Channel Islanders expanded their commerce-raiding interests on the basis of previous successes. See Bromley, 'New Vocation', 126-8.

5. In the 1793-1815 wars this trend was reversed as the privateering business contracted and centred increasingly on London and Liverpool, despite the accelerating growth of the shipping industry. See Appendices 7 and 8.

6. This 'bottleneck' might be broken by the utilisation of prize vessels; thus, the three largest units of the 1702-1712 Channel Island fleet were all captured from the French. See Bromley, 'New Vocation', 126. An infusion of London capital into outport ventures might also break the pattern; thus, Dartmouth's extraordinary interest in 'deep-water' privateering in the 1740s was partly financed by London merchants. Similarly, labour was relatively mobile and seamen might travel to ports where privateers were fitting out. See Rediker, *Devil and the Deep Blue Sea*, 79-83.

7. PRO, C 108/138. John du Grave to Patrick Galloway, 3 January 1703; Jamieson, 'Return to Privateering', 164.

8. Vaughan, *Voyages and Cruises*, xxxiv.

9. *Exeter Flying Post*, 24 July 1778.

10. Parkinson, *Rise of the Port of Liverpool*, 112, 130.

11. For instance, Newcastle emerged as one of Britain's leading shipowning ports in the second half of the eighteenth century. See S. P. Ville, 'Shipping in the Port of Newcastle, 1780-1800' *Journal of Transport History*, 9 (1988), 60-77. Yet it was not until 1779 that the *Antigallican* private man-of-war departed

Shields, 'being the first that ever sailed from this port'. *Newcastle Journal*, 13 March 1779.

12. Even the Channel Islands, the most committed of Britain's privateering communities, continued to engage in the Newfoundland fisheries and the carrying trades during wartime. See Bromley, 'New Vocation', 120.

Ten

'Private Interests Inseparable from . . . the Public Interests of the British Nation'?

By the eighteenth century, British privateering was clearly not the 'characteristic form of maritime warfare' that it had been in the 1580s and 1590s.[1] With the development of state navies, private commissioned vessels were no longer a decisive factor in the sea war as the strategic failure of the French *guerre de course* illustrated so well. Indeed, from the Seven Years' War onwards, it would seem that the decline in the scale of the average British commerce-raiding venture, together with the continuing wartime expansion of the Royal Navy, rendered privateering activity ever more marginal to the outcome of the intensifying Anglo-French struggle. This does not signify, however, that the operations of the 11,000 or so vessels commissioned during the 'long' eighteenth century were devoid of any military ramifications. On the contrary, the potential utility of the business as a tool of war was such that the state did more than just sanction the activity throughout the century—it positively advocated it, both in the language of 'encouragement' adopted by Parliament and the Admiralty in the various enabling and regulatory measures, and in practice with the abolition of the Crown's share in prizes and the provision of bounties for captors of enemy vessels-of-war.

In this positive approach to the commerce-raiding business, the government embraced the unbridled enthusiasm of the staunchest proponents of the activity—the owners and setters-out of privateers. Thus, to the *Observator*, mouthpiece of the mercantile class in the early eighteenth century, privateering represented one of the 'props of this island, being both so useful & necessary to trade & navigation, and to the poor of these kingdoms'.[2] Later in the century, the proprietors of the

Antigallican spoke for all privateering capitalists as they identified their own 'private interests [with] the Honour of His Majesty, and the public interests of the British Nation'.[3] A sense of 'satisfaction that we designed a service to our King and Country'[4] permeated the pronouncements of this interest group, reaching a peak in 1783, perhaps, with the boastful assertion of an anonymous Liverpool merchant that

> the whole fleet sent against the Spanish Armada in the reign of Elizabeth only measured 31,385 tons and was manned by 15,072 seamen. The town of Liverpool therefore by their private ships-of-war formed a greater force during the contest with the colonies than the whole nation, unanimously zealous was able to equip under the portent of the government of Elizabeth.[5]

The privateering endeavour of these patriotic and partial commentators was held to serve the nation in the damage that it inflicted upon enemy trade, and in the protection it afforded to home commerce. In the first respect, the sentences of the Prize Court indicate that the commissioned fleet contributed significantly to the prize total, with 3,065 common condemnations effected by privateering venturers in the 1702–1783 era. Though naval condemnations were undoubtedly of a higher average value, in number they exceeded the privateering 'catch' by just 495 over the same period; indeed, in the American Revolutionary War, the commissioned fleet was more effective in the prize war, recording 1,312 condemnations as opposed to the 1,021 enemy properties sentenced to the King's ships. In relation to 'inputs', however, the privateering 'output' appears less impressive. Thus, the 3,065 prizes fell to a total fleet of 6,987 commissioned vessels, a 'productivity rate' of 0.44 prizes per privateer; in other words, over half—considerably so, given the occurrence of multiple successes—of the craft licensed between 1702 and 1783 did not participate in prize-taking activity. Wide regional variations, reflecting the scale and complexion of local privateering activity, were apparent within the national picture, as the Channel Islanders returned an overall average of two prizes per commissioned vessel, while, at the other extreme, venturers in eastern England recorded a comparable rate of 0.12.[6] Broadly speaking, therefore, it was only a limited number of privateers, set forth from particular ports and localities, which actively wrought destruction upon the enemy's trade.

The impact of privateering enterprise, however, is understated in these figures. Not only do they neglect the condemnations emanating from disputed cases and the properties sentenced in the Vice-Admiralty Courts, but they also ignore the costs incurred by enemy shipowners and consignees as a consequence of the repeated searches which delayed their shipments, of the detention of suspected vessels and cargoes, and of the need to sail in convoy through waters frequented by licensed predators. Moreover, the strategic implications of this business are disguised, for the figures take no account of the disposition of the privateering effort or of the quality of prizes taken. Clear benefits, for instance, accrued from the interception of naval stores bound from the Baltic to the dockyards of France and Spain by privateersmen operating in the Channel Narrows and off the French coast. Here, John Mascall's privateers fed hungrily on neutral traders carrying hemp, pitch, tar and timber for Louis XIV's war effort, while, in the 1750s, these waters witnessed the harassment of Dutch, Scandinavian and Spanish merchantmen by a host of 'small ships, vessels, or boats' set forth in the wake of the 'Rule of the War of 1756'. Yet it was in the American Revolutionary War that this form of predation reached its height, assuming an heroic place in the maritime war according to MacPherson; thus,

> the maritime force of Great Britain alone was capable of maintaining the arduous conflict against the fleets of Spain, France and America and even the British privateers constituted a naval force sufficient to curb the attempts of the subjects of the neutral powers to convey warlike stores to the enemies of Great Britain.[7]

Supplies of consumer goods were similarly diverted or delayed as a consequence of privateering operations, an important consideration in the eyes of eighteenth-century mercantilist warmongers. Witness the sufferings of the coastal populations of Brittany and Normandy at the hands of the Channel Island *corsaires*; intense during the Spanish Succession War, the dearth and misery which resulted from this predation in subsequent conflicts was such that French plans to invade the islands were hatched in 1759 and 1778. Commissioned vessels also contributed to the isolation of the enemy's colonial possessions; in the Caribbean, for example, 'our Men-of-War and Privateers have so sharp a look out, that the French can't get any ships with stores to their islands'.[8] Likewise, in European waters, there were indications that 'deep-water' predators played a significant part in cutting the enemy's lines of supply; thus, in the Seven Years' War, 'English privateers, backed up by men-of-war in the neighbourhood, made a chain through which the [French colonial] trade could hardly escape.'[9] Though this was co-incidence—rather than co-ordination—of effort between the state and private naval forces, the clear inference is that private men-of-war materially assisted in the decisive blockade of France's Atlantic ports during 1757 and 1758.

The enemy's colonies, as well as his colonial trade, were occasionally subject to privateering attack. In the opening decades of the eighteenth century, for instance, Spanish American settlements were stormed by the 'expeditionary' forces of Dampier, Rogers and Shelvocke; if these assaults were motivated by plunder rather than military strategy, they represented a further erosion of the anachronistic commercial monopoly claimed by Spain in the New World and a forcible expression of Britain's emergence as the most dynamic mercantile power of the era. In subsequent years, and in different theatres, commissioned vessels featured at the margins of the imperial struggle. The seizure of a French outpost 'on the backside of Newfoundland' by three private men-of-war in 1745,[10] assaults upon the French island of St Bartholomew and the Dutch West India territories of Demerara and Essequibo by small fleets of Bristol privateers in the American Revolutionary War,[11] and, on a slightly different tack, the delivery of valuable supplies to the besieged garrison of Gibraltar by the 'letter of marque' *Mercury* in February 1782, all served to demonstrate the occasional utility—and versatility—of these 'additional forces' in the war for the colonies.

While Captain Conway Heighington's service in running the Gibraltar blockade was rewarded by the Admiralty with a lieutenancy in the Royal Navy,[12] there were many other instances in which Their Lordships had reason to be grateful to privateersmen. Cargoes of military stores were sometimes taken by commissioned vessels; thus, the *San Pedro* and the *Santa Zerriaco*, both laden with arms and ammunition for the Jacobite insurrectionists, were intercepted in two separate engagements by 'deepwater' private ships-of-war in 1745,[13] while in the following decade, the *Bien Aquiese* and her cargo of 'bombs, bomb shells, soldier's cloaths, etc' was taken in her passage from La Rochelle to the Mississippi by the *King of Prussia* and *Tyger* private men-of-war.[14] Enemy men-of-war were frequently distracted and occasionally taken by 'deep-water' commerce-raiders, as the seizure of the *Glorioso* illustrated; moreover, naval vessels like the *Solebay* and the *Winchelsea* were re-captured by private ships-of-war,[15] while intelligence of enemy shipping movements was frequently conveyed to the Admiralty in the form of dispatches taken out of privateering prizes or in reports compiled by privateersmen, notably the Channel Islanders, operating close to French roadsteads.[16]

As well as these various offensive attributes, privateering venturers were quick to stress the protective qualities of their enterprise. In 1708, for instance, this claim so impressed the government that it conceded its tenth-share in prizes, and offered bounties for the capture of enemy predators, as privateers were encouraged to augment the cruisers and convoys appointed to frustrate the French *guerre de course*. Thereafter, investment in privateering was regularly advocated as 'a piece of national service', the incentive of a 'good return to the owners' serving to 'defend our trade'[17] and

> infallibly secure our Commerce from French and Spanish depredations . . . our Trade flourishing and our Navigation protected.[18]

These assertions can be tested, to some degree, by recourse to the vouchers submitted by claimants of head money in respect of vessels-of-war condemned to the state and private naval forces. Though privateering venturers did not always claim the bounties to which they were entitled, it is clear that the Navy was predominant in this aspect of the prize war. Men-of-warsmen were in receipt of 88 per cent of the 979.5 bounties awarded to British captors between 1739 and 1783; in monetary terms, this amounted to an even greater share—94 per cent of the £613,482 10s paid—an indication of the greater average strength of the vessels-of-war taken by His Majesty's ships. Such prizes, moreover, represented 38.1 per cent of the Navy's return in the 1739–1783 period, while the privateering 'catch' included 117 enemy *corsaires* and men-of-war, just 5.6 per cent of the commissioned fleet's condemnations.[19]

If these figures imply that privateering venturers exaggerated their role in curtailing the enemy's predatory capability, there were other ways in which their business might contribute to the security of home trade. The primary function of a significant segment of the privateering fleet was the safe delivery of cargo, for 'armed traders' and 'specialist vessels' were commissioned to stiffen the crew's defensive resolve, as well as its predatory opportunism, by instilling into the employment contract the prospect of a share in the proceeds of any assailant taken. Intrinsic to these activities, therefore, was a measure of protective self-sufficiency. Many of these licensed merchantmen were large vessels 'armed and manned for the special reason of running without convoy',[20] though the carriage of a letter of marque was not a formal requirement for these 'runners' until 1798.[21] On occasion, such ships combined forces as a further safeguard; thus, 'having agreed to associate together for their mutual safety', the masters of the *Quebec* of Bristol, the *Nelly* of Lancaster and the *Nelly* of Liverpool 'appointed Captain Dawson of the *Marlborough*, commodore' for their homeward passage from St Kitts;[22] similar arrangements prevailed aboard vessels returning from the Mediterranean, four Turkeymen departing Leghorn in company 'exceedingly well manned and prepared for defence, should they be attacked';[23] the vessels of the chartered trading companies, moreover, regularly sailed from Hudson's Bay or the Far East in small consortships to enhance their powers of resistance. Thus, whether operating independently or in small fleets, 'letters of marque' tended to meet most of their own defensive requirements; though this probably added to the risks involved in their trading activities, it also served to lessen the protective burden borne by the Navy, thereby releasing resources for deployment elsewhere.

This burden was further eased in that privateers sometimes acted as convoys, escorting merchantmen both in conjunction with, or in the stead of, naval vessels. In 1779, for instance, four 'specialist letters of marque'—the *Active*, the *Carnatic*, the *Castor* and the *Tom*—were loaded with provisions at Cork for the use of His Majesty's troops in the West Indies. While the delivery of such a cargo was itself of some military utility—and an indication of the worth of this branch of the privateering business in the American Revolutionary War—these armed victuallers were

> not only of sufficient force to defend themselves against any enemy they were likely to meet with in their voyage, but were thought capable of strengthening and assisting His Majesty's ships appointed to convoy the Merchant Ships to the West Indies, and of affording Protection to the unarmed Ships in Company with them.

Accordingly, the vessels were detailed to assist HMS *Leviathan* in her convoy duties, with each provided with battle orders, signals and instructions commensurate with their elevated status as escorting, rather than escorted, ships.[24] The *Falmouth*, a commissioned 'advice boat in government service', acted in a similar capacity in accompanying 'the trade' from Plymouth to Portsmouth,[25] while licensed revenue cutters were often required to ward off the enemy privateers which from time to time infested coastal waters and threatened local trade.

Should the protective provisions of the state be found wanting, privateering venturers themselves might shoulder some responsibility for defending their wider commercial interests. This occurred in respect of particular localities; thus, the private man-of-war *Liverpool* was equipped specifically to secure the commerce of the Mersey from Thurot's naval force in 1759, though such was the reputation of the French commander that only a handful of men volunteered to serve in the ship and the laudable venture foundered.[26] Merchants concerned in a particular trade might also seek to safeguard their investments. In 1744, for instance, Yarmouth's fishing merchants fitted out, by subscription,

> two privateers of 12 carriage guns each, called the *Terrible* and the *Defence*, in order to cruize on that coast to protect the fishing trade from the insults of the French privateers.[27]

With similar designs,

> the gentlemen concerned in the corn trade have opened up a subscription for fitting out a large privateer to cruize against the French; and as they have the cargoes of most of the corn vessels from all parts of England consigned to them, it is also to serve to convoy those vessels, and see them safe into the port of London.[28]

There was even a report that private men-of-war were deployed to protect overseas trade; thus,

> four privateers are now fitting out at Deptford and Chatham, and are ordered to sail with all convenient speed, to cruize about the Bermuda islands, in order to protect the homeward-bound West-Indiamen from the American privateers.[29]

By dint of such ventures and, more significantly, the outset of 'letters of marque', private individuals added to the defensive resources of the state. This, together with the destruction visited upon enemy commerce in the pursuit of private profit, represented the 'service' which venturers persistently claimed to render to the nation, and the potential which the state sought to realise in its sponsorship of the activity. There were reservations, however, about the true extent of this utility. Thus, in seeking to stimulate privateering enterprise, governments invariably prescribed a series of instructions, prohibitions and penalties for the good conduct of the business, implying that reprisals, to be effective as a tool of maritime war, needed to be restrained and channelled against legitimate targets.

Naval officers, moreover, supposedly the practical beneficiaries of a flourishing privateering force, were generally sceptical as to the military efficacy of the commerce-raiding business. Frequently, indeed, their misgivings surfaced as open hostility. Vernon, for instance, declared that those seeking 'to serve in privateers . . . are generally as far from an inclination to serve the public that the public service is their greatest detestation.'[30] In the Seven Years' War, criticism was widespread as naval officers opined that privateers in home waters were no more than smugglers, while more serious complaints arose from the piratical behaviour of privateersmen in the Mediterranean and in the Caribbean, where their 'atrocious conduct . . . brought stain upon the nation's character'.[31] Much later, Nelson added to the condemnation, remarking that 'the conduct of all privateers is, as far as I have seen, so near piracy that I only wonder any civilised nation can allow them.'[32]

Seemingly, therefore, the noble intentions of commerce-raiding promoters might all too easily disintegrate before the lawlessness of their fellow venturers at sea. Yet these observations say more about relations between men-of-warsmen and privateersmen than they do about levels of indiscipline in the privateering business as a whole. In practice, it was competition and friction rather than co-operation and harmony which characterised dealings between the two services. While the naval officer generally saw the privateering venturer as an unruly irritant, a scavenger intent on profiting by the rich pickings left in the wake of the King's ships, from the other side, it was in the guise of policeman, press master or rival in the prize war that the man-of-warsman appeared to his privateering 'ally'. At the core of these conflicting perceptions, there lay the issues of prize, time and labour—assets which were invariably in short supply during wartime. On the assumption that the Navy employed them more efficiently, it may be argued that privateering enterprise, in diverting warlike resources away from their most utilitarian employment, was essentially detrimental to the military effort.

Whether or not this was actually the case is beyond a definitive, objective answer. However, the elements involved in such a judgement are abundantly clear. Prize money, for instance, rewarded men in both services and was clearly an important incentive for potential volunteers. It was also a source of mutual jealousy and distrust. While a degree of specialisation and complementarity is evident in the distribution of prizes, with naval vessels taking more of the enemy's ships-of-war, and privateers concentrating upon his merchantmen, there was still a substantial degree of overlap and duplication of predatory effort as naval and licensed vessels cruised the same waters and pursued the same quarry. Tension naturally ensued when income was at stake, with resentment particularly strong among men-of-warsmen; duty-bound to escort mercantile craft, engage the enemy's fleets or blockade his ports, they must have found it galling that privateersmen were not only free to cruise for prizes but often sought to prey upon vessels rendered defenceless by naval attacks upon convoys. Head money represented a poor consolation for the cargoes lost to privateering rivals in such circumstances. Even on the occasions when state- and privately-owned vessels combined to effect a seizure, there was frequently discord between the joint-captors; the *Royal Family* venturers, for instance, felt aggrieved that the *Russell*'s men were awarded the bulk of the *Glorioso* prize,[33] while it was in the Prize Appeals Court that HMS *Leviathan*'s company was forced to yield a share of a prize deceitfully denied to the *Active* privateer,[34] and here, also, that HM's cutter *Pheasant* was obliged to withdraw her claim to *De Twee Gesusters*, a prize to the *Providence* and *Spitfire* of Dartmouth.[35]

If such instances did little to foster a sense of common purpose amongst naval and privateering interests, a less obvious bone of contention was the time and effort expended by the Navy in policing the disorderly elements of the commissioned fleet. This might arise in the line of duty, the 'commanders of all the King's ships', for instance, being ordered to search for the infamous privateersman John Patrick 'and to take him out of his ship wherever they met with him'.[36] It could occur almost unwittingly, as private men-of-war like the *Centurion* were ordered by their owners to Spithead where the very presence of men-of-war and the press was deemed sufficient to instil order and deter any deserters among their men.[37] More normally, it was on an incidental basis that men-of-warsmen were called upon to administer discipline to privateersmen. Thus, 29 mutineers were subdued and arrested as their private ship-of-war, the *Princess Augusta*, fell in with a naval frigate;[38] James Verco was unfortunate enough to meet with HMS *Daphne* shortly after relieving a Dutchman of his cargo, and was duly arrested;[39] a similar encounter at sea revealed to the captain of HMS *Berwick* that the *Dreadnought* privateer was harbouring stolen and smuggled goods;[40] while, on land, it was a 'passing' press gang which subdued the angry and menacing survivors of the *Winchelsea*'s crew as they sought compensation from the owners and managers of the venture.[41]

Such encounters might result in offenders like the men of the *Dreadnought* being pressed into naval service. Here, the issue of discipline which sometimes divided privateersmen and naval seamen impinged upon the question of labour recruitment, the most serious area of conflict between the two services. Seafarers were generally at a premium in wartime as the massive requirements of the Navy added to the normal demands of the overseas and coastal trades, and the fishing industry. The privateering business exerted a further pressure on supply, with additional hands shipped aboard 'letters of marque' and entire crews enlisted for service in private men-of-war. As Appendix 2 indicates, the 'extra' burden imposed on the seafaring labour market by the promoters of 'Channel' and 'deep-water' commerce-raiders fluctuated widely and rapidly over the course of a war. At its peak, however, recruitment for private men-of-war accounted for a significant proportion of the maritime workforce. In September 1744, for instance, some 10,632 men were required in the predatory business, 13.2 per cent of an estimated total of 80,500 mariners employed at sea during that year; similarly, the 11,331 privateersmen sought in October 1757 represented 11.4 per cent of the seafarers currently working aboard British vessels, while a notional complement of 19,465 seamen was deployed aboard the nation's private ships-of-war in February 1781, approximately 14 per cent of a seaborne workforce which extended to almost 138,000 men.[42]

With a monthly average of 47,202, 63,259 and 98,269 seafarers borne for pay in the Navy during 1744, 1757 and 1781 respectively,[43] it is clear that the privateering business, at its height, attracted a significant number of potential men-of-warsmen away from the King's service. Moreover, many of these men were experienced mariners, the skilled workers which the Navy sought above all others. Thus, in 26 crew lists submitted to the Navy Office between 1739 and 1783, 995 of the 3,761 privateersmen rated were described as 'able', with 398 recorded as 'ordinary', 856 as 'landman' and 310 as 'boy'. As the unskilled ranks of 'landman' and 'boy' constituted 31 per cent of this sample, over two-thirds of the men listed—37 per cent rated as 'able' or 'ordinary' seamen, together with the officers and specialist crew members who comprised 32 per cent of the complements considered—had some seafaring expertise.[44]

The muster rolls further indicate that the vast majority of privateersmen were British in origin. In the *Royal Family* squadron's second cruise, for example, 87.2 per cent of 617 men of known nationality hailed from the British Isles—with Irishmen particularly numerous—despite the fact that the vessels were re-fitted in Lisbon.[45] Though such detail is lacking in other privateering crew lists, the dominance of anglicized names is striking; in contrast, names redolent of foreign birth are conspicuously few, with clarifications such as 'Turk', 'Dutchman', 'black boy' or 'Portuguese' entered to underline their rarity.[46] These data offer little support to the contention that private men-of-war relied heavily upon 'foreigners, landmen and criminals';[47] indeed, it would be surprising if this had been so, for privateering promoters, unlike the Lords of the Admiralty, were not compelled to fit out their vessels. They were principally concerned to make profits, and the availability and quality of labour was clearly a factor in their decision to invest in commerce-raiding. Moreover, a deficient or sub-standard crew might prove counter-productive and a reason for abandoning a venture; such an option seemed attractive to the owners of the *Sarah Gally* as they warned their captain,

> we can never expect any good of these people . . . if they will not goe a Cruseing on the French coast or westward. We desire you on receit hereof to discharge all such as will not goe & get others in their roome & if you can't gett enough to man the Gally discharge them all & lay her up, for we will not be eaten up by such people that will never loose the sight of their own Chimney's smoake.[48]

Undoubtedly, therefore, the privateering business served to compound the Navy's recurrent wartime manning problem, as large numbers of skilled seafarers worked—for part of a war at least—in the commissioned fleet. The competition between the two services which inevitably arose in this situation was less than perfect, for various regulatory measures and recruitment agencies operated to divert the flow of labour in one direction or the other. Privateering promoters, for instance, were inhibited by the issue of protections which safeguarded their crews from impressment but also imposed a ceiling upon the number of men they might recruit. Occasionally, certain types of venture were limited specifically to release men for the Navy,[49] and there were also restrictions regarding the quality of labour, with privateer commissions sometimes stipulating that landmen should comprise a proportion—usually a third, but sometimes three-quarters—of the ship's company.[50] In these provisions, the state's concern to encourage and maximise the utility of privateering enterprise without impairing the naval service is evident; while protections reserved a minimum number of men for private men-of-war, the forced enlistment of inexperienced men was designed to provide able men for the King's ships and to realise the privateering sector's potential as a nursery of seamen.

The manpower crisis apparent in each of the major eighteenth-century naval conflicts could never be fully resolved given the vast and sudden disparity which opened up between demand and supply. Though market forces operated to increase the flow of seafarers, with wages rising in the mercantile marine, including the 'letter of marque' branch of the privateering business, and bounties paid to encourage men to volunteer for private or naval ships-of-war, other means were deployed to enhance the supply and modify the distribution of men between the maritime sectors. Accordingly, crimpage was widely used by merchant shipowners, while the state used the Impress Service to intervene profoundly and controversially in the workings of the market. If crimps were notably adept at providing men-of-warsmen with drink and lodging, and then a berth in a private man-of-war, press-masters quickly saw the potential in heavily-manned commissioned vessels, and their tenders regularly greeted predators in the approaches to home ports. A deep, mutual antipathy arose out of this issue, with naval officers castigating the dubious tactics of privateering promoters,[51] and venturers, in their turn, expressing their bitterness in various ways. Thus, indignant owners such as Francis Ingram complained to the Admiralty of the injury inflicted upon the *Enterprize*'s cruise by impressment at sea;[52] cautious commanders like Captain Gardner of the *King of Prussia* hid their best men in the hold on sighting a man-of-war;[53] privateersmen such as George Clarke and Jenkin Thomas, injured by a press gang, sued for compensation from their assailants;[54] while the men of the *Eagle* and the *Sampson* were themselves the aggressors, both crews resorting to arms in their respective attempts to fend off press gangs in Cardiff and New York.[55]

In turning their weapons against the forces they were intended to abet, these privateersmen—whose labour was keenly sought by the Navy—illustrated vividly the problems of regulation and wastage of resources which might afflict their enterprise and which so concerned their naval critics. Yet these were isolated, well-publicised incidents, the culprits being swiftly brought to justice, their liberty curtailed and their right of reprisal extinguished. In this, they were atypical, for very few privateersmen were tried in the criminal law courts during the eighteenth century,[56] while those who appeared in the civilian tribunals of Prize and Chancery were generally examined as to the nationality of detained property or the distribution of prize funds rather than alleged acts of depredation. This might imply a poor detection rate; it might reflect the 'pusillanimity'—genuine or strategically convenient—of the authorities;[57] more likely, however, the relative silence of the legal record was due to the simple fact that the great majority of British privateersmen exerted their belligerent energies against legitimate targets. Whether defending or attempting to apprehend cargoes, it was self-interest which motivated these efforts, an incentive which co-incided, by and large, with the state's general aim of strengthening Britain's commercial interest at the expense of foreign rivals. If this private enterprise was essentially and increasingly marginal to the military outcome of the maritime struggle, and incurred indirect costs in the resources it attracted away from the public naval force, its contributions to the trade war were many and significant; moreover, as a rare and potentially lucrative opportunity for gain, the privateering business was of some importance in the wartime economies of many British ports.

Notes

1. Andrews, *Elizabethan Privateering*, 6.
2. *Observator*, 10 June 1702.
3. *Journals of the House of Commons*, 33 (1770-72), 521.
4. PRO, C 103/130. Richard Taunton to Thomas Hall, 15 January 1746.
5. LRO, 942 HOL 10, 406.
6. Starkey, thesis, 346.
7. MacPherson, *Annals of Commerce*, III, 668.
8. *Penny London Post, or Morning Advertiser*, 23 January 1745.
9. Pares, *War and Trade*, 360. Corbett, *England in the Seven Years' War*, II, 8, comes to the same conclusion.
10. *London Evening Post*, 5 February 1745.
11. Damer Powell, *Bristol Privateers*, 252-3, 267-8.
12. Damer Powell, *Bristol Privateers*, 276-7.
13. Damer Powell, *Bristol Privateers*, 173-4.
14. *London Chronicle*, 29 March 1757.
15. The *Winchelsea*, 24 guns, was retaken by the *Duke of Cornwall* of Bristol. See Damer Powell, *Bristol Privateers*, 201.
16. In so doing, privateersmen were following their instructions to inform the Admiralty of their 'captures and proceedings [and] whatsoever shall occur unto them or be discovered and declared to them or found out by them by examination of or correspondence and conference with mariners or passengers of or on the ships or vessels taken . . . touching or concerning the designs of the enemy or any of their fleets, ships, vessels or parties and of the stations, seas, ports and places of their interests therein'. Artcile 7, 'Instructions to Privateers', 17 March 1777. PRO, HCA 26/60. The Channel Islanders' particular utility in this respect is discussed by Raban, 'War and Trade', 135-9; and Jamieson, 'Return to Privateering', 152.
17. PRO, C 103/130. Richard Taunton to Thomas Hall, 2 August 1746.
18. *Lloyd's Evening Post and British Chronicle*, 17 February 1762.
19. PRO, ADM 43/2-30.
20. PRO, HCA 45/12. Case of *La Misercordia*.
21. 38 George III, c.76.
22. Damer Powell, *Bristol Privateers*, 280.
23. *Exeter Flying Post*, 27 August 1779.
24. PRO, HCA 45/9, 12. Case of *La Misercordia*.

25. PRO, ADM 43/11(2).
26. Williams, *Liverpool Privateers*, 134-5.
27. *Country Journal, or Craftsman*, 7 July 1744.
28. *Exeter Flying Post*, 2 October 1778.
29. This report appeared in the *Old Exeter Journal, or Weekly Advertiser*, 15 August 1776, some eight months before commissions were issued against the Americans. I am indebted to Stephen Fisher for this reference.
30. Quoted in Baugh, *Naval Administration*, 20.
31. Quoted in Rodger, *Wooden World*, 185-6.
32. Quoted in Minchinton, 'Piracy and Privateering', 300.
33. PRO, C 103/130. Richard Taunton to Thomas Hall, 14 November 1747, 9 January 1748.
34. PRO, HCA 45/9.
35. PRO, HCA 45/12.
36. Damer Powell, *Bristol Privateers*, 210.
37. PRO, C 103/130. Richard Taunton to Thomas Hall, 9 January 1745. Taunton lamented that a failure to get to the high seas had resulted in the unruly behaviour of the *Centurion*'s men; thus, he related, 'I am sorry our *Centurion* could not reach over for had we got our men in deep water they would have been governed 'till they had finished the Cruise & got to the Downs'.
38. Damer Powell, *Bristol Privateers*, 157.
39. PRO, HCA 45/12.
40. *Newcastle Chronicle*, 9 June 1781.
41. PRO, C 103/130. Richard Taunton to Thomas Hall, 26 August 1747.
42. These estimates of seafaring employment levels are based on a number of sources; for the mercantile marine, 'An Account of the Number of Seamen . . .' for 1740 to 1766 in BL, Add Mss 38,340, f.17, was used in conjunction with R. Davis, 'Seamen's Sixpences. An Index of Commercial Activity, 1697-1828' *Economica*, XXIII (1956), 328-43, and the Navigation Accounts in PRO, CUST 17/1-9; for the Navy, the *Journals of the House of Commons* were used, together with Lloyd, *British Seaman*, 286-90.
43. *Journals of the House of Commons*, XXIV (1744-1745), 769; XXVIII (1757-1761), 128; the 1781 figure is drawn from Lloyd, *British Seaman*, 286-90.
44. PRO, ADM 43/2-30. Most of these muster rolls relate to 'deep-water' private ships-of-war, with 17 drawn from the 1739-1748 war, five from the 1756-1762 war and four from the American Revolutionary War. These were the only crew lists to rate the men.
45. PRO, ADM 43/13(2). See Appendix 6, Table 5.
46. PRO, ADM 43/3(2), *Hardwicke*'s list, 1745; PRO, ADM 43/5(2), *Tygress*' list, 1745; PRO, BT 98/39, *Betsey*'s muster roll, 1779; SMV, Muster Rolls, *Tryal*'s hospital bill, 1780.
47. Rodger, *Wooden World*, 185.
48. PRO, C 108/138. Creagh & Fallet to Patrick Galloway, 2-3 March 1703.
49. For instance, 'letters of marque' were restricted in 1695, while the 1759

prohibition of 'Channel' privateers was partly designed to release men for the Navy. See Gradish, *Manning in the Seven Years' War*, 48-9.

50. In 1695, it was stipulated that landmen should constitute three-quarters of a privateering crew. See the letter of marque declarations in PRO, HCA 26/2. In later wars, landmen were to comprise one-third of complements. See the 'Instructions to Privateers', 4 June 1756, No. 12. PRO, HCA 26/5.
51. See Rodger, *Wooden World*, 185.
52. LRO, Accounts Books of the *Enterprize*, 387 MD 10.
53. Damer Powell, *Bristol Privateers*, 222.
54. Damer Powell, *Bristol Privateers*, 158.
55. Damer Powell, *Bristol Privateers*, 206, 231-2.
56. Between 1700 and 1750, for instance, only four of the 60 cases of mutiny identified by Rediker, *Devil and the Deep Blue Sea*, 308-09, occurred in privateering vessels. The index of cases collected in PRO, HCA 1—the records of the criminal division of the Admiralty Court—suggests that very few privateersmen were tried at the Old Bailey.
57. Rodger, *Wooden World*, 186, condemns the Administration for its weakness in the face of privateering abuses. However, in the Seven Years' War, it suited the government to allow privateering venturers a free hand in their dealings with neutral shipping, proscribing the activity only when war with the Dutch threatened. This brinkmanship angered Bristol's merchants who claimed that they had been encouraged to seize Dutch carriers, which were subsequently released as the Administration changed tack. See Damer Powell, *Bristol Privateers*, 184-5.

Eleven

'The Finest Opportunity'?

As an impermanent aspect of commercial life, privateering enterprise had a limited impact upon the development of the British economy in the eighteenth century. There are no grounds to assert, for instance, that resources invested, or profits generated, in the commerce-raiding business were instrumental in significantly accelerating or retarding the process of industrialisation.[1] Nor is there any reason to suspect that the setting forth of commissioned vessels influenced the long-run growth of ports or regions in the way that the Atlantic staples conditioned the early expansion of Bristol, Liverpool and Glasgow, or the coal trade underlay the maritime economy of the North East. However, during the regular and prolonged intervals in which reprisals were permissible, privateering activity constituted an integral part of the British shipping industry, a further option for merchant capitalists to exploit in the search for profit and a rare chance for seafarers to share directly in the product of their labour. As such, this 'privat interest in Publick War'[2] assumed a place within a dynamic sector of the economy at critical junctures when more conventional forms of commercial capital accumulation might be jeopardised by the state of hostilities.

In this context, the privateering business was significant in various ways. It stimulated the supply of ships and seafarers, the productive resources upon which the shipping industry depended. Thus, as one anonymous contemporary observed,

> merchants were induced to invest their Capital in the gainful employment of building ships ... for Privateers [which] when Peace returned were employed in Traffic or Fishery.[3]

Similarly, by regularly attracting landmen and boys to the sea, private men-of-war contributed to the long-term accretion of the seafaring population evident in the eighteenth century, an important attribute in the eyes of governments bent on the 'encouragement of seamen' and shipowners anxious to generate an ample, low-cost labour supply. Equally, of course, such benefits were offset by the physical losses incurred in the quest for prizes. Commerce-raiding was a high-risk activity, its belligerent, violent character exacerbating the normal perils of sailing ship operation. Accordingly, private ships-of-war might be taken or sunk by the enemy, or lost to the sea as a result of over-crowding or sailing too close to unknown shores—calamities which inevitably took their toll on the privateering workforce.

Whether the net impact of privateering activity on factor supply was positive or negative is incalculable. However, given its intermittent character, it is clear that the business of reprisal could never generate sufficient resources to sustain itself; rather, privateering promoters looked to the market for vessels, outfitting resources and seafarers—the capital and labour they required in considerable quantities. While it generally competed with the Navy for such 'inputs'—especially labour—commissioned enterprise enjoyed a complex, symbiotic relationship with the shipping industry. In one guise, it was virtually synonymous with an important part of the 'merchant's service', for the majority of 'letters of marque' were employed as 'runners', overseas trading vessels sailing without naval escort and equipped with commissions to append a predatory dimension to their voyages. To the extent that this prize-taking facility afforded some incentive for shipowners to proceed with a venture despite the hazards of war, and entailed the deployment of extra men and armaments, this form of privateering enterprise served to stimulate commercial activity. In another manifestation, however, the privateering business competed directly with the commercial sector, as private men-of-war placed an additional burden on the supply of maritime resources already depleted by the demands of the Navy. If this rendered the transport of cargo less tenable, there were other occasions when the aggression of the enemy severely curtailed trading operations; commerce-raiding might counter the commercial downswing in these instances, with shipowners and seafarers utilising their idle resources in an attempt to profit from the trade of enemy subjects.

The privateering business thus assumed a number of roles in the maritime economy during wartime, acting to encourage, to rival, or to supplant more regular forms of shipping activity. 'Letters of marque' were the most stable element of the commissioned fleet, with vessels working according to the seasons and the commodity markets—as far as the enemy would allow—and not the prize-taking prospects thrown up by the vacillating state of the war. Concentrated in London and the larger outports, these were also the least important units of the privateering business in terms of the net addition to commercial activity accruing from their operations; quite simply, it is probable that many of these traders would have sailed—on different routes, perhaps—if peace rather than war had prevailed, while only minor structural modifications were required to convert a foreign-going merchant ship into an 'armed trading vessel', few, if any, being specifically built or purchased for the purpose.

Concurrently, of course, the owners of such licensed merchantmen may well have held shares in one or more of the private men-of-war set forth to prey upon enemy commerce. More volatile than the 'letter of marque' sector, and with no parallel activity in peacetime, the overtly predatory arm of the privateering business was clearly of some import to the economies of many maritime districts. It was only in the early months of 1781, however, that the outset of 'Channel' and 'deep-water' commerce-raiders impinged upon commercial activity on anything approaching a national scale. Thus, with some 453 predators active in February 1781,

> it became almost impossible to find vessels sufficient to export the corn . . . a great proportion of the British mercantile shipping being at this time withdrawn from the purposes of trade by being converted into privateers or transports.

To alleviate this situation, bounties were offered to encourage neutral shippers to carry British corn.[4] Meanwhile, Daniel Eccleston's lament to his brother in Antigua suggests that the West India trade was similarly afflicted; thus,

> you will have now a prospect of a fine crop, and I wish I could send you a small vessel and cargo to bring part of it home, but since the commencement of the Dutch War, the demand for vessels be so great for privateers, and they have sold so high that there's no medling with 'em. I suppose there never was such a general spirit for privateering in either this or any other nation before; every little coasting sloop or even fishing smack that has the least appearance for sailing is now eagerly purchased at 500 per cent more than the intrinsick value and converted to that use.[5]

While such conversions clearly exerted immense pressure on the shipping market and inhibited the flow of trade, the sudden increase in demand for privateersmen—from 1,517 in November 1780 to a peak of 19,465 in February 1781—placed a further burden on the seafaring labour market at a time when the Navy's manning requirements were still rising.

Though the intense privateering 'mania' precipitated by the grant of reprisals against the Dutch soon expired—by July 1781 only 65 private men-of-war and 3,210 privateersmen were still operational—this burst of privateering activity was unprecedented in its scale and impact, and unique in its nationwide character.

At other times, the 'spirit of privateering' was less pervasive, serving to initiate local surges of commerce-raiding activity. Such upturns might be 'demand-led', with the bright prospects afforded by predatory enterprise persuading investors and seafarers to shift their resources from commercial operations into private men-of-war. In the case of labour, for instance, commerce-raiding ventures engaged the services of an annual average of 5,014, 6,078 and 6,329 privateersmen in the relatively active periods of 1744-1748, 1756-1758 and 1778–1781 respectively. As yearly means of 24,453, 23,345 and 32,459 seafarers were employed in British foreign-going and coastal traders at these junctures,[6] it would seem that the predatory business accounted for an important element of the labour force at times when merchant shipowners, as well as the Navy, generally struggled to raise complements.

Though it is unlikely that this short-term quest for speculative profits seriously impaired British commercial growth in the long run, the diversion of seafarers and other resources away from trading operations may well have had a detrimental local impact, serving to exacerbate weaknesses in the competitive position of a port in relation to rival maritime communities. In this sense, Bristol's extensive interests in 'deep-water' private ships-of-war during the hostilities of 1744–1748 and 1756–1758 may well have contributed to—or been a reflection of—the port's declining share in the Atlantic staple trades in the face of competition from Liverpool, Glasgow, Lancaster and elsewhere. Significantly, merchants and shipowners from these ports, notably from Liverpool, concentrated on commerce—and 'letters of marque'—at such critical junctures, exploiting the advantages of a northerly situation to emerge from the calamities of war with an enhanced share of the trades in slaves and Caribbean produce.

Local bursts of commerce-raiding activity did not always compete with the more regular trades for available 'inputs'. Instead, the outset of private men-of-war might consume resources 'laid up' due to the adverse trading conditions of war, thereby effecting an increase in the commercial activity of a port. Dartmouth's economy, for instance, was heavily dependent on the Newfoundland fisheries, a business that was highly vulnerable to enemy attack in the North Atlantic, to the impressment of its labour force at home and to the closure of markets for codfish in Catholic Europe.[7] When these depressive factors held sway, leading Western Adventurers such as the Holdsworths, the Newmans, the Sparkes, Leigh & Pinson, and Peter Ougier employed idle capital in the privateering business. Accordingly, in the 1740s, Dartmouth's merchants exhibited a keen interest in 'deep-water' private ships-of-war, while in the American Revolutionary War, their heirs and successors continued to follow the predatory fashion of the day and invested in a fleet of less powerful commerce-raiding craft. The local labour force was similarly redeployed, with shipmasters such as Thomas Goldsmith, Andrew Pidgely and Peter Tessier, whose service in the Newfoundland trade was long and regular, commanding more predatory undertakings with the onset of the American Revolutionary War.[8]

Commerce-raiding fulfilled a similar counter-cyclical function in Liverpool during this conflict. The collapse of the Atlantic staple trades as a result of enemy naval and privateering activity rendered many of the port's overseas trading vessels temporarily redundant. As early as 1775, shipowners in the slave trade were attempting to reduce costs by imposing a wage cut on their workforce, an action which provoked a serious riot amongst seafarers who attacked the town's merchants in their own Exchange.[9] If this incident suggests some correlation between unemployment and heightened social tension, it also helps to explain why Liverpool's merchants were so keen to embrace the opportunities presented by the issue of privateer commissions against the colonial rebels in April 1777 and, more significantly, the grant of reprisals against French commerce in August 1778. While an added inducement to fit out trading vessels, or 'letters of marque', was afforded in 1777, in the following year some of the slack within the port's economy was taken up by the outset of over 100 private ships-of-war and 'cruise and voyage' ventures. Accordingly, in November 1778, the Earl of Derby, was able to inform the House of Lords that

> Liverpool would have been ruined but for the success of its privateers; their efforts had indeed been remarkably fortunate but had the case been otherwise the town would have felt the war most severely.[10]

Thus, the commerce-raiding business might serve to alleviate the depressions which wartime entailed for many ports, just as it could add to the pressure on resources in local economies boosted by the onset of hostilities. Though the evidence is somewhat sparse, an impression of the gross value of 'inputs' into this activity can be gleaned from various sources. In Appendix 3, the sums expended on the outfit of 10 predatory ventures are related to crew size and the duration of the project as stated in the letter of marque declarations. Despite vast differences in the scale and character of these undertakings, some consistency is apparent in the monthly cost per man of their initial outfits. Thus, promotional expenditures—entailing the cost of the vessel, her armaments, stores and victuals—ranged from the £3 4s incurred by the owners of the *Enterprize* to the £8 15s laid out by the proprietors of the *Antigallican*, with five of the observations grouped around the mean of £5 10s per man per month.[11] If this average figure is applied to the aggregate manpower requirements of the predatory fleets derived from Appendix 2,[12] sums of £641,366, £1,587,102, £1,368,636 10s and £1,713,085 were evidently spent on the outfit of 'Channel' and 'deep-water' private men-of-war in the four major wars of the 1702–1783 period.[13]

Such calculations neglect the capital consumed in the course of cruises by way of depreciation, vessel repairs and replenishment of supplies; most significantly, however, they take no account of the value of the labour engaged in commerce-raiders, a form of investment in the sense that most privateersmen served for a share in the profits rather than a wage. On the assumption that the minimum stake held by each of these seafarers was the wage he would have earned in the Royal Navy, some notion can be gained of the worth of labour 'inputs' into the privateering business. Thus, some 116,612, 288,564, 248,843 and 311,470 man-months were worked in the predatory vessels commissioned during the major conflicts under review; applying a rate of 16s 6d to the 30 per cent of these totals assumed to be landmen, and the able seamen's monthly wage of 22s 6d to the remainder,[14] the notional value—or the gross opportunity cost—of privateering labour amounted to £120,693 6s in the 1702–1712 conflict, £298,663 16s in the Austrian Succession War, £257,252 9s 6d in the 1756–1762 conflict, and £322,371 9s in the American Revolutionary War. In sum, therefore, resources with a minimum value of £0.75m, £1.8m, £1.6m and £2.0m were invested in the predatory elements of the commissioned fleets of the 1702–1783 era.

These 'inputs' were important to the maritime economies of localities where the 'spirit of privateering' prevailed. Whether new-built or converted from other employments, the outfit of private men-of-war brought work and income to shipwrights; it generated business for sailmakers, coopers, ropemakers and other artisans in the shore-based maritime trades; it consumed the produce and services of iron founders, armourers and gunsmiths; and it created demand for victuals, provisions and the sundry other supplies necessary to sustain a heavily-manned vessel-of-war. By dint of these 'knock-on' effects, therefore, the outset of commerce-raiders concerned not only the venturers directly involved in predatory operations, but also those engaged in a myriad of auxiliary maritime employments.

The 'output' of the privateering business also held wide-ranging ramifications for the maritime community, though the product and its significance varied with the function of the individual venture. As most 'letters of marque' were engaged in trading operations, the bulk of the earnings they generated came in the form of freights charged for the carriage of cargo—gains which were forthcoming regardless of the commission issued for the vessel. Thus, the returns accruing specifically from the licensed status of the armed merchantman were limited to the prize goods occasionally taken by these vessels and the income earned by trading ventures launched largely because of the prize-taking facility afforded by the acquisition of a privateer commission. In sum, therefore, 'armed traders' and 'specialist vessels'—always a significant proportion of the privateering fleet—added little to the earnings of the shipping industry by virtue of their inherent commerce-raiding dimension.

Private men-of-war, on the other hand, were set forth to appropriate vessels and goods from foreign ownership, an extraordinary source of income distinct from, and supplemental to, the returns generated by the normal transportation services provided by the mercantile marine. This unusual product can be viewed from a number of perspectives. At the macro-economic level, it would seem that the vessels and goods taken from the subjects of a rival state added only marginally to Britain's national income in the eighteenth century. One estimate suggests that the prize earnings of the commissioned fleet in Queen Anne's War represented less than 0.5 per cent of the value of the nation's foreign trade.[15] If the gains of later wars were probably greater—due to the the higher average value of prizes—it is nevertheless clear that commerce-raiding activity did not lead to the injection of major quantities of capital into the economy as it had done in the 1580s and 1590s.[16] Moreover, there is no evidence to suggest that the transformation effected by the integration of prize Dutch bulk-carriers into the mid-seventeenth-century shipping stock was in any way repeated in the following hundred or so years.[17]

At the local level, however, commerce-raiding returns assumed some significance to consumers, merchants and producers. In the centres of predatory activity, prize goods added to commodity supplies, though the spasmodic character of their procurement dictated that such supplements were somewhat irregular and largely unrelated to demand. Gluts occurred, with market prices falling to the benefit of purchasers and the disadvantage of merchants engaged in the shipment and importation of the newly-abundant commodity. In 1779, for instance, news from the Channel Islands inferred that the local sugar market was overstocked; thus,

> 'tis said that there are 20,000 hogsheads of French prize sugars now in the several warehouses and magazines of the islands of Guernsey and Jersey, which amount, at only £20 per hogshead, to £400,000.[18]

The shipping market, and the business of shipbuilders, might be similarly affected by an influx of prize vessels. For example, in the wake of the privateering 'mania' of 1780–1781, newspaper advertisements imply that West Country ports were crowded with ships for sale as venturers attempted to sell their erstwhile private men-of-war and recently acquired 'prizes made free'. As a consequence, demand for locally-built vessels must have fallen, a presumption supported by the fact that 35 prize vessels—6.4 per cent of the region's mercantile fleet—were still owned in South Devon ports in 1790; moreover, the registration of 74,742 tons of prize shipping, 6.6 per cent of all English tonnage at this time, suggests that this was by no means a local phenomenon.[19]

Naturally, captors themselves suffered if the disposal of their prizes depressed the local market. Efforts were therefore made to find a lucrative mart, a quest which involved the landing of goods at ports where shortages were thought to exist, rather than at home bases. Channel Island venturers appear to have been adept at locating a favourable market price, disposing of goods in a range of mainland ports as opportunity offered.[20] Alternatively, captors might attempt to bring their wares to the attention of a wider audience, advertising auctions of prize properties in a range of newspapers and distributing sale catalogues via a number of brokers.[21] Provincial venturers often employed agents in London to bring local auctions to the notice of the large metropolitan market; thus, the cargo of *Die Lieffde* was to be sold at Hatton's Coffee House in Dartmouth, where

> goods may be viewed any time fourteen days previous to day of sale. Catalogues will be timely delivered, and samples may be seen at the warehouses in Dartmouth; and at Messrs. Vaughan, Winne, and Margetson's, London.[22]

Likewise, the disposal of particularly valuable cargoes—the spices and treasures brought home by the *Duke* and the *Dutchess*, the bullion taken by the *Duke* and the *Prince Frederick*, or the East India goods of the *Carnatic*[23]—was normally accomplished in the capital, where purchasing power was more extensive and prices were generally higher.

To those responsible for the apprehension of such goods, of course, the proceeds of the various prize sales and auctions represented an income, the reward for which they risked their capital or their labour. Whether the gross returns generated from this source exceeded the total sums invested in private men-of-war—whether the business of reprisal was profitable in an overall sense—is uncertain due to the limitations of the available evidence relating to prize values. However, estimates of the gross profits earned by particular facets of the predatory fleet present an optimistic view of its profitability. Thus, the aggregate takings of Channel Island venturers in Queen Anne's War have been assessed at up to £350,000,[24] while a contemporary list compiled in Liverpool in 1779 indicates that prizes with a gross value of just over £1m were taken by the port's licensed fleet in 1778–1779.[25] In both instances, the total proceeds of a part of the predatory force amounted to approximately half of the aggregate value of 'inputs' consumed by private ships-of-war in the two respective conflicts.[26]

Estimates of the gross prize return inevitably disguise the distribution of profits between the many and varied units of the commerce-raiding business. In fact, the dispersal of returns was highly uneven, with venturers experiencing widely differing fortunes in their efforts to realise the speculative gains that predation offered. At one extreme, the risks undertaken in fitting out, or serving aboard, private ships-of-war might produce a negative return. Such an outcome might ensue from a barren cruise; that approximately 40 per cent of the 1,201 'Channel' and 823 'deep-water' predators set forth in the 1702–1783 period failed to achieve a prize condemnation, and numerous captors effected just a single seizure, perhaps of limited value, suggests that unproductive cruises were commonplace.[27]

Moreover, a relatively high casualty rate attended the operations of private men-of-war, with ventures coming to variety of premature and costly ends.[28] The elements took their toll on predatory craft much as they did on other forms of sailing vessel; thus, the 'privateer of force' *Inspector* 'sprang a leak in a brisk gale' and was grounded in Tangier Bay, while the *Minerva* was totally lost in a hurricane during her 'cruising voyage' in the Caribbean, and the *Alert* of Liverpool was stranded off Whitehaven just 11 days into her 'deep-water' cruise.[29] Disasters also occurred in calmer weather, with overcrowding and poor shiphandling contributing to the sinking of the *Somerset* in the Bristol Channel on her maiden voyage, the oversetting of the *Bellona* of Exeter as she proceeded past Dawlish with a boat full of women alongside, and the capsize of the newly-launched *Pelican* as she paraded up and down the Mersey with 200 celebrating seafarers and guests on board.[30] Enemy action could be similarly devastating, of course. 'Smart' engagements with hostile ships-of-war obliged privateers such as the *Vulcano* of Exeter and the *Lion* of Bristol to undergo costly repairs,[31] while less fortunate craft like the *Tygress* of Dartmouth, the *Bacchus* of London and the *Old England* of Bristol were either taken or sunk by French naval vessels.[32]

Financial losses arising from such calamities might be considerable. Richard Taunton, for instance, was £2,000 the poorer as a consequence of the *Fame*'s 'expeditionary' debacle;[33] the demise of the *Tartar*'s cruise left her managing owners with debts of £10,000 on an initial investment of £14,000;[34] while the £10,000 spent in the Spanish law courts by the proprietors of the *Antigallican* in their forlorn attempt to reclaim a confiscated prize effectively doubled the outfitting costs of the venture.[35] Though generally uninsured, most investors were nevertheless able to ride such misfortunes by virtue of the organisational structures established to spread the risks inherent to commerce-raiding activity. Few, if any, sank their entire worth into the outfit of a single private man-of-war. Instead, partnerships, companies and popular subscriptions encouraged many to invest relatively small amounts of capital in such ventures without diminishing their interest in other commercial activities, while the device of shareholding allowed more committed speculators to participate in a number of predatory undertakings.

Privateer owners' liabilities were also reduced by the practice of enlisting seafarers on a 'no purchase, no pay' basis. While this limited the labour costs of the unsuccessful promoter, it meant that privateersmen sacrificed the wages currently and readily available in the mercantile marine and the Navy. John Brohier, a lieutenant in the *Fame*, was clearly aware of this opportunity cost in his melodramatic reflections on the ill-fated cruise; thus,

> I long to be out of the Sea of Troubles & Misfortunes which I have been involved in these near 3 years past, having for the fruits of my labour lost all that time [and] impaired my health more than 15 years in Europe would have done.[36]

Brohier's experience also points to the physical losses associated with the commerce-raiding business. While privateersmen, like other seafarers, were susceptible to disease, accident and the occasional bolt of lightning,[37] they were further endangered by the occupational hazards of serving in vessels that were sometimes overburdened and always liable to come under enemy fire. Human casualties were therefore higher than those suffered in commercial vessels; thus, the 'melancholy accidents' which befell the *Prince George,* the *Inspector* and the *Somerset* claimed 114, 96 and 76 lives respectively,[38] while the weapons of the French and the Spaniards left at least 19 of George Shelvocke's men dead and wounded, wrought carnage upon the crew and passengers of the *Duke of Tuscany,*[39] and accounted for countless others in the 'warm' exchanges which punctuated many a cruise. Survivors of losing encounters, moreover, might be incarcerated in a French prison where many a harrowing letter was written—and eagerly published in the press at home—about the miserable conditions endured by privateersmen as they awaited a cartel ship and their release;[40] worse still, perhaps, the seafaring venturer, like the men of the *Inspector,* might fall into the hands of the Moors, to be brutalised, enslaved or, like 'Peter Mason, a black', converted to the 'Mahometan' faith.[41]

If human and capital resources were wasted in these unfortunate undertakings, there were ventures, at the other extreme, which proved to be highly profitable. It is probable that the *Lewis Erasmus* and the *Marquis D'Antin* constituted the most valuable prize taken by British private ships-of-war in the eighteenth century. These register-ships were worth between £700,000 and £800,000 according to James Talbot, captain of the *Prince Frederick,*[42] joint-captor with the *Duke*; if, as seems likely, this was a reasonably accurate evaluation,[43] the rate of return on this investment—assuming that some £20,000 had been spent on the initial outfit[44]—was in the order of 3,500 per cent. Some of these gains generated further commerce-raiding income in that they were invested in the *Royal Family* squadron, the most powerful and costly venture mounted during the period. With George Walker—owner of 3 per cent of the crew's moiety as quarter master of the fleet, and 14 shares as its Commodore —due a total of £2,878 from the fleet's second cruise, a net prize fund of almost £191,000 resulted from this eight-month sortie, a five-fold return on the estimated outfitting costs of the venture.[45]

Such success was neither confined to the large-scale element of the business, nor to the 1740s. In Queen Anne's War, for instance, the celebrated 'expedition' commanded by Woodes Rogers returned net proceeds of approximately £106,000, against a capital investment of £13,188 13s 6d,[46] while substantial sums were generated, if never accounted for, in the subsequent circumnavigation led by George

Shelvocke in 1719.[47] Later in the century, net receipts of £72,158 accrued from the capture of the *Carnatic* by the *Mentor*, a 'compleat new frigate' set forth on a 'cruising voyage' largely because her builder, Peter Baker, had been unable to find a purchaser for his 370-ton vessel.[48] In the 'Channel' sector, meanwhile, gross earnings were less spectacular, though in relation to the costs of the diminutive predator profits could be quite outstanding, with Guernsey and Jersey venturers occasionally earning 'excellent' rates of return of up to 700 per cent per annum from this 'lucrative' business.[49] Yet it was on the mainland that perhaps the best expression of the potential profitability of this enterprise occurred; thus, the 40-ton *Snap Dragon* of Dartmouth, set forth at an expense of £157 10s, generated net proceeds of £21,088 3s 5d from the capture of the Dutch West Indiaman *Die Lieffde*, a return which, in its itself, serves to explain the scale and character of the privateering 'mania' of 1780–1781.[50]

The profits of the successful cruise were divided amongst the fortunate venturers according to the articles of agreement governing each enterprise. Initially, the net prize fund was split between the owners of the vessel and those investing their labour power in the project. As Appendix 4 indicates, privateering capitalists normally owned at least 50 per cent of the net proceeds, the share of individual investors corresponding to the stake each held in the venture. Accordingly, successful sole owners and partners in small companies might amass considerable fortunes; thus, George Campbell of Liverpool established a landed estate on the basis of his commerce-raiding profits, while William Boats—alleged to have greeted a prize with a cry of 'Billy Boates, born a beggar, die a lord!'— accumulated at least £30,000 from the prizes of the *Ellis* and the *Gregson*,[51] and Peter Baker shared over £54,000 with his son-in-law John Dawson on the condemnation of the *Carnatic* (see Appendix 5). In larger companies, of course, the investor's proportionate reward diminished along with his risk, though such consortia generally promoted the large-scale ventures capable of apprehending the more valuable prizes. The £70,000 earned by the owners of the *Duke* and the *Dutchess*, for instance, was divided into 256 parts belonging to 17 shareholders,[52] while the owners' moiety of £95,000 accruing from the *Royal Family* squadron's second cruise was parcelled into 120 lots and distributed amongst at least six investors.[53]

Commerce-raiding contracts regularly entitled privateer owners to shares in the crew's prize fund. In Bristol, for instance, promoters generally held a share in the men's moiety for each carriage gun mounted, a right which amounted to 4.4 per cent of the earnings of the *Blandford*'s people, and 6.3 per cent of the prize money due to the *Dreadnought*'s crew. (see Appendix 4). Promoters also appointed themselves as agents for the ship's company and extracted a commission from the gross account for their services. While this device effectively reduced the crew's earnings, it also enabled privateer owners to control the administration of the crew's interest. Here, the superficial collaboration between capital and labour fostered by the profit-sharing basis of the privatering business sometimes evaporated as the class tensions which increasingly marked the shipping industry at large came to the surface.[54] Conflict was particularly apparent in the large-scale enterprises as owners exploited their powerful position —both within the organisation, and in relation to the law—to defraud the seafarers and fellow venturers who worked their vessels. Thus, all manner of managerial sophistry denied Woodes Rogers and his men their full reward until many years after the establishment of a prize fund,[55] while the owners of the *Duke* and the *Prince Frederick* allegedly imposed new and harsher articles upon their crews just after embarkation, embezzled captured property in Kinsale, and maliciously delayed the payment of prize monies.[56] Concurrently, these same promoters —Jalabert, Nevill, Belchier, *et al*—summarily reduced the advance-money offered to the *Royal Family*'s men,[57] and subsequently cheated George Walker of his earnings from the cruise, having the 'gallant Commodore' thrown into prison as a bankrupt in 1756.[58]

If such chicanery occasionally jeopardised the privateersman's reward, it is nevertheless clear that service in a private man-of-war presented seamen and landmen with a rare, perhaps a once in a lifetime, chance to earn a substantial capital sum. Employed for most of their working lives on a wage labour basis, with the restrictions on their earnings capacity that such a system entailed, seafarers were naturally attracted by the prospect of a direct share in the produce of their labour—an inducement which persuaded many to join the Navy. Those enlisting in private men-of-war worked in a range of ventures possessed of differing attributes and prospects. In the 'Channel' sector, crews were generally drawn from the vessel's home port and its environs;[59] the physical hazards they faced were generally limited by the restricted range and duration of cruises and the inability of the typical prey to offer serious resistance; though prize funds, if established, were normally small, they were distributed amongst relatively few shareholders, thereby increasing the value of each man's stake so that in ventures

having but a small number of shares, there is a pleasing prospect of the ship's company making their fortunes in a very short time.[60]

Conversely, service in 'deep-water' predators was often dangerous, with longer cruises and attacks upon well-defended enemy craft invariably leading to higher casualties, while share values were depressed by the recruitment of large complements (see Appendix 4). Yet these were the ventures capable of taking the valuable elements of Bourbon trade and generating prize funds vast enough to enrich even the landmen and boys in their companies. Consequently, 'seamen flocked from all quarters to enter on board' the *Boscawen* 'privateer of force',[61] while the managers of the *Royal Family* squadron were able to recruit nearly 1,000 men in Bristol at an advance of 5 guineas each despite the establishment of a seafarers' 'Combination' to defend the 15 guineas originally offered.[62]

The profitable potential of the commerce-raiding business was realised by some seafarers. 'Channel' privateersmen occasionally enjoyed large windfall gains; thus, the proceeds of *Die Lieffde* yielded a first dividend of £3,000 for the crew of the *Snap Dragon*, with Captain Thomas Goldsmith receiving £600, his lieutenants earning £300 each, and the ship's people gaining in the region of £60 to £90 per man for three months' work.[63] Significant sums of prize money were sometimes added to the wages normally earned by Channel Island privateersmen,[64] profits which propelled men such as Edward le Brun from 'captain' to 'esquire'.[65] Large-scale projects might prove even more remunerative. At least £615 per share was paid out to the companies of the *Duke* and the *Prince Frederick* for six months' labour,[66] a reward which represented the aggregate earnings of an able seaman working for nearly 35 years in the mercantile marine at a high peacetime wage of 30 shillings per month. Shares in the eight-month cruise of the *Royal Family* were worth nearly £95,[67] over ten times the total wages an able seaman in the Navy might earn in the same period. The company of the *Mentor* fared still better, for most were discharged after one month and 25 days of her first cruise with prize vouchers valued at the rate of £109 per share.[68]

Though these privateersmen were undoubtedly the fortunate few, their extravagent gains—achieved during relatively short terms of service— not only demonstrated the viability of privateering activity, but also exemplified the essential rationality of the commerce-raiding business. Thus, in taking great physical risks, and forsaking income from safer employments, privateersmen might attain immense wealth. That many deemed this gamble worthwhile was suggested by John Brohier; despite losing three years' wages and damaging his health, this lieutenant's chief complaint was that the failure of the *Fame's* 'expedition' had cost him the finest opportunity I shall ever have of making my fortune.[69]

In presenting seafarers—and shipowners—with this fleeting and extraordinary opportunity for profit, British privateering enterprise assumed a significant place in the maritime economy of the eighteenth century.

Notes

1. Wickens, 'Economics of Privateering', comes to a similar conclusion in his examination of the impact of privateering earnings on Guernsey's economy in the American Revolutionary War.
2. Lord Stairs, President of the Court of Session of Scotland, 1681. Quoted in Graham, dissertation, 1.
3. BL, Add Mss, 38,432, f.59.
4. MacPherson, *Annals of Commerce*, III, 657.
5. LSF, Temp Mss 140/1. Daniel Eccleston to Isaac Eccleston, 31 January 1781. I am grateful to Maurice Schofield for bringing this information to my attention, and to the Library Committee of the Religious Society of Friends for permitting me to cite the letter.
6. These estimates are based on the returns of the Sixpenny Office in the 'Account of the Number of Seamen . . .' in BL, Add Mss, 38,340, f.17, the Navigation Accounts in PRO, CUST 17/1-9, and Davis, 'Seamen's Sixpences'.
7. See Matthews, 'West Country-Newfoundland Fishery'.
8. See the Dartmouth Muster Rolls for 1770-1776 in PRO, BT 98/3-5, and the letter of marque declarations.
9. Parkinson, *Rise of the Port of Liverpool*, 125-8; and R. B. Rose, 'A Liverpool Sailors' Strike in the Eighteenth Century' *Transactions of the Lancashire and Cheshire Antiquarian Society*, 68 (1958), 86.
10. *Morning Chronicle and London Advertiser*, 28 November 1778.
11. This suggests that British private men-of-war were more expensive to fit out than their colonial counterparts, for an estimated £1 9s per man per month was spent on Pennsylvania's commerce-raiders. Swanson, 'Profitability of Privateering', 54.
12. Re-armaments were undoubtedly less expensive than initial outfits. That vessels re-armed and operating under new commissions are included in these estimates tends to exaggerate aggregate investment; however, this is counter-balanced by the omission of re-armed vessels acting under the original letter of marque.

13. These crude measures of fixed privateering capital indicate that the privateering business accounted for a relatively small portion of the gross stock of British shipping, which has been valued at £12m for 1760, rising to £22m in 1800 (at 1851-1860 replacement cost). C. H. Feinstein, 'Capital Formation in Great Britain' in P. Mathias and M. M. Postan, eds, *Cambridge Economic History of Europe* (1978), VII, pt 1, 42.

14. These were the net rates of pay per lunar month in the Navy. Rodger, *Wooden World*, 125. The structure of the labour force is based on an analysis of the muster rolls in PRO, ADM 43/2-30. Specialist crew members and officers have been included with the able seamen, though they always earned a higher rate of pay.

15. Meyer, 'English Privateering, 1702-1713', 44-5.

16. See Andrews, *Elizabethan Privateering*. In 1746, however, the owners of the *Duke* and the *Prince Frederick* apparently lent £700,000 of their profits from the seizure of two register-ships to the Government. See Vaughan, *Voyages and Cruises*, xxxiv-xxxv.

17. See Davis, *Shipping Industry*, 12-13.

18. *Morning Chronicle and London Advertiser*, 15 April 1779.

19. PRO, CUST 17/12. Some of these prizes were taken in earlier wars, while some were taken by naval vessels.

20. Bromley, 'Channel Island Privateers', 450.

21. See the July and August editions of the *Sherborne and Yeovil Mercury* for a range of advertisements relating to prize sales.

22. *Sherborne and Yeovil Mercury*, 7 September 1781. In another instance, samples of *De Negotie en Zeevart*'s cargo were sent from Dartmouth to London at a cost of £2 0s 10d. PRO, HCA 42/140.

23. The prize goods returned by the *Duke* and the *Dutchess* were auctioned in at least nine sales held at the Marine Coffee House, Birchin Lane, London. PRO, C 104/36(2). Various London auction houses handled the disposal of the *Carnatic*'s cargo. See PRO, C 114/36.

24. Bromley, 'New Vocation', 123.

25. LRO, 942 HOL 10, 411.

26. Analysis of the rates of return earned by colonial privateers in the 1740s indicates that commerce-raiding was a profitable activity for those who took prizes. See Swanson, 'Profitability of Privateering'.

27. This estimate is based on the letter of marque declarations and the Prize Court sentences.

28. For instance, Press, *Bristol Seamen*, 16, estimates that roughly one-third of Bristol's commissioned vessels set forth in the 1756-1762 and 1777-1783 wars were captured, lost or sunk. However, he understates the size of Bristol's licensed fleets in these conflicts; thus, rather than a total of 276 vessels, 458 commissioned ships belonged to the port in the two wars. The true casualty rate was therefore just under 20 per cent.

29. T. Troughton, *Barbarian Cruelty* (Exeter, 1788); Damer Powell, *Bristol*

Privateers, 277; PRO, BT 98/39.

30. Damer Powell, *Bristol Privateers*, 166; *Exeter Flying Post*, 10 September 1779; Williams, *Liverpool Privateers*, 304-05.
31. *Penny London Post, or Morning Advertiser*, 20 January 1745; Damer Powell, *Bristol Privateers*, 272-3.
32. Ford, 'List of Some Briefs', 100; *Penny London Post, or Morning Advertiser*, 31 January 1745; Damer Powell, *Bristol Privateers*, 278-9.
33. PRO, C 103/130. Richard Taunton to Thomas Hall, 26 August 1747.
34. Jamieson, 'Return to Privateering', 159-60.
35. *Journals of the House of Commons*, 29 (1761-1764), 469-70.
36. PRO, C 103/130. John Brohier to his brother, 4 January 1747.
37. In the muster roll of the *Marlbro'* of Liverpool, William Brookes is recorded as 'killed by lightening' on 6 August 1778. PRO, BT 98/39.
38. *Gentleman's Magazine*, XV (1745), 418; Troughton, *Barbarian Cruelty*; Damer Powell, *Bristol Privateers*, 166. See Press, *Bristol Seamen*, 15-6, for mortality rates aboard Bristol privateers.
39. Perrin, *Voyage Round the World*, xx-xxii; Damer Powell, *Bristol Privateers*, 202-03.
40. For instance, see James Connor's letter in *Felix Farley's Bristol Journal*, 6 August 1757.
41. Troughton, *Barbarian Cruelty*. When the *Inspector* grounded in Tangier Bay, 'the Moors came down upon us, like ravenous beasts to devour their prey'; in all, 96 of the 183-strong crew were drowned or killed, seven, including Captain Richard Veale, were enslaved, 21 turned 'Mahometan', eight died in prison, and 51 were released after three or four years' imprisonment.
42. *Gentleman's Magazine*, XV (1745), 419.
43. Disgruntled crew members petitioned the House of Commons in 1749 and 1750 concerning prize money withheld by the agents. Yet dividends amounting to £615 per share had been paid by 1750; if this is multiplied by the shareholding current in the vessels during the *Royal Family*'s second cruise, (see Appendix 6, Table 3) the crew's moiety of the net prize fund equalled £239,542 10s, the total fund amounting to £479,085. As these are net figures, money was allegedly still in the agents' hands, and the complement was 45 men stronger in 1745, Talbot's estimates appear quite reasonable. *Journals of the House of Commons*, XXVI (1750), 104-05.
44. This estimate includes the *Prince George*, of 134 men, which sank before the squadron reached its cruising station. With 244 on board the *Prince Frederick*, and 150 in the *Duke*'s company, the total complement of 528 men was victualled for six months. Thus, capital costs amounted to an estimated £17,424, while labour to the value of £3,279 was notionally engaged.
45. Walker never received his share of these spoils due to the 'mean rascality' of the owners. See Vaughan, *Voyages and Cruises*, xlviii-xlix. The computations are based on the share distribution given in PRO, ADM 43/13(2). See Appendix 6.

46. Complex accounts relating to the cruise are preserved in PRO, C 104/36(2). The net proceeds cited are taken from the Master in Chancery's General Report of 28 July 1714, though various minor issues were undecided at this point.
47. Perrin, *Voyage Round the World*, xvii-xix.
48. J. H. Porter, *Carnatic Halls since 1779* (Liverpool UP, 1969) 1. See Appendix 5.
49. Bromley, 'New Vocation', 144-7; Jamieson, 'Return to Privateering', 171-2; Wickens, 'Economics of Privateering', 386-7.
50. PRO, HCA 42/135.
51. Williams, *Liverpool Privateers*, 92-4, 484-5.
52. PRO, C 104/36.
53. PRO, C 103/130. Richard Taunton's correspondence with Thomas Hall indicates that the *Royal Family* squadron was divided into 120 parts, and infers that there were numerous shareholders besides the six managers of the venture.
54. See Rediker, *Devil and the Deep Blue Sea*, for an analysis of class relations in the Anglo-American maritime world of the early eighteenth century.
55. See the Master in Chancery's General Report in PRO, C 104/36(2); and Rogers, 'Woodes Rogers's Privateering Voyage'.
56. *Journals of the House of Commons*, XXV (1749), 941.
57. *Penny London Post, or Morning Advertiser*, 2, 9 April 1746.
58. Vaughan, *Voyages and Cruises*, xlix. William Belchier, one of the managers of the *Royal Family* venture, sat on the Parliamentary Committee on bankcruptcy which took evidence from George Walker.
59. For instance, the crew of the *Good Intent* of Looe comprised 64 men, most of whom hailed from the Looe/Polperro district, though Captain Sharrock Jenkings and seven other Jenkings' were from St Mawes. Cornwall County Museum, Truro. Ledger Book of Zephaniah Job, ZJ 7; F. Perrycoste, 'Gleanings from the Records of Zephaniah Job' *Cornish Times* (1929). I am grateful to James P. Derriman for these references.
60. Damer Powell, *Bristol Privateers*, 288.
61. Vaughan, *Voyages and Cruises*, 40.
62. *Penny London Post, or Morning Advertiser*, 2 April 1746. Bristol was 'suddenly alarmed by a great body of sailors who had risen to the number of at least 2,000 . . . ascended Brandon Hill, and . . . entered into a solemn Combination that not one should take less than the 15 guineas, on Pain of being immediately hung up on a gallows they talked of erecting on the said Hill . . . from thence they all came in a formidable body into the City, and patrolled the streets with their Colours flying, armed with Bludgeons and huzzaing in a very loud manner'. The men eventually dispersed in good order after 'breaking a few windows, and throwing some Baskets of Potatoes, etc, about the Streets'. On 9 April 1746, the *Penny London Post* reported that 'upwards of 400 men (being those who lately came from France) have

accepted of the Five Guineas Advance Money, and are gone on board the Privateers, which are fallen down the Road; but those of the Combination, it seems, still abide by their former Resolutions'.

63. Newman Papers. Peter Ougier to Lydston Newman, 1782. I am grateful to Mrs Ray Freeman for this information. Each share was worth £8, indicating that the Captain owned 75 shares, and 37.5 were held by each of the lieutenants. It therefore seems likely that seamen owned between 8 and 12 shares.

64. See Wickens, 'Economics of Privateering' for a discussion of the distribution of Channel Island prize funds.

65. Bromley, 'New Vocation', 141.

66. *Journals of the House of Commons*, XXVI (1750), 104-05.

67. This computation is based on the sum owed to Commodore Walker (Vaughan, *Voyages and Cruises*, xliv) and the share distribution given in PRO, ADM 43/13(2) and presented in Appendix 6.

68. PRO, C 114/36. See Appendix 5. Captain John Dawson and the bulk of his crew, 70 of whom hailed from Chester, entered on board the *Mentor* on 26 September 1778; though some remained in her service, the majority were discharged in London on 20 November 1778, to be replaced by a fairly cosmopolitan company including Danes and Swedes as well as Londoners. PRO, BT 98/39.

69. PRO, C 103/130. John Brohier to his brother, 4 January 1747.

Appendix 1

Primary Source Materials: Problems and Methods

1. Letter of Marque Declarations (PRO, HCA 25 and 26)

Declarations regarding the characteristics of each vessel commissioned in the High Court of Admiralty from 1689 to 1815 exist in the Public Record Office, Chancery Lane, London. The majority comprise the 104 volumes of the HCA 26 series, though a significant number—those made under warrant in the outports, and all those offered from December 1808—are preserved with their respective bail documents in HCA 25. Over 23,000 declarations were made before the Court during the 'long' eighteenth century, providing details of the tonnage, crew size, armaments, equipment, officers and owners of every privately-owned British vessel authorised to seize enemy sea-borne property during this time. The scale and regional distribution of 'inputs' into the privateering business, particularly in terms of the number of vessels commissioned, can be assessed from this rich source. Problems arise in such an analysis, however, for these declarations were essentially legal documents and not a record of business activity. That a fresh licence was required on a change in captaincy or ownership generated a considerable quantity of duplicate declarations, a complication compounded by the Court's practice of granting reprisals separately against each adversary in 1744, and from 1777 onwards; commissions were issued 'until further orders' and therefore no account is given of the vessels lost or redeployed before the cessation of hostilities; doubts as to the accuracy and reliability of the data arise out of inconsistencies between declarations ostensibly for the same vessel; the port in which a vessel was registered is not specified in declarations made prior to 1759; moreover, and perhaps most seriously, it is only rarely that the declarations directly indicate the true occupation of the vessel to be commissioned.

To facilitate analysis of the declarations, a computer file was established,[1] containing details of the tonnage, crew size, number of guns carried, victualling period, home port (deemed to be the usual place of residence in pre-1759 declarations) and ship's name cited by each applicant for a privateer commission. Sorting this data by war, by home port, by date of application and by ship's name permitted the ready identification of many duplicate declarations, for declarants commonly offered the same information in respect of vessels commissioned against two or more enemies at the same Court hearing. In less clear-cut cases, 'actual vessels' were segregated from 're-commissions' by a comparison of the captaincy and ownership details given in the declarations, while in some instances a resort was had to supplementary sources, especially newspapers. By such means, a 'stock' of commissioned vessels was calculated for each port in each war, a static figure which takes no account of vessels leaving the business in the course of a conflict, or of vessels re-commissioned for second or subsequent ventures under new management. While this provides an uncertain guide to the scale of privateering activity at any given point in a war, a good impression as to the fluctuating rate of predatory enterprise can be gained by ordering the commissions and re-commissions relating to private men-of-war by date of application and victualling period (see Appendix 2).

The relationship between declared tonnage and crew size has been utilised in this study to indicate the intent of venturers—whether predatory or commercial—in setting forth commissioned vessels. That these variables are somewhat imprecise is suggested by the proliferation of rounded figures, and the contradictions which occur between declarations apparently relating to the same vessel. Such inaccuracies are relatively minor, and reflect the erratic nature of tonnage measurement prior to the Act of General Registry in 1786, as well as the fact that crew sizes were generally cited before recruitment had been completed. In general, they do not detract from the analysis of relative manning levels, for declarants tended to offer figures approximating to the intended strength of their ventures. While this is clear in comparable source materials—for instance, newspaper accounts, head money vouchers, muster rolls, and other Prize Court records—there appears to have been no incentive to encourage declarants to falsify their statements. Accordingly, a broad assessment of the structure of the privateering business can be attained from the letter of marque declarations.

2. Prize Court Sentences (PRO, HCA 34)

The 'final and definitive' sentences of the London Prize Court are used in this study to assess the 'output' of the privateering business. It is only feasible, however, to consider the number of prizes condemned using this source, for the value of properties so sentenced is rarely given. Moreover, there are inconsistencies in the data relating to the different wars. Prior to 1777 only the sentences deriving from cases of common condemnation are collected. In the American Revolutionary War, however, interlocutory decrees pertaining to properties disputed by claimants—and the final sentences of such cases—are also included. Thus, it is necessary to eliminate the interlocutory decrees, and to note the judgements which concluded these cases, to obtain a comparative view of the prize return. Properties apprehended in the Western Hemisphere are a further uncertain feature of the prize analysis; in the 1702–1712 war, for instance, seizures effected in Newfoundland waters were adjudicated at Doctors' Commons, but in later wars similar prosecutions were generally undertaken in the Vice-Admiralty Courts. As few of the records of these colonial hearings have survived, the extent of prize-taking by British-based privateers in the Caribbean and off the eastern seaboard of North America is unknown. Any consequent understatement is probably most serious for the American Revolutionary War for it was in the conflict that the trans-Atlantic 'cruising voyage' mode of operation was at its height.

Nevertheless, with these reservations in mind, the prize sentences offer the only consistent measure of the prize-taking successes of privateering venturers in the 1702–1783 period as a whole. They provide details of the date of condemnation, the name of the prize vessel and that of her master, the captor's identity and status, whether naval or private, the name of the successful commander, and also the port into which the prize was carried. A comparative view of the prize-taking performance of the Navy and the commercial fleet can thus be gained while the regional distribution of privateering prizes can be ascertained by establishing the captor's home port from the letter of marque declarations. Such results often differ from figures derived from other sources, notably the various incomplete lists prepared for the Customs Commissioners in the 1702–1712 and 1739–1748 wars; in general it appears that the Prize Court sentences understate the level of prize-taking activity due to the exclusion of disputed cases, though a similar pattern of prize condemnation emerges from the various series.

3. Prize Papers (PRO, HCA 32, 42 and 45)

The prize papers comprise the documents produced before the Prize Court (HCA 32) or the Court of Prize Appeals (HCA 42), in the process of prize adjudication. They include the various allegations, attestations, claims, examinations and affadavits presented to the Court, as well as any ship's papers taken out of the captured vessel and entered as exhibits. The evidence submitted varied from case to case. In some instances, when the prize had been abandoned by her crew, the papers are very sparse, consisting of an allegation that a ship, often *Name Unknown*, had been captured and was liable to condemnation as legal prize; other vessels yielded an array of papers—bills of lading, *congés*, *lettres de marque*, muster rolls, log books, letters and diaries—which were produced before the judge to help determine the status of the arrested property. Valuable information as to the location and circumstances of a seizure, the nationality, tonnage and crew size of a prize, together with her cargo and occupation can be gleaned from this material, particularly from the preparatory examinations of witnesses to the seizure. However, this is a vast and inconsistent body of data; thus, a sample of cases brought by London captors was taken for this study, adding detail and colour to the basic evidence provided by the letter of marque declarations and the prize court sentences.

In cases where captor or claimant appealed against the decision of the Prize Court, a similar range of evidence was presented before the Court of Prize Appeals. Indeed, in some instances there is considerably more detail, for the property at stake was often appraised or sold prior to the final sentence of the Court, and a valuation of the prize goods—necessary to estimate the security required—is included with the exhibits. In addition, the exhibits submitted to the higher court by appellants and respondents were printed and, for the 1756–1762 and 1777–1783 wars, the case books (HCA 45) provide a comprehensive view of the arguments and evidence, though not always the final decision, relating to disputed cases.

4. Head Money Vouchers (PRO, ADM 43)

In 1708, to encourage naval seamen and privateersmen to attack and apprehend enemy men-of-war and *corsaires*, the government offered a bounty of £5 for every man alive on board a captured vessel-of-war at the commencement of the decisive engagement. Details of these head money payments comprise the ADM 43 series. A comparative analysis of the effectiveness of the state and private arms of the naval force in the limitation of the enemy's maritime threat can be undertaken using this source. Moreover, valuable information concerning the structure of commerce-raiding ventures, and the size and composition of privateering crews, can also be gained, for claimants—the agents appointed by owners and crew—were required to submit articles of agreement to substantiate their right to claim, as well as a muster roll of the men entitled to share in the bounty.

These data tend to understate the significance of privateers as captors of enemy vessels-of-war, for the documents submitted in support of claims were sometimes retrieved by agents on the payment of the bounty. Moreover, head money was not awarded automatically, but on the submission of a proper claim by the captors' agent, and it seems probable that some decided not to lodge a claim, particularly in respect of relatively small prizes. Accordingly, no record of a bounty payment exists regarding the capture of known privateers such as the *Guipuscoa*, the *Nuestra Senora de la Escalivitia Santo Antonio e Almas* or the *Kouli Kan* (see PRO, HCA 32/113(1), 139, 155). Naval agents, on the other hand, were engaged specifically to perform such duties, while the claims they handled were generally much more valuable. The Head Money Vouchers therefore offer a fuller reflection of the Navy's contribution to the capture of enemy warships.

5. Newspapers

Contemporary newspapers exhibited a keen interest in privateering during the eighteenth century. Reports of desperate engagements with the enemy, news of extraordinary seizures or losses, extracts from the correspondence of privateersmen and owners, recruitment notices and advertisements of privateers or their prizes for sale were regularly published in the mercantile press from the 1740s onwards. Such information adds much detail and flavour to a quantitative analysis of the Prize Court records. It must be treated with some caution, however, for newspapers, then as now, were more interested in the sensational than the mundane and thus the day-to-day routine of the privateersman's work—the forlorn pursuit of the unidentified sail, the search and release of the innocent neutral, the interminable struggle with wind and sea—passed unnoticed as readers were offered tales of bloody encounters, mutinies and acts of an unusually courageous or scandalous nature. Moreover, the newspaper's sources of information were often the opinions of interested parties or correspondents of rumour and gossip. It would be unwise, therefore, to place too much faith in these reports, especially those relating to prize values; though reflecting the significance of a seizure—as in the case of the *Carnatic*—they frequently inflated the worth of the prize by a considerable margin.

Note

1. The computer file was established by Walter E. Minchinton. Subsequently, a number of researchers in the Department of Economic History at the University of Exeter added to the file which was enlarged, modified and completed by the author.

Appendix 2

Monthly Activity Rates of Private Men-of-War, 1702–1783

The number and regional distribution of commissioned vessels can be calculated from the letter of marque declarations. Such an analysis provides a comparative view of the licensed fleet over a war as a whole rather than an assessment of the rate of commerce-raiding activity at any given point. Further analysis of the declarations, however, yields a more dynamic picture of the course of the private war-at-sea. Clearly, venturers could not legitimately proceed until a letter of marque had been issued; moreover, though commissions were valid until further orders, ventures were limited in duration, the articles of agreement invariably stipulating the number of months a cruise was to last. As the declarations were dated and declarants were obliged to state the length of time, in months, for which their vessel was victualled, an indication of the start and end of each undertaking is given. This is only a notional picture, however; though the available comparisons suggest that declared victualling periods concurred with the contractual length of cruises, the date of application for a commission was rarely the date of a vessel's embarkation. Moreover, it is a view of intentions rather than actualities, for no account is taken of the premature loss, capture or re-deployment of vessels or of the craft worked by crews of more or less than the strength declared; equally, no consideration is given to the second or subsequent cruises of vessels operating under the same commission—a factor which leads to particular understatement in the 1702–1712 war[1]—though the inclusion of re-commissions helps to mitigate this omission, especially for the American Revolutionary War when licences against each enemy were granted.

The analysis is limited to private men-of-war, with the 'expeditionary' vessels included in the 'deep-water' totals. The month of application for the commission is deemed to have been the first full month of operation in each case. 'Channel' refers to privateers declared as 99 tons burthen or less, with crews in the ratio of up to and including 2.5 tons per man. The 'deep-water' category comprises vessels exceeding 100 tons burthen with manning ratios of 2.5 tons per man or less, as well as ventures declared to be enlisting 100 seafarers or more. 'Specialist' vessels exhibiting these characteristics have been excluded.

Note

1. Bromley, 'New Vocation', 119.

War of the Spanish Succession, 1702–1712

		'Channel'		'Deep-Water'		Total	
		No	Men	No	Men	No	Men
1702	Jun	13	443	3	260	16	703
	Jul	13	468	4	360	17	828
	Aug	8	303	10	740	18	1043
	Sep	7	239	14	1010	21	1249
	Oct	12	444	15	1110	27	1554
	Nov	11	404	17	1330	28	1734
	Dec	10	365	15	1270	25	1635
1703	Jan	13	414	17	1510	30	1924
	Feb	13	424	18	1670	31	2094
	Mar	12	401	19	1610	31	2011
	Apr	8	220	21	1780	29	2000
	May	7	210	15	1210	22	1420
	Jun	6	179	14	1110	20	1289
	Jul	6	174	13	1180	19	1354
	Aug	5	184	12	1070	17	1254
	Sep	6	220	11	1030	17	1250
	Oct	12	459	10	930	22	1389
	Nov	8	314	10	930	18	1244
	Dec	8	314	8	740	16	1054
1704	Jan	7	285	7	610	14	895
	Feb	8	310	8	720	16	1030
	Mar	7	270	8	720	15	990
	Apr	9	319	8	710	17	1029

		'Channel'		'Deep-Water'		Total	
		No	Men	No	Men	No	Men
1704	May	9	319	6	480	15	799
	Jun	7	234	7	630	14	864
	Jul	7	230	6	530	13	760
	Aug	8	260	5	450	13	710
	Sep	13	481	3	310	16	791
	Oct	13	481	2	230	15	711
	Nov	15	577	2	230	17	807
	Dec	15	600	2	230	17	830
1705	Jan	14	571	4	480	18	1051
	Feb	12	461	4	480	16	941
	Mar	18	571	5	560	23	1131
	Apr	20	641	4	440	24	1081
	May	18	554	6	590	24	1144
	Jun	8	286	6	550	14	836
	Jul	10	347	7	650	17	997
	Aug	12	437	7	650	19	1087
	Sep	11	417	5	440	16	857
	Oct	5	175	5	440	10	615
	Nov	8	275	3	290	11	565
	Dec	10	354	4	390	14	744
1706	Jan	10	340	3	220	13	560
	Feb	7	245	4	350	11	595
	Mar	5	185	3	310	8	495
	Apr	7	285	2	240	9	525
	May	8	335	2	240	10	575
	Jun	6	260	2	240	8	500
	Jul	3	110	2	240	5	350
	Aug	3	140	2	220	5	360
	Sep	2	95	1	120	3	215
	Oct	5	180	1	120	6	300
	Nov	7	270	2	200	9	470
	Dec	8	272	2	200	10	472
1707	Jan	9	317	3	275	12	592
	Feb	5	145	2	155	7	300
	Mar	8	246	2	155	10	401
	Apr	4	120	2	155	6	275
	May	3	90	2	160	5	250
	Jun	2	65	2	160	4	225
	Jul	4	165	2	160	6	325
	Aug	6	228	3	336	9	564
	Sep	3	103	2	256	5	359

		'Channel'		'Deep-Water'		Total	
		No	Men	No	Men	No	Men
1707	Oct	4	123	2	256	6	379
	Nov	5	190	2	256	7	446
	Dec	4	132	2	256	6	388
1708	Jan	6	182	2	256	8	438
	Feb	7	219	2	256	9	475
	Mar	11	368	3	230	14	598
	Apr	12	428	5	500	17	928
	May	16	544	6	570	22	1114
	Jun	16	560	4	420	20	980
	Jul	12	386	4	420	16	806
	Aug	4	125	5	500	9	625
	Sep	8	295	5	500	13	795
	Oct	8	325	5	500	13	825
	Nov	5	175	3	370	8	545
	Dec	19	778	4	450	23	1228
1709	Jan	23	908	4	450	27	1358
	Feb	25	891	5	490	30	1381
	Mar	18	649	5	490	23	1139
	Apr	19	648	3	220	22	868
	May	16	605	3	220	19	825
	Jun	9	345	3	220	12	565
	Jul	6	285	3	220	9	505
	Aug	12	465	5	420	17	885
	Sep	15	535	7	620	22	1155
	Oct	15	535	7	620	22	1155
	Nov	10	365	6	540	16	905
	Dec	8	360	7	690	15	1050
1710	Jan	12	545	9	900	21	1445
	Feb	13	535	7	700	20	1235
	Mar	10	350	7	830	17	1180
	Apr	8	275	9	910	17	1185
	May	8	295	7	770	15	1065
	Jun	8	295	7	720	15	1015
	Jul	7	210	9	980	16	1190
	Aug	5	135	10	1110	15	1245
	Sep	9	233	11	1130	20	1363
	Oct	8	191	8	900	16	1091
	Nov	10	254	8	900	18	1154
	Dec	8	351	7	770	15	1121
1711	Jan	8	413	7	770	15	1183
	Feb	10	510	5	550	15	1060

		'Channel'		'Deep-Water'		Total	
		No	Men	No	Men	No	Men
1711	Mar	8	340	6	710	14	1050
	Apr	7	255	6	790	13	1045
	May	6	245	7	920	13	1165
	Jun	10	460	6	820	16	1280
	Jul	11	520	7	1020	18	1540
	Aug	11	490	8	1100	19	1590
	Sep	10	360	7	950	17	1310
	Oct	9	300	7	950	16	1250
	Nov	10	330	6	880	16	1210
	Dec	9	363	4	600	13	963
1712	Jan	8	340	6	622	14	962
	Feb	8	328	6	552	14	880
	Mar	7	250	9	882	16	1132
	Apr	10	335	9	892	19	1227
	May	9	375	8	822	17	1197
	Jun	3	135	8	732	11	867
	Jul	4	175	10	972	14	1147
	Aug	3	150	8	752	11	902

War of the Quadruple Alliance, 1718-1720

		'Channel'		'Deep-Water'		Total	
		No	Men	No	Men	No	Men
1718	Dec	—	—	—	—	—	—
1719	Jan	—	—	2	250	2	250
	Feb	—	—	2	250	2	250
	Mar	1	30	2	250	3	280
	Apr	1	30	2	250	3	280
	May	5	182	2	250	7	332
	Jun	5	212	4	410	9	622
	Jul	6	242	4	410	10	652
	Aug	4	142	4	410	8	552
	Sep	2	90	4	410	6	500
	Oct	2	90	4	410	6	500
	Nov	3	150	4	410	7	560
	Dec	1	30	4	410	5	440
1720	Jan	1	30	4	410	5	440
	Feb	1	30	4	410	5	440

War of the Austrian Succession, 1739-1748

		'Channel'		'Deep-Water'		Total	
		No	Men	No	Men	No	Men
1739	Jul	—	—	—	—	—	—
	Aug	1	40	—	—	1	40
	Sep	1	40	1	80	2	120
	Oct	1	40	1	80	2	120
	Nov	1	40	1	80	2	120
	Dec	1	40	1	80	2	120
1740	Jan	1	40	1	80	2	120
	Feb	—	—	1	80	1	80
	Mar	—	—	1	80	1	80
	Apr	—	—	1	80	1	80
	May	—	—	1	80	1	80
	Jun	—	—	1	80	1	80
	Jul	—	—	1	80	1	80
	Aug	1	40	1	80	2	120
	Sep	1	40	2	250	3	290
	Oct	1	40	2	250	3	290
	Nov	1	40	2	250	3	290
	Dec	1	40	2	250	3	290
1741	Jan	1	40	2	250	3	290
	Feb	1	40	3	380	4	420
	Mar	1	40	2	230	3	270
	Apr	1	40	3	300	4	340
	May	1	40	3	300	4	340
	Jun	2	68	2	170	4	238
	Jul	2	68	2	170	4	238
	Aug	1	28	2	170	3	198
	Sep	—	—	2	200	2	200
	Oct	—	—	1	130	1	130
	Nov	—	—	2	230	2	230
	Dec	—	—	1	100	1	100
1742	Jan	—	—	1	100	1	100
	Feb	—	—	1	100	1	100
	Mar	—	—	1	100	1	100
	Apr	—	—	3	350	3	350
	May	—	—	2	250	2	250
	Jun	—	—	3	330	3	330
	Jul	—	—	3	330	3	330
	Aug	—	—	3	330	3	330

		'Channel'		'Deep-Water'		Total	
		No	Men	No	Men	No	Men
1742	Sep	—	—	4	390	4	390
	Oct	—	—	3	360	3	360
	Nov	—	—	3	360	3	360
	Dec	—	—	2	180	2	180
1743	Jan	—	—	2	180	2	180
	Feb	—	—	2	180	2	180
	Mar	—	—	1	120	1	120
	Apr	—	—	—	—	—	—
	May	—	—	1	110	1	110
	Jun	—	—	1	110	1	110
	Jul	—	—	1	110	1	110
	Aug	—	—	1	110	1	110
	Sep	—	—	2	235	2	235
	Oct	—	—	2	235	2	235
	Nov	—	—	2	235	2	235
	Dec	—	—	3	585	3	585
1744	Jan	—	—	3	585	3	585
	Feb	—	—	3	585	3	585
	Mar	—	—	3	585	3	585
	Apr	10	470	21	2910	31	3380
	May	15	760	34	4784	49	5544
	Jun	22	1084	43	5902	65	6986
	Jul	15	763	47	6617	62	7380
	Aug	10	453	56	8457	66	8910
	Sep	13	654	64	9978	77	10632
	Oct	13	659	60	9318	73	9977
	Nov	11	635	58	9238	69	9873
	Dec	5	330	53	8520	58	8850
1745	Jan	5	300	51	8170	56	8470
	Feb	6	340	49	7420	55	7760
	Mar	6	320	49	7770	55	8090
	Apr	6	225	45	7410	51	7635
	May	13	635	46	8000	59	8635
	Jun	13	625	50	8179	63	8804
	Jul	12	605	52	8389	64	8994
	Aug	10	480	46	7749	56	8229
	Sep	11	540	41	7119	52	7659
	Oct	10	486	39	7110	49	7596
	Nov	8	376	33	6035	41	6411
	Dec	6	326	26	4895	32	5221
1746	Jan	4	196	20	4045	24	4241

		'Channel'		'Deep-Water'		Total	
		No	Men	No	Men	No	Men
1746	Feb	5	286	18	3265	23	3551
	Mar	7	331	19	3405	26	3736
	Apr	8	331	18	2995	26	3326
	May	7	256	18	2620	25	2876
	Jun	9	416	17	2470	26	2886
	Jul	8	416	19	2740	27	3156
	Aug	6	270	19	2940	25	3210
	Sep	3	160	20	3020	23	3180
	Oct	2	100	21	3320	23	3420
	Nov	—	—	18	2830	18	2830
	Dec	2	130	19	2900	21	3030
1747	Jan	7	335	19	2920	26	3255
	Feb	8	365	17	2770	25	3135
	Mar	11	445	14	2070	25	2515
	Apr	15	668	14	1885	29	2553
	May	24	1077	16	2225	40	3302
	Jun	28	1284	22	3340	50	4624
	Jul	23	1064	23	3270	46	4334
	Aug	27	1237	22	3190	49	4427
	Sep	29	1337	26	4030	55	5367
	Oct	36	1507	26	3980	62	5487
	Nov	27	1125	27	4070	54	5195
	Dec	18	805	22	3510	40	4315
1748	Jan	18	775	18	2910	36	3685
	Feb	21	754	23	3730	44	4484
	Mar	22	799	21	3460	43	4259
	Apr	24	850	24	3670	48	4520
	May	19	625	19	2940	38	3565
	Jun	15	455	15	2070	30	2525

Seven Years' War, 1756-1762

		'Channel'		'Deep-Water'		Total	
		No	Men	No	Men	No	Men
1756	Jun	30	941	21	2790	51	3731
	Jul	32	1007	23	3090	55	4097
	Aug	26	989	25	3230	51	4219
	Sep	23	928	25	3685	48	4613

		'Channel'		'Deep-Water'		Total	
		No	Men	No	Men	No	Men
1756	Oct	20	880	26	3925	46	4805
	Nov	24	1025	32	5575	56	6600
	Dec	20	950	38	5715	58	6665
1757	Jan	24	1180	36	5595	60	6775
	Feb	25	1130	42	6345	67	7475
	Mar	25	1050	39	6070	64	7120
	Apr	25	965	41	5885	66	6850
	May	24	960	36	5285	60	6245
	Jun	25	1035	40	6005	65	7040
	Jul	22	885	51	7365	73	8250
	Aug	27	1010	57	8665	84	9675
	Sep	27	1060	64	9025	91	10085
	Oct	26	985	70	10346	96	11331
	Nov	17	670	56	8206	73	8876
	Dec	18	715	50	7246	68	7961
1758	Jan	20	725	45	6965	65	7690
	Feb	19	692	36	5695	55	6387
	Mar	21	792	34	4865	55	5657
	Apr	26	930	30	3775	56	4705
	May	32	1120	31	4255	63	5375
	Jun	33	1070	31	4220	64	5290
	Jul	38	1245	27	3600	65	4845
	Aug	44	1435	32	4070	76	5505
	Sep	41	1310	27	3170	68	4480
	Oct	39	1265	29	3480	68	4745
	Nov	33	1160	25	2760	58	3920
	Dec	33	1050	19	1950	52	3000
1759	Jan	29	920	14	1390	43	2310
	Feb	31	1105	13	1310	44	2415
	Mar	33	1080	10	1030	43	2110
	Apr	35	1198	11	1300	46	2498
	May	34	1163	9	1300	43	2463
	Jun	23	790	9	1300	32	2090
	Jul	25	849	10	1400	35	2249
	Aug	18	595	11	1661	29	2256
	Sep	14	470	11	1691	25	2161
	Oct	8	305	8	1351	16	1656
	Nov	6	220	6	990	12	1210
	Dec	3	130	6	840	9	970
1760	Jan	—	—	4	480	4	480
	Feb	—	—	3	330	3	330

		'Channel'		'Deep-Water'		Total	
		No	Men	No	Men	No	Men
1760	Mar	3	140	2	200	5	340
	Apr	4	160	2	200	6	360
	May	3	140	2	170	5	310
	Jun	5	164	2	170	7	334
	Jul	5	164	2	170	7	334
	Aug	5	164	2	170	7	334
	Sep	2	34	1	70	3	104
	Oct	2	34	1	70	3	104
	Nov	2	34	—	—	2	34
	Dec	—	—	—	—	—	—
1761	Jan	—	—	—	—	—	—
	Feb	—	—	—	—	—	—
	Mar	1	32	—	—	1	32
	Apr	1	32	—	—	1	32
	May	2	72	—	—	2	72
	Jun	1	40	1	60	2	100
	Jul	1	40	2	120	3	160
	Aug	1	40	2	120	3	160
	Sep	1	40	3	190	4	230
	Oct	1	40	3	190	4	230
	Nov	—	—	3	190	3	190
	Dec	—	—	2	130	2	130
1762	Jan	5	179	10	1224	15	1403
	Feb	11	386	14	1874	25	2260
	Mar	11	406	18	2304	29	2710
	Apr	12	397	23	3244	35	3641
	May	11	335	22	3184	33	3519
	Jun	5	150	22	3264	27	3414
	Jul	4	110	15	2320	19	2430
	Aug	4	110	12	1810	16	1920
	Sep	5	122	11	1830	16	1952
	Oct	2	42	8	1370	10	1412
	Nov	1	12	8	1370	9	1382

American Revolutionary War, 1777–1783

		'Channel'		'Deep-Water'		Total	
		No	Men	No	Men	No	Men
1777	Apr	—	—	—	—	—	—
	May	—	—	—	—	—	—

		'Channel'		'Deep-Water'		Total	
		No	Men	No	Men	No	Men
1777	Jun	—	—	—	—	—	—
	Jul	—	—	—	—	—	—
	Aug	—	—	—	—	—	—
	Sep	—	—	—	—	—	—
	Oct	—	—	—	—	—	—
	Nov	—	—	2	110	2	110
	Dec	1	30	2	110	3	140
1778	Jan	1	30	3	170	4	200
	Feb	3	71	4	230	7	301
	Mar	4	104	7	420	11	524
	Apr	7	209	10	640	17	849
	May	12	379	7	460	19	839
	Jun	16	516	8	545	24	1061
	Jul	21	736	11	705	32	1441
	Aug	45	1554	38	2764	83	4318
	Sep	61	2142	55	4354	116	6496
	Oct	74	2597	74	6314	148	8911
	Nov	64	2430	77	6154	141	8584
	Dec	53	2111	82	6899	135	9010
1779	Jan	39	1567	88	7714	127	9281
	Feb	34	1395	78	7204	112	8599
	Mar	29	1181	77	6734	106	7915
	Apr	34	1320	77	6779	111	8099
	May	27	1020	69	5760	96	6780
	Jun	36	1478	68	5980	104	7458
	Jul	43	1729	96	8264	139	9993
	Aug	37	1497	104	8923	141	10420
	Sep	25	1034	100	8523	125	9557
	Oct	19	808	96	8453	115	9261
	Nov	18	788	91	8208	109	8996
	Dec	19	733	86	7818	105	8551
1780	Jan	12	468	56	4984	68	5452
	Feb	14	527	46	3954	60	4481
	Mar	10	369	45	4054	55	4423
	Apr	24	820	47	4169	71	4989
	May	27	842	42	3749	69	4591
	Jun	24	742	35	3104	59	3846
	Jul	24	763	35	3254	59	4017
	Aug	22	658	30	2850	52	3508
	Sep	19	524	23	2095	42	2619
	Oct	12	252	17	1510	29	1762

		'Channel'		'Deep-Water'		Total	
		No	Men	No	Men	No	Men
1780	Nov	12	277	14	1240	26	1517
	Dec	133	3952	64	5254	197	9206
1781	Jan	328	10051	100	8042	428	18093
	Feb	342	10518	111	8947	453	19465
	Mar	301	9505	104	8662	405	18167
	Apr	243	7718	96	7985	339	15703
	May	227	7280	95	7895	322	15175
	Jun	149	4726	57	4565	206	9291
	Jul	41	1240	24	1970	65	3210
	Aug	19	469	14	1300	33	1769
	Sep	14	367	11	985	25	1352
	Oct	11	326	11	1055	23	1381
	Nov	9	276	10	935	19	1211
	Dec	9	294	9	865	18	1159
1782	Jan	11	333	8	770	19	1103
	Feb	10	307	6	480	16	787
	Mar	14	418	5	281	19	699
	Apr	17	445	3	161	20	606
	May	22	538	3	161	25	699
	Jun	16	431	3	161	19	592
	Jul	14	319	2	96	16	415
	Aug	13	363	2	91	15	454
	Sep	12	354	4	215	16	569
	Oct	8	256	4	215	12	471
	Nov	7	161	4	215	11	376
	Dec	4	92	4	215	8	307
1783	Jan	3	66	4	245	7	311

Appendix 3

Outfitting Costs

Venture	Tons	Men	Months	Outfitting Costs £	Cost per man per month £
1. *Royal Family*	1530	850	8	40000	5.88
2. *Tartar*	600	220	9	14000	7.07
3. *Duke/Dutchess*	600	270	12	13188.6	4.07
4. *Antigallican*	450	200	6	10500	8.75
5. *Sheerness*	450	200	6	8000	6.67
6. *Enterprize*	215	106	12	4083.66	3.21
7. *Conquerant*	100	80	3	801.6	3.34
8. *Roebuck*	50	30	3	450	5
9. *Esperance*	18	30	2	356.16	5.94
10. *Snap Dragon*	40	10	3	157.5	5.25
					5.52

Sources: The tonnage, crew size and victualling periods are taken from the letter of marque declarations. In the case of the *Enterprize*, the strength of the company given in the muster roll in LRO, Account Book of the *Enterprize*, differs significantly from the relevant declaration and therefore has been preferred. Outfitting costs are taken from the following sources:

1. PRO, C 103/130.
2. Jamieson, 'Return to Privateering', 159.
3. PRO, C 104/36.
4. *Journals of the House of Commons*, 29 (1761–1764), 469; 33 (1770–1772), 520.
5. *Bristol Oracle*, 4 October 1746.
6. LRO, Account Book of the *Enterprize*, 387 MD 45.
7. Bromley, 'New Vocation', 118.
8. Jamieson, 'Return to Privateering', 164.
9. Bromley, 'New Vocation', 118.
10. DRO, Seale Papers, Draft of Agreement made between John Seale and Peter Ougier, 1781.

Appendix 4

Share Values

The crew's portion of the net proceeds of a prize was divided into shares, with the holding of each member of the company varying according to his rank. In this table, the value of a single share in a net prize fund of £10,000—the minimum worth of the oft-cited 'capital' prize—is calculated for privateering ventures of differing types and strengths. Able seamen were allocated a whole share in all the ventures cited save the *St George*, in which they owned two shares. With the exception of the *Mentor* (PRO, C 114/36) the information is derived from the Articles of Agreement and Muster Rolls preserved in the Head Money Vouchers (PRO, ADM 43).

Venture	% owned by crew[a]	Crew size	Number of shares[b]	Value of share in £10,000
Private ships-of-war				
				£
Royal Family	44(6)	853	1008.57	4.36
St George	42(8)	205	480	8.75
Blandford	50	212	298.25 (26)	16.76
Sheerness	50	252	286.25 (26)	17.47
King George	40.6(9.4)	107	210.5	19.29
Brutus	40(10)	93	185.75	21.53
Alexander	50	143	200.65 (24)	24.92
Tryal	50	141	183.25 (18)	27.29
Duke of Cumb'd	50	164	180.5	27.70
Adventure	50	88	142.5	35.09
Ranger	42(8)	66	109.75	38.27
Eagle	50	94	128	39.06
Dreadnought	50	50	127.75 (16)	39.14
Fame	50	51	84.5	59.17

Venture	% owned by crew[a]	Crew size	Number of shares[b]	Value of share in £10,000

'Cruise and Voyage'

Venture	% owned by crew[a]	Crew size	Number of shares[b]	Value of share in £10,000
Brittannia	15.6(9.4)	88	137.25 (22)	11.37
Mentor	25	116	165.5	15.11
Deal Castle	25	108	101	24.75

'Armed Trading Vessel'

Sarah	25	47	67.5	37.04

'Specialist Vessels'

Falmouth (Govt)	33.33	120	182.75	18.24
Assistance (Customs)	50	21	34.5	144.93

a Figures in brackets denote the percentage of the crew's portion owned by the captain. In the case of the *Royal Family* squadron, the Commodore was allocated 3 per cent of the crew's moiety—2 per cent as quarter master of the fleet and 1 per cent as quarter master of the *King George*; the captains of the *Duke*, *Prince Frederick* and *Princess Amelia* were each allocated 1 per cent of the prize fund as quarter masters of their respective vessels.

b Figures in brackets denote the number of shares allocated to the carriage guns and owned in part or in full by the promoters of the venture. This provision was peculiar to Bristol ventures.

Appendix 5

Five Prize Accounts

The following accounts were presented to the Master in Chancery in respect of a 'Cause Unknown' and are preserved with sundry other exhibits in PRO, C 114/36. They relate to five prizes taken by Liverpool privateers in the autumn of 1778, the 'heyday' of the port's commerce-raiding experience; the first four were condemned to the *Ellis* and the *Gregson*, both owned by William Boats, while the *Carnatic* was captured by the *Mentor*, a 'cruise and voyage' venture set forth by Peter Baker and his son-in-law, Captain John Dawson. A summary of the *Carnatic's* accounts is presented here; the original extends to some 35 pages, with full details of the prize goods sold in nine auctions as well as a comprehensive breakdown of all the duties and charges incurred. Curiously, the total credits and debits amount to £113,053 14s 1d rather than the £114,053 14s 1d given in the original accounts. Though less extensive, the accounts of the other prizes appear to be arithmetically accurate.

1. Owners of the *Ville du Cap* in Account Curr't with Owners of the *Ellis* and *Gregson*

Dt 1778				£	s	d
Sep 18	To Cash pd		Riggers for docking	15	19	9
"	To do		Soldiers keeping Guard		19	10
24	To do		Sundry Boatage		5	
"	To do		For Beef & Liquor for the people	1	7	8
"	To do		Riggers	1	15	
"	To do		for Boots when at the Rock		5	
25	To do		for Drink		14	
26	To do		for cleaning the Cabin		7	
"	To do		unrigging her	2	19	1

Dt

1778				£	s	d
Oct 6	To cash paid		to carry Passenger home	10		
10	To	do	Pilotage	7	2	
Nov 13	To	do	Labourers	2	12	7
"	To	do	Expences at Custom House		14	6
21	To	do	Labourers discharging	2	17	
"	To	do	for Watching	1		
"	To	do	Labourers discharging	5	8	11
Dec 5	To	do	do do	4	19	
"	To	do	Watching etc	1	8	3
"	To	do	for discharging	5		
"	To	do	do (omitted 28 Nov)	7	15	6
1779						
Jan 16	To	do	Hy Forshaw for Commiss's	24	18	
"	To	do	Robt Moss, one of the Commiss's	10	10	
"	To	do	John Colquit do do	10	10	
"	To	do	Riggers		7	8
"	To	do	Charles Pole do do	7	7	
Apr 24	To	do	for Ale etc for Landwaiters	2	4	10
"	To	do	Proctor's Bill etc etc	96	3	3
"	To	do	Landwaiters	6	6	
"	To	do	Mr Lowndes for his attendance	5	5	
"	To	do	for a hatt & Shoes for Captain	1	3	
"	To	do	Passengers & Capt at Sundry Times	10		
May 6	To	do	Capt Pillet's Board Wages etc	14	9	7
"	To	do	Thomas Moore for suit of Cloathes	4	5	
"	To William Boats for 3/4 of Ballance			13760	14	5¾
"	To Captains & Crews for 1/4 do			4586	18	1¾
				£18614	12	0½

Cr

1779		£	s	d
Mar 4	By Net Sales of Sugar, Coffee, Cotton, Indigo & Rum	17507	10	0½
	By Charles Bromfield for said Ship's Hull & Materials	1100		
	By Pilotage p Contra (being twice charged)	7	2	
		£18614	12	0½

2. Owners of the *Eagle* in Account Curr't with Owners of the *Ellis*

Dt

1778				£	s	d
Oct 24	To Cash paid		for an Express from Kinsale	31	10	
"	To	do	for Potatoes for People in the Boat sent to Kinsale		5	
Nov 4	To	do	five men going to Kinsale	42		
"	To	do	three men from do	12	12	
"	To	do	Tripping the Anchor		10	6
6	To	do	Labourers		9	
"	To	do	Riggers	1	4	
13	To	do	Labourers	2	12	7
"	To	do	Watching	1	1	3
"	To	do	Labourers	2	16	2
"	To	do	Coach hire for Prisoners		10	6
Dec 5	To	do	Labourers	5	5	
19	To	do	do	3	9	
26	To	do	do		10	
1779						
Jan 9	To	do	Watching & Labourers	3	16	
16	To	do	Robert Moss, one Commissioner	10	10	
"	To	do	John Colquitt do	10	10	
"	To	do	Labourer		1	
"	To	do	Watching		18	3
Mar 24	To	do	Wm & Chas Pole, Commissioners	14	14	
"	To	do	Pilot Boat to Kinsale (24 Oct)	31	10	
May 3	To	do	Beef for Men in Boat	3	16	5
"	To	do	Wm Earle & son for Locks, Bars	1	0	1
13	To	do	for taking up an Anchor	3	3	
"	To	do	give the French Captain	2	2	
"	To	do	the first man discov'g sd vessel	1	1	
"	To	do	John Wilson for Commiss' disb	10	4	10
"	To	do	Proctor's Bill etc etc	73	12	11
May 14	To	do	Jas Glover for Exp on Prisoners	1	4	
"	To	do	Carriage of Prisoner's Trunks		10	6
"	To Insurance from Kinsale to Liverpoole			284	5	
"	To Wm Boats for 3/4 ballance			4327	9	11¼
"	To Captain & Crew for 1/4 do			1442	9	11¾

£6327   13   11

Cr

1779			£	s	d
Mar 4	By Nt Sales of Sugar, Coffee, Cotton				
	& Indigo		5427	13	11
"	By Gill Slater for Hull Masts Yards etc		900		
			£6327	13	11

3. Owners of the snow *Genevieve* in Acct Currt with Owners of the *Gregson*

Dt

1778				£	s	d
Nov 5	To Cash pd		Tripping an Anchor		10	6
"	To	do	French Passenger, carry him home	10	10	
"	To	do	Coach Hire		10	6
"	To	do	for a Boat running out Warps etc		4	6
7	To	do	Riggers	2	16	2
13	To	do	Labourers	2	12	7
"	To	do	Watching & labour	1	1	3
28	To	do	for Labour		5	
Dec 19	To	do	do & Watching	1	15	
31	To	do	John Wilson for Commiss's & 4 Prisoners Eating etc	10		
1779						
Jan 15	To	do	for Labour		13	
16	To	do	Robt Moss Commiss's	10	10	
"	To	do	John Colquit do	10	10	
"	To	do	Watching & Labour	1	18	
Mar 24	To	do	Willm &Chas Pole Commiss's	14	14	
"	To	do	Captn of said Ship	2	2	
"	To	do	Labourers	7	8	6
"	To	do	do	1	1	4
"	To	do	do		10	
"	To	do	for discovering said Ship	1	1	
"	To	do	Proctor's Bill etc	73	5	7
May 14	To	do	Jas Glover for his Expences on Prisoners	3	2	6
"	To	do	do for Carriage of Trunks		10	9
"	To	do	for taking up an Anchor	3	3	

Dt

1779		£	s	d
May 14	To William Boats for 3/4 of Balance	1760	12	4¾
"	To Captain & Crew for 1/4 of do	586	17	5¾
		£2508	5	0½

Cr

1779		£	s	d
May 4	By Amount of Sundries as p Acct Sales	£2508	5	0½

4. Owners of the Ship *Prudent* in Account Current with the Owners of the *Gregson*

Dt

1778				£	s	d
Dec 2	To Cash pd	Riggers for Tides in the Channel		17	17	
5	To do	for Transporting, Watching etc		3	17	3
15	To do	Labourers & Watching		8	1	1
26	To do	Riggers & Watching		2	12	5
29	To do	taking up an Anchor		3	3	
1779						
Jan 9	To do	Riggers, Commiss's disb		20	1	9
16	To do	four Commissioners		35	14	
"	To do	Boatage		1	17	6
23	To do	Labourers &Watching		2	15	4
Feb 6	To do	Riggers &Labourers		4		
13	To do	Ale for Landwaiters			1	2
"	To do	Riggers &Watching		3	6	
"	To do	Labourers		2	19	6
18	To do	do		5	10	6
"	To do	Watching		1		
27	To do	Labourers			16	
Mar 13	To do	discovering the *Prudent*		1	1	
26	To do	Watching		1		
May 14	To do	James Glover for Expences on Prisoners		2	10	6
"	To do	Carriage of Prisoner's Trunks			10	9
"	To do	Pilotage & taking up an Anchor		7	7	3
Jun 3	To do	Dock duties		25	15	

Dt

1778				£	s	d
Jun 23	To do	Peter Bennett for Fresh Beef		3		9
Jul 6	To do	WB's Expences in London		31	10	
"	To Error p Acct Sales (of 40 Bags Coffee sold					
	Chas & Ed'd Hague)			83	11	10
"	To Cash pd	Proctor's Bill etc		71	10	9
"	To do	for Abatements of Coffee		3	7	6
"	To William Boats for 3/4 of the Ballance			10013	12	3½
"	To Captain & Ship's Crew for 1/4 do			3337	17	5
				£13696	7	6½

Cr

1779		£	s	d
	By Error p Contra	83	11	10
Apr 1	By Nt Sales of said Ship & Cargo	13612	15	8½
		£13696	7	6½

5. Summary of the Accounts of the *Carnatic*, prize to the *Mentor*, 1778

Principal Duties and Charges

	£	s	d
Paid Pilotage & Men to bring *Carnatic* from Downs to Longreach	488	11	8
Insurance on £47,000 @ 2 gs per cent & policies	989	7	6
do on £10,000 @ 1 g do	105	5	9
Paid George March, Proctor	138	15	
" Duties & Charges on Sale of Ship	141	15	6
" Wm Prince for Duties on Tobacco, Redwood etc	355	2	
" Wm & Geo Panter for Duty on Coffee & Pepper	249	11	6
To Palmer & Green for Duty on Tea	327	7	6
" Oswald, Godwin & Coles for Duty on Piece Goods	20267	6	6
" do do on Saltpetre	1841	7	6
" do do on Shellack	678	9	6
" do do on Cassia Ligna & Raw Silk	407	16	
" do do & Excise on Arrack	577	8	6

	£	s	d
To Oswald, Godwin & Coles for Commission & Charges on Seven Sales	952	13	3
" Wharfage, Landing, Housing, Weighing Saltpetre, Tea, Piece Goods	397	19	7
" Jos Denison for Collecting £109,690 10s 3d @ 1/2%	548	9	
" Agency on do @ 5%	5484	10	6
Total Duty and Charges paid at sundry times	37,532	10	3
To Amount divided } 3/4 to owners of Ship *Mentor*	54,118	10	0
£72,158 } 1/4 to Ship's Crew	18,039	10	0
To Amount of Bond & other Charges accruing since division of Prize Money	3,363	3	10
	£114,053	14	1

Ct

1779					£	s	d
Jan	13	By Amount of this Day's Sale			22,566	1	0
	27	By	do	this Day	6,763	5	0
	29	By	do	this Day	2,842	11	3
Feb	1	By	do	this Day	12,557	6	5
	18	By	do	this Day	21,521	6	2
Mar	11	By	do	this Day	7,982	12	6
	17	By	do	this Day	16,221	13	10
	18	By	do	this Day	7,102	4	9
May	25	By	do	this Day	12,133	9	4
		By Balance (over divided)			3,363	3	10
					£114,053	14	1

List of the *Mentor*'s Crew entitled to Prize Money from Ship *Carnatic*

Name	Shares	Amount	
		£	s
John Dawson (Captain)	16	1,744	0
John Whiteside	8	872	0
James Gibbons	6	654	0
Paul Gaulteer	6	654	0
John Harvy	6	654	0

Name	Shares	Amount £ s
Hugh Beck	6	654 0
John Jones	6	654 0
Thomas Lee	6	654 0
Charles Lowe Whytell	6	654 0
James Boulton	6	654 0
George Beck	4	436 0
Thomas Wright	4	436 0
Joshuah Whiteside	4	436 0
Francis Campbell	4	436 0
Simon Walsh	4	436 0
William Barnsey	4	436 0
John Peat	3	327 0
Augustus Marrivale	2	218 0
Francis McCarthy	2	218 0
William Roberts	1.25	136 5
Harvey Monson Tonberg	1.25	136 5
25 Seamen	1 each @ £109	2,725 0
70 Ordinary Seamen	0.5 each @ £54 10s	3,815 0
	165.5	18,039 10

Appendix 6

Crew Composition, *Royal Family* Private Ships-of-War, 1747

The following tables are derived from the 'Book of Rates' submitted by the managers of the *Royal Family* venture in respect of a claim for head money payable on the capture of the Spanish man-of-war *Glorioso*. Preserved in PRO, ADM 43/13(2), together with the Articles of Agreement relating to the squadron's second cruise, the 'Book of Rates' comprises

> an exact list of the Commanders, Officers, Seamen, landmen and Boys, who were on board the *King George, Prince Frederick, Duke, Princess Amelia & Prince George* Private Ships of warr under the Command of Commodore George Walker at the Taking of the following Prizes, viz *St Jean Baptiste*, Commanded by Mons. Jean Baptiste Regon taken on the 22nd of August 1747 The *St Christopher*, Captain Juan Tarden & the *St Magin*, Capt Manoel Marine both taken on the 4th of October 1747, The *Gloriosa*, Commanded by Don   Taken on the 8th October 1747 and the *St Agatha*, Captain Aricort Toyne taken on the 2nd November 1747, with their shares and proportions of shares as settled According to the Articles . . .

After successfully completing its first cruise of eight months, the *Royal Family* squadron was re-fitted at Lisbon in 1747. Fresh articles of agreement were prepared and signed at Lisbon on 27 May 1747, and new letters of marque were issued for four of the vessels. Declarations made on 15 March 1746 for the *King George* (PRO, HCA 26/24) and 6 May 1747 for the other ships (PRO, HCA 26/25), offer the following characteristics:-

	Commander	Tons	Guns	Men
King George (KG)	George Walker	500	26	300
Prince Frederick (PF)	Edward Dottin	480	30	220
Duke (D)	Robert Denham	300	20	130
Princess Amelia (PA)	Andrew Riddell	250	26	120
Prince George (PG)	Francis Davidson	70	10	60

Table 1

Complement by Station and Share Ownership[a]

Station	Shares	KG	PF	D	PA	PG
Commodore	14	1	—	—	—	—
Commander	14	1(5)[b]	1	1	1	1(7)
1st Lieutenant	7	1	1	1	1	1(5)
2nd Lieutenant	5	1	1	1	1	1
3rd Lieutenant	5	1	1	1	1	—
4th Lieutenant	4	1	1	1	1	—
Surgeon General	7	1	—	—	—	—
Purser General	5	1	—	—	—	—
Surgeon	4	1	1	1	1	1
Master	4	1	1	1	1	1(2)
Purser	3.5	—	1	—	—	—
Boatswain	3	1	1	1	1	1(2)
Carpenter	3	1	1	1	1	1(2)
Gunner	3	1	1	1	1	1(2)
Chaplain	4	1	—	—	—	—
Commodore's Cook	2	1	—	—	—	—
Ship's Cook	1-2	1	2	1	1	1
Captain's Cook	2	—	—	—	1	1(1)
Sailmaker	2	1	1(1)	—	1	—
Armourer	0.5-2	2	—	1	1	1
Surgeon's 1st Mate	2.5	1	1	1	1	1(2)
Surgeon's 2nd Mate	2	1	1	—	—	—
Master's 1st Mate	3	1	1	—	1	—
Master's Mate	2	4	2	2	2	1(1.5)
Prize Master	2.5	2	—	—	—	—
Prize Master, *Nimfa*[c]	7	1	—	—	—	—
Prize Master, *BC*[c]	3	1	—	—	—	—
Boatswain's Mate	1-2	5	4	2	2	2

Station	Shares	KG	PF	D	PA	PG
Carpenter's Mate	1.25-2	1	1	—	2	1
Gunner's Mate	2	2	2	2	2	2(1.25)
Midshipman	1.5-2	4	3	4	4	—
Cooper	2	1	1	—	1	1(1.25)
Commodore's Clerk	3	1	—	—	—	—
Captain's Clerk	2	—	1	—	1	1(1.5)
Purser's Clerk	2	1	—	—	—	—
Ship's Clerk	2.5	1	—	—	—	—
Commodore's Steward	2	1	—	—	—	—
Captain's Steward	1-2	—	1	1	1	—
Ship's Steward	2	1	1	1	1	1(1.25)
Commodore's Barber	1.5	1	—	—	—	—
Commodore's Taylor	1	1	—	—	—	—
Quarter Master	1.25	7	4	4	5	3(1)
Boatswain's Yeoman	1.25-1.5	1	1	—	1	—
Carpenter's Crew	0.5-1	1	4	1	2	—
Carpenter's Yeoman	0.5-1	1	1	—	1	—
Gunner's Crew	1	—	3	—	—	—
Gunner's Yeoman	1.25-2	1	—	1	1	—
Quarter Gunner	1.25	5	3	3	2	—
Armourer's Mate	0.5-1	—	—	1	1	—
Cooper's Mate	1	1	—	—	—	—
Surgeon's Assistant	1	1	—	—	—	—
Clerk's Assistant	1.5	1	—	—	—	—
Cook's Mate	1	—	—	1	—	—
Steward's Mate	1	1	—	—	1	—
Painter	1	1	—	—	—	—
Swabber	1	—	1	—	1	—
Captain Marines	5	1	1(7)	1	1	1
Lieutenant Marines	2	1	1	1	1	—
Sargeant Marines	1.5	2	1	1	1	1(1.5)
Corporal Marines	1	2	2	2	2	—
1st Musician	3	1	—	—	—	—
Musician	1-3.5	3	1	1	—	—
Drummer	0.75	—	—	—	1	—
Volunteer	1-2	4	—	—	—	—
Commodore's Servants	1	8	6	—	5	4
Officer's Servants	1	10	15	13	15	7
Able Seaman	1	51	29	17	22	7
Ordinary Seaman	0.75	48	20	24	8	7
Ordinary Seaman	0.5	1	—	—	—	—

Station	Shares	KG	PF	D	PA	PG
Landman	0.75	3	1	—	—	—
Landman	0.5	55	72	31	33	14
Landman	0.33	1	—	—	—	—
Sea Lad	1.5	—	—	—	—	1
Boys	0.5	4	—	—	—	1
Boys	0.33	4	—	—	—	2
Boys	0.25	9	17	2	15	2
Unspecified	0-3	3	3	1	—	—
		282	219	130	151	71

a   Figures in brackets denote the number of shares allocated to a particular station in cases where it differed from the rate current in the rest of the squadron. The shareholding presented is that in force at the capture of the first prize.

b   Commodore George Walker was commander of the *King George*. However, Frederick Hamilton, captain of the uncommissioned tender *Prince Edward* was included in the *King George*'s complement and allocated five shares. At least two other of the *Prince Edward*'s men were likewise included in the *King George*'s list, both Joseph Loadman and Myles Masterson drowning on 14 July 1747 while in the service of the 'PE'.

c   The *Nimfa* and the *Bon Conseijo* (*BC*) were taken during the latter stages of the *Royal Family*'s first cruise, though their prize masters remained in the *King George*'s complement.

Table 2

Summary of Crew Composition

	KG	PF	D	PA	PG	Total
'Qualities'[a]	85	56	42	53	26	262
Servants	18	21	13	20	11	83
Able Seamen	51	29	17	22	7	126
Ordinary Seamen	49	20	24	8	7	108
Landmen	59	73	31	33	14	210
Boys	17	17	2	15	6	57
Unspecified	3	3	1	0	0	7
	282	219	130	151	71	853

a   'Qualities' refers to the commanders, officers and crew members with a specified occupation. Most of these seafarers owned more than the single share allocated to the able seaman.

Table 3

Share Distribution[a]

	KG	PF	D	PA	PG	Total
'Qualities'	199	126.25	95.5	121.75	53.75	596.25
Servants	18	21	12.25	20	11	82.25
Able Seamen	50	28	17	22	7	124
Ordinary Seamen	34.25	15	18	6	5.25	78.5
Landmen	29.08	36.25	15.5	16	7	103.83
Boys	5.58	4.25	0.5	3.75[b]	3.16	17.24
Unspecified	6.5	0	0	—	—	6.5
	342.41	230.75	158.75	189.5	87.16	1008.57

a This table presents the share allocation as it stood at the capture of the first prize. Thus, it ignores increases in the shareholding of those promoted during the course of the cruise, while it includes the shares of those who subsequently perished in service. The shares of four deserters have been discounted.

b No share allocation was entered against the names of 12 of the 15 boys serving in the *Princess Amelia*; it is assumed that they owned one-quarter of a share, the rate designated for a boy in the Articles of Agreement.

Table 4

Crew Lost

	KG	PF	D	PA	PG	Total
Killed	3	2	0	0	0	5
Drowned	3	0	0	2	0	5
Died	7	3	0	1	0	11
Discharged	1	0	0	0	0	1
Deserted	2	1	1	0	0	4
	16	6	1	3	0	26

Table 5

Complement by Country of Origin and Station[a]

	Q	S	AB	OS	L	B	NK	Total
England	61	1	34	20	55	26	3	200
Wales	13	0	5	4	10	3	0	35
Scotland	21	6	2	3	2	0	0	34
Ireland	101	3	35	43	77	9	0	268
Channel Islands	0	0	1	0	0	0	0	1
Colonies	4	0	1	1	2	0	0	8
Foreign	8	5	14	9	21	13	1	71
Unspecified	12	55	17	4	12	4	2	106
	220	70	109	84	179	55	6	723

Q = 'Qualities'   S = Servants   AB = Able Seamen
OS = Ordinary Seamen   L = Landmen   B = Boys
NK = Rank unknown

a As the 'Country' column of her list was left blank, the *Duke*'s company of 130 seafarers is not considered in this analysis.

Table 6

Complement by Age[a]

	Observations	Average Age	Age Range
'Qualities'	171	27.4	15–68
Servants	22	16.6	14–19
Able Seamen	103	26.6	16–76
Ordinary Seamen	79	24.9	17–40
Landmen	168	23.7	17–52
Boys	51	16.5	13–19

a As the 'Age' column of her list was left blank, the *Duke*'s company of 130 seafarers is not considered in this analysis. Ages were not given for the Commodore, Commanders and Lieutenants of the squadron.

Appendix 7

Commissioned Vessels by Region, 1793–1801

Region	Number of commissions	Actual vessels
London	1649	580
Bristol	114	61
Liverpool	1691	630
Channel Is — Alderney (3) Guernsey (69) Jersey (100)	436	172
E England — Colchester (2) Harwich (3) Hull (7) Lynn (2) Newcastle (9) Shields (1) Stockton (1) Sunderland (2) Whitby (3) Yarmouth (3)	66	33
SE England — Chichester (2) Cowes (4) Deal (3) Dover (17) Faversham (2) Folkestone (5) Hastings (4) Portsmouth (5) Rochester (1) Romney (2) Rye (4) Shoreham (1) Southampton (8)	94	58
SW England — Dartmouth (15) Exeter (3) Falmouth (6) Fowey (8) Ilfracombe (2) Lyme (3) Penzance (3) Plymouth (10) Poole (2) St Ives (3) Topsham (1) Weymouth (13)	153	69
Wales & NW England — Lancaster (62) Milford (1) Ulverston (1) Whitehaven (1)	177	65
W Scotland — Ayr (1) Glasgow (12) Greenock (20) Wigtown (1)	84	34
E Scotland — Aberdeen (1) Dundee (2) Edinburgh (1) Leith (14)	32	18
Ireland — Cork (9) Dublin (5)	17	14
Overseas Bases — Antigua (1) Barbados (2) Bermuda (2) Bombay (2) Calcutta (1) Jamaica (10) Leghorn (2) Martinique (5) New Providence (1) Nova Scotia (2) St Vincent (2)	59	30
Port Unknown	41	31
	4613	1795

Figures in brackets denote actual vessels.
Source: PRO, HCA 25/123-61; HCA 26/73-5, 81-7, 94, 96-9, 104.

Appendix 8

Commissioned Vessels by Region, 1803-1815

Region	Number of commissions	Actual vessels
London	2152	599
Bristol	67	33
Liverpool	1267	401
Channel Is — Alderney (1) Guernsey (152) Jersey (76)	817	229
E England — Berwick (1) Boston (1) Colchester (2) Grimsby (2) Harwich (6) Hull (12) Newcastle (3) Whitby (1) Yarmouth (12)	110	40
SE England — Brighton (1) Chichester (3) Cowes (10) Deal (2) Dover (24) Folkestone (8) Gosport (1) Hastings (12) Newhaven (1) Portsmouth (8) Ramsgate (2) Rochester (3) Rye (5) Sandwich (2) Shoreham (2) Southampton (10) Sussex (1)	243	95
SW England — Barnstaple (2) Bridport (1) Dartmouth (10) Exeter (2) Falmouth (7) Fowey (18) Gweek (1) Ilfracombe (3) Looe (4) Lyme (2) Penzance (2) Plymouth (77) Poole (3) Scilly Isles (1) St Ives (2) Weymouth (16)	461	151
Wales & NW England — Lancaster (33) Milford (7) Swansea (1) Whitehaven (5)	103	46
W Scotland — Ayr (2) Glasgow (30) Greenock (78) Lamlash (1) Stornoway (1) Whithorn (1)	209	113
E Scotland — Dundee (2) Edinburgh (10) Elie (1) Islay (1) Leith (17)	73	31
Ireland — Belfast (3) Cork (2) Ireland (1)	7	6
Overseas Bases — Bombay (2) Calcutta (4) Dominica (2) Jamaica (6) Newfoundland (3) Nova Scotia (2) Quebec (1) St Christopher (1) St Lucia (1)	44	22
Port Unknown	60	44
	5613	1810

Figures in brackets denote actual vessels.

Source: PRO, HCA 25/162-209; HCA 26/71-2, 76-80, 88-93, 95, 100-04.

Bibliography

Primary Sources

Manuscript

British Library

Additional Manuscripts, Add Mss 38,430, 38,432

Public Record Office

Head Money Vouchers, ADM 43
Liverpool Muster Rolls, 1778–1780, BT 98/38-43
Chancery Masters' Exhibits, C 103-114
Plymouth Muster Rolls, 1776–1780, CUST 66/227
Letter of Marque Bonds, HCA 25
Letter of Marque Declarations, HCA 26
Prize Court Miscellany, HCA 30
Prize Papers, HCA 32
Prize Court Sentences, HCA 34
Court of Prize Appeals Papers, HCA 42
Court of Prize Appeals Case Books, HCA 45

Avon County Library

Papers of the *Southwell* Privateer, 24651

Devon Record Office

Seale Papers
Southcote Papers, 1032 F/Z 7

India Office Library

Index of Captain's Logs, 1702–1707, L/MAR/B

Liverpool Record Office

Account Books of the *Enterprize*, 387 MD 45
Holt and Gregson Mss, 942 HOL 10
Tuohy Papers, TUO

Society of Merchant Venturers, Bristol

Hospital Bill Muster Rolls, 1777–1783

Printed

Anderson, Adam, *An Historical and Chronological Deduction of the Origin of Commerce from the Earliest Accounts to the Present Day* (1754).

Anderson, William, *The London Commercial Dictionary and Seaport Gazatteer* (2nd ed., 1826).

Cobbett, William, *Cobbett's Parliamentary History of England* (1810).

Cooke, Edward, *A Voyage to the South Sea and Round the World* (1712).

Hardy, Charles, *Register of Ships Employed in the Service of the Honourable United East India Company* (1799) 2 vols.

Hutchinson, William, *A Treatise on Practical Seamanship* (Liverpool, 1777).

Hutchinson, William, *A Treatise founded upon Philosophical and Rational Principles towards Establishing Fixed Rules for the Best Form and Proportional Dimensions . . . of Merchant Ships* (Liverpool, 1791).

Journals of the House of Commons

Lambert, Sheila, ed., *House of Commons Sessional Papers of the Eighteenth Century* (Wilmington, Delaware: Scholarly Resources, 1975).

Marsden, Reginald G, *Select Pleas in the Court of Admiralty* (Selden Society, 1894 & 1897) 2 vols

MacPherson, David, *Annals of Commerce* (1805).

Morgan, William J, ed., *Naval Documents of the American Revolution* (Washington, DC: Naval History Division, Department of the Navy, 1980)

Postlethwayt, Malachy, *The Universal Dictionary of Trade and Commerce* (4th ed., 1774).

Rogers, Woodes, *Life Aboard a British Privateer in the Time of Queen Anne* (1712; reprinted Chapman and Hall, 1894).

Shelvocke, George, *A Voyage Round the World by way of the Great South Seas Performed in the Years 1719–1722* (1726; reprinted with an introduction by W G Perrin, Cassel, 1928).

The Voyages and Cruises of Commodore Walker (1760; reprinted with an introduction by Herbert S Vaughan, Cassel, 1928)

Troughton, Thomas, *Barbarian Cruelty. A Narrative of the Sufferings and Hardships endured by the crews of the* Inspector Privateer *and* Litchfield Man-of-War *shipwrecked on the Coast of the Dominions subject to the Emperor of Morocco* (Exeter, 1788)

Newspapers

Observator, 1702–1707
London Gazette 1702–1712, 1739–1748, 1756–1762, 1777–1783
Read's Weekly Journal or British Gazatteer, 1739–1748, 1756–1762
Daily Post, 1739–1748
Country Journal, or Craftsman, 1744
Gentleman's Magazine, 1745
Lloyd's Evening Post and British Chronicle, 1762
Public Advertiser, 1762
Morning Chronicle and London Advertiser, 1777–1783
Gazatteer and New Daily Advertiser, 1778
Exeter Flying Post, 1778–1782
Felix Farley's Bristol Journal, 1778–1781
Newcastle Chronicle, 1778–1782
Newcastle Courant, 1778–1782
Newcastle Journal, 1778–1781
Sherborne and Yeovil Mercury, 1778–1782

Secondary Sources

Works published in London, unless otherwise stated

Andrews, Kenneth R, *English Privateering Voyages to the West Indies, 1588–1595* (Cambridge UP, 1959)

Andrews, Kenneth R, *Elizabethan Privateering during the Spanish War, 1585–1603* (Cambridge UP, 1964)

Appleby, John C and Starkey, David J, 'The Records of the High Court of Admiralty as a Source for Maritime Historians' in David J Starkey, ed., *Sources for a New Maritime History of Devon* (Devon County Council, 1986) 70-86

Barbour, Violet F, 'Privateers and Pirates of the West Indies', *American Historical Review*, XVI (1911), 529-66

Baugh, Daniel, *British Naval Administration in the Age of Walpole* (Princeton UP, 1965)

Bromley, John S, 'The Channel Island Privateers in the War of the Spanish Succession' *Société Guernesiaise Report and Transactions*, XIV (1949), 444-78

Bromley, John S, 'The French Privateering War, 1702-1713' in Henry E Bell and Richard L Ollard, eds, *Historical Essays, 1600-1750, presented to David Ogg* (Black, 1963) 203-31

Bromley, John S, 'The Trade and Privateering of St Malo during the War of the Spanish Succession' *Société Guernesiaise Report and Transactions*, XVII (1964), 631-47

Bromley, John S, 'Some Zeeland Privateering Instructions: Jacob Sautijn to Captain Saloman Reynders, 1707' in Ragnhild Hatton and John S Bromley, eds, *William III and Louis XIV. Essays by and for Mark A Thomson* (Liverpool UP, 1968) 162-89

Bromley, John S, 'Prize Office and Prize Agency at Portsmouth, 1689-1748' in John Webb, Nigel Yates and Sarah Peacock, eds, *Hampshire Studies* (Portsmouth City Records Office, 1981) 169-99

[John S Bromley's works on privateering are collected in Bromley, John S, *Corsairs and Navies* (Hambledon Press, 1987)]

Cameron, Alan and Farndon, Roy, *Scenes from Sea and City. Lloyd's List, 1734-1984* (Lloyd's List, 1984)

Carter, Alice C, 'How to Revise Treaties without Negotiating: Common Sense, Mutual Fears and the Anglo-Dutch Trade Disputes of 1759' in Ragnhild Hatton and M S Anderson, eds, *Studies in Diplomatic History. Essays in Memory of David Bayne Horn* (Longman, 1970) 214-35

Carter, Alice C, *The Dutch Republic in Europe in the Seven Years' War* (Macmillan, 1971)

Carter, Alice C, *Neutrality or Commitment. The Evolution of Dutch Foreign Policy, 1667-1795* (Edward Arnold, 1975)

Clark, George N, 'English and Dutch Privateers under William III' *Mariner's Mirror*, VII (1921), 162-7, 209-17

Clark, George N, 'War Trade and Trade War' *Economic History Review*, first series, I (1927-1928), 262-80

Clark, George N, *The Dutch Alliance and the War against French Trade, 1688-1697* (Manchester UP, 1963)

Clowes, William Laird, *The Royal Navy. A History from the Earliest Times to the Death of Queen Victoria* (Sampson, Low, Marston and Co, 1897-1903) 7 vols

Corbett, Julian S, *England in the Seven Years' War. A Study in Combined Strategy* (Longmans, Green and Co, 1907) 2 vols

Corbett, Julian S, *England in the Mediterranean. A Study of the Rise of British Power within the Straits, 1603-1713* (Longmans, Green and Co, 1917)

328 *British Privateering in the Eighteenth Century*

Crowhurst, R Patrick, *The Defence of British Trade, 1689-1815* (Folkestone: Dawson, 1977)

Crowhurst, R Patrick, 'Profitability in French Privateering, 1793–1815' *Business History*, XXIV (1982), 48-60

Cullen, Louis, 'Privateers fitted out in Irish Ports in the Eighteenth Century' *Irish Sword*, III (1957–1958), 170-7

Damer Powell, John W, *Bristol Privateers and Ships of War* (Bristol: Arrowsmith, 1930)

Davies, Kenneth G, *Letters from Hudson's Bay* (Hudson's Bay Record Society, 1965)

Davis, Ralph, 'English Foreign Trade, 1660–1700' *Economic History Review*, second series, VI (1954), 150-66

Davis, Ralph, 'Seaman's Sixpences. An Index of Commercial Activity, 1697–1828' *Economica*, XXII (1956), 328-43

Davis, Ralph, 'English Foreign Trade, 1700-1774' *Economic History Review*, second series, XV (1962), 329-45

Davis, Ralph, *The Rise of the English Shipping Industry in the Seventeenth and Eighteenth Centuries* (Macmillan, 1962; reprinted Newton Abbot: David and Charles, 1972)

Davis, Ralph, *The Rise of the Atlantic Economies* (Weidenfeld & Nicolson, 1973)

Dull, Jonathon R, *The French Navy and American Independence* (Princeton UP, 1975)

van Dusen, Albert E, *The Trade of Revolutionary Connecticut* (Ann Arbor, Michigan: University Microfilms, 1974)

Faibisy, John D, *Privateering and Piracy. The Effects of New England Raiding upon Nova Scotia during the American Revolution, 1775-1783* (Ann Arbor, Michigan: University Microfilms, 1974)

Fisher, H E Stephen, *The Portugal Trade* (Methuen, 1971)

Fraser, J Alban, *Spain and the West Country* (Burn, Oates and Washbourne, 1935)

Gill, Conrad, *Merchants and Mariners of the Eighteenth Century* (Edward Arnold, 1961)

Graham, Gerald S, *Empire of the North Atlantic. The Maritime Struggle for North America* (University of Toronto Press, 1950; reprinted Oxford UP, 1972)

Hyde, Francis E, *Liverpool and the Mersey. An Economic History of a Port, 1700-1900* (Newton Abbot: David and Charles, 1971)

Jackson, Gordon, *Hull in the Eighteenth Century. A Study in Economic and Social History* (Oxford UP, 1972)

Jamieson, Alan G, 'American Privateers in the Leeward Islands, 1776-1778' *American Neptune*, XLIII (1983), 20-30

Jamieson, Alan G, ed., *A People of the Sea. The Maritime History of the Channel Islands* (Methuen, 1986)

Jarvis, Rupert C, 'Eighteenth-Century London Shipping' in William Kellaway and Albert E J Hollaender, eds, *Studies in London History presented to Philip Edmund Jones* (Hodder and Stoughton, 1969) 401-25

Jarvis, Rupert C, 'Ship Registry—1786' *Maritime History*, IV (1974), 12-30

Jenkins, Ernest H, *A History of the French Navy from its Beginnings to the Present Day* (MacDonald and Janes, 1973)

John, Arthur H, 'War and the English Economy, 1700–1763' *Economic History Review*, second series, VII (1955), 329-45

Jessup, Philip C and Deak, Francis, *Neutrality, its History, Economics and Law* (Columbia UP, 1935)

Keen, Maurice H, *The Laws of War in the Late Middle Ages* (Routledge and Kegan Paul, 1965)

Kendall, Charles W, *Private Men-of-War* (Philip Allen, 1931)

Kennedy, Paul M, *The Rise and Fall of British Naval Mastery* (Macmillan, 1976)

Laughton, John K, *Studies in Naval History* (Longmans, Green and Co, 1887)

Lee, C D, 'Alexander Selkirk and the Last Voyage of the *Cinque Ports Gally*' *Mariner's Mirror*, 73 (1987), 385-99

Lloyd, Christopher C, *The British Seaman, 1200–1860. A Social Survey* (Collins, 1968)

Lydon, James G, *The Role of New York in Privateering down to 1763* (Ann Arbor, Michigan: University Microfilms, 1958)

MacGregor, David R, *Merchant Sailing Ships, 1775-1815. Their Design and Construction* (Watford: Argus Books, 1980)

Mackesy, Piers, *The War for America* (Longmans, Green and Co, 1964)

de Madariaga, Isabel, *Britain, Russia and the Armed Neutrality of 1780* (Hollis and Carter, 1962)

Mahan, Alfred T, *The Influence of Sea Power upon History* (Sampson, Low, Marston and Co, 1889)

Marsden, Reginald G, 'Early Prize Jurisdiction and Prize Law in England' *English Historical Review*, XXVI (1911), 34-56

Marsden, Reginald G, *Law and Custom of the Sea* (Navy Records Society, 1915)

McGrath, Patrick, *The Merchant Venturers of Bristol* (Bristol: Society of Merchant Venturers of the City of Bristol, 1975)

Merriman, Reginald D, ed, *Queen Anne's Navy* (Navy Records Society, 1961)

Meyer, William R, 'Mascall's Privateers' *Archaeologia Cantiana*, XCV (1979), 213-21

Meyer, William R, 'English Privateering in the War of 1688 to 1697' *Mariner's Mirror*, LXVII (1981), 259-72

Meyer, William R, 'English Privateering in the War of the Spanish Succession, 1702-13' *Mariner's Mirror*, LXIX (1983), 435-46

Miller, Daniel A, *Sir Joseph Yorke and Anglo-Dutch Relations, 1774–1780* (The Hague: Mouton, 1970)

Minchinton, Walter E, ed., *The Growth of English Overseas Trade in the Seventeenth and Eighteenth Centuries* (Methuen, 1969)

Minchinton, Walter E and Starkey, David J, 'Characteristics of Privateers operating from the British Isles against America, 1777–1783' in Timothy J

Runyon, ed., *Ships, Seafaring and Society. Essays in Maritime History* (Wayne State UP, 1987) 251-74

Mollat, Michel, ed., *Course et Piraterie* (Paris: Commission Internationale d'Histoire Maritime, 1976) 2 vols

Owen, John H, *War at Sea under Queen Anne, 1702–1709* (Cambridge UP, 1938)

Pack, Stanley W, *Sea Power in the Mediterranean. A Study of the Struggle for Sea Power in the Mediterranean from the Seventeenth Century to the Present Day* (Arthur Baker, 1971)

Pares, Richard, *War and Trade in the West Indies, 1739–1763* (Oxford: Clarendon Press, 1936)

Pares, Richard, *Colonial Blockade and Neutral Rights, 1739–1748* (Oxford: Clarendon Press, 1938; reprinted Philadelphia: Porcupine Press, 1975)

Parkinson, Cyril N, *The Trade Winds. A Study of British Overseas Trade During the French Wars, 1793–1815* (George Allen and Unwin, 1948)

Parkinson, Cyril N, *The Rise of the Port of Liverpool* (Liverpool UP, 1952)

Porter, Jeffrey H, *Carnatic Halls since 1779* (Liverpool UP, 1969)

Press, Jonathan, *The Merchant Seamen of Bristol, 1747–1789* (Bristol UP, 1976)

Raban, Peter, 'War and Trade in the Mid-Eighteenth Century' *Société Guernesiaise Report and Transactions,* (1986), 131-63

Rediker, Marcus, *Between the Devil and the Deep Blue Sea. Merchant Seamen, Pirates and the Anglo-American Maritime World, 1700–1750* (Cambridge UP, 1987)

Richmond, Herbert, *Statesmen and Sea Power* (Oxford UP, 1946)

Rodger, Nicholas A M, *The Wooden World. An Anatomy of the Georgian Navy* (Collins, 1986)

Rogers, Bertram M H, 'Dampier's Voyage of 1703' *Mariner's Mirror*, X (1924), 367-81

Rogers, Bertram M H, 'The Privateering Voyages of the *Tartar* of Bristol' *Mariner's Mirror*, XVII (1931), 236-43

Rogers, Bertram M H, 'Woodes Rogers's Privateering Voyage of 1708–11' *Mariner's Mirror*, XIX (1933), 196-211

Smith, H A, 'The Declaration of Paris in Modern War' *Law Quarterly Review*, LV (1939), 237-49

Stark, Francis R, *The Abolition of Privateering and the Declaration of Paris* (New York: Columbia UP, 1897)

Starkey, David J, 'British Privateering against the Dutch in the American Revolutionary War, 1780–1783' in H E Stephen Fisher, ed., *Studies in British Privateering, Trading Enterprise and Seamen's Welfare, 1775-1900* (University of Exeter, 1987) 1-17

Starkey, David J, 'The Economic and Military Significance of British Privateering, 1702–1783' *Journal of Transport History*, 9 (1988), 50-9

Statham, Edward, *Privateers and Privateering* (Hutchinson, 1910)

Sutherland, Lucy S, *A London Merchant, 1695–1774* (Oxford UP, 1962)

Swanson, Carl E, 'The Profitability of Colonial Privateering: Reflections on

British Colonial Privateers during the War of 1739–1748' *American Neptune,* XLII (1982), 36-56

Swanson, Carl E, 'American Privateering and Imperial Warfare, 1739–1748' *William and Mary Quarterly,* third series, XLII (1985), 357-82

Symcox, Geoffrey, *War, Diplomacy and Imperialism, 1618–1763* (New York: Harper and Row, 1973)

Syrett, David, *Shipping and the American War, 1775–1783. A Study of British Transport Organisation* (Athlone Press, 1970)

Thomas, E G, 'Captain Buckle and the Capture of the *Glorioso' Mariner's Mirror,* LXVIII (1982), 49-56

Walker, Geoffrey J, *Spanish Politics and Imperial Trade, 1700–1789* (Macmillan, 1979)

Wickens, Peter L, 'The Economics of Privateering. Capital Dispersal in the American War of Independence' *Journal of European Economic History,* 13 (1984), 375-95

Willan, Thomas S, *The English Coasting Trade, 1600–1750* (Manchester UP, 1967)

Woolf, Maurice, 'Eighteenth-Century London Jewish Shipowners' *Transactions of the Jewish Historical Society of England,* XXIV (1974), 198-204

Unpublished Theses

Brown, John W, 'British Privateering during the Seven Years' War, 1756–1762' (unpublished MA dissertation, University of Exeter, 1978)

French, Christopher J, 'The Trade and Shipping of the Port of London, 1700–1776' (unpublished PhD thesis, University of Exeter, 1980)

Graham, Eric J, 'Privateering. The Scottish Experience' (unpublished MA dissertation, University of Exeter, 1979)

Meyer, William R, 'The Scale of English Privateering in the Wars of William and Anne' (unpublished MA dissertation, University of Exeter, 1979)

Starkey, David J, 'Liverpool Privateering, 1702–1783' (unpublished MA dissertation, University of Exeter, 1979)

Starkey, David J, 'British Privateering, 1702–1783, with particular reference to London' (unpublished PhD thesis, University of Exeter, 1985)

Swanson, Carl E, 'Predators and Prizes. Privateering in the British Colonies during the War of 1739–1748' (unpublished PhD thesis, University of Western Ontario, 1979)

Index

Unless otherwise stated, cited ships are British commissioned vessels

Printed and bound by CPI Group (UK) Ltd, Croydon, CR0 4YY

23/04/2025

14660988-0001